SHAKESPEARE'S
LATE
TRAGEDIES

SHAKESPEARE'S LATE TRAGEDIES

A Collection of Critical Essays

Edited by
Susanne L. Wofford

Prentice Hall, Upper Saddle River, New Jersey 07458

Library of Congress Cataloging-in-Publication Data

Shakespeare's late tragedies : a collection of critical essays /
edited by Susanne L. Wofford.
    p. cm. — (New century views)
    Includes bibliographical references (p.).
    ISBN 0–13–807819–X
    1. Shakespeare, William, 1564–1616—Tragedies. 2. Shakespeare,
William, 1564–1616. Macbeth. 3. Macbeth, King of Scotland, 11th
cent.—In literature. 4. Shakespeare, William, 1564–1616.
Coriolanus. 5. Coriolanus, Cnaeus Marcius—In literature.
6. Shakespeare, William, 1564–1616. Antony and Cleopatra.
7. Cleopatra, Queen of Egypt, d. 30 B.C.—In literature.
8. Antonius, Marcus, 83?–30 B.C.—In literature. 9. Tragedy.
I. Wofford, Susanne Lindgren. II. Series.
PR2983.S4488   1996
822.3'3—dc20   95–10942
                                           CIP

Acquisitions editor: Tony English
Editorial/production supervision: Mary McDonald
Copy editor: Sherry Babbitt
Cover design: Karen Salzbach
Buyer: Mary Ann Gloriande

© 1996 by Prentice-Hall, Inc.
Simon & Schuster/A Viacom Company
Upper Saddle River, New Jersey 07458

Printed in the United States of America
10 9 8 7 6 5 4 3 2 1

ISBN 0-13-807819-X

Prentice-Hall International (UK) Limited, *London*
Prentice-Hall of Australia Pty. Limited, *Sydney*
Prentice-Hall Canada Inc., *Toronto*
Prentice-Hall Hispanoamericana, S.A., *Mexico*
Prentice-Hall of India Private Limited, *New Delhi*
Prentice-Hall of Japan, Inc., *Tokyo*
Simon & Schuster Asia Pte. Ltd., *Singapore*
Editora Prentice-Hall do Brasil, Ltda., *Rio de Janeiro*

Contents

Acknowledgments

In selecting the essays for this volume, I have benefited from the help of a number of friends and colleagues. I especially wish to thank Mihoko Suzuki, Janet Adelman, Marjorie Garber, and Heather James, whose advice and support were crucial to me; Richard Brodhead and Maynard Mack, for their excellent suggestions, patience, and continuing confidence in the project; my colleagues at the University of Wisconsin and at the Bread Loaf School of English, who gave me useful responses to an early version of my introduction; and my students at Yale, Wisconsin, and Bread Loaf, whose questions led me to rethink many of my conclusions in "The Body Unseamed," and whose responses to many of the essays included here helped me to shape the volume. In preparing the manuscript for press, I have been aided by three graduate student assistants at the University of Wisconsin: David Engelstad, who did some of the preliminary work; and Rebecca Schoenike and Hillary Arlen, whose help in checking manuscript details and in obtaining the needed permissions for essays and photographs was invaluable. To all three of them I owe my thanks. In proofreading the book, I benefited from the help of Brian Brindel and Margaret Quintanar. Thanks also is due to Mary McDonald, the production editor, Sherry Babbitt, the copy editor, and D. Anthony English, Senior Editor at Prentice Hall. My husband, Jacques Lezra, has given important advice, assistance, and support throughout the project. Finally, I wish to thank my sons, Gabriel and Nathaniel, who, although they did not know it, gave up vacation time on several occasions to allow me to finish this book.

Susanne Wofford
University of Wisconsin–Madison

SHAKESPEARE'S LATE TRAGEDIES

The Body Unseamed:
Shakespeare's Late Tragedies

Susanne L. Wofford

> Come, seeling Night,
> Scarf up the tender eye of pitiful Day,
> And, with thy bloody and invisible hand,
> Cancel, and tear to pieces, that great bond
> Which keeps me pale![1]
>
> *Macbeth,* 3.2.46–50

The question of the meaning and value of tragedy is one of the great issues that scholars, critics, and audiences have debated over the ages. This introduction will focus on this problem from only one angle—the representation of social and psychological fragmentation in *Macbeth, Coriolanus,* and *Antony and Cleopatra*—in order to describe part of what is particularly characteristic of late Shakespearean tragedy.

While tragedy often leads to a recognition of wisdom that emerges from suffering, it sometimes leads its audiences to question whether any certain understanding, for either the characters or the audience, has emerged from the violence enacted on stage. Shakespearean tragedy is located uncomfortably between these two possibilities, sometimes asserting value and sometimes questioning it—even questioning, sometimes, the authority of the monarch or of any transcendent truth. Shakespeare lived at a time when values and beliefs once considered absolute had suddenly come under intense political and religious questioning.[2] Some of the doubts expressed in his plays about what truths can be counted on reflect this historical moment—the Renaissance in a newly Protestant England—a time of extraordinary artistic and cultural excitement, volatility, and change.

---

[1]All quotations from Shakespeare are taken from the Arden editions of the plays: *Antony and Cleopatra,* ed. M. R. Ridley (1954; London: Methuen, 1986); *Coriolanus,* ed. Philip Brockbank (1976; London: Routledge, 1988); and *Macbeth,* ed. Kenneth Muir (1951; London: Routledge, 1988).

[2]For the importance of political, religious, and economic change in England to the development of tragedy, see Jonathan Dollimore, *Radical Tragedy: Religion, Ideology and Power in the Drama of Shakespeare and his Contemporaries* (Brighton, Sussex: Harvester, and Chicago: University of Chicago Press, 1984), from which a chapter is included in this volume (pp. 197–207); and Franco Moretti, "Tragedy and the Deconsecration of Authority," in *The Power of Forms in the English Renaissance,* ed. Stephen Greenblatt (Norman, OK: Pilgrim, 1982) 7–40.

1

The three late tragedies discussed in this volume rewrite the discovery that an apparently ordered and hierarchical universe has been broken or fragmented as dismemberment of a particularly bodily and literalized form. *Macbeth, Coriolanus,* and *Antony and Cleopatra*—three plays of extraordinary density, compression, and allusive power—share a fascination with dismemberment, with the tragic rending, tearing apart, or scattering of the body, material or corporate. A look at this aspect of these plays can help to identify their common assumptions and values, and to provide a broader speculation about Shakespeare's late tragic vision. Attending, then, to this knot of concerns, we discover first that in *Macbeth* and *Coriolanus,* this dismembering or scattering becomes difficult—indeed almost impossible—to heal, sew together, seam (in the vocabulary of *Macbeth*), or re-collect (a pun that reminds us that memory itself can be a form of re-membering dismembered parts). We discover, too, that *Antony and Cleopatra,* a tragedy that also has affinities with Shakespeare's late romances, can be understood as a dramatic articulation of the costs of gathering together or re-membering the body torn apart in *Macbeth* and *Coriolanus. Antony and Cleopatra* puts back together what in *Macbeth* and *Coriolanus* is scattered, but it does so through its own form of scattering and dispersion.

When speaking of the dismembering of the "body" in the late tragedies, I mean first the fictional bodies represented on stage—for instance, Macbeth's head or the various body parts that the witches throw into their cauldron, all of which play important parts in the spectacle as well as the poetic language of *Macbeth.* The body is also, however, the body politic—the corporate or civic body referred to in Menenius's Fable of the Belly in *Coriolanus*—and thus becomes a sign of several unities, including the dramatic. The body's "re-membering" is in these plays similarly more than a matter of plot, since it refers both to the question of memory and to the rhetorical, political, and poetic strategies by which any notion of the "whole"—any sense of totality or integrity—can be produced.

Macbeth

Macbeth explicitly takes place under the sign of a dismembered body part: the dissevered bloody head of the traitor invoked at the beginning of the play and literalized in its ending when MacDuff enters carrying Macbeth's bloody head. The opening description pictures Macbeth's heroism as specifically residing in his military strength, exemplified in his capacity to kill and behead the traitor. The captain, describing Macbeth's victory over the traitor Macdonwald early in the play, says:

> For brave Macbeth (well he deserves that name),
> Disdaining Fortune, with his brandish'd steel,
> Which smok'd with bloody execution,
> Like Valour's minion carved out his passage,
> Till he fac'd the slave;

Which ne'er shook hands, nor bade farewell to him,
Till he unseam'd him from the nave to th' chops,
And fix'd his head upon our battlements.

(1.2.16–23)

The metaphor of "unseaming" used so shockingly here implies that human beings, or men at least, are seamed, sewn together of fragments or parts made into a unity suddenly no longer essential but constituted. *Macbeth* somewhat nostalgically invokes the English King as healer of the body private and politic—the successful doctor missing in Scotland is found in the English King who can heal by the laying on of hands, an idealized version of the relation of part to whole—and so might seem to be merely dramatizing the political commonplace that while the healthy body politic is united under its head, the traitor no longer forms a part of this body. The dismemberment of the traitor represents dramatically and physically the situation his treachery has produced, as he is, bodily and materially as well as politically, dissevered from his head.

To use the metaphor of the body politic in this way fits with its political uses in the sixteenth and seventeenth centuries. Indeed, from Plato on the metaphor has been used to support hierarchies favoring rulers and those groups benefiting from a rigidly stratified social structure. One classic articulation of this metaphor as a political figure can be found in the Elizabethan "Exhortation Concerning Good Order and Obedience to Rulers and Magistrates," which declares that it is "God's ordinance, God's commandment, and God's holy will, that the whole body of every realm, and all the members and parts of the same, shall be subject to their head, the king."[3] The metaphor of the body politic appears somewhat differently in Menenius's Fable of the Belly in the beginning of *Coriolanus*, in which the nobles are called the "belly," a central symbolic part of a grotesque body.[4] Shakespeare takes this fable with the identification of the patricians as the belly from his sources, and he uses it to subject the patrician claims to a dramatic irony: although Menenius employs the metaphor to strengthen the aristocrats' position and to calm the rioting plebeians, his parable presents an image of how leadership can destroy the public good. They consume all the social wealth and fail to serve as the ruling head. On first glance, *Macbeth*, in contrast, appears to be a play that will invoke the metaphor of the realm as body politic in a more orthodox manner.

The contemporary power and clarity of this metaphor were evidenced in its real life employment by James VI of Scotland (though soon to become James I of England), against the Earl of Gowrie. Steven Mullaney describes this incident eloquently in his essay included in this volume:

[3]*Certain Sermons or Homilies Appointed to Be Read in Churches in the Time of the Late Queen Elizabeth of Famous Memory* (London: Society for the Promotion of Christian Knowledge, 1908) 211.
[4]On the grotesque body, see Mikhail Bakhtin, *Rabelais and his World*, trans. Helene Iswolsky (Bloomington: Indiana UP, 1984) 303–67; Peter Stallybrass and Allon White, *The Politics and Poetics of Transgression* (Ithaca: Cornell UP, 1986) 1–26; Peter Stallybrass, "Patriarchal Territories: The Body Enclosed," *Rewriting the Renaissance*, eds. M. Ferguson, M. Quilligan, and N. Vickers (Chicago: U of Chicago P, 1986) 123–42.

In 1600, violating ancient codes of hospitality and of fealty, the earl of Gowrie attempted
to murder James VI of Scotland while the sovereign was staying at Gowrie's house in
Perth. Gowrie and his accomplice were cut down in the attempt. . . . [The body of the
traitor] was transported to Edinburgh, presented to Parliament in a spectral session,
duly found guilty of treason, and then hanged, drawn and quartered, and exhibited—on
poles fixed at Edinburgh, Perth, Dundee and Stirling (p. 110).

The body unseamed, then, is first the body of the traitor, "unseamed" (as the
Captain says in *Macbeth*) to illustrate the way his own deeds have dissevered him
from his King and his society. Representing such a dismembered body on stage
would seem only to reinforce the political and moral hierarchies of the play.
Macbeth actually treats this metaphor in a more complicated way, for the kind of
moral certainty that it evokes is projected into the past or future but never made
fully present on stage. It is useful, however, to begin by taking the measure of the
play's more traditionalist vision of social unity before exploring the ways in which
Shakespeare qualifies this vision.

Such a political reading of Macbeth's unseaming of the traitor at first seems to
be strengthened by the association of the witches with dissevered fragments of
selves. The witches throw into their cauldron—and therefore presumably gain
some of their supernatural power from—many parts of different, dead wholes,
"Poison'd entrails" and other fragments of animal and human bodies:

Second Witch: Fillet of a fenny snake,
              In the cauldron boil and bake;
              Eye of newt, and toe of frog,
              Wool of bat, and tongue of dog,
              Adder's fork, and blind-worm's sting,
              Lizard's leg, and howlet's wing,
              For a charm of powerful trouble,
              Like a hell-broth boil and bubble. . . .
Third Witch: Scale of dragon, tooth of wolf;
              Witches' mummy; maw, and gulf,
              Of the ravin'd salt-sea shark;
              Root of hemlock, digg'd i' th' dark;
              Liver of blaspheming Jew;
              Gall of goat, and slips of yew,
              Sliver'd in the moon's eclipse;
              Nose of Turk, and Tartar's lips;
              Finger of birth-strangled babe,
              Ditch-deliver'd by a drab,
              Make the gruel thick and slab.
                        (4.1.12–19, 22–32)

The witches too are traitors of a sort: they are marginalized, uncanny figures
whose dependence on dismemberment, especially of the weak, the excluded, or
the socially marginal, seems symbolically appropriate. Each example of a body part
in this famous cauldron speech points to a double kind of fragmentation. The
witches make this broth of "powerful trouble" out of parts (liver, nose, lips, finger)

that point not only to the whole body once joined in life but to a now broken narrative. It is the "liver of blaspheming Jew," a fragment doubled in power by being part of a larger story of blasphemy, which the witches are reconstituting in their pot. The finger belongs not just to any baby but to one strangled at birth, and strangled not by any woman but by a prostitute, a "drab." Earlier in the play we heard of similar dismembered parts that seemed to point to lost wholes both corporal and narrative: "Here I have a pilot's thumb,/Wrack'd, as homeward he did come" (1.3.28–29). By holding the pilot's thumb the witch invokes the power to cause a "wrack," and the body part seems to be identified as a source of the witches' power. The account of the sailor being "wracked" while on his way "homeward" also suggests that the cutting off of the pilot's thumb serves as an image of castration, the cut that keeps the self or the even plot always severed from its home. One of the deeper terrors of *Macbeth* seems to be not, then, the dismemberment of the traitor in manly battle but the "wrack" associated with the witches' uncanny control, and possibly, by extension, a man's mutilation at the hands not of a man but of a female or, perhaps even worse, a doubly gendered embodiment of fate.

To shift talk of dismemberment into the witches' mouths and into their incantations is to move attention away from the play's initial example of unseaming, which was associated not with witchcraft but with heroic victory. This shift registers anxiety about the value given to acts of dismemberment on both sides of the moral line. *Macbeth* is a play that seems at times to distinguish clearly between benevolent, good characters and the ambitious, murderous protagonists—"this dead butcher, and his fiend-like Queen" (5.9.35)—yet it also exposes most of the "good" characters to a disturbing dramatic scrutiny that suggests that they may not be as different from Macbeth and Lady Macbeth as they first seem. Since the actual "unseaming" in the play is performed by one warrior on another, the witches' reliance on dismemberment as the source of their magic power initially makes us reconsider its meaning. It serves at first to keep Macbeth from being associated with dismembered body parts and deflects any tendency to question the value of the kind of dismemberment performed by the hero in battle, an action that defines a male ideal in much of the play.

The witches have a complicated and doubled relation to tragic dismemberment, however, as this example suggests, and their use of it in their spells provides a hint of why dismemberment is not so easily avoided in these plays. Since they could be said to sew, or *seam*, together present, past, and future, they present a figure of historical and temporal totality. If, as has been long argued, the witches are to be identified with the three fates, spinning and cutting the thread of life, an identification implied in the Anglo-Saxon *wyrd* (as in "the Weird Sisters," 1.3.32), meaning "fate" or "destiny," then they are figures from a mythic past, yet they act in the present by reading the future. The play presents them as drawing their powers from dismembered body parts, as if the function of the cauldron were to reconstitute from these parts a different whole, one that grants a special prophetic power to these uncanny, marginalized figures excluded from the body politic and from the political realm as it is represented in the play. The play establishes a contrast, then, between their capacity to read the future, which seems to involve seeing beyond the momentary fragment of history in which they are located, and the means to this prophetic vision, which is dismemberment. As in *Coriolanus*, where accepting one's identity as part of a larger social or civic whole is felt by the protagonist as an undoing of the self, in *Macbeth* Shakespeare seems to link fragmentation or disintegration with a potentially dangerous embodiment of the whole. In both plays, submission to an image of the whole and to one's destiny in time is felt to be a kind of dismemberment of the self, a loss that in each case may also bring a special sense of individual power, if at great personal cost.

The witches' power is uncanny, then, both because it seems to cross the boundary between the supernatural and the human, and because we cannot decide if their advice is destructive or benevolent, a seizing of Macbeth's power of choice or a means of connecting him to his historical role. Freud's account of the uncanny includes body parts as principal examples—decapitated heads and mutilated or dissevered hands that are felt to be uncanny because they draw attention to a totality that is present in thought (because they point to it) but *not there*.[5] The rhetorical figure Freud depends on here is the synecdoche—the figure that offers part for whole. The witches present to Macbeth a synecdoche of time: he sees the fragment and guesses wrongly about the whole to which it should point. His embrace of this fragment nonetheless ironically allows him to seize the historical moment and to try to make it his. This portrait of human agency reveals its impotence in the face of a whole that can never be fully known. *Macbeth* is a tragedy in part because it does not present any clearer or less ironized portrait of human agency.

Heroic self-assertion is associated in *Macbeth*, then, with dismemberment—literally, in the case of the ambitious treachery of the first Thane of Cawdor, and, at the end of the play, of Macbeth. This also occurs more metaphorically in the middle of the play when Macbeth returns to the witches and chooses to interpret a fragment of his destiny—that he is King—as the whole story, an interpretive choice that he makes in the face of an historical fate that, it becomes increasingly clear to him and to the audience, will frustrate his ambition and deny his heirs any "succession." The play presents Macbeth's hubristic seizing of the historical moment as both heroic and fatally flawed, and represents his will as divided.

In *Macbeth*, this divided self defines the tragic space proper to historical agency. Thus the witches, figures at the crossing of gender and class, of history and mythography, of aesthetics ("fair is foul and foul is fair") and politics, help to suggest the dangers of believing that the play's moral or political conclusions can be simple. They are, as Macbeth calls them, "imperfect speakers" (1.3.70), meaning principally that their utterances are incomplete—imperfect as in the imperfect tense in Romance languages, imperfect in announcing that they are historically

---

[5]See Sigmund Freud, "The Uncanny," in *The Standard Edition of the Complete Psychological Works of Sigmund Freud*, 24 vols., trans. James Strachey et al., ed. James Strachey (London: Hogarth, 1953–1974), 17:219.

unfinished, and imperfect in creating desire and frustrating satisfaction. Hence their very words reinterpret speech itself as imperfect, dismembered, always a scattering of discursive parts that do not convey the whole meaning. If the sentence of history or of an individual life is still unfinished, then it has no perfected meaning. It might even be "a tale/Told by an idiot, full of sound and fury,/Signifying nothing" (5.5.26–28), leading to momentary victory but not to the truer success represented by succession.

The dismemberment enacted and represented in *Macbeth* kills, then, but it also seems to allow for a resistance to the sort of moral and political closure that appears too easily to distinguish the good and the evil at the end of the play. By not uttering the whole sentence of history, the witches open Macbeth to a break with his own moral values and eventually to a form of political rebellion. *Macbeth* punishes that rebellion by branding Macbeth as evil, but it also enacts his fantasy of dismemberment, providing a more covert textual affirmation of this very destructive power. The tragic dismemberment is thus characterized as the destruction that undoes the self, and yet the play pictures in Macbeth an intense desire for that dismemberment, which he invokes as a kind of liberation in the passage I cited as epigraph:

> Come, seeling Night,
> Scarf up the tender eye of pitiful Day,
> And, with thy bloody and invisible hand,
> Cancel, and tear to pieces, that great bond
> Which keeps me pale!
>   (3.2.46–50)

The "great bond" to which Macbeth refers here has a wide allusive resonance: it can refer to "the bond by which Banquo and Fleance hold their lives from Nature,"[6] in which case Macbeth is kept pale at the fear of their succession; it can refer to the bond of life more generally, including that which binds Macbeth to his humanity (canceling "that great bond" often is used in Shakespeare to describe the act of someone about to lose his or her life); and it can refer to the moral law that keeps Macbeth pale—that is, afraid to commit murder. This latter interpretation is strengthened by the extended legal metaphor in the speech, for a bond is a legal document, imagined here as a parchment to be canceled and then torn. To have that bond torn by the powerful figure of Night is here represented as a liberation that will free Macbeth from these moral limits and perhaps also from his humanity itself. The audience is not invited to take Macbeth's point of view entirely here, but the play nonetheless articulates a tragic desire for freedom from social, moral, and political constraint, a desire with which we are covertly allowed to sympathize. The irony of the final scene, in which Macduff discourses about time being free (5.9.21) as he carries in Macbeth's bleeding head, strikes readers and audiences very forcefully.

---

[6]This quotation is cited by the New Arden edition from the New Clarendon edition. See the New Arden edition of *Macbeth*, p. 85, n. 49.

Coriolanus

Tragic dismemberment fills the language of the play *Coriolanus* and threatens to create its ending. At the end of the play the Volscians, who had been Coriolanus's worst enemies and then became his allies in his quest to conquer Rome, turn against him when they realize he has bowed to his mother's wish that he not attack Rome. Remembering the violence of his destruction of one of their cities, Corioles, the crowd shouts:

> Tear him to pieces! Do it presently!
> He killed my son! My daughter! He killed my cousin Marcus! He killed my father!
> (5.6.120–22)

Coriolanus is killed first by the conspirators, who draw their swords to prevent the angry crowd, which they have incited, from tearing him apart. This death is quite different from the ending in Plutarch's account of Coriolanus's death, Shakespeare's principal source for the play. A comparison between the two can help to expose the shocking quality of the crowd's role in the play's last scene. Here is Plutarch's account in Sir Thomas North's translation of 1579:

> those that were of the conspiracie, beganne to crie out that he [Coriolanus] was not to be heard, nor that they would not suffer a traytour to usurp tyrannicall power over the tribe of the Volsces, who would not yeld up his estate and authoritie. And in saying these wordes, they all fell upon him, and killed him in the market place, none of the people once offering to rescue him. Howbeit it is a clere case, that this murder was not generally consented unto, of the most part of the Volsces, for men came out of all partes to honour his bodie, and dyd honourably burie him, setting out his tombe with great store of armour and spoyles, as the tombe of a worthie persone and great captaine.[7]

Plutarch's Coriolanus is not threatened, as is Shakespeare's, by a crowd made up of all the people that urges he be torn to pieces. After the death, too, the versions diverge. Plutarch describes a recuperative gathering at the tomb that honors Coriolanus: men came "out of all partes" to join in the communal spectacle. In the play too Aufidius gestures toward remembering and honoring Coriolanus—"Yet he shall have a noble memory" (5.6.153)—but the scene is briefer and does not involve the sense of regret shared by the people. It seems diminished in comparison to Plutarch's collective reinstatement of Coriolanus's heroic identity and suggests that Shakespeare wanted to intensify the dramatic effect of the Volscian betrayal of Coriolanus.

The way in which Shakespeare's ending seems to deny Coriolanus heroic stature has disturbed both actors and directors who stage the play, which they have often altered quite considerably in order to avoid this ending—for instance, by cutting the death scene altogether or more often by making Coriolanus himself his own killer to give him more dignity. In a recent essay John Ripley describes several per-

---

[7]Plutarch's "Life of Coriolanus" is reprinted in the Appendix to the Arden edition of *Coriolanus*. This citation is from pp. 367–68.

formances that illustrate the felt need to make Coriolanus more heroic in his death or, if not, then to evoke audience sympathy by treating him with unusual violence:

> William Poel, in his 1931 revival, dropped the onstage assassination altogether. . . . Michael Benthall, in the 1954 production, cut all the text after the cry of "Kill, kill, kill, kill, kill him" (5.6.130), and staged the assassination itself as a ceremonial bloodletting. "Clad in a great scarlet cloak that is like a splash of blood on the world's face," wrote Harold Hobson, "[Richard Burton] stands with arms outstretched in front of the dark city doors of Corioli, and, in the attitude of a priest celebrating some tremendous ritual, is stabbed to death by his envious enemies" (*Sunday Times*, 28 Feb., 1954). . . . In 1938, at the Old Vic, Olivier punctuated his demise with a breathtaking plunge down a steep flight of stairs. Alan Howard, in the 1977 RSC [Royal Shakespearean Company] production, became his own executioner [by flinging himself on his own sword in Aufidius's hand]. . . . Calculated cruelty to Marcius has been an equally productive directorial ploy. In 1959, at the Shakespeare Memorial Theatre, Olivier lept backwards off a twelve-foot-high platform from which he was dangled by soldiers, head-downward, while he was stabbed. "I wanted something really nasty," Peter Hall told an interviewer; and he found his inspiration in the sordid dispatch of Mussolini (*Daily Express*, 8 July 1959).[8]

As this last staging shows, some directors have alluded dramatically to the crowd's desire to "tear him to pieces" (5.6.120), a line that alludes to an earlier scene in which Coriolanus's mother Volumnia talks about his son with his wife Virgilia and Valeria, a friend. Volumnia compares a bleeding wound to a mother's breast dripping with milk, although, unlike Lady Macbeth, Volumnia hardly seems to recognize the horror of her imagery:

> The breasts of Hecuba
> When she did suckle Hector, look'd not lovelier
> Than Hector's forehead when it spit forth blood
> At Grecian sword contemning.
> (1.3.40–43)

After this shocking comment, Valeria describes the kind of boy Volumnia and Virgilia are raising:

> *Valeria:*   O' my word, the father's son! . . . I saw him run after a gilded butterfly, and when he caught it, he let it go again, and after it again, and over and over he comes, and up again, catched it again; or whether his fall enraged him, or how 'twas, he did so set his teeth and tear it. Oh, I warrant how he mammocked it!
> *Volumnia:*   One on's father's moods.
> *Valeria:*   Indeed, la, 'tis a noble child.
> (1.3.57–67)

"Mammocking" means "to tear into fragments or shreds," although the word contains the uneasy echo of "mammary" and "mammal," as if already in a subter-

---

[8]John Ripley, " 'Physic for the Whole State': *Coriolanus* as Sacrificial Crisis," unpublished essay. Quotation used with the author's permission.

ranean connection the play is imagining a shredding of the breast.[9] This scene first introduces the topos of dismemberment, or "mammocking," in domestic terms, but it is Coriolanus who will eventually become associated with the butterfly. Cominius describes Coriolanus and his Volscian army as "boys pursuing summer butterflies" (4.6.95), a double comparison that presents the Romans as "flies" or "brats" but that also superbly diminishes Coriolanus's own self-presentation, for he had earlier compared himself to "a lonely dragon" (4.1.30). Menenius glosses this pattern of imagery toward the end of the play as he begins to realize that Coriolanus is the butterfly, now turned dragon:

> There is differency between a grub and a butterfly; yet your butterfly was a grub. This Martius is grown from man to dragon: he has wings: he's more than a creeping thing.
>
> (5.4.11–14)

When in the conclusion the crowd shouts, "Tear him to pieces" (5.6.120), the play completes this idea, showing that Coriolanus is in danger of becoming what he has torn apart. The Romans were first called butterflies as Coriolanus attacked them, and now he himself, the lonely dragon, risks having his wings "mammocked."

This threat to heroic dignity is only one of the most dramatic ways in which the play more broadly concerns itself with dismemberment. The play dramatizes the threats that the hero will be dismembered by the state, that the son will be destroyed and symbolically castrated by the mother, and that the state will be torn apart by the conflicting interests of its citizens, with the danger of civil unrest haunting the opening scenes. Indeed, Coriolanus complains to his mother that he will become like a eunuch or a woman if he compromises and goes to the marketplace:

> My throat of war be turn'd,
> Which choired with my drum, into a pipe
> Small as an eunuch, or the virgin voice
> That babies lull asleep!
>
> (3.2.112–15)

This dismembering of the body politic is predicted by the opening scene in which the plebeians, ready to revolt, are pacified with Menenius's Fable of the Belly, according to which "the senators of Rome are this good belly" (1.1.147), and the mutinying citizens are invoked through the person of the First Citizen as "You, the great toe" (1.1.154). This body politic is a grotesque body in Bakhtin's and Stallybrass's sense—all belly and consuming orifices, the "lower bodily stratum" occupying the position normally belonging to the head.[10] The distortion in the metaphor strikes even Menenius, who insists, "I may make the belly smile,/As

---

[9]Janet Adelman develops some of the implications of this connection in her essay in this volume (pp. 134–166), in which she describes the ways in which the link between milk and blood becomes a central symbolic interaction of the play.

[10]See n. 4 on p. 3.

well as speak" (1.1.108–9), where the explicit personification is accomplished by an imagined, already disfiguring transfer of parts and attributes—the smiling belly.

This body politic is scattered throughout the play. People are spoken of as body parts, while imagery of digestion represents the self-consumption and the self-destruction of this divided state. Coriolanus is called "a limb that has but a disease:/Mortal, to cut it off" (3.1.293–94) (as Menenius puts it), but cut it off is what the tribunes lead the people to do. We hear from Cominius that the state has a navel—"Even when the navel of the state was touch'd," Coriolanus comments, the citizens "would not thread the gates" (3.1.122–23)—and bowels, as his mother accuses Coriolanus of "tearing/His country's bowels out" (5.3.102–3). Moreover, in the scene in which the citizens give Coriolanus their voices, even this act seems to involve a separation of body and voice. Coriolanus plays on the notion that these voices have been literally given away, separated from the bodies that give them vibrance: "Here come moe voices./Your voices!" (2.3.124–25). The people have become nothing but voices; it is no wonder they need no bread. The often grotesque materializing of the metaphor of the body politic in the Roman scenes reminds us that the threat to the hero is part of a greater fragmenting of what should be a source of unity: the Roman state.

In this play, the symbolic universe is itself imagined as having a body so that it too can be torn apart. Body parts are scattered through the air in Menenius's admission that he is "one that converses more with the buttock of the night than with the forehead of the morning" (2.1.50–52), where not only the personified times have been rent but the sequence of day and night itself is imagined as a body scattered. In Volumnia's final speech to Coriolanus, we again hear of the dismembering of the air—or of time—in a line designed to describe the quality of Coriolanus's heroism:

> Speak to me, son:
> Thou hast affected the fine strains of honour,
> To imitate the graces of the gods,
> To tear with thunder the wide cheeks o'th'air.
> (5.3.148–51)

The trope of personification functions here not merely to give body to the inanimate or abstract but to embody it so as to tear it apart. If dismemberment is the principal political and figurative action of this tragedy, as of *Macbeth* and *Antony and Cleopatra*, then a kind of reverse personification is one of its informing figures of speech, a trope where the giving of face dismembers and disfigures. Like the action of the gods (for Coriolanus is being compared to Jupiter here), the trope tears with thunder the wide cheeks of the air.

If everything is scattered about, one supposes that a unity preceded this dismemberment, and one can similarly ask if any move toward a reincorporation or a gathering together makes the closure. The person who embodies that unity—that which draws everything into it and consumes it, to use the metaphors of the play—is Volumnia, who represents not only the overwhelming mother from whom

Coriolanus has tried to separate himself through heroic action but the body politic itself, Mother Rome. Volumnia's odd relationship with her son is already adumbrated in her second line in the play, which begins, "If my son were my husband . . ." The sense in which Volumnia becomes a character who usurps or controls all of Coriolanus's attachments is suggested by her dominance in scenes involving his wife and is articulated with epigrammatic force in the central scene in Rome, where Volumnia convinces him to go to the marketplace: "I am in this/Your wife, your son, these senators, the nobles" (3.2.64–65). In insisting that he return to the marketplace, Volumnia appears to take away Coriolanus's sense of individual agency—his power of manhood as he has defined it. Here the mother usurps all relations in a terrifying example of what we might call civic incest.[11] If in the psychological plot Volumnia represents a too-powerful, engulfing mother, on a different symbolic level, then, she also represents Mother Rome, the collectivity to which Coriolanus should belong, and her actions show what Mother Rome does to her sons. The play then can be read as a strong critique of the corrupt Roman government that has produced such a deeply divided state, and of the heroic values demanded by Rome and espoused by Volumnia.

This picture of the whole—that gatheredness or collectedness of self and society that confers value and order—as being incestuous and as tending to betray, swallow, and engulf Coriolanus, provides the energy that generates the play's repeated dismemberments. *Coriolanus*, like *Macbeth*, is deeply marked by this symbolic economy—a unity that is found to be too complete and to draw into itself categories that must be kept separate (foul and fair, mother and son, son and husband, the individual and the state)—and thereby presents a horrifying picture of that totality that should serve to provide a center and source of meaning.

Macbeth and *Coriolanus* share this horrifying representation of the collective or the whole as destructive of individual desire and agency. In *Macbeth*, however, fantasies of dismemberment—both metaphoric and literal reminders of it—provide a covert means to advocate a freeing of the individual from social constraint, although these are also shown to be evil, whereas in *Coriolanus* fantasies of escape first center in heroic action that purports to defend the state and only later are shown to involve an attack on the state. If Coriolanus's expulsion from Rome is a kind of dismemberment—he is "a limb . . . /Mortal, to cut it off" (3.1.293–94)— then his attack on Rome is another, but this metaphor is only realized in the moment of his own death, where he receives the traitor's due, his dead body symbolizing the impossibility of any escape from the overwhelming "whole" of which he finally has to admit he is a part. So in *Coriolanus* escape is shown to be illusory

---

[11]One might add that the dramatic use of dismemberment is associated early on with similar questions about gender and maternal destructiveness through Euripides's use of the device in *The Bacchae*, where Pentheus's mother tears him to pieces while in a Dionysiac ecstatic trance. The notion that Volumnia becomes a figure for Rome is strengthened by the symbolic treatment of Corioli: passage through the city gates is imagined as both a rape and, in the other direction, a horrifying birth fantasy that allows Marcius to believe that he can be author of himself. On the two fantasies described here—of the overwhelming and all-consuming mother, and of birth from the city—see the essay by Adelman in this volume (p. 155).

while individual agency is again associated with the choice of fragmentation, for Coriolanus chooses to exile himself and thus to cut himself off from the body politic in order to protect his power to act as he believes is right.

Antony and Cleopatra

Antony and Cleopatra, a play that shares with Shakespeare's romances a celebration of the metaphoric dimension of action, nonetheless must be placed with these late tragedies that dramatize the inevitability that the heroic subject must come "unseamed." One measure of the play's tragic stature is the extent of its use of a symbolic economy similar to that which has been outlined for *Macbeth* and *Coriolanus*. If these two plays show why the tragic protagonist might need to escape suffocating or destructive totalities even at the risk of complete loss of self, *Antony and Cleopatra* can be read as a play that re-members and re-collects the dissevered tragic body in part by reimagining tragic dismemberment and the scattering of the self as bounty. It is a play about different kinds of union and dismemberment, where scattering or loss is made to point the way to a greater imagined whole. In its tragic vision, then, the play suggests that whatever affirmations remain are made possible only through what Antony calls "the very heart of loss" (4.12.29).

We might briefly approach the question of the relation of part to whole in this play by looking at the definition of the trope of synecdoche in George Puttenham's *Arte of English Poesie*, a rhetorical handbook published in 1589 in which the author gives English names and definitions for the classic rhetorical figures of thought and speech. Synecdoche is understood far more broadly in this Renaissance account than most modern definitions would allow, for Puttenham sees it as a system of tropes such as figurative foreshadowing, personification, relation of part to whole as well as of whole to part, and cause for effect. He gives the trope the English name of "Figure of quick conceit":

> the Greeks then call it *Synecdoche*, the Latines *sub intellectio* or understanding, for by part we are enforced to understanded the whole, by the whole part, by many things one thing, by one, many, by a thing precedent, a thing consequent.[12]

Puttenham gives the following examples of the trope:

> as when one would tell me how the French king was overthrown at Saint Quintans, I am enforced to think that it was not the king himselfe in person, but the Constable of Fraunce with the French kings power. Or if one would say, the towne of Andwerpe were famished, it is not so to be taken, but of the people of the towne of Andwerp, and this conceit being drawen aside, and (as it were) from one thing to another, it encombers the minde with a certaine imagination what it may be that is meant, and not expressed: as he that said to a young gentlewoman, who was in her chamber making herself unready,

---

[12]George Puttenham, *The Arte of English Poesie*, 1589 (1906; Kent, Ohio: Kent State UP, 1970 [facsimile]) 196. I have modernized the orthography but not the spelling.

Mistresse will ye give me leave to unlace your peticote, meaning (perchance) the other thing that might follow such unlasing. In the olde time, whosoever was allowed to undoe his Ladies girdle he might lie with her all night: wherfore, the taking of a womens maidenhead away, was said to undoo her girdle.[13]

The examples of synecdoche here include a personification, Antwerp for the people of Antwerp, and what we might call a metonymy, the king for his army or commanders. To call this a synecdoche in modern terms would be to make a political point: the king and his army are part of one collective whole, an idealized unity that the figure of speech establishes but that neither Macbeth nor Coriolanus experience with their armies. Puttenham's third example, the extraordinary synecdoche whereby "unlacing the peticote" means "taking the maidenhead," is an example of both metonymy (the peticote covers the woman's virginity but is not in any sense essentially a part of it) and Puttenham's unusual temporalized concept of synecdoche, which is also central to the way in which Antony and Cleopatra conceive of their deaths. Here the events that precede lead to those that follow where something not intrinsically related to a woman's body is treated as a part of it, and where the totality—the part of which this part is only a part—is the larger narrative action of the taking of the maidenhead. Puttenham's example seems to share a deep affinity with the movements of thought and image in *Antony and Cleopatra*, for it shows a movement toward an imagined whole that involves becoming *un*ready, being *un*laced, and *un*doing the maidenhead.

The idea of the body politic is already a synecdoche, since it imagines the individual subjects or citizens as parts of a whole that is somehow embodied in them. It is even more a synecdoche when the body politic is personified in an individual ruler, as when Antony, as he does so often, refers to Cleopatra as "Egypt"—a kind of hyperbole of incorporation. *Antony and Cleopatra* could then be said to take the notion of the body politic to universal proportions. Each of the protagonists is apotheosized and treated as embodying the whole universe in his or her body. This might be seen as the opposite of the dismembering action of tragedy, but in *Antony and Cleopatra* it is precisely this "incorporation" in a larger whole that undoes the self. This sense that the self is a synecdoche for some larger institution in which it figures but which it also embodies is perhaps felt most strongly in those moments when "Antony" and "Cleopatra" are treated as institutions to which the characters Antony and Cleopatra ought to remain loyal:

> Sir, sometimes, when he is not Antony,
> He comes too short of that great property
> Which still should go with Antony.
>   (1.1.57–59)

says Philo, explaining to Demetrius what appears to be a falling off from what he understands to be a Roman heroic standard. Yet Antony has just invoked this very sense of identity by claiming to achieve it especially in the moment when he is

[13]Puttenham, pp. 205–6.

stirred by Cleopatra (1.1.42–43). The definition of these institutions of "Antony" and "Cleopatra" thus is contested in the play, with the Romans insisting that the romantic Antony is not the Antony of heroic stature, while the lovers insist that Antony fulfills his heroic stature only in his passion, but the existence of the institution is never doubted. Antony finally can be defined only by the tautology Cleopatra utters: "Antony/Will be himself" (1.1.42–43). Even Antony and Cleopatra speak this language when they fear they are losing themselves: "I am Antony yet" (3.13.93), Antony insists after the loss at Actium, when he believes Cleopatra to have betrayed him to Caesar's messenger Thidias, asking "what's her name,/Since she was Cleopatra?" (3.13.98–99). The temporal paradoxes in these lines—I will be I (but am not yet), or I will still be I but won't be for long—point to the way in which Antony and Cleopatra are here shown to be parts of an institutionalized self.

Antony insults Cleopatra by saying that before she fell in love with him she had become merely the leftovers on the plates of Julius Caesar and Pompey:

> a morsel, cold upon
> Dead Caesar's trencher: nay, you were a fragment
> Of Gnaeus Pompey's.
>
> (3.13.116–18)

Thus when betrayal threatens, the imagined mythic whole crashes into small parts, as the image of the "morsel" again suggests the fragmentary, the partial. Later in the scene, when the lovers have been reconciled, Cleopatra concludes, "But since my lord/Is Antony again, I will be Cleopatra" (3.13.186–87). In each case, the invoking of this sense of institution—we might think of it as the myth of Antony and Cleopatra—comes with a reminder of a moment when the part has been split from that whole. The cost of submersion in this particular mythic totality will be death, the tragic dispersion of self.

The intimate imagined link between an ideal whole and the parts of the body is experienced by the lovers as an erotic reimagining of their body parts. In invoking the transcendent power of their love, Cleopatra, faced with Antony's imminent return to Rome, comments:

> when you sued staying,
> Then was the time for words: no going then;
> Eternity was in our lips, and eyes,
> Bliss in our brows' bent; none our parts so poor
> But was a race of heaven.
>
> (1.3.33–37)

Here their "parts"—lips, eyes, eyebrows—are sufficient to make present a unity that itself is heavenly. Eros links the fragments of the human body in time to "eternity." Yet Antony and Cleopatra also experience passion as dismembering or dispersing their powers metaphorically. For Antony, this dismemberment is sexual, if metaphoric: "O, thy vile lady!/She has robb'd me of my sword" (4.14.22–23), he tells Eros; and Cleopatra tellingly describes the urgency of her desire to send news to Antony in Rome by saying, "He shall have every day a several greeting,/Or I'll unpeople Egypt" (1.5.77–78). She sends "twenty several messengers" (1.5.62–63) to Antony each day and thus risks "unpeopling" her country. Here Cleopatra as "Egypt" will empty herself to keep her tie to Antony strong. These messengers point also to the role of metaphor, that trope that is a carrying across of a word or a meaning from one land to another. Cleopatra's messengers, like her metaphors, threaten a scattering of her power even as they express its source and quality. The scene that these lines conclude and the one in which Antony and Enobarbus discuss his plans to leave for Rome can serve as two comic examples early in the play of how the rhetoric of synecdoche, inclusion, and submersion of the part in the whole is linked throughout to, and indeed made possible by, an action of dismemberment and fragmentation that the lovers finally choose to embrace.

Antony's decision to leave for Rome is prompted by the news that his wife Fulvia has died. Although she caused him personal and political difficulties, once she is dead, Antony mourns her, commenting "she's good, being gone" (1.2.123). Here he adumbrates a politics and an erotics of loss in which value is created because of absence, loss, or death, with these terms thus marking the prerequisite part (and cause) that leads to the mythic whole. One of these examples is a passing political comment Caesar makes to try to explain to himself how Pompey can have become so powerful: "the ebb'd man, ne'er lov'd till ne'er worth love,/Comes dear'd, by being lack'd" (1.4.43–44). The "ebb'd man," his powers already beginning to be dispersed or diminished, is somehow all the more powerful in this play. But the more extended and important example of this movement from dispersion to imagined totality and back again to a kind of metaphoric dismemberment occurs in Enobarbus's joking description of Cleopatra as a kind of colossal body politic. Enobarbus has joked that if Antony leaves Egypt, he will kill "all our women": "if they suffer our departure, death's the word" (1.2.131–32). He continues the joke by playing on the double sense of "to die" in Renaissance English, where the phrase could also mean to achieve sexual consummation:

Antony:	I must be gone.
Enobarbus:	. . . Cleopatra catching but the least noise of this, dies instantly. I have seen her die twenty times upon far poorer moment: I do think there is mettle in death, which commits some loving act upon her, she hath such a celerity in dying.
Antony:	She is cunning past man's thought.
Enobarbus:	Alack, sir, no, her passions are made of nothing but the finest part of pure love. We cannot call her winds and waters sighs and tears; they are greater storms and tempests than almanacs can report. This cannot be cunning in her; if it be, she makes a shower of rain as well as Jove.

(1.2.133–49)

Cleopatra is pictured here, in a critique of lyric discourse, as a part of a larger body politic, a kind of colossus that is the whole world. Her celerity in dying, and her other forms of *un*doing and making herself *un*ready, produce a vision of a totality with divine omnipotence—she is as good as Jove (at least for producing rain).

Cleopatra the character is only a part of this transcendent whole, and yet in Enobarbus's quip her body somehow *is* the earth with its storms, so that the figurative and the literal have reversed position—"We cannot call her winds and waters sighs and tears," where the proper name for her letting out of breath is now "wind" and not "sighs," and what was once viewed as literal, as the action of the play—her tears and sighs at Antony's leaving—is to be read only as a metaphor for the cosmic convulsion to be produced by their separation (as if they really were Mars and Venus, joined in a love guaranteeing cosmic harmony, as this love affair was interpreted by Renaissance allegorists).

Enobarbus's joke continues, strangely linking imagery of cutting and dismembering with the colossal synecdoche of Cleopatra. The following passage shows how the play is beginning to turn images of cutting or dismembering around to attach to them a different meaning:

> *Antony:* Fulvia is dead.
> *Enobarbus:* Sir?
> *Antony:* Fulvia is dead.
> *Enobarbus:* Fulvia?
> *Antony:* Dead.
> *Enobarbus:* Why, sir, give the gods a thankful sacrifice. When it pleaseth their deities to take the wife of a man from him, it shows to man the tailors of the earth; comforting therein, that when old robes are worn out, there are members to make new. If there were no more women but Fulvia, then had you indeed a cut, and the case to be lamented: this grief is crown'd with consolation, your old smock brings forth a new petticoat, and indeed the tears live in an onion, that should water this sorrow.
>
> (1.2.154–68)

Here Enobarbus develops the conceit of the world as a tailor shop where the gods are the tailors, cutting new clothes out of old (with a bawdy sense throughout associated with both "member" and "cut"). In this tailor shop of the world, Fulvia is understood as part of the larger collective "women." If Fulvia were the only woman, to lose her would be to lose all—her death would be a cut—but as she is only a part of the larger whole, to lose her—that is, to have her cut from the whole—would be to gain (with the bawdy sense of "cut"), to bring forth (the birthing metaphor is especially apt) a new "petticoat"—and we know from Puttenham what such a garment represents. The totality—the collectivity of "women"—is reached here too through cutting, when the cutting is a metaphor for death. The cut that is also a sexual organ (the cut that might be penetrated when the petticoat is unlaced); the cutting of the body that is also the producer of pleasure; a scattering of the self that is also the reconfirmation of a totality—all these are characteristic jokes for *Antony and Cleopatra* that will be played out to their fullest and most literal sense in the play's ending.

Throughout the play, then, Shakespeare's bawdy language defines the tragic dialectic of submersion in a desired whole through a cutting or dismembering, a dialectic pitting pain with loss, hyperbole with incomplete or interrupted synecdoches. Thus in Act 1, scene 5, Cleopatra begins by thinking that Mardian, her eunuch, is free from the desire that drives her to think only of the absent Antony:

Cleopatra:	. . . I take no pleasure
	In aught an eunuch has: 'tis well for thee
	That, being unseminar'd, thy freer thoughts
	May not fly forth of Egypt. Hast thou affections?
Mardian:	Yes, gracious madam.
Cleopatra:	Indeed?
Mardian:	Not in deed, madam, for I can do nothing
	But what indeed is honest to be done:
	Yet have I fierce affections, and think
	What Venus did with Mars.
Cleopatra:	O Charmian!
	Where think'st thou he is now? Stands he, or sits he?
	Or does he walk? or is he on his horse?
	O happy horse to bear the weight of Antony!
	(1.5.9–21)

Mardian the eunuch is "unseminar'd" (without seed), while presumably Antony and Cleopatra are "seminar'd," and yet Egypt is described as the place where the "seedsman/Upon the slime and ooze scatters his grain,/And shortly comes to harvest" (2.7.21–23), an image whereby the scattering or dispersing of seed is the necessary condition for fertility. Mardian reenacts the cut that made him "unseminar'd" in his pun on "indeed," where he cuts the word in half, marking the division between the figurative "indeed" of Cleopatra and his literal inability. He "thinks" what Venus did with Mars—but doesn't do it in deeds. For Cleopatra, however, these two are one and the same: she moves without transition or explanation from the reference to Mars and Venus to Antony—"where think'st thou he is now?" She and Antony participate fully in the imagined love affair of Mars and Venus, in the face of which she feels no inadequacy at all, and yet she gets to this vision of erotic totality through the cut of Mardian. She makes love like Venus in deed—and that deed will also be a cutting off, a death.

For Antony, the play provides several beneficent examples of a scattering or dispersing that, while not overtly sexual, extend the play's treatment of fertility through scattering. The traits and actions that get named Antony's "bounty," including the scene in the marketplace in which he gives away the parts of his empire to Cleopatra's children, show the play's fascination with a kind of dismemberment that somehow leads to gain. While this scattering seems to be glossed in a comic vein by the image of the seedsman scattering his seeds, the ending of the play makes it clear that this scattering is also a radical self-undoing for Antony and that such fertility comes only with death.

This quality of Antony's perhaps also provides a way of reading the play's formal dispersion. With acts that have thirteen to fifteen scenes (Acts 3 and 4), most taking place in locations geographically distant from one another (Rome, Athens, Messina, Alexandria, a plain in Syria), the play seems to enact the very dispersion it discusses through the fiction. While this formal scattering could be said to suggest an epic scope and claim, the effect of this fragmenting of the action hardly seems one of imperial control or containment, and the play has been quite rightly characterized as making an anti-epic argument. The formal dismemberment of the dramatic unity, this scattering of the action, is the means by which the play functions—like Antony, not in spite of but because of the scattering of its parts.

Antony's "bounty" is most clearly linked to a capacity to reincorporate the world into a hyperbolic image of union in Cleopatra's dream vision of him after his death. The earlier comic examples of the topos of the body politic are matched here by the tragic turn of this trope, where we come to see the scattering or dismembering in a more literal, and more destructive, light. Cleopatra's dream vision of Antony as a Colossus or God standing over the whole world suggests that the cosmic totality he personifies has been achieved through "reaping"—death—but more importantly perhaps by the dispersion of self Antony experiences as he is "reaped":

> His legs bestrid the ocean, his rear'd arm
> Crested the world: his voice was propertied
> As all the tuned spheres, and that to friends:
> But when he meant to quail, and shake the orb,
> He was as rattling thunder. For his bounty,
> There was no winter in 't: an autumn 'twas
> That grew the more by reaping: His delights
> Were dolphin-like, they show'd his back above
> The element they lived in, in his livery
> Walk'd crowns and crownets: realms and islands were
> As plates dropp'd from his pocket.
> (5.2.82–92)

Incorporating the whole world, Antony's bounty—his giving away of riches, of seed, of kingdoms, even of the self—can somehow occur within this unity, and thus becomes a radical scattering always re-membered by hyperbole. The familiar and powerful paradoxes of this speech apply not only to mortality and human frailty, but to the particular play of whole and part, recollection and dismembering (or scattering), that characterizes the play. As a personification of a cosmic body politic, Antony nonetheless is already dispersing his parts—dropping realms and islands from his pockets. His "bounty" grew the more by reaping: the metaphorical labor in this play is to reimagine tragic dismemberment as occurring within this universalized self or even as making it possible.

In *Antony and Cleopatra*, then, synecdoche is rewritten as a tragic figure: the play radicalizes the desire expressed more indirectly in *Macbeth* and *Coriolanus* for a dismemberment or dispersion that might free the self from that which constrains it. Antony rejects Rome—"Let Rome in Tiber melt" (1.1.33)—several times in the play and most finally in his moment of suicide, as he rewrites the Dido and Aeneas story in his mind, imagining them together in the underworld waiting for his arrival with Cleopatra as their rivals. Here Antony implies that the Roman version of the story as told in that nation's great epic, *The Aeneid*, is simply wrong, and he makes the opposite choice: to stay and die with Cleopatra, his Dido. But this rewriting of Roman mythology still submits him to a destructive whole, though a different one: the mythic love affair with Cleopatra that has both dismembered him and freed him—from Rome, from heroic ascesis, from mortal limitation.

To say that the play radicalizes the symbolic economy described here is to suggest that it accepts and dramatizes more directly both the desire for dismemberment and its costs. It shows that submersion in a mythic whole may be both deeply feared and deeply desired, that such submersion can only come with the acceptance of the very dismemberment or dispersion of the self that seems to be its opposite, that it is both destructive and yet the only means to self-transcendence. It shows that being willing to accept and even seek death can become the only way to give a life the kind of heroic meaning that the two protagonists long for, the certainty that their love truly exceeds in value that of the love of any other lovers or even the claims of "Rome" itself.

Is a political valence brought to these plays by their dramatic representation of the violent fragmenting and dismembering of the body politic? All three, though in quite different ways, criticize the heroic military values that initially appear to define not only the protagonists' power but the plays' ideologies. *Macbeth* punishes the desire, expressed through and in the character of Macbeth, to achieve dominance of fate, time, and political fortune by the deeds of the hand, the kind of deeds that the hero is good at performing, with the tools he knows he can use. It thus hints at the threat posed by the military hero to the ordered society he supposedly protects, while dramatizing powerful desires, only apparently killed off in the ending, to unseat the king and seize the time. The play surreptitiously identifies the dismemberment—the decapitation of the body politic—as a source of unauthorized political power. *Coriolanus* even more powerfully indicts this military ideology as already a form of dismemberment, and uses dismemberment to show the destructive effects of the powers in control. The play's overt meditation on the metaphor of the body politic suggests that this state will need to be pulled apart before it can be reconstituted as a more functional, integrated body. All three of these plays then represent political fragmentation not merely to lament a lost order, threatened by heroic excess, but to celebrate that threat, no matter how destructive to the individual it may be. Simply because tragedies end in death—the tragic loading of the stage with dead bodies—and because they insist that we accept the true costs of action that transgresses human or political boundaries does not mean that they are celebrations of the order that was lost or of the boundaries that have been crossed. But one thing they do insist on is an honest accounting of what the disruption of social, familial, or psychic order may mean—a measuring of the costs of such rebellion that gives full weight to the possibility of complete disintegration of meaning and value implicit in such undoing.

In *Antony and Cleopatra* Shakespeare finally seems able to affirm the value of being gathered into a mythic totality, although the play insists that to be so is an act of self-destruction of apocalyptic significance, a marking out of the "new heaven and new earth" to which Antony refers in the first scene. These three plays then do not fully undermine our interpretive efforts or the characters' efforts to construct meaning, but they show that the connecting of part to whole—the re-collection of bodies, events, words—that such interpretive closure requires can be destructive and participates itself in the tragic process, and so they frustrate our desire for clarity and simplicity in tragic illumination. If in Greek tragedy we might be said to "suffer into truth," for Shakespeare truth sometimes seems to lie in suffering, in dismemberment, and in human mortality or loss. *Antony and Cleopatra* will assert that it is nonetheless truth, albeit changed by the element in which it lives—the "lie" of Cleopatra, the myth of history, the totality that gives meaning and kills, the breastfeeding mother who simultaneously provides an image of nurture and death:

> With thy sharp teeth this knot intrinsicate
> Of life at once untie: poor venemous fool,
> Be angry, and despatch. . . .
> 　　　　　　　　　Peace, peace!
> Dost thou not see my baby at my breast,
> That sucks the nurse asleep?
> 　　　　　(5.2.303–5, 308–9)

Shakespeare's tragic "knot intrinsicate"—intrinsic, intricate, tying truth and lies, soul and body, actor and impersonation, death and nurture, dispersion and synecdoche—provides a final image for a tragic form that makes dismemberment and death intrinsic to its order.

This book presents a range of contemporary readings of Shakespeare's late tragedies and their early seventeenth-century and their twentieth-century cultural contexts. One volume cannot do justice to the complexity and range of current work on these three plays, nor to the cultural and historic research being done on Shakespeare. Indeed, the choice of the New Century Views series to focus on three canonical Shakespeare plays to some extent requires the editor to select among the richness of recent studies of Shakespeare and Renaissance culture essays that are oriented toward reading and interpreting these texts. This volume itself, then, participates in the project of canonizing Shakespeare's plays, and in its focus on the *literary* text is quite traditional in its aims. Much recent work on the sixteenth–seventeenth century English theater, on the cultural and political meaning of these plays, on "Shakespeare" as a cultural construct, and on Shakespeare's cultural capital in the twentieth century does not focus on specific plays or on literary texts at all, so the essays collected here necessarily represent only some of the many intellectual projects underway in the field of Shakespeare studies. That said, it is hoped that the power and excitement of the contemporary debate can emerge from this selection. Many of the essays in the volume have become "classic" in the sense that they define a set of interpretive moves or questions on which writer after writer takes a stand, even if it is by using a different idiom or critical method, or by contesting the centrality of *these* questions and *these* answers in the first place. It is the aim of the volume to make accessible such classic arguments while providing examples of more recent work that similarly is shaping the discipline, and thus to enable its readers to carry on these debates all the more fruitfully.

The Jacobean Shakespeare: Some Observations on the Construction of the Tragedies

Maynard Mack

1

No account of Shakespeare's virtuosity as a dramatist, and more importantly as a tragic dramatist, would be complete without an effort to examine some of the principles of construction (often repeated from play to play but in such varying guises that they rarely command our conscious attention) which give his tragedies their distinctive "feel," their form and pressure. And the right place to begin, it seems to me, is with A. C. Bradley's pioneering analysis in the second of his famous lectures, published some ninety years ago. Bradley's concern was with what would today be called the clearer outlines of Shakespearean practice—the management of exposition, conflict, crises, catastrophe; the contrasts of pace and scene; the over-all patterns of rise-and-fall, variously modulated; the slackened tension after the crisis and Shakespeare's devices for countering this; and the faults.[1]

Bradley is quite detailed about the faults. Sometimes, he says, there are too rapid shiftings of scene and *dramatis personae*, as in the middle section of *Antony and Cleopatra*. Sometimes there is extraneous matter, not required for plot or character development, like the player's speech in *Hamlet* about the murder of Priam, or Hamlet's advice later to the same player on speaking in the theater. Sometimes there are soliloquies too obviously expositional, as when Edgar disguises himself to become Poor Tom in *King Lear*. Or there is contradiction and inconsistency, as with double time in *Othello*. Or flatulent writing: "obscure, inflated, tasteless," or "pestered with metaphors." Or "gnomic" insertions, like the

From Maynard Mack, *Everybody's Shakespeare: Reflections Chiefly on the Tragedies* (Lincoln: Nebraska U. P., 1993), 231–62. The title in this collection is "What Happens in Shakespearean Tragedy?" Essay first published as "The Jacobean Shakespeare: Some Observations on the Construction of the Tragedies," in Alvin Kernan, ed., *Modern Shakespearean Criticism* (New York: Harcourt Brace, 1970). The original footnotes have been renumbered. Reproduced by permission of the author.

[1]See chapter 1 of A. C. Bradley, *Shakespearean Tragedy*, 3rd. ed. (New York: St. Martin's Press, 1992; 1st published, 1904). The text of the plays used throughout this essay is that of the Pelican Shakespeare, *Complete Works of Shakespeare*, General Editor Alfred Harbage (Penguin Books, 1969).

Duke's couplet interchange with Brabantio in *Othello,* used "more freely than, I suppose, a good playwright now would care to do." And finally, to make an end, there is too often, he says, a sacrificing of dramatic appropriateness to get something said that the author wants said. Thus the comments of the Player King and Claudius on the instability of human purpose arise because Shakespeare "wishes in part simply to write poetry, and partly to impress on the audience thoughts which will help them to understand, not the player-king nor yet King Claudius, but Hamlet himself." These failings, Bradley concludes, belong to an art of drama imperfectly developed, which Shakespeare inherited from his predecessors and acquiesced in, on occasion, from "indifference or want of care."

Though Bradley's analysis is still the best account we have of the outward shape of Shakespearean tragedy, a glance at his list of faults and especially his examples reminds us that a vast deal of water has got itself under the critical bridges since 1904. It is not simply that most of the faults he enumerates would no longer be regarded as such, but would instead be numbered among the characteristic practices of Shakespearean dramaturgy, even at its most triumphant. Still more striking is the extent to which our conception of the "construction" of the tragedies has itself changed. The matters Bradley described have not ceased to be important— far from it. Still, it is impossible not to feel that he missed something—that there is another kind of construction in Shakespeare's tragedies than the one he designates, more inward, more difficult to define, but not less significant. This other structure is not, like his, generated entirely by the interplay of plot and character. Nor is it, on the other hand, though it has been fashionable to suppose so, ultimately a verbal matter. It is poetic, but it goes well beyond what in certain quarters today is called (with something like a lump in the throat) "the poetry." Some of its elements arise from the playwright's visualizing imagination, the consciousness of groupings, gestures, entrances, exits. Others may even be prior to language, in the sense that they appear to belong to a paradigm of tragic "form" that was consciously or unconsciously part of Shakespeare's inheritance and intuition as he worked.

At any rate, it is into this comparatively untraveled and uncharted territory of inward structure that I should like to launch some tentative explorations. I shall occasionally look backward as far as *Julius Caesar* (1599), *Richard II* (1595?–1597), and even *Romeo and Juliet* (1595–6); but in the main I shall be concerned here with the tragedies of Shakespeare's prime, from *Hamlet* (1600–1) to *Coriolanus* (1607–8). In these seven or eight years, Shakespeare's golden period, he consolidated a species of tragic structure that for suggestiveness and flexibility has never been matched.[2]

First, the hero. The Shakespearean tragic hero, as everybody knows, is an overstater. His individual accent will vary with his personality, but there is always a residue of hyperbole. This, it would seem, is for Shakespeare the authentic tragic

---

[2]The flexibility of the structure is witnessed by the amazing differences between the tragedies, of which it is, however, the lowest common multiple. In my discussion, I shall necessarily take the differences between the tragedies for granted and stress simply the vertebrate characteristics they share.

music, mark of a world where a man's reach must always exceed his grasp and everything costs not less than everything.

> Wert thou as far
> As that vast shore washed with the farthest sea,
> I should adventure for such merchandise.
>
> > (*Romeo*, 2.2.82)

> 'Swounds, show me what thou't do.
> Woo't weep? woo't fight? woo't fast? woo't tear thyself?
> Woo't drink up esill? eat a crocodile?
> I'll do't.
>
> > (*Hamlet*, 5.1.261)

> Nay, had she been true,
> If heaven would make me such another world
> Of one entire and perfect chrysolite,
> I'ld not have sold her for it.
>
> > (*Othello*, 5.2.144)

> Death, traitor! Nothing could have subdued nature
> To such a lowness but his unkind daughters.
>
> > (*Lear*, 3.4.68)

> Will all great Neptune's ocean wash this blood
> Clean from my hand?
>
> > (*Macbeth*, 2.2.59)

> I, that with my sword
> Quartered the world and o'er green Neptune's back
> With ships made cities, . . .
>
> > (*Antony*, 4.14.57)

> I go alone,
> Like to a lonely dragon, that his fen
> Makes feared and talked of more than seen.
>
> > (*Coriolanus*, 4.1.29)

This idiom is not, of course, used by the hero only. It is the language he is dressed in by all who love him and often by those who do not:

> This was the noblest Roman of them all . . .
> His life was gentle, and the elements
> So mixed in him that Nature might stand up
> And say to all the world, 'This was a man!'
>
> > (*Caesar*, 5.5.68)

> The courtier's, soldier's, scholar's, eye, tongue, sword,
> Th' expectancy and rose of the fair state,
> The glass of fashion and the mould of form,
> Th' observed of all observers, . . .
>
> > (*Hamlet*, 3.1.151)

Can he be angry? I have seen the cannon
When it hath blown his ranks into the air
And, like the devil, from his very arm
Puffed his own brother—and is he angry?
                    (*Othello*, 3.4.134)

   On the Alps
It is reported thou didst eat strange flesh,
Which some did die to look on.
                    (*Antony*, 1.4.66)

   Let me twine
Mine arms about thy body, whereagainst
My grainèd ash an hundred times hath broke,
And scarred the moon with splinters.
                    (*Coriolanus*, 4.5.107)

But by whomever used, it is a language that depends for its vindication—for the redemption of its paper promises into gold—upon the hero, and any who stand, heroically, where he does. It is the mark of his, and their, commitment to something beyond "the vast waters Of the petrel and the porpoise," as T. S. Eliot has it in *East Coker,* a commitment to something—not merely death—which shackles accidents and bolts up change and palates no dung whatever.

Thus the hyperbole of tragedy stands at the opposite end of a tonal scale from the hyperbole of comedy which springs from and nourishes detachment:

When I was about thy years, Hal, I was not an eagle's talent in the waist; I could have crept into any alderman's thumb-ring. (*I Henry IV*, 2.4.313)

O, she misused me past the endurance of a block! An oak but with one green leaf on it would have answered her; my very visor began to assume life and scold with her. (*Much Ado*, 2.1.214)

He has a son, who shall be flayed alive; then 'nointed over with honey, set on the head of a wasp's nest; then stand till he be three quarters and a dram dead; then recovered again with aqua-vitae or some other hot infusion. Then, raw as he is, and in the hottest day prognostication proclaims, shall he be set against a brick-wall, the sun looking with a southward eye upon him, where he is to behold him with flies blown to death. (*Winter's Tale*, 4.4.771)

Comic overstatement aims at being preposterous. Until it becomes so, it remains flat. Tragic overstatement, on the other hand, aspires to be believed, and unless in some sense it is so, remains bombast.

2

Besides the hyperbolist, in Shakespeare's scheme of things, there is always the opposing voice, which belongs to the hero's foil. As the night the day, the idiom of absoluteness demands a vocabulary of a different intensity, a different rhetorical and moral wave length, to set it off. This other idiom is not necessarily under-statement, though it often takes the form of a deflating accent and very often involves colloquialism—or perhaps merely a middling sort of speech—expressive of a suppler outlook than the hero's and of other and less upsetting ways of encountering experience than his hyperbolic, not to say intransigent, rigorism. "'Twere to consider too curiously, to consider so" (5.1.193), says Horatio of Hamlet's equation between the dust of Alexander and a bunghole, and this enun-ciates perfectly the foil's role. There is no tragedy in him because he does not consider "curiously"; there are always more things in earth and heaven than are dreamt of in his philosophy.

Each of the Shakespearean tragedies contains at least one personage to speak this part, which is regularly assigned to someone in the hero's immediate entourage—servitor, wife, friend. In *Romeo and Juliet* it is of course Mercutio, with his witty resolution of all love into sex. In *Julius Caesar* it is Cassius, whose restless urgent rhythms, full of flashing images, swirl about Brutus's rounder and abstracter speech, like dogs that bay the moon:

> *Brutus:*   I do believe that these applauses are
>   For some new honors that are heaped on Caesar.
> *Cassius:* Why, man, he doth bestride the narrow world
>   Like a Colossus, and we petty men
>   Walk under his huge legs and peep about
>   To find ourselves dishonorable graves.
>   (1.2.133)

In the famous forum speeches this second voice is taken over temporarily by Antony, and there emerges a similar but yet more powerful contrast between them. Brutus's prose—in which the actuality of the assassination is intellectualized and held at bay by the strict patterns of an obtrusively formal rhetoric, almost as though corporal death were transubstantiated to "a ballet of bloodless cate-gories"—gives way to Antony's sinewy verse about the "honorable men" (3.2.83), which draws the deed, and its consequence, the dead Caesar, ever closer till his own vengeful emotions are kindled in the mob.

In *Hamlet* the relation of foil to hero undergoes an unusual adaptation. Here, since the raciest idiom of the play belongs to the hero himself, the foil, Horatio, is given a quite conventional speech, and, to make the contrast sharper (Hamlet being of all the heroes the most voluble), as little speech as may be. Like his sto-icism, like his "blood and judgment"—"so well commeddled/That they are not a pipe for Fortune's finger/To sound what stop she please." (3.2.66)—Horatio's "Here, sweet lord" (3.2.50), "O, my dear lord," "Well, my lord" are, presumably (as the gentleman in *Lear* says of Cordelia's tears), "a better way" (4.3.19) than Hamlet's self-lacerating virtuosities and verbosities. But of course we do not believe this and are not meant to: who would be Horatio if he could be Hamlet?

Plainly, this is one of the two questions that all the tragic foils exist to make us ask (the other we shall come to presently). Who, for instance, would be Enobarbus, clear-sighted as he is, in preference to Antony? His brilliant sardonic speech, so useful while he can hold his own career and all about him in the comic focus of detachment, withers in the face of his engagement to ultimate issues, and he dies speaking with an imagery, accent, and feeling which are surely meant to identify him at the last with the absoluteness of the heroic world, the more so since his last syllables anticipate Cleopatra's:

> Throw my heart
> Against the flint and hardness of my fault,
> Which, being dried with grief, will break to powder,
> And finish all foul thoughts. O Antony,
> Nobler than my revolt is infamous,
> Forgive me in thine own particular,
> But let the world rank me in register
> A master leaver and a fugitive.
> O Antony! O Antony!
>
> (4.9.15)

Such unequivocal judgments are a change indeed on the part of one who could earlier rally cynically with Menas about "two thieves kissing" (2.6.96) when their hands meet.

King Lear is given two foils. The primary one is obviously the Fool, whose rhymes and riddles and jets of humor in the first two acts set off both the old king's brooding silences and his massively articulated longer speeches when aroused. But in the storm scenes, and occasionally elsewhere, one is almost as keenly conscious of the relief into which Lear's outrageous imprecations are thrown by the mute devoted patience of his servant Kent. For both foils—and this of course is their most prominent function as representatives of the opposing voice—the storm itself is only a storm, to be stoically endured, in the one case, and, in the other, if his master would but hear reason, eschewed:

> O nuncle, court holy-water in a dry house is better than this rain-water out o' door. Good nuncle, in; ask thy daughters blessing. . . . (3.2.10)

Doubtless the Fool does not wish to be taken quite *au pied de la lettre* in this—his talk is always in the vein of the false daughters', his action quite other. But neither for him nor for Kent does facing the thunder have any kind of transcendent meaning. In Lear's case, it has; the thunder he hears is like the thunder heard over Himavant in *The Waste Land;* it has what the anthropologists call "mana"; and his (and our) consuming questions are what it means—and if it means—and whose side it is on.

In my view, the most interesting uses of the opposing voice occur in *Macbeth* and *Othello*. In *Macbeth* Shakespeare gives it to Lady Macbeth, and there was never, I think, a more thrilling tragic counterpoint set down for the stage than that in the scene following the murder of Duncan, when her purely physical reading of what has happened to them both is met by his metaphysical intuitions. His "noise" (2.2.14) to her is just the owl screaming and the crickets' cry. The voice of one crying "Sleep no more!" (2.2.34) is only his "brainsickly" (2.2.45) fear. The blood on his hands is what "A little water clears us of" (2.2.66). "Consider it not so deeply" (2.2.29), she says at one point, with an echo of Horatio in the graveyard. "These deeds must not be thought/After these ways." But in the tragic world which always opens on transcendence, they must; and this she herself finds before she dies, a prisoner to the deed, endlessly washing the damned spot that will not out. "What's done cannot be undone" is a language that like Enobarbus she has to learn.

Othello's foil of course is Iago, about whose imagery and speech there hangs, as recent commentators have pointed out, a constructed air, an ingenious, hyperconscious, generalizing air, essentially suited to one who, as W. H. Clemen has said, "seeks to poison . . . others with his images."[3] Yet Iago's poison does not work more powerfully through his images than through a corrosive habit of abstraction applied in those unique relations of love and faith where abstraction is most irrelevant and most destructive. Iago has learned to "sickly o'er" the irreducible individual with the pale cast of class and kind:

> Blessed fig's-end! The wine she drinks is made of grapes. . . .
> (2.1.247)

> These Moors are changeable in their wills. . . . If sanctimony and a frail vow betwixt an erring barbarian and a supersubtle Venetian be not too hard for my wits . . .
> (1.3.344)

> Come on, come on! You are pictures out of doors,
> Bells in your parlors, wildcats in your kitchens,
> Saints in your injuries, devils being offended,
> Players in your housewifery, and housewives in your beds.
> (2.1.109)

> I know our country disposition well:
> In Venice they do let God see the pranks
> They dare not show their husbands.
> (3.3.201)

Othello's downfall is signaled quite as clearly when he drifts into this rationalized dimension—

> O curse of marriage,
> That we can call these delicate creatures ours,
> And not their appetites!
> (3.3.268)

—leaving behind his true vernacular, the idiom of "My life upon her faith!" (1.3.294) as when his mind fills with Iago's copulative imagery. Shakespeare seems to have been well aware that love is the mutual knowing of uniqueness. And also that there are areas of experience where, as a great saint once said, one must first believe in order that one may know.

---

[3] *The Development of Shakespeare's Imagery* (1951), 122.

3

To one who should ask why these paired voices seem to be essential ingredients of Shakespearean tragedy, no single answer can be given. They occur partly, no doubt, because of their structural utility, the value of complementary personalities in a work of fiction being roughly analogous to the value of thesis and antithesis in a discursive work. Partly too, no doubt, because in stage performance the antiphonal effects of the two main vocabularies, strengthened by diversity in manner, costume, placing on the stage, supply variety of mood and gratify the eye and ear. But these are superficial considerations. Perhaps we come to something more satisfactory when we consider that these two voices apparently answer to reverberations which reach far back in the human past. *Mutatis mutandis*, Coriolanus and Menenius, Antony and Enobarbus, Macbeth and Lady Macbeth, Lear and his Fool, Othello and Iago, Hamlet and Horatio, Brutus and Cassius, Romeo and Mercutio exhibit a kind of duality that is also exhibited in Oedipus and Jocasta (as well as Creon), Antigone and Ismene, Prometheus and Oceanus, Phaedra and her nurse—and also, in many instances in Greek tragedy, by the protagonist and the chorus.

If it is true, as can be argued, that the Greek chorus functions in large measure as spokesman for the values of the community, and the first actor in large measure for the passionate life of the individual, we can perhaps see a philosophical basis for the long succession of opposing voices. What matters to the community is obviously accommodation—all those adjustments and resiliences that enable it to survive; whereas what matters to the individual, at least in the heroic mood, is just as obviously integrity—all that enables a human being to remain an *individual*, one thing not many. The confrontation of these two outlooks is therefore a confrontation of two of our most cherished instincts, the instinct to be resolute, autonomous, free, and the instinct to be "realistic," adaptable, secure.

If it is also true, as I think most of us believe, that tragic drama is in one way or other a record of man's affair with transcendence (whether this be defined as gods, God, or, as by Malraux, the human "fate," which men must "question" even if they cannot control), we can see further why the hero must have an idiom—such as hyperbole—that establishes him as moving to measures played above or outside our normal space and time. For the *reductio ad absurdum* of the tragic confrontation is the comic one, exemplified in Don Quixote and his Sancho, where the comedy arises precisely from the fact that the hero only *imagines* he moves to measures above and outside our normal world; and where, to the extent that we come to identify with his faith, the comedy slides toward pathos and even the tragic absolute.

These considerations remain speculative. What is not in doubt is that dramaturgically the antiphony of two voices and two vocabularies serves Shakespeare well, and in one of its extensions gives rise to a phenomenon as peculiar and personal to him as his signature. Toward the close of a tragic play, or if not toward the close, at the climax, will normally appear a short scene or episode (sometimes more than one) of spiritual cross purposes: a scene in which the line of tragic speech and feeling generated by commitment is crossed by an alien speech and feeling very much detached.

Bradley, noting such of these episodes as are "humorous or semi-humorous," places them among Shakespeare's devices for sustaining interest after the crisis, since their introduction "affords variety and relief, and also heightens by contrast the tragic feelings." Another perceptive critic has noted that though such scenes afford "relief," it is not by laughter. "We return for a moment to simple people, a gravedigger, a porter, a countryman, and to the goings on of every day, the feeling for bread and cheese, and when we go back to the high tragic mood we do so with a heightened sense that we are moving in a world fully realized."[4]

To such comments we may add another. For the whole effect of these episodes does not come simply from variety or from the juxtaposition of bread and cheese with the high tragic mood; though these elements are certainly present in it. It arises, in the main, I think, from the fact that Shakespeare here lays open to us, in an especially poignant form, what I take to be the central dialogue of tragic experience. It is a dialogue of which the Greek dialogue of individual with community, the seventeenth-century dialogue of soul with body, the twentieth-century dialogue of self with soul are perhaps all versions in their different ways: a dialogue in which each party makes its case in its own tongue, incapable of wholly comprehending what the other means. And Shakespeare objectifies it for us on his stage by the encounter of those in whom, "changed, changed utterly," a terrible beauty has been born, with those who are still players in life's casual comedy. Hamlet and the gravediggers, Desdemona and Emilia, Cleopatra and the clown afford particularly fine examples of Shakespeare's technique in this respect.

In the first instance, the mixture of profoundly imaginative feelings contained in Hamlet's epitaph for Yorick—

> I knew him, Horatio, a fellow of infinite jest, of most excellent fancy. He hath borne me on his back a thousand times. And now how abhorred in my imagination it is! My gorge rises at it. Here hung those lips that I have kissed I know not how oft. Where be your gibes now? your gambols, your songs, your flashes of merriment that were wont to set the table on a roar? Not one now to mock your own grinning? Quite chapfall'n? Now get you to my lady's chamber, and tell her, let her paint an inch thick, to this favor she must come. Make her laugh at that. (5.1.173)

is weighed over against the buffoon literalism of the clown—

Hamlet:	What man dost thou dig it for?
First clown:	For no man, sir.
Hamlet:	What woman then?
First clown:	For none neither.
Hamlet:	Who is to be buried in't?
First clown:	One that was a woman, sir; but, rest her soul, she's dead
	(5.1.121)

[4]Bradley, *Shakespearean Tragedy*, p. 49; F. P. Wilson, *Elizabethan and Jacobean* (1945), 122.

—and against his uncompromising factualism too, his hard, dry vocabulary of detachment, without overtones, by which he cuts his métier down to a size that can be lived with:

> Faith, if 'a be not rotten before 'a die, . . . 'a will last you some eight year or nine year: a tanner will last you nine year. (5.1.154)

In this scene, Hamlet's macabre thoughts are not allowed to outweigh the clown. A case is made for factualism and literalism. Horatio is seen to have a point in saying it is to consider too curiously to consider as Hamlet does. A man must come to terms with the graveyard; but how long may he linger in it with impunity or allow it to linger in him? Such reckonings the opposing voice, whether spoken by the primary foil or by another, is calculated to awake in us: this is the second kind of question that it exists to make us ask.

In a sense, then, the implicit subject of all these episodes is the predicament of being human. They bring before us the grandeur of our nature, which contains, potentially, both voices, both ends of the moral and psychic spectrum. They bring before us the necessity of choice, because it is rarely given us to go through any door without closing the rest. And they bring before us the sadness, the infinite sadness of our lot, because, short of the "certain certainties" that tragedy does not deal with, we have no sublunar way of knowing whether defiant "heroism" is really more to be desired than suppler "wisdom." The alabaster innocence of Desdemona's world shines out beside the crumpled bedsitters of Emilia's—

Desdemona:	Wouldst thou do such a deed for all the world?
Emilia:	Why, would not you?
Desdemona:	No, by this heavenly light!
Emilia:	Nor I neither by this heavenly light.
	I might do't as well i' th' dark.
Desdemona:	Wouldst thou do such a deed for all the world?
Emilia:	The world's a huge thing; it is a great price for a small vice.
Desdemona:	In troth, I think thou wouldst not.
Emilia:	In troth, I think I should . . . who would not make her husband a cuckold to make him a monarch? I should venture purgatory for 't.
Desdemona:	Beshrew me, if I would do such a wrong
	For the whole world.
Emilia:	Why, the wrong is but a wrong i' th' world; and having the world for your labor, 'tis a wrong in your own world, and you might quickly make it right.
Desdemona:	I do not think there is any such woman

(4.3.62)

—but the two languages never, essentially, commune—and for this reason the dialogue they hold can never be finally adjudicated.

The same effect may be noted in Cleopatra's scene with the countryman who brings her the asps. Her exultation casts a glow over the whole scene of her death. But her language when the countryman has gone would not have the tragic resonance it has if we could not hear echoing between the lines the gritty accents of the opposing voice:

Give me my robe, put on my crown, I have
Immortal longings in me.
                    (5.2.279–80)

Truly I have him; but I would not be the party that should desire you to touch him, for
his biting is immortal: those that do die of it do seldom or never recover.
                                                                        (5.2.245)

The stroke of death is as a lover's pinch,
Which hurts, and is desired.
                    (5.2.294–95)

I heard of one of them no longer than yesterday; a very honest woman, but something
given to lie, as a woman should not do but in the way of honesty—how she died of the
biting of it, what pain she felt.
                                                                        (5.2.250–54)

            Peace, peace!
Dost thou not see my baby at my breast,
That sucks the nurse asleep?
                    (5.2.307–8)

Give it nothing, I pray you, for it is not worth the feeding.
                    (5.2.268–9)

The "worm"—or "my baby"; the Antony Demetrius and Philo see—or the
Antony whose face is as the heavens; the "small vice" (4.3.68) of Emilia—or the
deed one would not do for the whole world; the skull knocked about the mazzard
by a sexton's spade—or the skull which "had a tongue in it, and could sing once"
(5.1.71): these are incommensurables which human nature nevertheless must
somehow measure, reconcile and enclose.

4

We move now from "character" to "action," and to the question: what happens
in a Shakespearean tragedy? Bradley's traditional categories—exposition, conflict,
crisis, catastrophe, etc.—give us one side of this, but largely the external side, and
are in any case rather too clumsy for the job we try to do with them. They apply as
well to potboilers of the commercial theater as to serious works of art, to prose as
well as poetic drama. What is worse, they are unable to register the unique capacity of Shakespearean dramaturgy to hint, evoke, imply, and, in short, by indirections find directions out. The nature of some of Shakespeare's "indirections" is a
topic we must explore before we can hope to confront the question posed above
with other terms than Bradley's.

To clarify what I mean by indirection, let me cite an instance from *King Lear*.
Everybody has noticed, no doubt, that Lear's Fool (apart from being the King's
primary foil) gives voice during the first two acts to notations of topsy-turviness
that are not, one feels, simply his own responses to the inversions of order that

have occurred in family and state, but a reflection of the King's; or to put the matter another way, the situation is so arranged by Shakespeare that we are invited to apply the Fool's comments to Lear's inner experience, and I suspect that most of us do so. The Fool thus serves, to some extent, as a screen on which Shakespeare flashes, as it were, readings from the psychic life of the protagonist, possibly even his subconscious life, which could not otherwise be conveyed in drama at all. Likewise, the Fool's *idée fixe* in this matter, his apparent obsession with one idea (often a clinical symptom of incipient insanity) is perhaps dramatic shorthand and even sleight-of-hand for goings-on in the King's brain that only occasionally bubble to the surface in the form of conscious apprehensions: "O, let me not be mad, not mad, sweet heaven" (1.5.40). "O fool, I shall go mad!" (2.4.281). Conceivably, there may even be significance in the circumstance that the Fool does not enter the play as a speaking character till after King Lear has behaved like a fool and leaves it before he is cured.

Whatever the truth of this last point, the example of the Fool in Lear introduces us to devices of play construction and ways of recording the progress of inward "action," which, though the traditional categories say nothing about them, are a basic resource of Shakespeare's playwriting, and nowhere more so than in the tragedies. We may now consider a few of them in turn.

First, there are the figures, like the Fool, some part of whose consciousness, as conveyed to us at particular moments, seems to be doing double duty, filling our minds with impressions analogous to those which we may presume to be occupying the conscious or unconscious mind of the hero, whether he is before us on the stage or not. A possible example may be Lady Macbeth's sleepwalking scene. Macbeth is absent at this juncture, has gone "into the field" (5.1.4)—has not in fact been visible during two long scenes and will not be visible again till the next scene after this. In the interval, the slaying at Macduff's castle and the conversations between Malcolm and Macduff keep him before us in his capacity as tyrant, murderer, "Hell-kite," seen from the outside. But Lady Macbeth's sleepwalking (5.1) is, I think, Shakespeare's device for keeping him before us in his capacity as tragic hero and sufferer. The "great perturbation in nature" (5.1.9) of which the doctor whispers ("to receive at once the benefit of sleep and do the effects of watching"), the "slumb'ry agitation," the "thick-coming fancies That keep her from her rest" (5.3.38): these, by a kind of poetical displacement, we may apply to him as well as to her; and we are invited to do so by the fact that from the moment of the first murder all the play's references to sleep and its destruction have had reference to Macbeth himself.

We are, of course, conscious as we watch the scene that this is Lady Macbeth suffering the metaphysical aspects of murder that she did not believe in; we may also be conscious that the remorse pictured here tends to distinguish her from her husband, who for some time has been giving his "initiate fear" the "hard use" (3.4.143) he said it lacked, with dehumanizing consequences. Yet in some way the pity of this situation suffuses him as well as her, the more so because in every word she utters his presence beside her is supposed; and if we allow this to be true, not only will Menteith's comment in the following scene—

> Who then shall blame
> His pestered senses to recoil and start,
> When all that is within him does condemn
> Itself for being there
>
> (5.2.22)

—evoke an image of suffering as well as retribution, but we shall better understand Macbeth's striking expression, at his next appearance, in words that we are
almost bound to feel have some reference to himself, of corrosive griefs haunting
below the conscious levels of the mind:

> Canst thou not minister to a mind diseased,
> Pluck from the memory a rooted sorrow,
> Raze out the written troubles of the brain,
> And with some sweet oblivious antidote
> Cleanse the stuffed bosom of that perilous stuff
> Which weighs upon the heart?
>
> (5.3.40)

Such speeches as this and as Lady Macbeth's while sleepwalking—which we
might call umbrella speeches, since more than one consciousness may shelter
under them—are not uncommon in Shakespeare's dramaturgy, as many critics
have pointed out. *Lear* affords the classic examples: in the Fool, as we have seen,
and also in Edgar. Edgar's speech during the storm scenes projects in part his role
of Poor Tom, the eternal outcast; in part, Edmund (and also Oswald), the vicious
servant, self-seeking, with heart set on lust and proud array; possibly in part,
Gloucester, whose arrival with a torch the Fool appropriately announces (without
knowing it) in terms related to Edgar's themes: "Now a little fire in a wild field
were like an old lecher's heart" (3.4.105); and surely, in some part too, the King,
for the chips and tag-ends of Edgar's speech reflect, as if from Lear's own mind,
not simply mental disintegration, but a strong sense of a fragmented moral order:
"Obey thy parents; keep thy words' justice; swear not; commit not with man's
sworn spouse" (3.4.76).

But, in my view, the most interesting of all the umbrella speeches in the
tragedies is Enobarbus's famous description of Cleopatra in her barge. The triumvirs have gone offstage, Antony to have his first view of Octavia. When we see
him again, his union with Octavia will have been agreed on all parts (though not
yet celebrated), and he will be saying to her, with what can hardly be supposed
insincerity:

> My Octavia,
> Read not my blemishes in the world's report:
> I have not kept my square, but that to come
> Shall all be done by th' rule. Good night, dear lady.
>
> (2.3.4)

Then the soothsayer appears, reminds Antony that his guardian angel will always
be overpowered when Caesar's is by, urges him to return to Egypt; and Antony,

left alone after the soothsayer has gone, meditates a moment on the truth of the pronouncement and then says abruptly:

I will to Egypt:
And though I make this marriage for my peace,
I' th' East my pleasure lies.
(2.3.38)

There is plainly a piece of prestidigitation here. It is performed in part by means of the soothsayer's entry, which is evidently a kind of visual surrogate for Antony's own personal intuition. ("I see it in my motion, have it not in my tongue," [2.3.14] the soothsayer says, when asked for the reasons he wishes Antony to return; and that is presumably the way Antony sees it too: in his "motion," i.e., involuntarily, intuitively.) But a larger part is played by Enobarbus's account of Cleopatra. Between the exit of the triumvirs and the reappearance of Antony making unsolicited promises to Octavia, this is the one thing that intervenes. And it is the only thing that needs to. Shakespeare has made it so powerful, so colored our imaginations with it, that we understand the promises of Antony, not in the light in which he understands them as he makes them, but in the riotous brilliance of Enobarbus's evocation of Cleopatra. The psychic gap in Antony between "My Octavia" (2.3.4) and "Good night, dear lady," on the one hand, and "I will to Egypt" (2.3.38), on the other, is filled by a vision, given to us, of irresistible and indeed quasi-unearthly power of which the soothsayer's intuition is simply a more abstract formulation. Here again, by indirection, Shakespeare finds direction out.

Not all mirror situations in the tragedies involve reflection of another consciousness. Some, as is well known, emphasize the outlines of an action by recapitulating it, as when Edgar's descent to Poor Tom and subsequent gradual re-ascent to support the gored state echoes the downward and upward movement in the lives of both King Lear and Gloucester; or as when Enobarbus's defection to, and again from, the bidding of his practical reason repeats that which Antony has already experienced, and Cleopatra will experience (at least in one way of understanding Act 5) between Antony's death and her own. *Hamlet,* complex in all respects, offers an unusually complex form of this. The three sons, who are, in various senses, all avengers of dead fathers, are all deflected temporarily from their designs by the maneuvers of an elder (Claudius for Laertes and Hamlet; the King of Norway, inspired by Claudius, for Fortinbras), who in two cases is the young man's uncle.

There are of course important differences between these three young men which we are not to forget; but with respect to structure, the images in the mirror are chiefly likenesses. Hamlet, outmaneuvered by Claudius, off to England to be executed, crosses the path of Fortinbras, who has also been outmaneuvered by Claudius (working through his uncle) and is off to Poland to make mouths at the invisible event, while at the same moment Laertes, clamoring for immediate satisfaction in the King's palace, is outmaneuvered in his turn. Likewise, at the play's end, all three young men are "victorious," in ways they could hardly have foreseen. The return of Fortinbras, having achieved his objective in Poland, to find his "rights" in Denmark achieved without a blow, is timed to coincide with Hamlet's achieving his objective in exposing and killing the King and Laertes's achieving his objective of avenging his father's death on Hamlet. When this episode is played before us in the theater there is little question, to my way of thinking, but that something of the glow and martial upsurge dramatized in Fortinbras's entrance associates itself to Hamlet, even as Fortinbras's words associate Hamlet to a soldier's death. Meantime, Laertes, who has been trapped by the King and has paid with his life for it, gives us an alternative reflection of the Prince, which is equally a part of the truth.

5

Fortinbras's arrival at the close of *Hamlet* is an instance of an especially interesting type of mirroring to be found everywhere in Shakespeare's work—the emblematic entrance, and exit. Sometimes such exits occur by death, as the death of Gaunt, who takes a sacramental view of kingship and nation in *Richard II*, comes just as Richard has destroyed, by his personal conduct and by "farm[ing]" (1.4.45) his realm, the sacramental relationships which make such a view possible to maintain. Gaunt has to die, we might say, before a usurpation like his son's can even be imagined; and it is, I take it, not without significance that the first word of Bolingbroke's return comes a few seconds after we have heard (from the same speaker, Northumberland) that Gaunt's tongue "is now a stringless instrument" (2.1.149). Something similar, it seems clear, occurs with the death of Mamillius in *The Winter's Tale*. Sickening with his father's sickening mind, Mamillius dies in the instant that his father repudiates the message of the oracle; and though in the end, all else is restored to Leontes, Mamillius is not.

In the tragedies emblematic entrances and exits assume a variety of forms, ranging from those whose significance is obvious to those where it is uncertain, controversial and perhaps simply a mirage. One entrance whose significance is unmistakable occurs in the first act of *Macbeth*, when Duncan, speaking of the traitor Cawdor, whom Macbeth has slain, laments that there is no art to find the mind's construction in the face, just as the new Cawdor, traitor-to-be, appears before him. Equally unmistakable is the significance of the King's exit, in the first scene of *Lear*, with the man who like himself has put externals first, "Come, noble Burgundy" (1.1.266), he says, and in a pairing that can be made profoundly moving on the stage, the two men go out together.

But what are we to say of Antony's freedman Eros, who enters for the first time (at least by name) just before his master's suicide and kills himself rather than kill Antony? This is all from Plutarch's life of Antony; but why did Shakespeare include it? Did Eros's name mean something to him? Are we to see here a shadowing of the other deaths for love, or not? Or again, the carrying off of Lepidus, drunk, from the feast aboard Pompey's galley. Does this anticipate his subsequent fate? and if it does, what does the intoxication signify to which in this scene all the great men are subject in their degree? Is it ordinary drunkenness; or is it, like the drunkenness that afflicts Caliban, Trinculo, and Stephano in *The Tempest*, a species of self-intoxication, Shakespeare's subdued comment on the thrust to worldly power? Or again, what of the arrival of the players in *Hamlet?* Granted their role in the plot, does Shakespeare make no other profit from them? Are such matters as the speech on Priam's murder and the advice on acting interesting excrescences, as Bradley thought, or does each mirror something that we are to appropriate to our understanding of the play: in the first instance, the strange confederacy of passion and paralysis in the hero's mind,[5] in the second, the question that tolls on all sides through the castle at Elsinore: when is an act not an "act"?[6]

These are questions to which it is not always easy to give a sound answer. The ground becomes somewhat firmer underfoot, I think, if we turn for a concluding instance to Bianca's pat appearances in *Othello*. R. B. Heilman suggests that in rushing to the scene of the night assault on Cassio, when she might have stayed safely within doors, and so exposing herself to vilification as a "notable strumpet" (5.1.78), Bianca acts in a manner "thematically relevant, because Othello has just been attacking Desdemona as a strumpet"—both "strumpets," in other words, are faithful.[7] Whether this is true or not, Bianca makes two very striking entrances earlier, when in each case she may be thought to supply in living form on the stage the prostitute figure that Desdemona has become in Othello's mind. Her second entrance is notably expressive. Othello here is partially overhearing while Iago rallies Cassio about Bianca, Othello being under the delusion that the talk is of Desdemona. At the point when, in Othello's mental imagery, Desdemona becomes the soliciting whore—"Now he tells how she plucked him to my chamber" (4.1.139)—Bianca enters in the flesh, and not only enters but flourishes the magic handkerchief, now degenerated, like the love it was to ensure, to some "minx's," some "hobbyhorse's" token, the subject of jealous bickering. In the theater, the emblematic effect of this can hardly be ignored.[8]

Further types of mirroring will spring to every reader's mind. The recapitulation of a motif, for instance, as in the poisoning episodes in *Hamlet*. *Hamlet* criticism has too much ignored, I think, the fact that a story of poisoning forms the climax of the first act, a mime and "play" of poisoning the climax of the third, and actual poisoning, on a wide scale, the climax of the fifth. Surely this repetition was calculated to keep steady for Shakespeare's Elizabethan audiences the political and moral bearings of the play? We may say what we like about Hamlet's frailties, which are real, but we can hardly ignore the fact that in each of the poisoning episodes the poisoner is the King. The King, who ought to be like the sun, giving warmth, radiance, and fertility to his kingdom, is actually its destroyer. The "leperous distilment" (1.5.64) he pours into Hamlet's father's ear, which courses through his body with such dispatch, has coursed just as swiftly through

---

[5]See an important comment on this by H. Levin in *Kenyon Review* (1950), 273–96.

[6]See " 'The Readiness is All': *Hamlet*," in *Everybody's Shakespeare*, pp. 107–28, where I have commented on this point.

[7]See Robert B. Heilman, *Magic in the Web: Action and Language in 'Othello'* (Lexington: University of Kentucky Press, 1956), 180.

[8]Another emblematic entrance is the first entrance of the soothsayer in *Julius Caesar*.

the body politic, and what we see in Denmark as a result is a poisoned kingdom, containing one corruption upon another of Renaissance ideals. The "wise councilor," who is instead a tedious windbag. The young "man of honor," who has no trust in another's honor, as his advice to his sister shows, and none of his own, as his own treachery to Hamlet shows. The "friends," who are not friends but spies. The loved one, who proves disloyal (a decoy, however reluctant, for villainy), and goes mad—through poison also, "the poison of deep grief." The mother and Queen, who instead of being the guardian of the kingdom's matronly virtues has set a harlot's blister on love's forehead and made marriage vows "as false as dicers' oaths."

And most especially the Prince, the "ideal courtier," the Renaissance man— once active, energetic, now reduced to anguished introspection; a glass of fashion, now a sloven in antic disarray; a noble mind, now partly unhinged, in fact as well as seeming; the observed of all observers, now observed in a more sinister sense; the mold of form, now capable of obscenities, cruelty, even treachery, mining below the mines of his school friends to hoist them with their own petard. All this in one way or another is the poison of the King, and in the last scene, lest we miss the point, we are made to see the spiritual poison become literal and seize on all those whom it has not already destroyed:

> a Prince's Court
> Is like a common Fountaine, whence should flow
> Pure silver-droppes in generall: But if't chance
> Some cursed example poyson 't neere the head,
> Death, and diseases through the whole land spread.[9]

The lines are Webster's, but they state with precision one of the themes of Shakespeare's play.

Finally, in the tragedies as elsewhere in Shakespeare, we have the kinds of replication that have been specifically called "mirror scenes,"[10] or (more in Ercles's vein) scenes of "analogical probability."[11] The most impressive examples here are frequently the opening scenes and episodes. The witches of *Macbeth*, whose "foul is fair" (1.1.10) and battle that is "lost *and* won" (1.1.4) anticipate so much to come. The "great debate" in *Antony and Cleopatra*, initiated in the comments of Philo and the posturings of the lovers and reverberating thereafter within, as well as around, the lovers till they die. The watchmen on the platform in *Hamlet*, feeling out a mystery—an image that will re-form in our minds again and again as we watch almost every member of the *dramatis personae* engage in similar activity later on. The technique of manipulation established at the outset of *Othello*, the persuading of someone to believe something he is reluctant to believe and which

---

[9] *Duchess of Malfi*, 1.1.11–15.
[10] By H. T. Price, in *Joseph Quincy Adams Memorial Studies*, ed. J. McManaway (1948), 101 ff.
[11] See P. J. Aldus, *Shakespeare Quarterly* (1955), 397 ff. Aldus deals suggestively with the opening scene *of Julius Caesar.*

is not true in the sense presented—exemplified in Iago's management of both Roderigo and Brabantio, and prefiguring later developments throughout the play. *Lear* offers perhaps the best of all these instances. Here the "Nature" of which the play is to make so much, ambiguous, double-barreled, is represented in its normative aspect in the hierarchies on the stage before us—a whole political society from its *primum mobile*, the great King, down to lowliest attendant as well as a whole family society from father down through married daughters and sons-in-law to a third daughter with her wooers—and, in its appetitive aspect (which Edmund will formulate in a few moments) in the overt self-will of the old King and the hidden self-will, the "plighted cunning" (1.1.280) of the false daughters. As the scene progresses, the cycle of future events becomes all but visible as these hierarchies of the normative Nature, which at first looked so formidable and solid, crumble away in the repudiation of Cordelia, the banishment of Kent, the exit of Lear and Burgundy, till nothing is left standing on the stage but Nature red in tooth and claw as the false daughters lay their heads together.

6

I dwell on these effects of "indirection" in the tragedies because I believe that most of us as playgoers are keenly conscious of their presence. Perhaps I describe them badly, in some instances possibly misconceive them; but they are not my invention; this kind of thing has been pointed to more and more widely during the past nine decades by reputable observers. In short, these effects, in some important sense, are "there." And if they are, the question we must ask is, Why? What are they for? How are they used?

I return then to the query raised earlier: what *does* happen in a Shakespearean tragedy? Is it possible to formulate an answer that will, while not repudiating the traditional categories so far as they are useful, take into account the matters we have been examining?

Obviously the most important thing that happens in a Shakespearean tragedy is that the hero follows a cycle of change which is, in part, psychic change. And this seems generally to be constituted in three phases. During the first phase, corresponding roughly to Bradley's exposition, the hero is delineated. Among other things he is placed in positions that enable him to sound the particular timbre of his tragic music:

Not so, my lord. I am too much in the sun.
(*Hamlet*, 1.2.67)

Seems, madam? Nay, it is. I know not 'seems.'
(1.2.76)

My father's brother, but no more like my father
Than I to Hercules.
(1.2.152)

> My fate cries out,
> And makes each petty artere in this body
> As hardy as the Nemean lion's nerve.
>   (1.4.81)

Chiming against this we are also permitted to hear the particular timbre of the opposing voice, spoken by the foil as well as others:

> If it be,
> Why seems it so particular with thee?
>   (1.2.74)

> For what we know must be and is as common
> As any the most vulgar thing to sense,
> Why should we in our peevish opposition
> Take it to heart?
>   (1.2.98)

> What if it tempt you toward the flood, my lord,
> Or to the dreadful summit of the cliff
> That beetles o'er his base into the sea,
> And there assume some other horrible form,
> Which might deprive your sovereignty of reason
> And draw you into madness?
>   (1.4.69)

From now on, as we saw, these are the differing attitudes toward experience that will supply the essential dialogue of the play.

The second phase is much more comprehensive. It contains the conflict, crisis, and falling action—in short, the heart of the matter. Here, several interesting developments occur. The one certain over-all development in this phase is that the hero tends to become his own antithesis. We have met this already in Hamlet, in whom "the courtier's, soldier's, scholar's, eye, tongue, sword" (3.1.151) suffer some savage violations before the play is done. Likewise, Othello the unshakable, whose original composure under the most trying insults and misrepresentations almost takes the breath away, breaks in this phase into furies, grovels on the floor in a trance, strikes his wife publicly. King Lear, "the great image of authority" (4.6.155) both by temperament and position, becomes a helpless crazed old man crying in a storm, destitute of everything but one servant and his Fool. Macbeth, who would have "holily" (1.5.19) what he would have "highly," who is too full of the milk of human kindness to catch the nearest way, whose whole being revolts with every step he takes in his own revolt—his hair standing on end, his imagination filling with angels "trumpet-tongued" (1.7.19), his hands (after the deed) threatening to pluck out his own eyes—turns into the numbed usurper, "supped full with horrors" (5.5.13), who is hardly capable of responding even to his wife's death. The development is equally plain in Antony and Coriolanus. "The greatest prince o' th' world, The noblest" (4.15.54), finds his greatness slipped from him, and his nobility debased to the ignominy of having helpless emissaries whipped.

The proud and upright Coriolanus, patriot soldier, truckles in the marketplace for votes, revolts to the enemy he has vanquished, carries war against his own flesh and blood.

This manner of delineating tragic "action," though it may be traced here and there in other drama, seems to be on the whole a property of the Elizabethans and Jacobeans. Possibly it springs from their concern with "whole" personalities on the tragic stage rather than, as so often with the ancients and Racine, just those aspects of personality that guarantee the *dénouement*. In any case, it seems to have become a consistent feature of Shakespeare's dramaturgy and beautifully defines the sense of psychological alienation and uprootedness that tragic experience in the Elizabethan and Jacobean theater generally seems to embrace. Its distinctively tragic implications stand out the more when we reflect that psychic change in comedy (if indeed comedy can be said to concern itself with psychic change at all) consists in making, or in showing, the protagonist to be more and more what he or she always was.

In this second phase too, either as an outward manifestation of inward change, or as a shorthand indication that such change is about to begin or end, belong the tragic journeys. Romeo is off to Mantua, Brutus to the Eastern end of the Roman world, Hamlet to England, Othello to Cyprus, Lear and Gloucester to Dover, Timon to the cave, Macbeth to the heath to revisit the witches, Antony to Rome and Athens, Coriolanus to Antium.[12] Such journeys, we rightly say, are called for by the plots. But perhaps we should not be wrong if we added that Shakespearean plotting tends to call for journeys, conceivably for discernible reasons. For one thing, journeys can enhance our impression that psychological changes are taking place, either by emphasizing a lapse of time, or by taking us to new settings, or by both. I suspect we register such effects subconsciously more often than we think.

Furthermore, though it would be foolish to assign to any of the journeys in Shakespeare's tragedies a precise symbolic meaning, several of them have vaguely symbolic overtones—serving as surrogates either for what can never be exhibited on the stage, as happens with the mysterious processes leading to psychic change, which cannot be articulated into speech, even soliloquy, without losing their form-less instinctive character; or for the processes of self-discovery, the learning processes—a function journeys fulfill in many of the world's best-known stories (the *Aeneid*, the *Divine Comedy*, *Tom Jones*, etc.) and in some of Shakespeare's comedies. Hamlet's abortive journey to England seems to be an instance of the first category. After his return, and particularly after what he tells us of his actions while at sea, we are not surprised if he appears, spiritually, a changed man. Lear's and Gloucester's journey to Dover is perhaps an instance of the second category, leading as it does through suffering to insight and reconciliation.

During the hero's journey, or at any rate during his over-all progress in the second phase, he will normally pass through a variety of mirroring situations of the sort for-merly discussed (though it will be by us and not him that the likeness in the mirror is

---

[12]These are merely samples; other journeys occur that I have not named here.

seen). In some of these, the hero will be confronted, so to speak, with a version of his own situation, and his failure to recognize it may be a measure of the nature of the disaster to ensue. Coriolanus, revolted from Rome and now its enemy, meets himself in Aufidius's embrace in Antium. Hamlet meets himself in Fortinbras as the latter marches to Poland but does not see the likeness—only the differences. Lear goes to Goneril's and there meets, as everyone remembers, images of his own behavior to Cordelia. Thrust into the night he meets his own defenselessness in Edgar and is impelled to pray. Encountering in Dover fields, both Lear and Gloucester confront in each other an extension of their own experience: blindness that sees and madness that is wise. Macbeth revisits the witches on the heath and finds there (without recognizing them) not only the emblems of his death and downfall to come but his speciousness and duplicity. Antony encounters in Enobarbus's defection his own, and possibly, in Pompey, his own later muddled indecision between "honor" and *Realpolitik*. Othello hears the innocent Cassio set upon in the dark, then goes to re-enact that scene in a more figurative darkness in Desdemona's bedroom.

Sometimes, alternatively or additionally, the hero's way will lie through quasi-symbolic settings or situations. The heath in both *Macbeth* and *King Lear* is infinitely suggestive, even if like all good symbols it refuses to dissipate its *Dinglichkeit* in meaning. The same is true of the dark castle platform in Hamlet, and the graveyard; of the cliff at Dover and Gloucester's leap; of the "monument," where both Antony and Cleopatra die; and of course, as many have pointed out, of the night scenes, the storm, the music, the changes of clothing, the banquets. So much in Shakespeare's tragedies stands on the brink of symbol that for this reason, if no other, the usual terms for describing their construction and mode of action need reinforcement.

After the hero has reached and passed through his own antithesis, there comes a third phase in his development that is extremely difficult to define. It represents a recovery of sorts—in some cases, perhaps even a species of synthesis. The once powerful, now powerless king, will have power again, but of another kind—the kind suggested in his reconciliation with Cordelia and his speech beginning "Come, let's away to prison" (5.1.8); and he will have sanity again, but in a mode not dreamed of at the beginning of the play. Or, to take Othello's case, it will be given the hero to recapture the faith he lost,[13] to learn that the pearl really was richer than all his tribe and to execute quite another order of justice than the blinkered justice meted out to Cassio and the blind injustice meted out to Desdemona. Or again, to shift to Antony, the man who has so long been thrown into storms of rage and recrimination by the caprices of his unstable mistress receives the last of them without a murmur of reproach, though it has led directly to his death, and dies in greater unison with her than we have ever seen him live.

I believe that some mark of this nature is visible in all the tragedies. Coriolanus, "boy" though he is and in some ways remains, makes a triumphant choice (detract from his motives as we may), and he knows what it is likely to cost. Moreover, he

---

[13]See Helen Gardner's *The Noble Moor* (1956) and my " 'Speak of me as I am': *Othello*," in *Everybody's Shakespeare*, pp. 129–50.

refuses the way of escape that lies open if he should return now with Volumnia and Vergilia to Rome. "I'll not to Rome, I'll back with you," he tells Aufidius, "and pray you,/Stand to me in this cause" (5.3.198). The young man who after this dies accused of treachery—by Aufidius's treachery and the suggestibility of the crowd, as slippery in Corioli as Rome—cannot be thought identical in all respects with the young man who joined Menenius in the play's opening scene. He is that young man but with the notable difference of his triumphant choice behind him; and there is bound to be more than a military association in our minds when the Second Lord of the Volscians, seeking to quell the mob, cries, "The man is noble, and his fame folds in/This orb o' th' earth"; and again too when the First Lord exclaims over his body, "Let him be regarded/As the most noble corse that ever herald/Did follow to his urn" (5.6.123, 141). Even the monster Macbeth is so handled by Shakespeare, as has been often enough observed, that he seems to regain something at the close— if nothing more, at least some of that *élan* which made him the all-praised Bellona's bridegroom of the play's second scene; and everything Macbeth says, following Duncan's death, about the emptiness of the achievement, the lack of posterity, the sere, the yellow leaf, deprived of "that which should accompany old age,/As honor, love, obedience, troops of friends" (5.3.24), affords evidence that the meaning of his experience has not been lost on him.

To say this, I wish to make it clear, is not to say that every Shakespearean tragic hero undergoes an "illumination," or, to use the third term of Kenneth Burke's sequence, a Mathema or perception.[14] This is a terminology that seems to me not very useful to the discussion of tragedy as Shakespeare presents it. It is sufficient for my purposes to say simply that the phase in which we are conscious of the hero as approaching his opposite is followed by a final phase in which we are conscious of him as exhibiting one or more aspects of his original, or—since these may not coincide—his better self: as in the case of Antony's final reunion with Cleopatra, and Coriolanus's decision not to sack Rome.

Whether we then go on to give this phenomenon a specific spiritual signifi-cance, seeing in it the objective correlative of "perception" or "illumination," is a question that depends, obviously, on a great many factors, more of them perhaps situated in our own individual philosophies than in the text, and so, likely to lead us away from Shakespeare rather than toward him.

Clearly if Shakespeare wished us to engage in this activity, he was remiss in the provision of clues. Even in *King Lear,* the one play where some sort of regenera-tion or new insight in the hero has been universally acknowledged, the man before us in the last scene—who sweeps Kent aside, rakes all who have helped him with grapeshot ("A plague upon you murderers, traitors all;/I might have saved her . . ." [5.3.270]), exults in the revenge he has exacted for Cordelia's death, and dies self-deceived in the thought she still lives—this man is one of the most profoundly human figures ever created in a play; but he is not, certainly, the Platonic idea laid up in heaven, or in critical schemes, of regenerate man.

[14] *A Grammar of Motives* (1945), 38 ff.

7

I have kept to the end, and out of proper order, the most interesting of all the symbolic elements in the hero's second phase. This is his experience of madness. One discovers with some surprise, I think, how many of Shakespeare's heroes are associated with this disease. Only Titus, Hamlet, Lear, and Timon, in various senses, actually go mad. But Iago boasts that he will make Othello mad and in a way succeeds. Antony, it will be recalled, after the second defeat at sea, is said by Cleopatra to be

> more mad
> Than Telamon for his shield; the boar of Thessaly
> Was never so embossed.
>
> (4.13.1)

Caithness in *Macbeth* tells us that some say the king is mad, while "others, that lesser hate him,/Do call it valiant fury" (5.2.13–14). Romeo, rather oddly, enjoins Paris at Juliet's tomb to

> be gone. Live, and hereafter say
> A madman's mercy bid thee run away.
> (5.3.66)

Even Brutus, by the Antony of *Antony and Cleopatra,* is said to have been "mad."

What, if anything, one wonders, may this mean? Doubtless a sort of explanation can be found in Elizabethan psychological lore, which held that the excess of any passion approached madness, and in the general prevalence, through Seneca and other sources, of the adage: *Quos vult perdere Jupiter dementat prius.*[15] Furthermore, madness, when actually exhibited, was dramatically useful, as Shakespeare's predecessor Thomas Kyd had shown. It was arresting in itself, and it allowed the combination in a single figure of tragic hero and buffoon, to whom could be accorded the license of the allowed fool in speech and action.

Just possibly, however, there is yet more to it, if we may judge by Shakespeare's sketches of madness in *Hamlet* and *King Lear.* In both of these, madness is to some degree a punishment or doom, corresponding to the adage. Lear prays to the heavens that he may not suffer madness, and Hamlet asks Laertes in his apology before the duel to overlook his conduct, since "you must needs have heard,/How I am punished with a sore distraction" (5.2.217–18). It is equally obvious, however, that in both instances the madness has a further dimension, as insight, and this is true also of Ophelia. Ophelia, mad, is able to make awards of flowers to the King and Queen which are appropriate to frailties of which she cannot be supposed to have conscious knowledge. For the same reason, I suspect we do not need Dover Wilson's radical displacement of Hamlet's entry in 2.2, so as to enable him to over-

---

[15]"Whom Jove wishes to destroy he first makes mad."

hear Polonius.[16] It is enough that Hamlet wears, even if it is for the moment self-assumed, the guise of the madman. As such, he can be presumed to have intuitive unformulated awarenesses that reach the surface in free (yet relevant) associations, like those of Polonius with a fishmonger, Ophelia with carrion.

Lear likewise is allowed free yet relevant associations. His great speech in Dover fields on the lust of women derives from the designs of Goneril and Regan on Edmund, of which he consciously knows nothing. Moreover, both he and Hamlet can be privileged in madness to say things—Hamlet about the corruption of human nature, and Lear about the corruption of the Jacobean social system (and by extension about all social systems whatever)—which Shakespeare could hardly have risked apart from this license. Doubtless one of the anguishes of being a great artist is that you cannot tell people what they and you and your common institutions are really like—when viewed absolutely—without being dismissed as insane. To communicate at all, you must acknowledge the opposing voice; for there always is an opposing voice, and it is as deeply rooted in your own nature as in your audience's.

Just possibly, therefore, the meaning of tragic madness for Shakespeare approximated the meaning that the legendary figure of Cassandra (whom Shakespeare had in fact put briefly on his stage in the second act of *Troilus and Cressida*) has held for so many artists since his time. Cassandra's madness, like Lear's and Hamlet's—possibly, also, like the madness *verbally* assigned to other Shakespearean tragic heroes—contains both punishment and insight. She is doomed to know, by a consciousness that moves to measures outside our normal space and time; she is doomed never to be believed, because those to whom she speaks can hear only the opposing voice. With the language of the god Apollo sounding in her brain, and the incredulity of her fellow mortals ringing in her ears, she makes an ideal emblem of the predicament of the Shakespearean tragic hero, caught as he is between the absolute and the expedient. And by the same token, of the predicament of the artist—Shakespeare himself, perhaps—who, having been given the power to see the "truth," can convey it only through poetry—what we commonly call a "fiction" and dismiss.

---

[16]*What Happens in* "*Hamlet*" (1935), 103 ff.

"I Wooed Thee with My Sword": Shakespeare's Tragic Paradigms

Madelon Gohlke Sprengnether

Traditional textual interpretation founds itself on this particular understanding of metaphor: a detour to truth. Not only individual metaphors or systems of metaphors, but fiction in general is seen as a detour to a truth that the critic can deliver through her interpretation.

—Gayatri Chakravorty Spivak, translator's preface to Jacques Derrida, *Of Grammatology*

Much of what I am going to say about Shakespeare and about the possibility of a feminist psychoanalytic interpretation of literature, or, for that matter, of culture, depends on a reading of metaphor. It is metaphor that allows us to subread, to read on the margins of discourse, to analyze what is latent or implicit in the structures of consciousness or of a text. A serious feminist critic, moreover, cannot proceed very far without becoming paranoid unless she abandons a strictly intentionalist position. To argue sexism as a conscious conspiracy becomes both foolish and absurd. To pursue the implications of metaphor, on the other hand, in terms of plot, character, and possibly even genre, is to adopt a psychoanalytic strategy that deepens the context of feminist interpretation and reveals the possibility at least of a feminist psychohistory.

Metaphor provides a convenient entrance into a text, as it provides a point of departure for psychoanalytic interpretation because of the way in which vehicle consistently outdistances tenor. For instance, the following two lines from *A Midsummer Night's Dream*—"Hippolyta, I wooed thee with my sword,/And won thy love, doing thee injuries" (1.1.16–17)—convey far more than the simple prose explanation offered in my text: "Theseus had captured Hippolyta when he conquered the Amazons."[1] These lines, in which the sword may be the metaphoric equivalent of the phallus, in which love may be either generated or secured by hostility, and in which the two partners take up sadistic and masochistic postures

From Madelon Gohlke Sprengnether, "'I Wooed Thee with My Sword': Shakespeare's Tragic Paradigms." In Schwartz, Murray M., Coppélia Kahn, eds. *Representing Shakespeare: New Psychoanalytic Essays*. The Johns Hopkins University Press, Baltimore/London, 1980, pp. 170–87. Reprinted by permission of Johns Hopkins University Press and the author.

[1]*A Midsummer Night's Dream, The Complete Signet Classic Shakespeare*, ed. Sylvan Barnet (New York: Harcourt Brace Jovanovich, 1963, 1972), p. 530. Quotations from Shakespeare in this essay refer to this edition.

in relation to each other, are not irrelevant to the concerns of the play. They may be seen to reverberate in the exaggerated submission of Helena to Demetrius, in the humiliation of Titania by Oberon, in the penetration by violence of the language of love. They even bear an oblique relation to the "lamentable comedy" of *Pyramus and Thisbe,* the failed marriage plot contained within the larger structure of successful heterosexual union celebrated at the end of the play.

Metaphor may also elucidate character, as in the case of Claudio in *Much Ado,* whose speech is relatively poor in imagery until it erupts into his condemnation of Hero in the middle of the play. There he claims, among other things: "But you are more intemperate in your blood/Than Venus, or those pamp'red animals/That rage in savage sensuality" (4.1.58–60). It is Claudio's suspicious predisposition that composes this violent and disproportioned outburst. It is no accident that the "solution" to this conflict hinges on the fiction that Claudio has killed Hero through his slander. In this sense, the conventional marriage plot of Shakespeare's comedy may also be read metaphorically. The prospect of heterosexual union arouses emotional conflicts that give shape to the plot, unleashing a kind of violence that in the comedies remains symbolic, imagined rather than enacted.

In the following pages, I shall be considering the uses of metaphor in several related ways. In some instances, I will refer to the function of metaphor in individual discourse, assuming that it is this kind of highly charged imagistic expression that offers the most immediate clues to unconscious awareness, that metaphor in some sense structures awareness. I am assuming furthermore that metaphor may be seen to structure action, so that some features of plot may be regarded as expanded metaphors. Moving outward from this premise, I then want to consider the possibility that certain cultural fictions may be read metaphorically, that is, as expressions of unconsciously held cultural beliefs. I am especially interested in Shakespeare's tragedies, in what seem to me to be shared fictions on the part of the heroes about femininity and about their own vulnerability in relation to women—fictions interwoven with violence, which generate a particular kind of heterosexual dilemma.

The primacy of metaphor in the structures of individual consciousness, as in the collective fiction of the plot, appears in an early tragedy, *Romeo and Juliet,* where the failure of the play to achieve the generic status of comedy may be read as the result of the way heterosexual relations are imagined. In the conversation between the servants Sampson and Gregory, sexual intercourse, through a punning reference to the word maidenhead, comes to be described as a kind of murder:[2]

---

[2]Two critics have dealt specifically with the relationship between sex and violence in this play. A. K. Nardo notes that "To the youths who rekindle the feud on a point of honor, sex, aggression, and violence are inextricably united." While Juliet undergoes an extraordinary process of development, Nardo argues, she is ultimately unable to survive in this hostile atmosphere and is finally "thrust to the wall by the phallic sword her society has exalted." See "Romeo and Juliet Up against the Wall," *Paunch* 48–49 (1977): 126–32. Coppélia Kahn, in a more extensive consideration of this subject, relates the ethic of the feud, in which sex and violence are linked, to the patriarchal structure of the society, commenting on the extent to which the conclusion of the play, associating death with sexual consummation, is also contained within this structure. Fate is thus not only a result of powerful social forces but also of the individual subjective responses to these forces. See "Coming of Age in Verona," *Modern Language Studies* 8 (1977–78): 5–22.

Sampson: 'Tis all one. I will show myself a tyrant. When I have fought with the men,
           I will be civil with the maids—I will cut off their heads.
Gregory: The heads of the maids?
Sampson: Ay, the heads of the maids or their maidenheads. Take it in what sense
           thou wilt.

                                                                              (1.1.23–28)

To participate in the masculine ethic of this play is to participate in the feud, which defines relations among men as intensely competitive, and relations with women as controlling and violent, so that women in Sampson's language "being the weaker vessels, are ever thrust to the wall" (1.1.17–18). That Romeo initially rejects this ethic would seem to redefine the nature and structure of male/female relationships. What is striking about the relationship between Romeo and Juliet, however, is the extent to which it anticipates and ultimately incorporates violence.

Both lovers have a lively imagination of disaster. While Romeo ponders "some vile forfeit of untimely death" (1.4.111), Juliet speculates "If he is married,/My grave is like to be my wedding bed" (1.5.136–37). Premonition, for both, has the force of self-fulfilling prophecy. While Romeo seeks danger by courting Juliet and death by threatening suicide in the wake of Tybalt's death, Juliet, under pressure, exclaims: "I'll to my wedding bed;/And death, not Romeo, take my maidenhead!" (3.2.136–37). Read metaphorically, the plot validates the perception expressed variously in the play that love kills.

The paradigm offered by *Romeo and Juliet,* with some modifications, may be read in the major tragedies as well. Here the structures of male dominance, involving various strategies of control expressed in the language of prostitution, rape, and murder, conceal deeper structures of fear, in which women are perceived as powerful and the heterosexual relation is seen as either mutually violent or at least deeply threatening to the man.

Murder in the Bedroom: Hamlet *and* Othello

Hamlet's violent behavior in his mother's bedroom expresses some of the violence of his impulses towards her. Obsessed as he is with sexual betrayal, the problem of revenge for him is less a matter of killing Claudius than one of not killing his mother.[3] Hamlet's anger against women, based on his perception of his mother's conduct, finds expression in the language of prostitution in his violent outburst against Ophelia:

---

[3]Theodore Lidz represents Hamlet as torn between the impulse to kill his mother for having betrayed his father and the desire to win her to a state of repentance and renewed chastity. My reading of Hamlet is very much indebted to his analysis in *Hamlet's Enemy: Madness and Myth in "Hamlet"* (New York: Basic Books, 1975).

I have heard of your paintings, well enough. God hath given you one face, and you make yourselves another. You jig and amble, and you lisp; you nickname God's creatures and make your wantonness your ignorance. Go to, I'll no more on't; it hath made me mad. (3.1.143–48)

It is painting that makes women two-faced, which allows them to deceive, to wear the mask of chastity, while lust "Will sate itself in a celestial bed/And prey on garbage" (1.5.56–57). Like whores, they cannot be trusted. The paradox of prostitution in these plays is based on the masculine perception that the prostitute is not so much the victim as the agent of exploitation. If women are classed as prostitutes and treated as sexual objects, it is because they are so deeply feared as sexually untrustworthy, as creatures whose intentions and desires are fundamentally unreadable. Thus, while Helen in *Troilus and Cressida* is verbally degraded (the Trojans discuss her in terms of soiled goods and contaminated meat), she is, through her infidelity to Menelaus, the source of the sexual pride and humiliation that animates the entire conflict between the two warring nations. Honor among men, in this play, though it takes the form of combat, is ultimately a sexual matter, depending largely on the fidelity or infidelity of women. For a man to be betrayed by a woman is to be humiliated or dishonored. To recover his honor he must destroy the man and/or woman who is responsible for his humiliation, for placing him in a position of vulnerability.

In *Hamlet,* it is the player queen who most clearly articulates the significance attributed to feminine betrayal. "A second time I kill my husband dead/When second husband kisses me in bed" (3.2.188–89). It hardly matters whether Gertrude was implicated in the actual death of Hamlet. Adultery is itself a form of violence and as great a crime. Hamlet, who reacts as an injured husband in seeking revenge against Claudius, also seeks retribution against his mother. Not having any sanction to kill his mother, however, he must remind himself to "speak daggers to her, but use none" (3.2.404). That his manner suggests physical violence is confirmed by Gertrude's response: "What wilt thou do? Thou wilt not murder me?/Help, ho!" (3.3.22–23). It is at this point that the violence Hamlet seeks to contain in his attitude towards his mother is deflected onto another object presumed to be appropriate.

This single act of displaced violence, moreover, has further ramifications in terms of Hamlet's relation to Ophelia, whose conflicted responses to the fact that her lover has killed her father increase the burden of double messages she has already received from the men in the play, culminating in her madness and death. It is not his mother whom Hamlet kills (Claudius takes care of that) but Ophelia. Only when she is dead, moreover, is he free to say clearly that he loved her. Similarly Othello, in whom the pathology of jealousy, the humiliation and rage that plague the man supposedly dishonored by the woman he loves, are more specifically and vividly portrayed, will say of Desdemona late in the play: "I will kill thee,/And love thee after" (5.2.18–19).

If I seem to be arguing that the tragedies are largely about the degeneration of heterosexual relationships, or marriages that fail, it is because I am reading the development from the comedies through the problem plays and the major tragedies in terms of an explosion of the sexual tensions that threaten without rupturing the surface of the earlier plays. A woman's power throughout is less social or political (though it may have social and political ramifications) than emotional, expressed in her capacity to give or to withhold love. In a figure like Isabella, the capacity to withhold arouses lust and a will to power in someone like Angelo, whose enforcing tactics amount to rape. In Portia, the threat of infidelity, however jokingly presented, is a weapon in her struggle with Antonio for Bassanio's allegiance. Male resistance, comic and exaggerated in Benedick, sullen and resentful in Bertram, stems from fears of occupying a position of weakness, taking in essence a "feminine" posture in relation to a powerful woman.

The feminine posture for a male character is that of the betrayed, and it is the man in this position who portrays women as whores. Since Iago occupies this position in relation to Othello, it makes sense that he seeks to destroy him, in the same way that Othello seeks to destroy the agent of his imagined betrayal, Desdemona. There is no reason to suppose, moreover, that Iago's consistently degraded view of women conceals any less hostile attitude in his actual relations with women. He, after all, like Othello, kills his wife. The difference between the two men lies not in their fear and mistrust of women, but in the degree to which they are able to accept an emotional involvement. It is Othello, not Iago, who wears his heart on his sleeve "for daws to peck at" (1.1.62). Were it not for Othello's initial vulnerability to Desdemona, he would not be susceptible to Iago's machinations. Having made himself vulnerable, moreover, he attaches an extraordinary significance to the relationship: "And when I love thee not,/Chaos is come again" (3.3.91–92); "But there where I have garnered up my heart,/Where either I must live or bear no life,/The fountain from the which my current runs /Or else dries up" (4.2.56–59).

Once Othello is convinced of Desdemona's infidelity (much like Claudio, on the flimsiest of evidence), he regards her not as a woman who has committed a single transgression but as a whore, one whose entire behavior may be explained in terms of lust. As such, he may humiliate her in public, offer her services to the Venetian ambassadors, pass judgment on her, and condemn her to death. Murder in this light is a desperate attempt to control. It is Desdemona's power to hurt that Othello seeks to eliminate by ending her life. While legal and social sanctions may be invoked against the prostitute, the seemingly virtuous woman suspected of adultery may be punished by death. In either case, it is the fear or pain of victimization on the part of the man that leads him to victimize women. It is those who perceive themselves to be powerless who may be incited to the acts of greatest violence.

The paradox of violence in *Othello*, not unlike that in *Macbeth*, is that the exercise of power turns against the hero. In this case, the murder of a woman leads to self-murder, and the hero dies attesting to the erotic destructiveness at the heart of his relationship with Desdemona: "I kissed thee ere I killed thee. No way but this,/Killing myself, to die upon a kiss" (5.2.357–58). If murder may be a loving act, love may be a murdering act, and consummation of such a love is possible only through the death of both parties.

"Of Woman Born": Lear *and* Macbeth

The fantasy of feminine betrayal that animates the drama of *Othello* may be seen to conceal or to be coordinate with deep fantasies of maternal betrayal in *Macbeth* and *Lear.*[4] Here the emphasis falls not so much on the adult heterosexual relation (though there are such relations) as on the mother/son or the fantasy of the mother/son relation. In these plays, to be feminine in the masculine consciousness is to be powerless, specifically in relation to a controlling or powerful woman. For Lear, rage as an expression of power acts as a defense against this awareness, while tears threaten not only the dreaded perception of himself as feminine, and hence weak, but also the breakdown of his psychic order:

> Life and death, I am ashamed
> That thou hast power to shake my manhood thus!
> That these hot tears, which break from me perforce,
> Should make thee worth them. Blasts and fogs upon thee!
> (1.4.298–301)

> You think I'll weep.
> No, I'll not weep.
> I have full cause of weeping, but this heart
> Shall break into a hundred thousand flaws
> Or ere I'll weep. O Fool, I shall go mad!
> (2.4.279–83)

> O, let me not be mad, not mad, sweet heaven!
> Keep me in temper; I would not be mad!
> (1.5.45–46)

It is not Lear who annihilates his enemies, calling down curses on the organs of generation of Goneril and Regan, but rather he who is being banished by the women on whom he had depended for nurturance. It is they who are the agents of power and destruction, allied with the storm and he, like Edgar, who is "unaccommodated man," a "poor, bare, forked animal," naked and vulnerable. That the condition of powerlessness gives rise to compassion in Lear is part of his dignity as a tragic hero. It does not, however, alter his perceptions of women as either good or bad mothers. Moreover, if the banishment of Cordelia initiates a process by which Lear becomes psychotic, it may be argued that her return is essential to the restoration of his sanity. The presence or absence of Cordelia, like Othello's faith in Desdemona's fidelity, orders the hero's psychic universe. When Cordelia dies, Lear must either believe that she is not dead or die with her, being unable to withstand the condition of radical separation imposed by death.

[4]Murray M. Schwartz discusses the difficulty of the hero's recognition of his relation to a nurturing woman in "Shakespeare through Contemporary Psychoanalysis," in *Representing Shakespeare: New Psychoanalytic Essays*, eds. Murray Schwartz and Coppélia Kahn (Baltimore: Johns Hopkins University Press, 1980), pp. 21–32. While Lear's dilemma, according to Schwartz, results from a "refusal to mourn the loss of maternal provision," Macbeth's difficulty may be seen as the result of an attempt to usurp maternal functions and to control the means of nurturance himself.

In *King Lear,* the most powerful image of separation, of the child who is banished by his mother, is that of birth. "We came crying hither:/Thou know'st, the first time that we smell the air/We wawl and cry" (4.6.178–80). In this sense, the mother's first act of betrayal may be that of giving birth, the violent expulsion of her infant into a hostile environment. In other passages, a woman's body itself is perceived as a hostile environment:

> But to the girdle do the gods inherit,
> Beneath is all the fiend's.
> There's hell, there's darkness, there is the sulphurous pit.
> (4.6.126–29)

> The dark and vicious place where thee he got
> Cost him his eyes.
> (5.3.174–75)

Intercourse imaged as violent intrusion into a woman's body may be designed to minimize the cost.

If it is birth itself—the condition of owing one's life to a woman and the ambivalence attending an awareness of dependence on women in general—that structures much of Lear's relations to his daughters, *Macbeth* may be read in terms of a systematic attempt by the hero to deny such an awareness. The world constructed by Macbeth attempts to deny not only the values of trust and hospitality, perceived as essentially feminine, but to eradicate femininity itself.[5] Macbeth reads power in terms of a masculine mystique that has no room for maternal values, as if the conscious exclusion of these values would eliminate all conditions of dependence, making him in effect invulnerable. To be born of woman, as he reads the witches' prophecy, is to be mortal. Macbeth's program of violence, involving murder and pillage in his kingdom and the repression of anything resembling compassion or remorse within, is designed, like Coriolanus' desperate militarism, to make him author of himself.

The irony of *Macbeth,* of course, is that in his attempt to make himself wholly "masculine" or uncontaminated, so to speak, by the womb, he destroys all source of value: honor, trust, and—to his dismay—fertility itself. It is his deep personal anguish that he is childless. The values associated with women and children, which he considers unmanly, come to be perceived as the source of greatest strength. In this play, it is procreation rather than violence that confers power—"the seeds of Banquo kings!" (3.1.70). To kill a child or to imagine such an act, as Lady Macbeth does in expressing contempt for her husband's vacillations, is to betray not only the bonds of human society but to betray one's deepest self. To reject the conditions of weakness and dependence is to make oneself weak and dependent. Macbeth's relentless pursuit of power masks his insecurities, his anxieties, and ultimately his impotence. *Macbeth,* more clearly than any of the other tragedies (with the possi-

---

[5]My discussion of the ways in which masculinity and femininity are perceived in this play is indebted to Cleanth Brooks' classic essay on *Macbeth* in *The Well Wrought Urn* (London: Dobson Books, 1968), pp. 17–39. For Brooks, it is Macbeth's war on children that reveals most clearly his own weakness and desperation. Ultimately the issue of manliness, for Brooks, is related to the theme of humanity or lack of it, but he does not raise questions about masculine and feminine stereotypes.

ble exception of *Coriolanus*), enacts the paradox of power, in which the hero's equation of masculinity with violence as a denial or defense against femininity leads to his destruction.

Macbeth's attempt to avoid the perception of Lear that "we cry that we are come/To this great stage of fools" (4.6.182–83), that the human infant is radically defenseless and dependent on the nurturance of a woman, gradually empties his life of meaning and leads to his perception of it as "a tale/Told by an idiot . . . /Signifying nothing" (5.5.26–28). Of all the tragic heroes, moreover, he is the most isolated in his death, alienated from himself, his countrymen, his queen. He has become what he most feared, the plaything of powerful feminine forces, betrayed by the "instruments of darkness," the three witches.

"The Heart of Loss": Antony and Cleopatra

Interwoven into the patriarchal structure of Shakespeare's tragedies is an equally powerful matriarchal vision. They are even, I would argue, aspects of one another, both proceeding from the masculine consciousness of feminine betrayal. Both inspire a violence of response on the part of the hero against individual women, but more importantly, against the hero's perception of himself as womanish, in which he ultimately hurts himself. The concurrence of these themes is particularly evident in *Antony and Cleopatra*, a play that both recalls the ritual marriage conclusion of the comedies as it deepens the sexual dilemma of the tragic hero.

Antony's relation both to Cleopatra and to Caesar may be read in terms of his anxieties about dominance, his fear of self-loss in any intimate encounter. Early in the play, Cleopatra uses this perception to her advantage by suggesting that for Antony to respond to the Roman messengers is to acknowledge his submission either to Caesar or to Fulvia. Her own tactics, of course, are manipulative and a form of dominance that Antony himself recognizes: "These strong Egyptian fetters I must break/Or lose myself in dotage" (1.2.117–18). The advice of the soothsayer to Antony concerning his proximity to Caesar is similar in structure if not in content: "near him thy angel/ Becomes afeard, as being o'erpow'red" (2.3.20–21). When Antony returns to Egypt, he is in effect "o'erpow'red" by Cleopatra: "O'er my spirit/Thy full supremacy thou knew'st" (3.11.58–59); "You did know/How much you were my conqueror, and that/My sword, made weak by my affection, would/ Obey it on all cause" (3.11.65–68). Antony, like Romeo earlier, perceives himself as having been feminized by love: "O sweet Juliet,/Thy beauty hath made me effeminate/And in my temper soft'ned valor's steel!" (*Rom.* 3.1.115–17). "O, thy vile lady!/She has robbed me of my sword" (*Ant.* 4.14.22–23).

If affection makes Antony weak, it also makes him suspicious of Cleopatra's fidelity: "For I am sure,/Though you can guess what temperance should be,/You know not what it is" (3.13.120–22). He falls easy prey to the conviction that Cleopatra has betrayed him to Caesar, making him a subject of sexual as well as political humiliation. "O, that I were/Upon the hill of Basan to outroar/The horned herd!" (3.13.126–28). In this light, Cleopatra becomes a "witch," a "spell," a "triple-turned whore":

O this false soul of Egypt! This grave charm,
Whose eye becked forth my wars, and called them home,
Whose bosom was my crownet, my chief end,
Like a right gypsy hath at fast and loose
Beguiled me, to the very heart of loss.
What, Eros, Eros!

                                                                     (4.12.25–30)

Antony, under the power of erotic attachment, feels himself, like Othello, to have
been utterly betrayed. Under the impact of this loss, moreover, his sense of psychic integrity begins to disintegrate: "here I am Antony,/Yet cannot hold this visible shape, my knave" (4.14.13–14). Chaos is come again.

While the fiction of Cleopatra's death restores Antony's faith in her love, it does
not restore his energy for life. Rather, the withdrawal of her presence destroys any
vestige of interest he has in the world of the living. "Now all labor/Mars what it does;
yea, very force entangles/Itself with strength" (4.14.47–49). It is Cleopatra who not
only dominates Antony's emotional life but invests his world with meaning. The fact
that she—unlike Juliet, Ophelia, Desdemona, Cordelia, and Lady Macbeth—dies so
long after her lover, not only reveals her as a complex figure in her own right, but
also attests to her power to give imaginative shape to the hero's reality.

Cleopatra in many ways is the epitome of what is hated, loved, and feared in a
woman by Shakespeare's tragic heroes. She is, on the one hand, the woman who
betrays, a Circe, an Acrasia, an Eve, the Venus of *Venus and Adonis*. To submit to
her or be seduced by her is to die. She is the player queen, for whom adultery is
also murder. She is a Goneril, a Lady Macbeth, a nonnurturing mother. What she
takes, on the other hand, she also has the power to give. She is imaginative, fertile,
identified with the procreative processes of the Nile. If Antony lives in our imagination, it is because of her "conception" of him. In this sense, she, like Desdemona
and Cordelia, is the hero's point of orientation, his source of signification in the
world. Union with her is celebrated as a curious comic counterpoint to the tragic
structure of double suicide and also portrayed as a literal impossibility. Moreover,
for this sexually powerful woman to escape censure, the fate of a Cressida or a
Helen, she must negate her own strength; she must die. While Theseus' phallic
sword in Antony's hands turns against him, Cleopatra, like Juliet, will accept death
"as a lover's pinch,/Which hurts, and is desired" (5.2.295–96). Throughout
Shakespeare's tragedies, the imagery of heterosexual union involves the threat of
mutual or self-inflicted violence.

Looked at from one angle, what Shakespeare's tragedies portray is the anguish
and destruction attendant on a fairly conventional and culturally supported set of
fictions about heterosexual encounter. The tragedies, as I read them, do not themselves support these fictions, except to the extent that they examine them with
such acute attention. The values that emerge from these plays are, if anything,
"feminine" values dissociated from the traditional masculine categories of force
and politics, focused instead on the significance of personal relationships or the
fact of human relatedness: the values of feeling, kinship, loyalty, friendship, and
even romantic love. That the recognition of these values entails the destruction of

the hero and everyone who matters to him attests perhaps to a kind of cultural determinism, or at least to the very great difficulty of reimagining habitual modes of behavior. It is the basis in cultural fictions of certain kinds of heterosexual attitudes to which I now wish to turn.

On the Margins of Patriarchal Discourse

Shakespeare's tragic paradigms offer the possibility of a deconstructive reading of the rape metaphor that informs Theseus' words to his captured queen.[6] Violence against women as an aspect of the structure of male dominance in Shakespeare's plays may be seen to obscure deeper patterns of conflict in which women as lovers, and perhaps more importantly as mothers, are perceived as radically untrustworthy. In this structure of relation, it is women who are regarded as powerful and men who strive to avoid an awareness of their vulnerability in relation to women, a vulnerability in which they regard themselves as "feminine." It is in this sense that one may speak of a matriarchal substratum or subtext within the patriarchal text. The matriarchal substratum itself, however, is not feminist. What it does is provide a rationale for the structure of male dominance in Shakespeare's tragedies, while it provides an avenue of continuity between these plays and the comedies in which women more obviously wield power.

The preceding analysis may be seen, moreover, to parallel the movement of psychoanalytic theory from an emphasis on oedipal to preoedipal stages of development. Roughly speaking, the shift has occurred in terms of a decrease of concern with father-son relations and a corresponding increase of concern with mother-son relations.[7] Certainly it may be said that the theories of object-

---

[6]I would assent to the following description by Gayatri Spivak of the task of deconstruction: "To locate the promising marginal text, to disclose the undecidable moment, to pry it loose, with the positive lever of the signifier; to reverse the resident hierarchy, only to displace it; to dismantle in order to reconstitute what is always already inscribed. Deconstruction in a nutshell." See Jacques Derrida, *Of Grammatology*, translator's preface (Baltimore: Johns Hopkins Univ. Press, 1976), p. lxxvii. While Spivak points out that there is no end to this process, in that the work of deconstruction is itself subject to deconstruction, she also notes that "as she deconstructs, all protestations to the contrary, the critic necessarily assumes that she at least, and for the time being, means what she says" (p. lxxvii). While it may not be strictly necessary to borrow this terminology for the reading I am proposing, it may be useful to observe that any large-scale reinterpretation, from a minority position, of a majority view of reality must appear at least in the eyes of some as a "deconstruction."

[7]Although the shift from father to mother is clear in the work of such theorists as John Bowlby, Melanie Klein, Margaret Mahler, and D. W. Winnicott, the child or infant, partly for grammatical reasons, tends to be regarded as male. Here, the problem inherent in the use of the masculine pronoun to refer to both sexes emerges. Textually speaking, the construction often obscures a shift of consideration from the development of the infant, male or female, to the exclusive development of the male infant. This convention is related to the cultural assumption by which the male of the species is taken as a norm, of which the female then becomes a variant. To remove this convention would not merely introduce a stylistic awkwardness (for some people at least), but it would also reveal a fundamental awkwardness in the structure of the author's argument. While the use of the male pronoun often *is* used generically to indicate both men and women, it as frequently serves to exclude consideration of the female without calling attention to the process by which she has been removed from the discussion.

relations, narcissism, schizophrenia, and separation-individuation have more to do with the child's early relations with the mother than with the father. Whether or not these theories are read in consonance with Freud's formulation of the Oedipus complex, the shift in focus relocates the discussion of certain issues. This relocation in turn reveals new interpretive possibilities. Specifically, it reopens the question of femininity.

A deconstructive reading of the rape metaphor in Shakespeare's tragedies leads directly or indirectly to a discussion of the masculine perception of femininity as weakness. The "macho" stance thus becomes a form of "masculine protest," or a demonstration of phallic power in the face of a threatened castration. It is for the male hero, however, that femininity signifies weakness, while actual women are perceived by him as enormously powerful, specifically in their maternal functions. It is not the female herself who is perceived as weak, but rather the feminized male. To project this problem back onto women—as Freud does in his discussions of femininity, in which the little girl perceives herself as castrated—is to present it as incapable of resolution.[8] If femininity itself is defined as the condition of lack, of castration, then there is no way around the masculine equation that to be feminine is to be castrated, or as Antony puts it, to be robbed of one's sword.

It is the so-called masculine consciousness, therefore, that defines femininity as weakness and institutes the structures of male dominance designed to defend against such an awareness. Shakespeare's tragedies, as I read them, may be viewed as a vast commentary on the absurdity and destructiveness of this defensive posture. However, while Shakespeare may be said to affirm the values of feeling and vulnerability associated with femininity, he does not in dramatic terms dispel the

---

[8]Although Freud approaches the subject of femininity from different angles in his three major discussions of it, there is no question that he links the process of feminine development indissolubly to the recognition on the part of the little girl that she is castrated. It would seem at least reasonable to argue, however, that the presence or absence of a penis is of far greater significance to the boy or man, who feels himself subject to the threat of its removal, than it could ever be to the girl or woman, for whom such a threat can have little anatomical meaning. I wonder too, why, in Freud's argument, a little girl would be inspired to give up the manifestly satisfying activity of masturbation on the basis of the illusion of a loss—the assumption perhaps that she might have had more pleasure if she had once had a penis, of which she seems mysteriously to have been deprived?

The problem that gives rise to these baroque speculations is of course Freud's assumption that there must be some reason why the little girl would withdraw her love from her mother in order to bestow it upon her father. Freud can imagine no other reason than the little girl's recognition of her own inferiority and thus "penis envy," and her resentment of her mother, equally deprived, for not having provided her with the desired organ. There can be no heterosexual love, in this account, without the theory of feminine castration. One can understand, from this vantage point, why Freud was reluctant to give it up. See "Some Psychical Consequences of the Anatomical Distinction Between the Sexes," "Female Sexuality," and "Femininity," in *The Standard Edition of the Complete Psychological Works of Sigmund Freud*, ed. and trans. James Strachey et al., 24 vols. (London: Hogarth Press, 1953–74), pp. 19, 21, 22, 241–60, 221–46, 112–35. For various critiques of Freud, see also Roy Schafer, "Problems in Freud's Psychology of Women," *Journal of the American Psychoanalytic Association* 22 (1974): 459–85; Jean Strouse, ed., *Women and Analysis* (New York: Grossman Press, 1974); Jean Baker Miller, ed., *Women and Psychoanalysis* (Baltimore: Penguin, 1973).

anxiety surrounding the figure of the feminized male. At this point, I would say that dramatic metaphors intersect with cultural metaphors.[9]

Freud's views of femininity may be useful to the extent that they articulate some deeply held cultural convictions. In one sense, what they do is reveal the basis of some powerful cultural metaphors, so powerful in fact that they continue to find formulation in the midst of our vastly different social and intellectual context. In the midst of profound structural changes in habits of philosophic and scientific thinking, as a culture we cling to the language of presence and absence, language and silence, art and nature, reason and madness, to describe the relations between the terms masculine and feminine. It is as though the breakdown of hierarchical modes of thought, of vertical ways of imagining experience, finds its deepest resistance in our habits of imagining the relations between the sexes. Some, like the Jungian James Hillman, would even argue that in order to effect real changes in our intellectual formulations of reality, we must find ways of reimagining femininity.[10] Sexual politics may lie at the heart of human culture, of our constantly shifting and evolving world views.

The preceding discussion, of course, rests on assumptions to which Freud would not have subscribed, chief among them a hypothesis concerning the relation between cultural metaphors and the concept of a cultural unconscious. What I would like to propose is that the notion of the unconscious may be culture specific—that is, the guiding metaphors of a given society or culture may legitimately be seen to express the structure of its unconscious assumptions, just as the metaphoric structure of individual discourse may be seen to convey some of the unconscious freight of a given life. If [Thomas] Kuhn is correct in assuming that scientific revolutions are the result of paradigm shifts or profound changes in our habits of imagining the world, then it may also be possible to consider the unconscious implications of certain habits of imagining.[11] Literary conventions may then be viewed as aspects of these imaginative habits, as codifications of a certain spectrum of unconscious attitudes, at the same time that they change and evolve, live and die according to their relation to the society out of which they arise and to which they respond. Cultural changes, to pursue the implications of Kuhn's argument, are in effect profound metaphoric changes, which in turn involve changes in the structuring of the unconscious.

In this light, literary history may be read psychologically. The questions one might ask, then, would concern the spectrum of psychic needs served by specific conven-

[9]One might wish to argue that social, psychic, and literary structures are so intimately interwoven that the relation between plot and culture is like that between Hamlet and his fate, between a text that is given and one that is generated, enacted, in part chosen. With this in mind, one might begin to speak of "patriarchal plots," the complex set of figures by which western culture has elaborated its relation to the structures by which it lives. The question then becomes the extent to which a powerful social movement warps, flexes, alters, and reimagines these essential structures and how genres are born and transformed.

[10]James Hillman, *The Myth of Analysis: Three Essays in Archetypal Psychology* (Evanston, Ill.: Northwestern Univ. Press, 1972), pp. 215–98.

[11]Thomas Kuhn, *The Structure of Scientific Revolutions* (Chicago: Univ. of Chicago Press, 1966).

tions and genres. Tracing the uses of a convention would then also yield a literary version of psychohistory. To offer an example close to the subject of this essay, I would like to pursue briefly some of the ramifications of the rhetoric of courtly love.

It is interesting to observe the language of Denis de Rougemont, who is so careful to situate the courtly love phenomenon in a historical sense, when he refers to the rhetorical trope of love as war: "There is no need, for example, to invoke Freudian theories in order to see that the war instinct and eroticism are fundamentally allied: it is so perfectly obvious from the common figurative use of language."[12] Obvious to whom? Is the war instinct, for instance, perceived as an aspect of the feminine psyche? Here the common (and to many readers unquestioned) assumption that reference to the male of the species includes women may be seen to obscure a process by which a fundamentally "masculine" attitude is proposed as a universal norm. More important, however, is the interpretive process by which de Rougemont reads a metaphor specific to a certain set of conventions, albeit powerful ones, as an unalterable aspect of the unconscious life of the species: "All this confirms the natural—that is to say, the physiological—connexion between the sexual and fighting instincts."[13]

It is this supposedly natural "connexion between the sexual and fighting instincts" that structures the language of the courtly love lyric, as it structures the language of sexual encounter in Shakespeare. To term this rhetoric "conventional" is not to demean it but rather to call attention to its psychological power, to which de Rougemont himself assents, at the same time that one recognizes its mutability, its historicity. Images of sexual intercourse as an act of violence committed against a woman run deep in our culture. The depth and persistence of these images, however, may tell us more about the anxieties of a culture in which femininity is conceived as castration and women are perceived paradoxically as a source of maternal power than it does about the actual or possible relations between the sexes.

Toward a Feminist Discourse

And, as I have hinted before, deconstruction must also take into account the lack of sovereignty of the critic himself. Perhaps this "will to ignorance" is simply a matter of attitude, a realization that one's choice of evidence is provisional, a self-distrust, a distrust of one's own power, the control of one's vocabulary, a shift from the phallocentric to the hymeneal.

—Gayatri Chakravorty Spivak, translator's preface to Jacques Derrida, *Of Grammatology*

---

[12]Denis de Rougemont, *Love in the Western World,* trans. Montgomery Belgion (New York: Harcourt Brace, 1956), p. 243. I have chosen the passages from de Rougemont because they are central to the elucidation of the courtly love tradition and because they are so clearly, though unintentionally, biased. A more contemporary (and more complex) example of the same kind of bias might be found in the concluding chapters of Leo Bersani's *A Future for Astyanax: Character and Desire in Literature* (Boston: Little, Brown, 1977).

[13]de Rougemont, p. 244.

Literary history, finally, is an aspect of cultural history. Both attest to changing patterns of awareness, to the constant refiguring of our relation to our specific location in time and space, to our own historicity. If individual history, as Ortega y Gasset writes, may be conceived as a process of casting and living out or living through metaphors of the self, is it not possible to imagine cultural history in similar terms?[14] To interpret these metaphors, to read on the margins of discourse, is not only to engage in a process that is characteristic of psychoanalytic interpretation but also to become engaged in a fundamentally historical process, that of making what is unconscious conscious and thus altering and displacing the location of the unconscious. This process, obviously akin to that of psychotherapy, is not to be perceived statically as an attempt to eliminate the unconscious but rather to dislodge it, to transform its metaphoric base.

Psychoanalytic theory in this sense may also be read in the historical dimension, as a means of reading the unconscious figurings of a given life within a specific cultural moment. As such, it will of course be subject to change and will to some extent serve the interests of the society that supports it. I am not here arguing against psychoanalytic theory in any sense but rather *for* a recognition of its historicity.[15] While Freud's elaboration of the Oedipus complex may have served to assuage the neurotic dilemmas of his society, it does not serve the needs of contemporary feminism. In a society like ours, in which most women can expect to work for a significant part of their lives and to bear fewer than three children, the interpretive myths offered by Freud for women are increasingly pathological. In order to be useful, the theory must bear a demonstrable relation to perceived reality. To argue that the social reality of women should be altered to fit the theory is not only reactionary but naive. It would make more sense to pursue the directions of contemporary psychoanalytic theory toward a redefinition of femininity, assuming, as I do, that implicit within the current focus on the mother/child relation is a reawakening of interest in the question of femininity. There are even some theorists, like Dorothy Dinnerstein, who would argue that such a reformulation is necessary for cultural survival, given the political destructiveness of the masculine ethic.[16]

[14][José] Ortega y Gasset, *History as a System, and Other Essays Toward a Philosophy of History* (New York: W. W. Norton, 1961), pp. 165–233.

[15]The following articles make a case for the relevance of Freud's personal history to the structure of his thought: Arthur Efron, "Freud's Self-Analysis and the Nature of Psychoanalytic Criticism," *The International Review of Psychoanalysis* 4 (1977): 253–80; Jim Swan, "*Mater* and Nannie: Freud's Two Mothers and the Discovery of the Oedipus Complex," *American Imago* 31 (1974): 1–64; Patrick Mahony, "Friendship and Its Discontents," unpublished paper presented to the Canadian Psychoanalytic Society, Montreal, May 19, 1977. Freud's instrument of self-analysis, from the point of view of these critics, becomes a double-edged sword, a manifestation of his genius for the articulation of the structural principles of his own psyche, as well as a measure of the necessary limitation of his method. Murray Schwartz elucidates this point further in "Shakespeare through Contemporary Analysis," cited in note 4. Juliet Mitchell might be seen to treat this subject on a large scale in *Psychoanalysis and Feminism* (New York: Pantheon Books, 1974), when she argues that the Oedipus complex acts as a structural representation of the psychic organization of patriarchal society.

[16]Dorothy Dinnerstein, *The Mermaid and the Minotaur: Sexual Arrangements and Human Malaise* (New York: Harper and Row, 1976).

What then, in psychoanalytic terms, would constitute the beginnings of feminist discourse? How is a woman, according to the painful elaborations of Julia Kristeva and others, to avoid the Scylla of silence or madness and the Charybdis of alienated or masculine discourse?[17] Gayatri Spivak has lately been suggesting that what we need is something like a Copernican revolution: from the phallocentric formulation of femininity as absence to a gynocentric language of presence.[18] If it makes sense that the male child should perceive his own sex as primary and difference as an inferior version of himself, then it makes as much sense that the little girl should also initially perceive her sex as primary. That each sex should take itself as the norm is perhaps part of the Ptolemaic universe of children, which must undergo several stages of decentering before maturity. Not to undergo this process of decentering is to elaborate structures in which dominance becomes the mask of weakness and submission a subversive strategy in the mutual struggle for power. For a woman to read herself obliquely through the patriarchal discourse as "other" is to assent to this structure. For a critic, male or female, to read this discourse as representative of the true nature of masculinity or femininity is to accept this structure. For a feminist critic to deconstruct this discourse is simultaneously to recognize her own historicity and to engage in the process of dislocation of the unconscious by which she begins to affirm her own reality.

[17]Julia Kristeva, who seems to accept the Lacanian explanation of the process of the child's induction into the symbolic order in western culture, presents the position of women within this construct as one of agonized conflict. See the opening chapters of *About Chinese Women*, trans. Anita Barrows (New York: Urizen Books, 1977). Shoshana Felman discusses the problem of defining a feminist discourse within a masculine ethic in "Women and Madness: The Critical Phallacy," *Diacritics* 4 (1975): 2–10.

[18]This statement derives from remarks made by Gayatri Spivak near the end of a session at the 1977 convention of the Midwest Modern Language Association. She spoke of "the womb as a tangible place of production," as the point of departure for a new discourse of femininity.

Lying Like Truth: Riddle, Representation, and Treason in Renaissance England

Steven Mullaney

I

In 1600, violating ancient codes of hospitality and of fealty, the Earl of Gowrie attempted to murder James VI of Scotland while the sovereign was staying at Gowrie's house in Perth. Gowrie and his accomplice were cut down in the attempt. But according to *Gowries Conspiracie,* printed in the same year *cum privilegio Regis,* the Earl's corpse bore its wounds strangely. It refused to bleed until James, while searching the body for letters that might provide a clue to a deed inexplicable as that of a man acting under his own power and volition, discovered a "close parchment bag" in Gowrie's pocket and removed it. Immediately blood gushed from the corpse. Nature resumed its course, and with nature and James once more in control, the body of the traitor was once again free, and once again subject to natural and human laws. It was free, that is, to be transported to Edinburgh, presented to Parliament in a spectral session, duly found guilty of treason, and then hanged, drawn and quartered, and exhibited—on poles fixed at Edinburgh, Perth, Dundee, and Stirling. Gowrie's bag was found to be "full of magicall characters, and words of inchantment, wherein, it seemed, he put his confidence."[1]

Today we are uncertain which to be most incredulous about—the documented spectacle of execution, or the preternatural detail of this "devil's writ," as York describes the "oracles . . . hardly attained and hardly understood" that he snatches from Southwell's hand in *2 Henry 6* (1.4.69). Both are significant aspects of the representation of treason in the age, however. The traitor stands at an uncertain threshold of Renaissance society, athwart a line that sets off the human from the demonic, the natural from the unnatural, and the rational from the enigmatic and obscure realm of unreason. Treason is a twice-monstrous act: it is something awesome and terrifying in a way we find difficult to conceive—although period

From *English Literary History,* Vol. 47, No. 1, pp. 32–47. The Johns Hopkins University Press, Baltimore/London (1980). Reproduced by permission of Johns Hopkins University Press and the author.

[1]*Gowries Conspiracie* (1600); printed in *Harleian Miscellany* (London, 1808), II, 345.

accounts, such as those describing the mood of London after the discovery of the Gunpowder Plot in 1605,[2] testify to its tumultuous repercussions even in failure—but it is monstrous, too, in that it is something made to show and reveal itself in both speech and spectacle. The fate of the Gunpowder conspirators provides but one example of a sequence that was typical, and could be described as the penal variety of a "King's Triumphs": first the confessions, then a procession through the city and an exhibition so that the populace could come to see the traitors "as the rarest sorts of monsters; fools to laugh at them, women and children to wonder, and all the common people to gaze."[3] In treason's procession as in the King's the city itself is the stage, and its streets form the scene for a mobile representation of power and authority. In the royal procession, however, the King himself appears and passes through a series of elaborate archways that provide, with their emblems and devices, a running commentary on his presence and his power. In chains as a sign and demonstration of that power, the traitor is himself a living gloss upon it and needs no further interpretation. But if his course is not graced in advance with the handiwork of the city's guilds, his wake is afterwards hung with treason's emblems. The final stage and ultimate performance of treason, often accompanied by a second, public confession, was of course on the scaffold, where the traitor was hanged and drawn and quartered for further display in death, according to a custom whose ritual was as much dramatic as it was juridical.[4]

There are suggestive analogies to be drawn between the one scaffold and the other—between the spectacle of the traitor on the platform of public execution and on the stage—but it would be wrong to equate the two. It is not that one is real, however, while the other is a mere show. Each belongs to the ritual and representation of treason in the Renaissance, but with a crucial difference. It is not treason that speaks from the place of execution, and in a sense it is no longer the body of the traitor that is painstakingly subjected to the law, and so shown to be human and natural once again. Confession and execution mark the return of the traitor to society and to himself, even in death. "Nothing in his life," as Malcolm says of the repentant Cawdor's execution, "Became him like the leaving it" (1.4.7).[5] His death was fitting and becoming, in a sense, because it was only in leaving life that he again became *himself* and achieved again a certain decorum of self—as Gowrie did even in death when his bag of riddles was removed. Confession, execution, and dismemberment, unsettling as they may seem, were not so much punishment of the traitor as they were the demonstration that what had been a traitor was so no longer, and that what had set him off from man and nature had been—like Gowrie's bag—lifted from him. When the body bleeds, treason has been effaced; execution is treason's epilogue, spoken by the law. In

[2]John Nichols, *The Progresses . . . of James the First* (London, 1828), II, 38–43.
[3]*The King's Booke* (1605); cited in Henry N. Paul, *The Royal Play of Macbeth* (New York: Macmillan & Co., 1950), p. 230.
[4]Here and elsewhere I am indebted to Michel Foucault, *Discipline and Punish: The Birth of the Prison*, trans. Alan Sheridan (New York: Pantheon, 1977).
[5]All quotations are from the Arden *Macbeth*, ed. Kenneth Muir (London: Methuen & Co., 1951).

histories of the period, however, treason presents us with a more equivocal figure; on stage, it is something closer to treason itself that is enacted, and that speaks.

II

It is during the country troubles of Henry VIII that the language of treason begins, like masterless men, to come under renewed legislative scrutiny. Like so much else in the unsteady movement from a feudal to a nascent capitalist economy, it is within the antitheses of city and country, court and country that treason is defined. It is a country matter and a vagabond act in its own right—the act of one without a proper master, or one who denies his master as proper.[6] In 1534, with Henry's Statute 26, the explicit questioning of the King's authority becomes a matter of high treason, punishable by death. Making speech a capital offense provoked a long-lasting dispute with Parliament, one whose outlines can be traced through the years by the successive repeals and re-enactments of the law. But whenever troubles arise, what you say again becomes an affair of life and death. The *Act for the punishment of diverse treasons* (1552) follows a time of pronounced civil strife, and again defines as guilty of high treason anyone who "by open preaching, express words, or sayings do expressly, directly and advisedly set forth and affirm that the King that here is is an heretic, schismatic, tyrant, infidel, or usurper of the crown."[7]

But the rebel is rarely so accommodatingly forthright. He "troubleth by biwaies," as Sir John Cheeke writes in *The Hurt of Sedicion* (1569): he wins others over to his cause not by outright, identifiable and therefore governable lies, but by relying upon and taking advantage of the multiple senses of things, whether actions or words. The rebel or traitor is not a plain dealer, quite the opposite. "He cannot plainely withstand and useth subtiltie of sophistrie," Cheeke continues, "mistaking the thing, but persuading men's minds, and abusing the plaine meaning of the honest to a wicked end of religious overthrow."[8] Cheeke confronts not treason's lie—so much is assumed—but the problem of its persuasiveness and the difficulty of identifying it in the making, before the damage is done and the rabble roused. Treason lies, but it lies like truth—as it must do. Underlying Cheeke's description of the traitor as one who makes verbal abuse a transitive act (whose primary object is always an indirect one—it abuses *to*) is the assumption that men could not be persuaded to rebellion by reason or by proper argument—that treason is explicable only as reason deluded or seduced, deceived by an abuser of words.

[6]See E. K. Chambers, *The Elizabethan Stage* (Oxford: Clarendon Press, 1923), I, 269–79, for the extension of the Vagabond Act to players in 1572.

[7]In Arthur Kinney, *Elizabethan Backgrounds: English Historical Documents of the Age of Elizabeth I* (Hamden, Conn.: Archon, 1975), V, 480.

[8]In [Raphael] Holinshed, *Chronicles of England, Scotland, and Ireland* (1580?; rpt. London: J. Jonson, 1807–08), III, 1009. Cheeke is included in full by Holinshed, pp. 987–1011.

Yet if the traitor abuses words, he is also abused by them. Among the causes of the Yorkshire uprising of 1549, amid a discussion of the rebels' grievances and evil dispositions, Holinshed notes that "an other cause was, for trusting to a blind and fantasticall prophecie, where with they were seduced, thinking the same prophecie shuld come to passe, by the rebellions of Norffolke, of Devonshire, and other places."[9] The Yorkshire rebels were as much the victims of this "fantasticall prophecie" as they were its agents, and they were undone by the riddle that led them on with the hope of success. Here we encounter a recurrent topos in accounts of treason. As an explanation of cause the prophecy doesn't explain—it displaces the source of seduction from the rebels to an oracular utterance—but it does account for the actions of all, both the mob and its head. Something like Zeno's paradox operates in discussions of the cause of rebellion: an infinite regress of others who are to blame, the abusers or seducers, opens out into a series from which the figure of the Other ultimately crystallizes, and the note of the preternatural often begins to sound. But such riddles also highlight the fact that, for the Renaissance, treason is by definition a self-consuming act. "What commonwealth is it then," Cheeke asks the rebel, "to doo such abhominable enterprises after so vile a sort, that yee hinder that good yee would doo, and bring in that hurt yee would not, and so find that yee seek not, and follow that yee lose, and destroie yourselves by follie . . . and so not onlie overfloweth us with the miserie, but also overwhelmeth you with the rage thereof?"[10] Given the enormity of his rebellion, the traitor too must have been somehow deceived. He is caught by a riddle or prophecy in an equivocal space between the truth and a lie, and he will prove his own ruination one way or the other—for the monstrosity and enigma of his act is that it threatens the foundations of order itself, and even in success could not survive the catastrophe it plots. The prophecy that gives a false and impossible hope of success to treason embodies its inevitable defeat, but it does not prescribe a limit to treason's catastrophe: facing a triumph that may well prove to be pyrrhic, authority is little consoled by treason's riddling delusion or the guarantee of its inevitable doom.

In these prophecies and riddles what we might dismiss as mere superstition constitutes in fact a rhetoric of rebellion. "When we speak or write doubtfully, that the sence may be taken in two ways," we are guilty, according to George Puttenham, of *ambiguitas*—or in the Greek, of *amphibology*.[11] Puttenham ranks amphibology as the worst abuse or vice in rhetoric, and his definitions and examples are standard ones. What distinguishes *The Arte of English Poesie* from its fellow handbooks of rhetoric is a two-fold digression warning of the social and political threat posed by the figure of amphibology. If the traitor is an ambiguous figure for Holinshed, the vice or trope of amphibology is for Puttenham the figure of treason itself.

---

[9]Holinshed, p. 985.
[10]Holinshed, pp. 1004–05.
[11]*The Arte of English Poesie* (1589; rpt. Westminister: A. Constable & Co., 1895), p. 267. [All future references to this edition will be included parenthetically in the text.]

Puttenham relates amphibology not to sophistry, as Cheeke did, but to a pre-Socratic past that is oracular as well as pagan.[12] "These doubtfull speeches were used much in old times by their false Prophets as appeareth by the Oracles of *Delphos* and of the *Sybilles* prophecies devised by the religious persons of those days to abuse the superstitious people, and to encomber their busie braynes with vaine hope and vaine fear." Yet the punning prophecies of amphibology are also found closer to home, since "all our old British and Saxon prophecies be of the same sort, that turne them on which side ye will, the matter of them may be verified." Nor are they simply relics of bygone days, for amphibologies return willfully to trouble both the still developing national language and the security of the state itself:

> [They] carryeth generally such force in the heades of fonde people, that by the comfort of those blind prophecies many insurrections and rebellions have beene stirred up in this Realme, as that of *Jacke Strawe*, and *Jacke Cade* in *Richard* the secondes time, and in our own time by a seditious fellow in Norffolke calling himself Captaine Ket, and others in other places of the Realme, lead altogether by certain propheticall rymes, which might be constred [*sic*] two or three wayes as well as that whereunto the rebelles applied it. (Book 3, Chapter 22, p. 267)

According to period accounts the rebellion led by Robert Kett in 1549 was guided from beginning to end by "fayned prophecies" that seemed to promise success to the rebels' cause but were in fact "as ambiguous as those uttered by older and more famous soothsayers." Obscure or doubtful as the riddles were, they possessed a persuasive force. "Still there was a charm, and mystery, a mighty power to them."[13] Kett's rebellion was a massive one. Following a minor enclosure riot at Attleborough in June of 1549, villagers gathered at Wymondham on July 7 to celebrate an annual festival and attend a play in honor of Thomas of Canterbury.[14] More fences were torn down by the gathered crowd. A landlord himself, Kett joined the mob after his own fences were lost, organized it and led it as an army eventually numbering 16,000 men in a successful siege on Norwich. Locally impressed and royal troops were defeated, a royal pardon offered and rejected. When Kett found himself under attack by 11,000 troops under the Earl of Warwick it was an amphibological riddle that determined the course of what was intended to be a strategic retreat:

---

[12]On oracular possession and rhetoric, see Plato's *Phaedrus*, 244 A–E. Aristotle discusses the relation between amphibology and oracles, citing a duplicitous prophecy from Herodotus (*Rhet.* 1407 A–B); see also Quintillian, *Institutio Oratoria* 7.9, and Cicero, *De Divinatione* 2.56.

[13]Frederic W. Russell, *Kett's Rebellion in Norfolk* (London, 1859), p. 142. Russell is a useful compilation of period accounts, chiefly Southerton (1549) and Nevylle. Holinshed also describes the prophetic elements of the uprising. For a modern study, see Julian Cornwall, *Revolt of the Peasantry 1549* (London & Boston: Routledge & K. Paul, 1977).

[14]The uprising thus provides a context for the frequent charges made later in the century, that playhouses served as sites for the hatching of treasonous plots. Playhouses "give opportunity to the refuze sort of evill disposed & ungodly people . . . the said Stage Plaies beeinge the very places of theire Randevous appoynted by them to meete with such other as wear to ioigne with them in theire designes & mutinous attemptes, beeinge also the ordinarye places for maisterles men to come together and recreate themselves." *The Lord Mayor and Aldermen to the Privy Council*, July 28, 1597; in Chambers, IV, 321.

The country gnoffes, Hob, Dick, and Hick
With clubbes and clouted shoone
Shall fill the vale
Of Dussindale
With slaughter'd bodies soon.[15]

Fill the vale they did: the oracle was fulfilled, although the bodies in the vale proved not to be, as the rebels had presumed they would, those of Warwick's men. The riddle of treason lies, it seems, in the riddle itself. A riddle, a prophecy, a double meaning, an unsettling pun: "when a sentence may be turned both wayes," Abraham Fraunce says of amphibole, "so that a man shall be uncertayne what way to take."[16] The image is that of a crossroads where the only right route to take is both at once. Choose one route or reading and the crossroads will return to haunt you—as it did Oedipus, a regicide and riddle-ridden man, and as it often did the traitor, who found his final resting place there, at the crossroads.[17] A lie can be defined or outlawed, a veiled message unveiled. But these riddles, prophecies, or amphibologies involve something other than treason lying or disguising itself.[18] They exceed and usurp the intentions of the traitor himself, bifurcating choice and intentionality. Surprisingly, no source is suggested for the prophecy in cases such as Kett's, no agent demonic or otherwise is even obliquely mentioned. The traitor is seduced by a language without origin.

But if amphibology seduces the traitor, it also presents authority with a considerable dilemma, and with it we move into a linguistic sphere the law cannot control. There is a recognition of a certain power in language here, one which for all its aura of superstition and country lore is associated with decidedly real struggles and threats to the power of the throne. National tongues were not without their role in exercising and expanding that power. "Language," as the Bishop of Avila remarked in 1492, "is the perfect instrument of empire."[19] Yet if we find in the Renaissance an increasing awareness and deployment of the power of language— power in a real sense, as a weapon for conquest and control—we also find in it a charting of the boundaries of rule, beyond which authority can only watch and listen to treason's amphibolic spectacle.

---

[15]Russell, p. 142.

[16]*The Lawyers Logicke* (1588; rpt. Menston: Scholar Press, 1969), p. 27.

[17]Amphibology is, according to Jean-Pierre Vernant, a wellspring of Greek tragedy and most prominent in *Oedipus Rex;* see *Mythe et Tragédie en Grèce Ancienne* (Paris: F. Maspero, 1972), pp. 21–40, 101–31.

[18]When the country matter of treason tunnels under the foundations of the State itself in the Gunpowder Plot, we may have an example of the conspirators invoking and attempting to use this "country confidence" to their advantage. In his letter to the Tower with instructions for the interrogation of Guy Fawkes, James inquires about the circulation of a "crewallie villanouse pasquil . . . which spake something of harvest and prophesied my destruction." Cited in B. N. De Luna, *Jonson's Romish Plot* (Oxford: Clarendon Press, 1967), p. 223, n. 1.

[19]Cited by Stephen J. Greenblatt in his excellent "Learning to Curse: Aspects of Linguistic Colonialism in the Sixteenth Century," in *First Images of America*, ed. Fredi Chiapelli (Berkeley: Univ. of Calif. Press, 1976), p. 562.

III

In December of 1604 the Gowrie plot was briefly exhumed as *Gowrie*, a lost play performed at least twice by the King's Players and then banned with a minor rebuke to the company for having thus brought the King to the scaffold.[20] While the direct representation of the King on stage might risk displeasure or imprisonment, the staging of treason—preternatural or regicidal as it might be—did not, and we can assume that Gowrie's "magicall characters, and words of inchantment" made their appearance in the play. Some two years after presumably performing in *Gowrie*, a year after the Gunpowder Plot of 1605, one of the King's Players turned to Holinshed for the plot of a play rich in such elements, in which a Scottish King is assaulted by a kinsman and a subject—while in "double trust," as James was in 1600. *Macbeth* is perhaps the fullest literary representation of treason's amphibology in its age. In 1606 it was performed for James at court: authority watched, and listened. On stage is a Scotland rapidly succumbing to misrule, lamented and viewed from an English perspective by its former countrymen—a description that fits the perspective of Malcolm and his fellow refugees from Macbeth's bloody reign, but one that fits the perspective of James as well, as he viewed the play. The Scotland on the scaffold is one preliminary to the intersection of James' line with Scottish royalty, but prophetic of it; it is also a Scotland interfused with contemporary concerns of the English court. But the fusion of times and places is not without its unsettling prospects from the vantage point of the throne.

Nearing the end of his fantastic career, Macbeth pauses and looks back down the way he has come, recognizing behind him the doubtful crossroads and the way not taken in the riddles that once made him resolute, bloody and bold:

> I pull in resolution; and begin
> To doubt th'equivocation of the fiend,
> That lies like truth.
>
> (5.5.42)

He has recognized the amphibology in the witches' riddles—the duplicitous sense of "wood" in the one prophecy wherein he put his confidence—and he will soon come to know that "none of woman born" was not the impossible and inhuman reference he took it for, but rather paltered with him in a double sense of "born." In Macbeth's recognition the audience finds a peculiar one of its own. For recognizing amphibology where one expected something more univocal has been the experience of the audience since Macbeth's drunken Porter made his entrance, so upsetting to Coleridge, and gave us his topical pronouncement. "Faith, here's an equivocator, that could swear in both the scales against either scale; who committed treason enough for God's sake, yet could not equivocate to heaven" (2.3.9).

---

[20]The play and its problems at court are known only from a letter of Dec. 8, 1604, cited in Chambers, I, 328.

In 1606 the topical reference was a clear one, since Father Garnet's equivocation during his trial for complicity in the Gunpowder Plot was still an active and much publicized concern. While the reference was clear, however, the *relation* of Garnet's equivocation to the play was not. In its narrow historical context, "equivocation" has been of inestimable aid in dating *Macbeth*, but of doubtful use as a key to the entanglements of truth, lie, and treason in the play.[21] What Shakespeare gives us is not treason's lie—something the court might well have expected, something it could regulate, define, control, and perhaps anticipate—but treason's amphibology. Not Garnet's equivocation, but an equivocation that lies like truth.

According to James, Garnet lied. According to the Church he relied upon a theologically valid duplicity known as equivocation or mental reservation—qualifying his spoken utterances with unspoken emendations, forming a true if mixed response to the questions put him. In the eyes (or ears) of God, he had not lied. During the sixteenth century the Church promulgated and defended such equivocation as a strategy for Catholics to employ when caught between conflicting demands for loyalty to Protestant rulers and to Rome, and it is equivocation as such—as mental reservation—that the audience of *Macbeth* had well in mind. The theological treatises on equivocation that begin with St. Raymond's *Summa* (1235) describe mental reservation, however, as a secondary, narrower form of equivocation.[22] The term used for its primary form is amphibology. The Church had better sense, however, than to recommend punning under oath as a pragmatic strategy for Catholics who had to skate between the truth and a lie. Although theologically sound, puns and amphibologies would be of dubious value if *control* of a situation was paramount. As our tales of treason suggest, amphibology resists control. Indeed, psychoanalytic theory draws an antithetical relationship between control and amphibology, since it is through parapraxes and puns that the unconscious breaches the defenses of the conscious mind.[23]

When Thomas James refers to Garnet in 1612, he echoes Fraunce's syntax and image of amphibole as a crossroads where choice is bifurcated, but it is an empty echo. "Al his Equivocations, wherein his tongue runs one way, and his meaning another, that you know not where to find him."[24] The intentions of the speaker *rule* here: mental reservation resides and resolves itself in the conscious intentions of the speaker. In *Macbeth*, from its foul-and-fair opening to the senseless slaughter of Macduff's family in an effort to crown, as Macbeth says, his "thoughts with acts," intention, act, and language are unruly, a matter of words unencompassed by definitions of truth and lie that "palter with us in a double sense" and that exceed Macbeth's intentions and his efforts to control, both compelling and undoing his resolution.

---

[21]See Paul (n. 3), pp. 226–48.
[22]See *The Catholic Encyclopaedia* under "Mental Reservation" for a full chronology.
[23]Relevant texts would be Freud's *The Psychopathology of Everyday Life* (New York: W. W. Norton & Co., 1965) and *Jokes and Their Relation to the Unconscious* (New York: W. W. Norton & Co., 1960). Of the work of Jacques Lacan, see *Ecrits*, trans. Alan Sheridan (New York: W. W. Norton & Co., 1977), pp. 146–79

[24]*The Jesuits Downfall;* cited in Frank L. Huntley, "*Macbeth* and the Background of Jesuitical Equivocation," *PMLA* 79 (1964): 400, n. 45.

Shakespeare does not, then, merely project the concerns of the moment onto the screen of Scotland's past. When finally admitted by the Porter, Macduff questions him, and the doorkeeper responds in "multitudinous antitheses," glossing his previous reference to mental reservation with a demonstration of amphibology in comic guise, culminating in an (un)resolving pun on "lie":

> *Macduff:* What three things does drink especially provoke?
> *Porter:* Marry, sir, nose-painting, sleep, and urine. Lechery, sir, it provokes, and unprovokes: it provokes the desire, but it takes away the performance. Therefore, much drink may be said an equivocator with lechery: it makes him, and it mars him; it sets him on, and it takes him off; it persuades him, and disheartens him; makes him stand to, and not stand to: in conclusion, equivocates him in a sleep, and, giving him the lie, leaves him.
>
> (2.3.27)

It is when Macbeth returns to the heath and seeks out the three hags for a second set of prophecies that Shakespeare's design with equivocation and the interplay of times and places comes into its most dramatic focus. After hearing the riddles, Macbeth witnesses the "show of eight Kings" from Banquo's line. They form a procession that leads prophetically offstage to the royal audience they will culminate in, and the last of them holds a glass in his hand, presumably to catch the countenance of the King. Genealogy and prophecy are made manifest in a visible display, but there is another genealogy in the air as well, one heard rather than seen. Juxtaposed to the projection of James' line, the witches' riddles complicate its complimentary gesture with what amounts to a genealogy of treason and equivocation: the equivocation the audience knows, defined by James as treason's dissembling lie, has been contextualized or traced back to the less than reassuring figure of treason and rebellion we have been charting in this essay.

Amphibology marks an aspect of language that neither treason nor authority can control. It is a power that cannot be trammelled up, mastered, or univocally defined, but it is a power: it compels and moves the speaker or auditor. From the perspective of authority, it does so illicitly—that is, in the place of authority and laws of State, reason, or sense. It is not when Macbeth lies but when the language he would use instead masters him that the power of amphibology strikes us, and its effects are not confined to the witches' riddles.

Language behaves strangely and impulsively in the play, as if with a will of its own. At times Macbeth seems to stride the blast of his own tongue, not so much speaking as he is spoken by his words and their insistent associations. A submerged current propels his speech even when Macbeth dissembles, and it surfaces during his description of the murdered Duncan in the form of a disassembled pun:

> . . . his gash'd stabs look'd like a breach in nature
> For ruin's wasteful entrance: there, the murtherers,
> Steep'd in the colour of their trade, their daggers
> Unmannerly breech'd with gore.
>
> (2.3.113)

The breach that is an opening in Duncan's flesh—allowing what is outside to intrude, spilling all that should remain within—returns to the mind's eye and ear when "breech'd" succeeds it so closely. The first suggests or prompts the second in something closer to free association than logical progression of thought.[25] Wound and unmannerly covering, the intrusion of the one homonym upon the other acts as a pun often does, making visualization of an image difficult. The breeches of gore are themselves breached: one image haunts the other, and we are uncertain what way to take.

With the amphibolic riddle, taking one course through it does not eliminate the other; in his own moving and self-persuading language, Macbeth relies and rides upon gliding significations of words, often with a powerful effect. Authority can either watch and listen to such motions, or it can engage them. In *Macbeth*, Shakespeare develops an unsettling affiliation between treason's spectacle and its audience. To engage treason's motions is to participate in them, threatening the otherwise clear antithesis that would seem to hold between rule and misrule and revealing the latter to be less the antithesis of rule than its alternating current, its overextension and in a sense its consequence. In England with Macduff, Malcolm dissembles. He lies about his own character and tarnishes his reputation, confident that when the test of his compatriot has been made he can remove this mask of misrule as easily as he donned it. But once on his face, it leaves a lasting impression. For Macduff the experience is a discomposing one, for it reveals a family resemblance between authority and its other where no relation was expected. When Malcolm strips away the mask and swears, "my first false speaking/Was this upon myself" (4.3.130), Macduff hesitates, uncertain whether it is Malcolm honest and pure or Malcolm profligate who declares such an absolute division between his lies and his truths. The line he draws and the need to draw it are equally difficult for Macduff to align with his notions of a true ruler: "Such welcome and unwelcome things at once,/'Tis hard to reconcile" (4.3.138).

The words could have been spoken by Macbeth before Duncan's murder, when still on the heath and wondering how to reconcile the foul and fair tidings of the witches' greetings. Both a metaphor and a pun call for a simultaneous perception of likeness and difference, but unlike a metaphor, a pun cannot be reduced to a simile—as Aristotle said any metaphor could be—in order to clarify the lines of its similitude. Amphibology lies *like* truth: similitude here is reason's dilemma, not its exegetical or legal solution. An interplay of likeness and difference, amphibology is less readily ruled than are the antitheses of authority.

---

[25]See Cleanth Brooks, "The Naked Babe and the Cloak of Manliness," in *The Well-Wrought Urn* (New York: Harcourt, Brace & World, 1947), pp. 38ff. Brooks is interested in the imagistic unity of the play; "breach" and its gliding interference with the "breech'd" daggers, which are related to the clothes-motif of *Macbeth*, receive no comment.

IV

Amphibology belongs to treason's spectacle. What is effaced by the time of treason's orderly procession and meticulous execution under the law is something more than a rhetorical figure or mere wordplay, as we understand such terms today. When amphibology surfaces in histories or on the stage it is accorded a power that is generative rather than controlling or restraining. It is something the traitor gives himself up to, and a part of what is generated out of it is the traitor's arc of rebellion. In his study of the "uncomic puns" in *Macbeth*—"breach" could be added to it— Kenneth Muir suggests such puns possess a generative power since lost to dramatic language, but he approaches them strictly within the history of literary language and the stage. Characteristic of Shakespearean drama, most pronounced in *Macbeth* yet absent from the stage after the Restoration, the uncomic pun is a part of what separates Shakespeare's language from ours: "The Restoration dramatists were admirably lucid, but their use of language was, in the last resort, unimaginative. The banishing of the pun except for comic purposes was the symbol of a radical defect: it was a turning away from the genius of the language."[26]

Muir's thesis is a striking one, but a part of what separates Shakespeare's language from ours is the (an)aesthetization that has taken place, when amphibology thus resurfaces as a purely linguistic phenomenon whose significance is both entirely aesthetic and even limited to a single genre. For Puttenham the domain of amphibology and the threat posed by it are considerably broader, as they were for the later seventeenth century—which did more than "turn away" from its *genius linguae*. Indeed, the age subsequent to Shakespeare brought language under its full and controlled scrutiny, not as a spectacle but as something to chart, analyse, regulate, and even legislate into a clear and ordered discourse.[27] Modern grammars, prose style, and ideas of translation stem from the efforts of the Royal Society and others to master language, but the ordering and deployment of discourse is also a phenomenon inseparable from the creation of the modern State.[28] The consequences for the figure of the traitor, dramatic and rhetorical, are beyond the bounds of this essay but relevant to it. What I have called amphibology, Puttenham also describes as ambiguity. I avoid the more familiar term because of its familiarity. Ambiguity, too, has enjoyed considerable popularity as an aesthetic

[26]"The Uncomic Pun," *Cambridge Journal* 3 (1950): 484. Comic or not, paronomasia lacks the *force* associated with amphibology, even in its etymology. Fraunce's "amphibole" is actually the most correct form, in that the word's root (*bole*) is not swallowed up by the *-logos* suffix. Meaning both to strike on all sides and to be struck on all sides, "amphibole" is itself an amphibole.

On the relation of *comic* puns and figures of sedition, see Robert Weimann, *Shakespeare and the Popular Tradition in Theatre*, trans. R. Schwartz (Baltimore: Johns Hopkins Univ. Press, 1978), esp. pp. 135–48.

[27]See R. F. Jones, "Science and English Prose Style in the Third Quarter of the Seventeenth Century," in *Seventeenth-Century Prose*, ed. Stanley E. Fish (New York: Oxford Univ. Press, 1971), pp. 53–90, for an account of Joseph Glanvill's day before the bar of the Royal Society. Originally an imitator of Browne, Glanvill revised all his works, expunging metaphors and figures, then came before a full session of the Society for their approval, openly confessing the error of his ways and vowing not to stray from the path of a clear style again.

[28]See Michel Foucault, *The Order of Things* (New York: Vintage Books, 1971), esp. pp. 78–208.

phenomenon in this century. What the Latin fails to suggest—partly in its etymology, but more importantly in its modern usage—is the unruly but generative force associated with treason's figure. But the Greek term *becomes* unfamiliar. Its strangeness is an historical occurrence, and it seems more than a coincidence of history or philology that it is during the seventeenth century when it begins to decline in usage and gives way to the familiar but relatively pallid "ambiguity."

Charting the course a more orderly commonwealth must take, Hobbes broadly attacks figurative language in *Leviathan,* often eliding metaphor with ambiguity as equivalent vices. While he employs the more familiar term, the figure of treason still informs his use, in 1651, of "ambiguity." "Metaphors, and senslesse and ambiguous words," he writes, "are like *ignes fatui;* and reasoning upon them, is wandering amongst innumerable absurdities; and their end [is] contention, and sedition."[29] Less clearly but still perceptibly, the association of treason and amphibology enters into Johnson's discussion of Shakespeare's wordplay. The quibble—a pun or a riddle—fascinates and seduces Shakespeare, acting upon him like an *ignis fatuus* or one of Atalanta's irresistible apples, but something more threatening also darkens its appeal:

> A quibble is to Shakespeare, what luminous vapors are to the traveller; he follows it at all adventures, it is sure to lead him out of his way, and sure to engulf him in the mire. It has some malignant power over his mind, and its fascinations are irresistible. . . . A quibble is the golden apple for which he will always turn aside from his career, or stoop from his elevation. A quibble, poor and barren as it is, gave him such delight, that he was content to purchase it, by the sacrifice of reason, propriety, and truth. A quibble was to him the fatal Cleopatra for which he lost the world, and was content to lose it.[30]

A *malignant* power, seductive and alluring, charming us out of all propriety and property. The gods of one age tend to become the demons of the succeeding one: here, it is the author of treason's spectacle that has himself become the figure of the traitor, undone by treason's rhetoric.

Like his author but unlike Cawdor, Macbeth dies unrepentant. As a staging of treason, *Macbeth* is a rather full portrait. At its opening, in the deaths of Glamis and Cawdor, different versions of treason's final performance are described. At its close the play returns to the question of treason's representation and its proper stage, and from that question derives its penultimate dramatic impetus. We witness a new aspect of the traitor. Macbeth has run his bloody course and stands undone but no longer deluded, facing Macduff but refusing to engage with his doom. As we near the point of the traitor's effacement it is fitting that Macduff goads his rival into action with a reminder that treason has another stage, and that its monstrosity fully realizes itself only in defeat:

> Then yield thee, coward,
> And live to be the show and gaze o' th' time:
> We'll have thee, as our rarer monsters are,

[29]*Leviathan*, ed. C. B. Macpherson (Harmondsworth: Penguin, 1972), pp. 116–17.
[30]*Preface to Shakespeare*, in the Yale *Complete Works*, ed. Arthur Sherbo (New Haven: Yale Univ. Press, 1968), VII, 74.

> Painted upon a pole, and underwrit,
> "Here you may see the tyrant."
> (5.8.23)

Macduff threatens a life in captivity and a gallows procession which, staged in effigy, can be infinitely repeated—and viewed by Macbeth himself. Macbeth chooses instead to die in renewed rebellion. When he exits it is as a warrior and a traitor, in arms. Macduff returns, bearing his head: the traitor is no more. But the appearance of Macbeth's head transforms the stage it bloodies. To the audience the visage is a familiar one, but it is also one proper to a different setting. Macbeth's head in a sense doubles the stage, and we end in a visual representation of the verbal pun: one scaffold portrayed upon the boards of the other, in a closing reformation of treason's spectacle.

Macbeth: The Male Medusa

Marjorie Garber

> *"towards his design*
> *Moves like a ghost"*

By the superstitious on and off the stage, *Macbeth* has always been considered an unlucky play.[1] Actors have been known to refuse to wear a cloak or carry a sword that has been used in a *Macbeth* production.[2] Inside the theatre, it is said, even in the wings and dressing rooms, they will not mention the name of the play, or the names of any of its characters. They call it "the Scottish play" or "that play" or "the unmentionable." Macbeth's death is referred to as "the death," and Lady Macbeth as "the Queen." Those who unwittingly or carelessly break these unspoken rules, and quote from the "Scottish play" behind the scenes, are obliged to perform a time-honored ritual to remove the "curse." The offender must go out of the dressing room, turn around three times, spit, knock on the door three times, and beg to be admitted. It may be that this ceremony of exorcism derives in some way from the knocking at the gate in the Porter scene (2.3), or from the witches' custom of cursing in threes, or perhaps from the incantation of those same witches when Macbeth approaches them on the heath: "By the pricking of my thumbs,/Something wicked this way comes./Open, locks,/Whoever knocks!" (4.1.44–47). An alternative method of removing the curse is said to be to quote from *The Merchant of Venice*—especially Lorenzo's benison to the departing Portia: "Fair thoughts and happy hours attend on you!" (3.4.41). *Merchant* is considered a particularly lucky play, and thus to provide an antidote for the malign powers of *Macbeth*.

Interestingly enough, if we are to believe in stage history, those powers seem to have been considerable. In the first production of the play outside England, in 1672, the Dutch actor playing Macbeth was at odds with the actor playing Duncan over the affections of the latter's wife—who was cast in the role of Lady Macbeth.

From Marjorie Garber, *Shakespeare's Ghost Writers: Literature as Uncanny Causality* (New York: Methuen, 1987), pp. 88–123. Reproduced by permission of Routledge, Chapman and Hall and the author. The essay printed here is a shortened version of the original.

[1]See *The Riverside Shakespeare*, ed. G. Blakemore Evans (Boston: Houghton Mifflin, 1974). Unless noted, all citations from the plays are to this edition.

[2]For this and subsequent information about *Macbeth* and theatrical superstition I am indebted to Richard Huggett, *Supernatural on Stage: Ghosts and Superstitions of the Theater* (New York: Taplinger Publishing Company, 1975), pp. 153–211. I was witness to the Stratford, Ontario, incident (July 1980).

One evening the murder scene was particularly bloody, and "Duncan" did not appear for his curtain call. Afterwards it was discovered that a real dagger had been used. The former "Macbeth" served a life sentence for murder.

In more modern times the curse has apparently been equally lively. Laurence Olivier played the title part in 1937. First he lost his voice. Then the sets were found to be far too large for the stage. Finally he narrowly escaped death when a heavy weight plummeted from above and demolished the chair in which he had just been sitting. The show went on.

In the 1942 production starring—and directed by—John Gielgud there were no fewer than four fatalities. Two of the witches, the Duncan, and the scenic designer all died in the course of its run. The set was then repainted and used for a light comedy, whereupon the principal actor of that play promptly died.

Orson Welles filmed the play in 1946. When the film was finished, he discovered that the Scots accent he had insisted his actors acquire was totally incomprehensible to the audience. The entire sound track had to be recorded again.

When Charlton Heston played the part he had a serious motorcycle accident during rehearsals, after which there was much backstage murmuring about the "curse." The production was staged outdoors, and Heston was required to ride a horse in the opening scene. At the first performance he rushed from the stage, clutching his tights and whispering urgently, "Get them off me. Get them off me." The tights, it seemed, had been dipped in kerosene, either accidentally or on purpose, so that the heat from the horse inflicted painful burns. To add insult to injury, the audience responded to the play as if it were a comedy, laughing uproariously throughout the last act, and redoubling their laughter when Macduff appeared with Macbeth's severed head, which had been closely modeled on Heston's own.

Actors have occasionally been tempted to defy the curse, chanting lines from the play in unison in their dressing rooms just to see what would happen. This occurred in 1974 at the Bankside Theater, which was then performing in a tent. The result was a huge and sudden rainstorm, which short-circuited the electricity and made the entire stage a deathtrap. Then the canvas roof of the tent collapsed—fortunately just after the audience had made its way out. The entire theatrical season for the following year had to be cancelled.

On another occasion the young actress playing Lady Macbeth declared shortly after the dress rehearsal that she did not believe in the curse. The next day she decided she had been playing the sleepwalking scene wrong, keeping her eyes open when they ought properly to be shut. At the first performance she entered with her eyes closed and fell fifteen feet into the orchestra pit. She climbed back to the stage and continued the scene.

But the show has not always gone on. The great Russian director Constantin Stanislavski, who greatly admired *Macbeth,* mounted an elaborate production for the Moscow Arts Theater. During the dress rehearsal the actor playing Macbeth forgot his lines and—as was the custom in the Russian theater—came down to the prompt box at the front of the stage to get his cue. There was no word from the prompter. Irritably he tried again; still no word. A third try; nothing. At last he peered into the box, only to find the aged prompter dead—but still clutching the script. Stanislavski, no less a fatalist than his countrymen Chekhov and Dostoevsky, cancelled the production immediately. It—like the prompter—was never revived.

Stories of this kind are legion. People have been injured or killed, and productions seriously disrupted. The play is not only thought to be unlucky—on the face of things it actually has been unlucky, and actors today continue to believe in the curse. Recently, a tourist visiting the Stratford Festival in Ontario, Canada, innocently mentioned the name of the play while standing on the stage; the tour guide, a member of the company, quickly crossed himself.

What is there about Shakespeare's *Macbeth* that provokes so strong a response, and so heightened a defense? The answer is not hard to locate, for the play is itself continually, even obsessively, concerned with taboo, with things that should not be heard and things that should not be seen, boundaries that should not be crossed— and are. One of the principal themes of *Macbeth* is the forbidden, the interdicted, that which a man (or woman) may not with safety see or do. As much as it seeks to repress this acknowledgment, the play's *subject* is the uncanny and the forbidden—and its ancillary, covering subject is the need to repress or deny that fact. There *is* something uncanny going on here. Thus attempts to explain away the evidence of stage history have about them an engagingly overdetermined air of rationalization—a deliberate insistence upon finding the "facts"—as if these would dispel the numinous effect. Thus it is asserted that the role of Macbeth is so large, and the stage action so busy, with swordfights, entrances and exits (especially at the end of the play, when Birnam wood comes to Dunsinane) that accidents are just bound to happen—an explanation that explains nothing at all.

"Research" has also been brought to bear on the suppression of this troubling history of performance. We are informed, for example, that the witches' brew concocted in Act 4 was based on an actual recipe known to the witches of Shakespeare's native Warwickshire—a region famous for its practice of witchcraft.[3] Since the public enunciation of these secret ingredients—"fillet of a fenny snake," "eye of newt and toe of frog," not to mention "liver of blaspheming Jew" and "finger of birth-strangled babe"—would constitute a kind of inverse blasphemy, like the use of Christian artifacts in the Black Mass, disastrous or "unlucky" events might well ensue.

Ingenious "solutions" of this kind, with their spurious but reassuring documentation (the "real" recipe; the "original" witches, now safely dead) invite us to take refuge in the happy bromide that "accidents are bound to happen," as if such uncomfortable formulae could, by their very familiarity, produce comfort—or at least eliminate the sneaking suspicion that there is more going on in *Macbeth* than is dreamt of in anyone's philosophy. But such deferrals will not stay in place. The play is itself transgressive, and insists upon the posing of pertinent thought-troubling questions.

---

[3]Huggett, pp. 162–63.

What is the relationship of the play to its stage history? In what sense can *Macbeth* be said to be about this kind of transgression and dislocation? Are these seeming "accidents" part of the play's affect—and also of its subject?—something let out to wander, to cross the borders between safety and danger, play and "reality," like a sleepwalker or a persistent wandering ghost: Lady Macbeth's somnambulistic nightmare, or Banquo's unsettling, extraneous, and persistent presence at the banquet? The more we wish to pack her safely offstage and thus to bed, to banish him from his usurped place at table, the more we see how much the play resists such easy resolutions, such comfortable conclusions about the dramatic role of dramatic presentations. The story *of* the play reflects the story *in* the play.

"wicked dreams abuse
The curtain'd sleep"

Macbeth presents us with what is in effect a test case of the limits of representation. The boundary between what is inside the play and what is outside it (in its performances, in its textual resonances) is continually transgressed, and marked by a series of taboo border crossings: sleep/waking, male/female, life/death, fair/foul, heaven/ hell, night/morning. It is perhaps no accident that the Porter scene, itself a theatrical presentation of the transgressive limit or boundary, has aroused so much critical interest. It may indeed be the case that all stories about the uncanny are stories about the repression of the uncanny. In his essay on "The Uncanny" Freud discusses the strategy of the writer who lulls his reader into a false sense of security which he then deliberately transgresses or violates: "He takes advantage, as it were, of our supposedly surmounted superstitiousness; he deceives us into thinking that he is giving us the sober truth, and then after all oversteps the bounds of possibility."[4] Something of the same emotion is reflected in De Quincey's famous remarks "On the Knocking at the Gate in *Macbeth*" (1823), and even more acutely in Mallarmé's "La Fausse Entrée des Sorcières dans *Macbeth*" which takes De Quincey as a point of departure. Mallarmé is fascinated by the witches' uncanny presence, so different from the bold transgressive knock at the gate. *"Rien, en intensité, comparable aux coups à la porte répercutés dans la terreur; mais ici, au contraire, un évanouissement, furtif, décevant la curiosité."*[5] "Something comes only to vanish, furtive, disappointing all curiosity." He lays stress on the fact that the witches do not *enter*, are not described as entering the scene in the ordinary way of actors—instead they *appear: extra-scéniquement*, uncannily present.

---

[4]Sigmund Freud, "The Uncanny," in *Studies in Parapsychology*, ed. Philip Rieff, trans. Alix Strachey (New York: Macmillan, 1963), p. 57.
[5]Stéphane Mallarmé, *La Fausse Entrée des Sorcières dans Macbeth*, in *Crayonné au Théâtre, Oeuvres Completes* (Paris: Pléiade, 1945), p. 348. I am indebted to Barbara Johnson for calling this essay to my attention, and for the translation.

Overture sur un chef-d'oeuvre: comme, en le chef-d'oeuvre, le rideau simplement s'est levé, une minute, trop tôt, trahissant des menées fatidiques.
   Cette toile qui sépare du mystère, a, selon de l'impatience, prématurement cédé—admis, en avance sur l'instant réglementaire, la cécité commune à surprendre le geste éffarouché de comparses des ténèbres—exposé, dans une violation comme fortuite, pour multiplier l'angoisse, cela même qui parassait devoir rester caché, tel que cela *se lie par derrière et effectivement à l'invisible: chacun scrute et dérange, parmi l'éclair, la cuisine du forfait, sans le chaudron futur aux ingrédients pires que des recommandations et un brusque au revoir.*

[The overture to a masterpiece: as if, in the masterpiece, the curtain had simply risen a minute too soon, betraying fateful goings-on.
   That canvas that separates mystery off has somehow, through some impatience, prematurely given way—admitted, anticipating upon the regulation moment, the common blindness to surprise the startled gesture of the cronies of darkness—exposed, in a seemingly fortuitous violation, so that anxiety is compounded, the very thing that seemed to have to remain hidden, such that *that* is knotted up from behind and effectively to the invisible; everyone examines and disturbs, in the lightning, the kitchen in which the deed is cooking, without the future cauldron with its ingredients worse than recommendations, admonitions, prophecies and a brusque vow to meet again.]

In Mallarmé's vision of the scene, we have a *theatrical* transgression—the curtain lifts too soon, the witches and their malign powers are prematurely exposed in a "fortuitous violation." Like an antemasque, the first encounter of the witches seems indecently to invite the spectator behind the scenes, into the kitchen, to the source of creative energy and dramatic power before it unfolds in its proper place. "The very thing that seemed to have to remain hidden" is revealed, examined, and disturbed. The spectator sees—indeed is compelled to see, by the timely-untimely lifting of the curtain—what should not be seen. *Une violation comme fortuite*—a fortuitous, but also a somehow fortunate violation.

Macbeth is full of such moments of transgressive sight and concomitant, disseminated violation. Repeatedly the play—through its chief protagonist—theorizes about the uncanny, while at the same time resolutely determining to ignore it, to cover it over or repress it.

> This supernatural soliciting
> Cannot be ill; cannot be good. If ill,
> Why hath it given me earnest of success,
> Commencing in a truth? I am Thane of Cawdor.
> If good, why do I yield to that suggestion
> Whose horrid image doth unfix my hair
> And make my seated heart knock at my ribs,
> Against the use of nature? Present fears
> Are less than horrible imaginings:
> My thought, whose murther yet is but fantastical,
> Shakes so my single state of man that function
> Is smother'd in surmise, and nothing is
> But what is not.
>   (1.3.130–42)

"Supernatural soliciting"; "function . . . smother'd in surmise"; "nothing is but what is not." Yet in the next moment Macbeth resolves that "If chance will have me king, why, chance may crown me/Without my stir" (143–44). Notice that it is a horrid "image" that transfixes him (by "unfixing" his hair and setting his heart to "knocking"—a physiological anticipation of the unnatural knocking in the Porter scene). The boundary between a thing and its reflection is constantly being transgressed, here and elsewhere in the play. Good/ill; natural/supernatural; single/double; function/surmise; is/is not. "Nothing," a present absence, emerges from this internal debate as the one palpable substantive. But as much as Macbeth tries to contain these speculations, to know and dissemble the uncanny, it will out. Murder will out.

Consider another key passage about boundary transgression, knowledge and identity. Prior to the murder of Duncan, Macbeth is still vacillating, debating the trajectory of murder and the priority of particular taboos: against slaying a kinsman; against slaying a king; against slaying a guest; tacitly against parricide, the double murder of king and father.

> If it were done, when 'tis done, then 'twere well
> It were done quickly. If th'assassination
> Could trammel up the consequence, and catch
> With his surcease, success; that but this blow
> Might be the be-all and the end-all—here,
> But here, upon this bank and shoal of time,
> We'ld jump the life to come. But in these cases
> We still have judgment here, that we but teach
> Bloody instructions, which, being taught, return
> To plague th'inventor. This even-handed justice
> Commends th'ingredience of our poison'd chalice
> To our own lips. He's here in double trust:
> First, as I am his kinsman and his subject,
> Strong both against the deed; then, as his host,
> Who should against his murtherer shut the door,
> Not bear the knife myself.
>
> (1.7.1–16)

"Shut the door"; but it is precisely this door, this portal, threshold, or boundary, which cannot be shut. The keen knife that, in Lady Macbeth's pregnant phrase, must "see not the wound it makes" (1.5.52) will pierce the blanket of the dark— and the limits of the stage. The stage history of the play is in effect the acting out of the play's own preoccupation with boundary transgression. It is not extrinsic or anecdotal; it is the matter of the play itself.

A particularly striking instance of this transgressive violation occurs, as we have noticed, in the sleepwalking scene, which encodes an onstage audience: Lady Macbeth's Waiting-Gentlewoman, horrified by the events of previous nights, has called a Doctor of Physic to observe her lady's actions. "What, at any time, have you heard her say?" asks the Doctor (5.1.12–13). "That, sir," replies the Waiting-Gentlewoman, "which I will not report after her" (14). "Neither to you," she answers, "nor any one, having no witness to confirm my speech" (17–18). What she has heard is unspeakable, unrepeatable. At this point the sleeping Lady Macbeth appears, tries to wash invisible blood from her hands, and in half a dozen other words and actions reveals that she and her husband are guilty of the murders. Not only Duncan, but Banquo and the family of Macduff have all been their victims. And the response of the Doctor and Waiting-Gentlewoman is once again expressed in terms of taboo. "You have known what you should not," he reproaches her (46–47), and she replies roundly, "She has spoke what she should not, I am sure of that; heaven knows what she has known" (48–49). Notice "should not" here—not "cannot." The unspeakable knowledge is transgressive, interdicted. The audience in the theater, which has experienced these horrors once, now relives them through new eyes and ears. As the scene closes the Doctor confirms the sense of impotent dismay that is felt by both audiences, onstage and off, declaring, "My mind she has mated, and amaz'd my sight./I think, but dare not speak" (78–79).

"My mind she has mated"—that is, checkmated, stunned, stupefied—"and amaz'd my sight." Consider how very frequently in the play this kind of perturbation in nature takes place. As we have seen, Macbeth is paralyzed when he contemplates the murder of Duncan. Having committed the murder, he cannot bear to look upon his victim: "I am afraid to think what I have done;/Look on't again I dare not" (2.2.48–49). The vision of the dagger he sees before him (2.1), the blood-boltered ghost of Banquo (which, like the dagger, is invisible to everyone on the stage save Macbeth himself), and the apparitions produced by the witches are all literally amazing sights, sights that are taboo, forbidden, dangerous. "Seek to know no more" (4.1.103) counsel the witches. But Macbeth is deaf to their instruction. "I will be satisfied. Deny me this,/And an eternal curse fall on you!" (104–5). With extraordinary hubris he threatens to lay a curse upon the very creatures who themselves possess the power of malediction. And when they ironically comply with his demands he misinterprets what he sees and hears, and brings upon himself defeat and death. The whole play is in one sense at least a parade of forbidden images gazed upon at peril, and it inscribes an awareness of this, a preoccupation with it. Through "the sightless couriers of the air" it "blow(s) the horrid deed in every eye" (1.7.23–24). "My mind she has mated, and amaz'd my sight." There is one dramatic moment, early in the play, in which the act of gazing on the taboo is explicitly described, and it is a moment which I think has a crucial significance for the pattern and meaning of Shakespeare's play. I refer to the moment—and the manner—in which Macduff announces the death of Duncan.

The time is early morning. Macduff and Lennox, two loyal liegemen, have arrived to see the King at his request. They knock on the Porter's door, waking him and prompting the famous and disquieting comparison of Macbeth's castle to hell itself. "If a man were porter of Hell Gate, he should have old turning the key" (2.3.1–3). For Macduff and Lennox the crossing of this threshold is a transgressive act, a fatal journey from the familiar to the forbidden, a rite of dreadful passage from which they will return greatly changed.[6]

---

[6]Huston Diehl, in "Horrid Image, Sorry Sight, Fatal Vision: The Visual Rhetoric of *Macbeth*," *Shakespeare Studies* 16 (1983): 191–203, comments on the problematics of reading the play, contrasting Macduff's ethical reading of the dead body of Duncan with Macbeth's rejection of the spiritual and ethical, and noting the audience's participation in the act of seeing and interpreting.

Admitted, they are welcomed by their host, Macbeth, who shows them the way to the king's chamber. And it is from that chamber that Macduff emerges, a moment later, with words of horror on his tongue. "O horror, horror, horror! Tongue nor heart/Cannot conceive nor name thee!" (63–64). Again the event is said to be unspeakable—it cannot be told. But equally important, it cannot be looked upon.

> Approach the chamber, and *destroy your sight*
> *With* a *new Gorgon.* Do not bid me speak;
> See, and then speak yourselves.
>   Awake, awake!
> Ring the alarum-bell! Murther and treason!
> Banquo and Donalbain! Malcolm, awake!
> Shake off this downy sleep, death's counterfeit,
> And look on death itself! Up, up, and see
> The great doom's image! Malcolm! Banquo!
> As from your graves rise up, and walk like sprites,
> To countenance this horror! Ring the bell.
>   (2.3.71–80) (my italics)

The Gorgon of classical mythology turned those who looked upon her to stone. To Macduff the sight of the dead king is "a new Gorgon" that will do the same to Duncan's subjects—a monstrous vision that will amaze their sight. What is this reference to "a new Gorgon" doing in the play?

"our rarer monsters"

The most famous of the Gorgons was Medusa, one of three sisters in Greek mythology, whose hair was said to be entwined with serpents, whose hands were brass, their bodies covered with scales, their teeth like boars' tusks.[7] When gazed upon, they turned the onlooker to stone. The first two Gorgons, Stheno ("The Mighty One") and Euryale ("Wide-leaping") were immortal, and seem to have nothing really to do with the myth beyond multiplying the fearsome power of the terrible and petrifying female image from one to the favorite number for monstrous females, three . . . as with the Graiai, or Spirits of Eld; the Moirai, or Fates; and the Charities, or Graces. The two supernumerary Gorgons disappear almost immediately from most accounts, leaving the focus on the third, the mortal Gorgon, Medusa, whose name—significantly enough for *Macbeth*—means "the Queen."

I arrive to talk about Medusa at a moment when considerable attention has been paid to this myth—particularly by Freud and by theorists influenced by him. I will therefore first run briefly through the myth in such a way as to highlight those aspects of it that are important for my purposes, then touch upon the readings of Freud and others, and how they pose, or counterpose, some difficul-

---

[7]H. J. Rose, *A Handbook of Greek Mythology* (New York: E. P. Dutton, 1959), pp. 29–30.

ties and unresolved questions in contextualizing the Medusa story within *Macbeth*. Once again I hope to show that the unresolved questions are precisely at issue in the play. Specifically, the initial difficulty of applying Freud's reading of the Medusa head as a fearful sighting of the female genitals indicates a site of resistance and underscores the way in which gender undecidability and anxiety about gender identification and gender roles are at the center of *Macbeth*—and of Macbeth.[8]

In classical mythology the story of Medusa is one of the exploits of the hero Perseus, the son of Zeus and of a mortal woman, Danae. For reasons that need not concern us here mother and son were exiled from their native country and came to the land of a certain king, Polydectes. Polydectes lusted after Danae, and sent her inconvenient son Perseus off to fetch the head of Medusa, hoping—and expecting—that he would never return from this dangerous exploit. But Perseus was favored by the gods, especially Athena, the virgin goddess of wisdom and war, who advised him how to proceed. To gain access to the Gorgons (still described as three, although only Medusa's head was his object) he first visited another triad of figures, the Graiai, who are thought to be either the sisters or the sentries of those Gorgons. The Graiai, gray-haired from birth, are considered by modern commentators to represent the personified spirits of old age. They had only one eye and one tooth among them, and by trickery Perseus stole both, agreeing to return them only when he received in exchange a magic cap, which made him invisible; magic shoes, which made him swift; and a magic wallet, in which he might carry the severed head. When the time came he approached Medusa with his back turned, looking at her image as it was reflected in his shield rather than directly, and was thus able to decapitate her without being turned to stone. Once he achieved this feat he made use of the head as a weapon, turning to stone those who dared to oppose him. Ultimately he gave the head to his patroness, Athena, who wore it thereafter on her aegis.

Thus the head of Medusa, so horrible in life, becomes in death an apotropaic talisman, a means of warding off evil. Throughout Greek and Roman art the Medusa head—with grinning mouth, staring eyes, and protruding tongue—appears as a protective ornament, whether worn on armor, carved on statues of Athena, or incised on tombstones. In fact the head as a talisman seems to have preceded the myth, and perhaps to have generated it. Jane Ellen Harrison writes persuasively that

> in her essence Medusa is a head and nothing more; her potency only begins when her head is severed; she is in a word a mask with a body later appended. The primitive Greek

---

[8]What is the relationship between anxiety of gender and the anxiety generated by an application of Freud's theory? Is the Medusa head like a King Charles head for modern critical theory, a whimsical obsession, always turning up where least wanted and expected? Or is it, in fact, a radical of this play's dramatic subtext, everywhere present because everywhere absent, something we fall in love with because we fear to look on it? Medusa, after all, was a figure of surpassing beauty—it is for this reason, according to some versions of the story, that Athena had her killed, and annexed (while disabling) her beauty by depicting the head on her shield.

knew that there was in his ritual a horrid thing called a Gorgoneion, a grinning mask with glaring eyes and protruding beast-like tusks and pendant tongue. How did this Gorgoneion come to be? A hero had slain a beast called the Gorgon, and this was its head. Though many other associations gathered round it, the basis of the Gorgoneion is a cultus object, a ritual mask misunderstood. The object comes first; then the monster is begotten to account for it; then the hero is supplied to account for the slaying of the monster.[9]

Thus Homer speaks of the Gorgon as a disembodied head, whether he is describing an ornament or an actual monster. Agamemnon carries a shield embossed with the staring face of the Gorgon (*Iliad* 11.36), Hector glares with the Gorgon's stark eyes (*Iliad* 8.349), and Odysseus fears lest Persephone send a Gorgon-head from deeper hell to afright him, and flees to his ship (*Odyssey* 11.634).

If the Gorgon's heads in effect precede and preempt the bodies that support them, in what sense can we say of Macbeth that *his* real potency only begins when his head is severed, and he becomes an apotropaic object? Before we come to consider the terrifying heads of Shakespeare's *Macbeth*, it may be useful to consider what some of his contemporaries thought of the Medusa myth, and the degree to which there was a consciousness of that myth in Western Europe, and especially in England.

Renaissance mythographers, when they contemplated the story of Medusa, saw plainly allegorical meanings. The influential Italian mythographer Caesare Ripa, in his *Iconologia,* interpreted the head of the Medusa as "a symbol of the victory of reason over the senses, the natural foes of 'virtu,' which like physical enemies are petrified when faced with the Medusa."[10] The real battle was within the warring elements of the self. Thus Mantegna represents *Philosophia* in the form of Minerva with a shield bearing a Medusa mask, to represent wisdom's control of the senses.[11] The degree to which this interpretation accords with the spirit of *Macbeth* is made manifest in the two speeches we have already considered: Macbeth's first long aside, which begins, "This supernatural soliciting/Cannot be ill; cannot be good" (1.3.130–31), and the remarkable soliloquy that begins Act 1, scene 7 ("If it were done, when 'tis done, then 'twere well/It were done quickly" [1–2]). Like Lady Macbeth's open eyes and closed sense in the sleepwalking scene, this speech refuses to look where it is going, to see where it is headed—and so in effect it beheads itself, and "falls on th'other" (28), yielding to the very transgressive energy it struggles so hard to contain.

Francis Bacon, in a treatise called *De sapientia veterum,* or *The Wisedome of the Ancients,* titled his interpretation of the Medusa story "Perseus, or Warre." The Medusa was an emblem of tyranny, against which the just warrior should fight.

[9]Jane Ellen Harrison, *Prolegomena to the Study of Greek Religion* (Cambridge: Cambridge University Press, 1922; rpt New York: Meridian Books, 1955), p. 187.
[10]Caesare Ripa, *Iconologia* (Florence, 1613), p. 182.
[11]Walter Friedländer, *Carvaggio Studies* (Princeton, N.J.: Princeton University Press, 1955), p. 88.

There must bee a care that the motives of Warre bee just and honorable; for that begets an alacrity . . . in the soldiers that fight. . . . But there is no pretence to take up arms more pious than the suppression of Tyranny, under which yoake the people loose their courage, and are cast downe without heart and vigour, as in the sight of Medusa.[12]

Bacon also has interesting things to say about the Graiai, whom he identifies as "treasons which may be termed the Sisters of Warre." They are "descended of the same stocke, but far unlike in nobilities of birth; for Warres are generall and hero-icall, but Treasons are base and ignoble."[13] "Perseus [Bacon continues] therefore was to deale with these Greae for the love of their eye and tooth. Their eye to dis-cover, their tooth to sowe rumors and stirre up envy, and to molest and trouble the minds of men."[14] Once again, we have forbidden sight and forbidden language. The Graiai in this reading bear a suggestive resemblance to the weird sisters, sim-ilarly consulted, and similarly—though again reluctantly—helpful to the hero in his quest. The Old English word *wyrd* means Fate, and it has been conjectured by Holinshed and others that the weird sisters may represent the "goddesses of des-tiny"; Holinshed also reports that they resembled "creatures of elder world."[15] In any case the threeness of the witches (and indeed the murderers) calls to mind the ritual trios of Graiai and Gorgons, all relentless and unrepentant in their dealings with mortal men.

Another English mythographer, Alexander Ross, sees Medusa as an emblem of the dangerous power of women: "the sight of these Gorgones turned men into stones; and so many men are bereft of their sense and reason, by doting too much on women's beauty."[16] Ross also comments on the fact that not only Perseus but his entire family were made into constellations, remarking that by this fact it was possible to see "how one worthy person doth enoble a whole family."[17]

For James I the allegorization of the Medusa story would have had potentially disquieting political—and personal—implications. In his political writings James continually recurred to the image of the King as head of state: thus he writes in the *Basilikon Doron* of the King as a "publicke person" to whose "preseruation or fall, the safetie or wracke of the whole common-weale is necessarily coupled, as the body is to the head";[18] in a speech to the first English Parliament (19 March 1603) he declared, "I am the Husband, and the whole Isle is my lawfull Wife; I am the Head, and it is my Body,"[19] and in *The Trew Law of Free Monarchies* (1598) he likewise articulates, and embellishes, this figure:

---

[12]Francis Bacon, *The Wisedome of the Ancients,* trans. Arthur Gorges (London, 1619), p. 41.

[13]ibid., p. 43.

[14]ibid., p. 44.

[15]Richard Hosley, ed., *Shakespeare's Holinshed* (New York: G. P. Putnam, 1968), p. 17. An excerpt from Holinshed's *Chronicles of Scotland* appears in Kenneth Muir, ed., *Macbeth,* The Arden Shakespeare (London: Methuen, 1962), pp. 170–88.

[16]Alexander Ross, *Mystogogus Poeticus* (London, 1647), p. 103.

[17]ibid., p. 213.

[18]*The Political Works of James I, reprinted from the Edition of 1616,* ed. Charles Howard McHwain (Cambridge, Mass.: Harvard University Press, 1918), p. 29.

[19]ibid., p. 272.

> And for the similitude of the head and the body, it may very well fall out that the head will be forced to garre cut off some rotten members (as I haue already said) to keep the rest of the body in integritie: but what state the body can be in, if the heade, for any infirmitie that can fall to it, be cut off, I leaue it to the readers iudgement.[20]

The decapitation of the state, the severing of the head from the body politic, was at the same time unimaginable, and offered to the reader (or audience) to imagine. Yet in James' own recent memory there had been such a beheading and such a severance, of a monarch "set high upon a skaffolde"—or, as later editions of the *Basilikon Doron* would emend the phrase, "on a stage, whose smallest actions and gestures, all the people gazingly doe behold":[21] the public beheading of his mother, Mary Queen of Scots, on February 8, 1587. The fate of Mary haunts the *Basilikon Doron,* so much so that in his introduction to later editions the King felt it necessary to excoriate the "malicious" critics who claimed that "in some parts [of the *Basilikon Doron*] I should seeme to nourish in my minde, a vindictive resolution against *England,* or at the least, some principals there, for the Queene my mothers quarrell";[22] in the treatise itself he urges Prince Henry to pay particular heed to the Fifth Commandment, to honor his father and his mother, alluding to the just retribution that had fallen upon "all them that were chiefe traitours to my parents . . . I mean specially by them that serued the Queene my mother."[23] (The editor of James' political writings comments without irony that the religious and civil disorders of the time "had been brought to a head by the execution of Mary Stuart in 1587."[24])

In the *Basilikon Doron,* addressed to his son as presumptive heir, James distinguishes—in passages that have often been linked to *Macbeth*—between the characteristics of the "good King" and those of the "vsurping Tyran."[25] For James, a usurping tyrant like Macbeth, who deserves to have his head struck off and exhibited to the people ("live to be the show and gaze o' th' time! . . . painted upon a pole, and underwrit,/'Here may you see the tyrant.'" 5.8.24–27), would indeed be a sort of male Medusa. The play covers over and represses or displaces the figure of the decapitated Mary, so offensive and so omnipresent to the King's imagination, "set high upon a skaffolde," and substitutes for it the appropriate and politically necessary decapitation of Macbeth: "Behold where stands/Th'usurper's cursed head" (5.9.20–21).

Not only mythographic and political but also archaeological evidence speaks to these questions. The architectural remains of Roman Britain include a remarkable number of Medusa heads.[26] Coffins, tombstone pediments, antefixes, floor mosaics, and pottery all bear Medusa masks, as do bronze jugs, jug-handles, and visor-masks, skillets intended for religious and sacrificial use, rings, coins, pen-

---

[20]ibid., p. 65.
[21]ibid., p. 43.
[22]ibid., p. 6.
[23]ibid., p. 21.
[24]ibid., p. xxviii.
[25]ibid., pp. 18ff.
[26]J.M.C. Toynbee, *Art in Britain Under the Romans* (Oxford: Clarendon Press, 1964), *passim.*

dants, and *phalerae* (small glass or metal disks, often awarded as gifts to soldiers of the Roman armies)—to say nothing of statues and relief carvings of the goddess Minerva (the Roman counterpart of Athena) with the head of Medusa displayed on her aegis. The function of these decorations, like those of their Greek predecessors, is in most cases clearly apotropaic; the figured jet pendants, for example, were obviously intended to ward off evil from their wearers, the *phalerae* to protect the soldiers in battle, and the tomb and coffin Medusas to safeguard the dead.

But among these numerous Medusas there were a few which differed crucially from the traditional representation, for they are manifestly *male*. Three certain examples of the male Medusa have been found in England, and others have been tentatively identified. Carved on a pediment for a tombstone at Chester is a bearded and moustached male head with severely patterned hair and eight writhing snakes framing its face. "It is, in fact," writes J.M.C. Toynbee, "a kind of male Medusa."[27] An antefix or roof ornament from Dorchester bears the mask of another bearded Medusa, and coins from the reign of Tincommius (ca. 20 B.C.–5 A.D.) carry full-faced Medusa masks which are "very probably bearded."[28] But the most celebrated of the British male Medusas is the second or third century sculpted pediment on the Temple of Sulis-Minerva at Bath. Toynbee, cataloguer of the 1961 London Exhibition of Art in Roman Britain, asserts

> That the glaring mask on the boss of the central, dominating shield of the Bath pediment is, to some extent, at any rate, intended, despite its masculinity, to depict the Medusa of Minerva is certain. Of this the wings and snakes in the hair are clinching evidence; the owl beside the shield was specifically Minerva's bird; the temple was dedicated to her as conflated with the Celtic Sulis; and to Minerva, as the child of Jupiter, oak-wreaths are appropriate. The Bath face, with its trap-like mouth, lined, scowling brows, and huge, deeply drilled, and penetrating eyes, is, indeed, very different from the normal, feminine Medusa of Hellenistic and Roman art. All the same, wild, glowering, frowning faces, sometimes set on round shields, were not unknown in Roman art in Mediterranean lands.[29]

Indeed, other representations of the male Medusa are to be found in the Mediterranean area, specifically at Rome, Petra, and Hatra in Mesopotamia (now Al Hdr, Iraq).[30]

Toynbee's description of the striking mouth, brows, and eyes on the pediment at Bath brings sharply to mind another decorative architectural motif that also involves a glaring male beard, often with gaping mouth and protruding tongue. I refer to the foliate head or leaf mask which gained enormous popularity in England and throughout Western Europe during the Romanesque and medieval periods. These remarkable images, with leaves sprouting from their faces, can be

---

[27]ibid., p. 136.
[28]ibid., p. 32.
[29]J.M.C. Toynbee, *Art in Roman Britain* (London: Phaidon Press, 1962), p. 163.
[30]Nelson Glueck, *Deities and Dolphins: The Story of the Nabataeans* (New York: Farrar, Straus & Giroux, 1965), pp. 80–84.

found virtually everywhere in English medieval churches, from fonts to tombs, corbels and capitals to arm rests. Known in Britain chiefly as the Green Man, this often sinister and frightening figure appears, among other places, in Exeter, Ely, Lincoln, and Winchester Cathedrals, and in the Church of the Holy Trinity in Coventry, Warwickshire—not a great distance from Shakespeare's home in Stratford-upon-Avon.[31] The Green Man, although he seems in some ways an odd choice for ecclesiastical ornamentation, in fact embodies a warning against the dark side of man's nature, the devil within: "For all flesh is as grass, and all the glory of man as the flower of grass. The grass withereth, and the flower thereof falleth away" (1 Peter 1:24).

Foliate head and Medusa head, one monster with hair and beard of leaves, the other with snaky locks; both are in effect conquered, tamed, and appropriated as symbols by religions to which they were originally antipathetic. Medusa was considered Athena's antitype, "a hostile Pallas who could sometimes be united with her . . . and sometimes regarded as an antagonist being detested by the goddess herself."[32] So closely are they associated that Euripides calls Athena "Gorgon" twice in his plays. The rational goddess can also be an irrational monster; wisdom can be transformed to war: "There's no art/To find the mind's construction in the face" (*Macbeth* 1.4.11–12). As for the Green Man, a type of the male Medusa, he is terrifying precisely because he is, and is not, man. And, as I hope to show, Macbeth too becomes a male Medusa. To see why, it may be helpful to return to Freud.

"Bloody instructions, which, being taught, return To plague th'inventor"

Freud's essay on "The Uncanny" is uncannily pertinent to *Macbeth,* although—as we have already seen—Freud repeatedly denies or represses that pertinence by disclaiming any direct relationship between the literary appearance of ghosts and apparitions and the *Unheimlich* or uncanny. The affect of uncanniness, we have noted, is for Freud a kind of "morbid anxiety" that derives from "something repressed which *recurs*"; this uncanny is in reality nothing new or foreign, but "something familiar and old-established in the mind that has been estranged only by the process of repression."[33] Thus he is moved to agree with Schelling that the uncanny is something which ought to have been kept concealed but has nonetheless come to light—something concealed because of the protective mechanism of repression.

---

[31] Kathleen Basford, *The Green Man* (Ipswich, Suffolk: D. S. Brewer, 1978), pp. 9–22.
[32] Karl Otfried Müller, *Introduction to a Scientific Study of Mythology,* trans. Leitch (London, 1844). Cited in Burton Feldman and Robert D. Richardson, Jr., *The Rise of Modern Mythology* (Bloomington: Indiana University Press, 1972), p. 420.
[33] Freud, "The Uncanny," p. 47.

Associated with such sensations as intellectual uncertainty whether an object is alive or not, the fear of the evil eye and of "the omnipotence of thoughts,"[34] instantaneous wish-fulfillment, secret power to do harm, and the return of the dead,[35] the uncanny is nothing less than the thematized subtext of Shakespeare's *Macbeth*. For example, the "moving grove," Birnam wood en route to Dunsinane, is precisely the kind of phenomenon about which it is difficult to judge—is it animate or inanimate, natural or unnatural? The audience knows, because it is told directly in Act 5, scene 4, that the soldiers have hewn down boughs, and carry them before them—not as an uncanny spectacle but as military camouflage, that they may better scout out the numbers of the enemy, and hide their own troop strength. The rational explanation is given to us directly, and apparently explains the stratagem. But does it? With the witches' prophecy inevitably in mind, we may count the ironic fulfillment as itself uncanny. Macbeth's appalled presentiment of doom identifies the moving grove as a reified, dramatized catachresis.

> I pull in resolution, and begin
> To doubt th'equivocation of the fiend
> That lies like truth. "Fear not, till Birnam wood
> Do come to Dunsinane," and now a wood
> Comes toward Dunsinane.
>   (5.5.41–45)

The uncanny, says Freud, is also linked to the well-documented phenomenon of the double—whether through telepathic communication between persons, so that one "identifies himself with another person, so that his self becomes confounded, or the foreign self is substituted for his own"—as in the case of Macbeth and Lady Macbeth—or through the "constant recurrence of similar situations, a same face, or character-trait, or twist of fortune, or a same crime, or even a same name recurring throughout several consecutive generations." Manifestations of the uncanny appear in the witches' riddling prophecies, the puzzling, spectacular apparitions, the walking of trees and sleepers, the persistent sense of doubling that pervades the whole play: two Thanes of Cawdor; two kings and two kingdoms, England and Scotland themselves doubled and divided; two heirs apparent to

---

[34]The "omnipotence of thoughts" ascribed to witches could be a self-elected characteristic, concomitant to certain modern mental disorders like schizophrenia—or a more ordinary outgrowth of loneliness and superstition. Thus Reginald Scot in his *Discovery of Witchcraft* (1584) describes them: "One sort of such as are said to be witches are women which be commonly old, lame, blear-eyed, pale, foul, and full of wrinkles; poor, sullen, superstitious, and papists; or such as know no religion: in whose drowsy minds the Devil hath gotten a fine seat; so as, what mischief, mischance, calamity, or slaughter is brought to pass, they are easily persuaded the same is done by themselves, imprinting in their minds an earnest and constant imagination thereof. . . .

The witch . . . expecting her neighbors' mischances, and seeing things sometimes come to pass according to her wishes, curses, and incantations . . . being called before a Justice, by due examination of the circumstances is driven to see her imprecations and desires and her neighbors' harms and losses to concur, and as it were to take effect: and so confesseth that she (as a goddess) hath brought such things to pass." Cited in G. B. Harrison, ed., *Shakespeare: The Complete Works* (New York: Harcourt, Brace & World, 1952), pp. 1644–45.

[35]Freud, "The Uncanny," p. 46.

Duncan; the recurrent prefix "Mac" itself which means "son of"; the sexually ambiguous witches replicated in the wilfully unsexed Lady Macbeth; Macbeth and Banquo on the battlefield "As canons overcharg'd with double cracks, so they/Doubly redoubled strokes upon the foe" (1.2.37–38); Duncan as the Macbeths' guest, "here in double trust" (1.7.12), their ostentatious hospitality as Lady Macbeth points out, "in every point twice done, and then done double" (1.6.15). Macbeth believes the witches' prophecies (and believes that he interprets them correctly), but he will "make assurance double sure" by killing Macduff, thus bringing down sure disaster upon himself. The witches or weird sisters, he will later assert, are "juggling fiends" "that palter with us in a double sense" (5.8.19; 20), and we hear them chant their litany of "double, double, toil and trouble" (4.1.10; 20; 35). The mode of involuntary repetition, which we saw embodied in Lady Macbeth's futile acting out of the events of the play, determines dramatic action from Macbeth's first reported action to his death at the close. In Act 1, scene 2, a "bloody man," the sergeant just returned from battle, reports Macbeth's valiant victory over a traitorous rebel, "the merciless Macdonwald." "Brave Macbeth," says the sergeant,

> (well he deserves that name),
> Disdaining Fortune, with his brandish'd steel,
> Which smok'd with bloody execution,
> (Like Valor's minion) carv'd out his passage
> Till he fac'd the slave;
> Which nev'r shook hands, nor bade farewell to him,
> Till he unseam'd him from the nave to th'chops,
> And fix'd his head upon our battlements.
> (16–23)

The play thus begins with the (offstage) head of a rebel fixed upon the battlements, as it will end with another rebellion, another battle, and "the usurper's cursed head" held aloft by Macduff. The sergeant's phrase, "bloody execution" encapsulates the doubleness, since execution here means both deed and death, and points ahead to the "If it were done" soliloquy (1.7.1). Thus, Macbeth performs in the first, offstage battle what might be aptly described as "bloody instructions, which, being taught, return/To plague th'inventor" (1.7.9–10), imagistically "carv[ing] out" the patterns of his own retributive death.

Significantly, Freud singles out as well a series of metonymic objects, dislocated body parts—several of which appear as prominent stage properties in Elizabethan and Jacobean drama: "Dismembered limbs, *a severed head,* a hand cut off at the wrist, feet which dance by themselves—all these have something peculiarly uncanny about them . . . As we already know, this kind of uncanniness springs from its association with the castration-complex."[36] For Freud, indeed, the castration-complex is intrinsic to uncanniness wherever it appears. The severed head so central to *Macbeth* (and its Medusa associations) is only one instance of this pervasive

---

[36]ibid., p. 397.

pattern of underlying meaning. Doubling, too, is linked to castration anxiety: "the 'double' was originally an insurance against destruction of the ego. . . . This invention of doubling as a preservation against extinction has its counterpart in the language of dreams, which is fond of representing castration by a doubling or multiplication of the genital symbol."[37] Again, he comments that "It often happens that male patients declare that there is something uncanny about the female genital organs."[38] Later, in his essay on "Medusa's Head" (1922), he will point out that the representation of Medusa's hair by snakes in works of visual art is another manifestation of the castration complex:

> however frightening they may be in themselves, they nevertheless serve actually as a mitigation of the horror, for they replace the penis, the absence of which is the cause of the horror. This is a confirmation of the technical rule according to which a multiplication of penis symbols signifies castration.[39]

The "Medusa's Head" essay has achieved a certain prominence in recent theoretical discussions, in part because of Neil Hertz's provocative article "Medusa's Head: Male Hysteria under Political Pressure" in the Fall 1983 issue of *Representations,* and the replies to it by Catherine Gallagher and Joel Fineman in the same issue of that journal.[40] The key passage here is Freud's explanation of "the horrifying decapitated head of Medusa":

> To decapitate = to castrate. The terror of Medusa is thus a terror of castration that is linked to the sight of something. Numerous analyses have made us familiar with the occasion for this: It occurs when a boy, who has hitherto been unwilling to believe the threat of castration, catches sight of the female genitals, probably those of an adult, surrounded by hair, and essentially those of his mother.
>
> The hair upon Medusa's head is frequently represented in works of art in the form of snakes, and these once again are derived from the castration complex. It is a remarkable fact that, however frightening they may be in themselves, they nevertheless serve as a mitigation of the horror, for they replace the penis, the absence of which is the cause of the horror. This is a confirmation of the technical rule according to which a multiplication of penis symbols signifies castration.
>
> The sight of Medusa's head makes the spectator stiff with terror, turns him into stone. Observe that we have here once again the same origin from the castration complex and the same transformation of affect! For becoming stiff means an erection. Thus in the original situation it offers consolation to the spectator: he is still in possession of a penis, and the stiffening reassures him of the fact.
>
> If Medusa's head takes the place of a representation of the female genitals, or rather if it isolates their horrifying effects from the pleasure-giving ones, it may be recalled that displaying the genitals is familiar in other connections as an apotropaic act. What arouses horror in oneself will produce the same effect upon the enemy against whom one is

[37]ibid., p. 40.

[38]ibid., p. 51.

[39]Sigmund Freud, "Medusa's Head," in *Sexuality and the Psychology of Love,* ed. Philip Rieff (New York: Macmillan, 1963), p. 212.

[40]See Neil Hertz, *The End of the Line* (New York: Columbia University Press, 1985), pp. 161–215.

seeking to defend oneself. We read in Rabelais of how the Devil took to flight when the woman showed him her vulva.

The erect male organ also has an apotropaic effect, but thanks to another mechanism. To display the penis (or any of its surrogates) is to say: "I am not afraid of you. I defy you. I have a penis." Here, then, is another way of intimidating the Evil Spirit.[41]

The desire to rewrite the female first as castration then as erection has seldom been so clearly expressed. In *Macbeth*, too, gender assignments are constantly in doubt, in flux, and in the way.

We may note that the brief 1922 piece on "Medusa's Head," the 1927 essay on "Fetishism," and the longer essay on "The Uncanny" (1919) all return or double back upon this fear of castration and its relationship to the sight of the female genitals, the mythologized version of which is Medusa's severed head. In this context it is particularly interesting to take note of Freud's own implicit strategy of repression or denial in "The Uncanny" as manifested in his gentle but firm correction of E. Jentsch's interpretation of Hoffmann's tale with which "The Uncanny" begins. Jentsch had maintained, in what is described as "a fertile but not exhaustive paper,"[42] that uncanny effects in literature are produced by uncertainty as to whether a particular figure in the story is a human being or an automaton. This, says Freud, is not in fact what produces uncanniness in "The Sand-Man." It is not, or not only, "the theme of the doll, Olympia, who is to all appearance a living being" that gives Hoffmann's tale its "quite unparalleled atmosphere of uncanniness," but rather "the theme of the Sand-Man who tears out children's eyes,"[43] and the Sand-Man's association with fears of castration and the castrating father. Yet when he turns to the subject of other imaginative literature, Freud makes a similar move in the direction of a misleading detail. Twice in his essay he specifically mentions Shakespeare's plays, and prominent among them, *Macbeth;* on both occasions, as we have seen, he denies that the presence of "spirits, demons and ghosts"[44] or "ghostly apparitions" in themselves impart to the play an aspect of the play's uncanniness. I quote again:

> The souls in Dante's *Inferno* or the ghostly apparitions in *Macbeth* or *Julius Caesar*, may be gloomy and terrible enough, but they are no more really uncanny than is Homer's jovial world of gods. We order our judgement to the imaginary reality imposed on us by the writer, and regard souls, spirits and spectres as though their existence had the same validity in their world as our own has in the external world. And then in this case too we are spared all trace of the uncanny.[45]

What Freud in effect denies here, in the case of Shakespeare, is the real uncanniness at the center of the play, which is provoked not by the ghosts and apparitions in *Macbeth* but rather by the "morbid anxiety" produced by "something

[41]Freud, "Medusa's Head," pp. 212–13.
[42]ibid., p. 20.
[43]ibid., pp. 31–32.
[44]ibid., p. 35.
[45]ibid., p. 57.

repressed which *recurs*"[46]—an idea, fear, or fantasy that is continually undergoing a process of repression or denial. "This uncanny is in reality nothing new or foreign, but something familiar and old-established in the mind that has been estranged only by the process of repression."[47] Summing up his findings, Freud catalogues them, and in doing so names practically every major theme in *Macbeth*: "animism, magic and witchcraft, the omnipotence of thought, man's attitude to death, involuntary repetition, and the castration-complex comprise practically all the factors which turn something fearful into an uncanny thing."[48] By the terms of this anatomy, *Macbeth* is *the* play of the uncanny—the uncanniest in the canon.[49]

For Macbeth the dramatic character, uncanniness, the "something repressed which recurs," is figured not only in the witches and Banquo's ghost, but also, perhaps most strikingly, in the fear of castration, which he repeatedly expresses in the form of gender anxiety:

Macbeth:	I dare do all that may become a man;
	Who dares do more is none.
Lady Macbeth:	What beast was't then
	That made you break this enterprise to me?
	When you durst do it, then you were a man;
	And to be more than what you were, you would
	Be so much more the man.

(1.7.46–51)

Lady Macbeth's sexual taunts here and elsewhere in the play have about them the painful familiarity of an old story, an efficacious and destructive strategy of attack upon his masculinity, his male identity.[50] "You would/Be so much more the man." But what is *more* than man? Is it, in this play of border transgressions, equivalent to being woman? or some androgynous combination of the genders, like the bearded witches or the "unsexed" Lady Macbeth herself?

This same conversation repeats itself in a yet more agonized form when Macbeth is confronted by the Medusa head of Banquo at the banquet in Act 3, scene 4.

Macbeth:	Thou canst not say I did it; never shake
	Thy gory locks at me . . .

(49–50)

---

[46]ibid., p. 47.

[47]ibid.

[48]ibid., p. 49.

[49]For a useful and persuasive discussion of the consanguinities of Shakespearean and Freudian models of psychic representation in *Macbeth*, see David Willbern, "Phantasmagoric *Macbeth*," *English Literary Renaissance* 16 (1986): 520–49. Willbern deals succinctly with the problem of Shakespeare's uncanny prefiguration of Freud: "In brief," he writes, "Shakespeare dramatizes what psychoanalysis theorizes" (p. 544), and again, "Shakespeare prefigures Freud: drama enacts what theory affirms" (p. 545).

[50]For another discussion of *Macbeth*, gender anxiety, and androgyny, see Robert Kimbrough, "Macbeth: The Prisoner of Gender," *Shakespeare Studies* 16 (1983): 175–90.

Lady Macbeth:	*—Are you a man?*
Macbeth:	Ay, and a bold one, *that dare look on that*
	Which might appall the devil.
Lady Macbeth:	O proper stuff!

This is the very painting of your fear;
This is the air-drawn dagger which you said
Led you to Duncan. O, these flaws and starts
(Impostors to true fear) would well become
A woman's story at a winter's fire,
Authoriz'd by her grandam. Shame itself,
Why do you make such faces? When all's done,
You *look* but on a stool.

                                                        (57–67) (my italics)

Macbeth (to Ghost):	Avaunt, *and quit my sight!* let the earth hide thee!

Thy bones are marrowless, thy blood is cold;
Thou hast no speculation in those eyes
Which thou dost glare with!

Lady Macbeth [to assembled lords]:	Think of this, good peers,

But as a thing of custom. 'Tis no other;
Only it spoils the pleasure of the time.

Macbeth:	*What man dare, I dare.*

Approach thou like the rugged Russian bear,
Th'armed rhinoceros, or th'Hyrcan tiger,
Take any shape but that, and my firm nerves
Shall never tremble. Or be alive again,
And dare me to the desert with thy sword;
If trembling I inhabit them, protest me
The baby of a girl. Hence, horrible shadow!
Unreal mock'ry, hence!   (Exit Ghost)
          Why, so; *being gone,*
I am a man again.

                                                        (92–106) (my italics)

Macbeth [to Lady Macbeth]:	You make me strange

Even to the disposition that I owe,
When now I think you can behold such sights,
And keep the natural ruby of your cheeks,
When mine is blanch'd with fear.

                                                        (111–15) (my italics)

"Daring" here becomes the play's trope of transgression, and also Macbeth's desperate and self-defeating rhetorical equivalent of masculinity in action. Lady Macbeth taunts him with "Letting 'I dare not' wait upon 'I would,'/Like the poor cat i' th'adage" (1.7.44–45), giving the word an aphoristic context; the "poor cat" contrasts ironically with the "beast" that broke the murder plan to her, and also to the Hyrcan tiger, the Russian bear, and the armed rhinoceros, just as "the baby of a girl" contrasts with the bold "man" he claims to be. Lady Macbeth's scathing reference to female storytelling, womanish narrative, and female authority and lineage neatly encapsulates all his fears, providing a devastating alternative to the bold male historical chronicle in which he would like to act, as well as to the paternal authority symbolized by Duncan, by the desire for heirs to the throne, and by the tacit and powerful figure of the father-king James I. Likewise the references to proliferation of dangerous gazings and forbidden sights in this scene ("never shake/Thy gory locks at me"; "a bold one, that dare look on that/Which might appall the devil"; "Avaunt, and quit my sight"; "Thou hast no speculation in those eyes/Which thou dost glare with"; "Take any shape but that, and my firm nerves/Shall never tremble"; "Hence, horrible shadow!/Unreal mock'ry, hence!"; "you can behold such sights,/And keep the natural ruby of your cheeks/When mine is blanch'd with fear") call attention to the underlying theme of the Medusa complex. Notice that Lady Macbeth can, in his view, look with impunity on that which reduces him to unmanned fright. Why? Because she is "unsexed"? Because she is a woman? Because she has no "manhood" to protect?

"Unsex me here"

With its gaping mouth, its snaky locks, and its association with femininity, castration, and erection, Medusa's head ends up being the displacement upward neither of the female nor of the male genitals but of gender undecidability as such. *That* is what is truly uncanny about it, and it is that uncanniness that is registered in the gender uncertainties in *Macbeth*. Yet Freud (along with virtually all other commentators on Medusa as well as on *Macbeth*, including recent feminist critics) enacts the *repression* of gender undecidability. Freud's text is positively acrobatic in its desire to reassign decidable difference, to read the Medusa figure in terms of castration anxiety and penis display, and to locate fetishism as an identifiable variant of this same anxious and repressive process. Shakespeare's play, however, resists such assignment, resists even the present-day tendency to see the play in terms of male homosocial bonding or anxiety about female power.[51] Power in *Macbeth* is a function of neither the male nor the female but of the suspicion of the undecidable. The phallus as floating signifier is more powerful than when definitely assigned to either gender.

---

[51]For a strong and appealing presentation of this case, see Janet Adelman, " 'Born of Woman': Fantasies of Maternal Power in *Macbeth*," in *Cannibals, Witches, and Divorce: Estranging the Renaissance*, ed. Marjorie Garber (Baltimore: Johns Hopkins University Press, 1986), pp. 90–121. [This essay appears in revised form in the essay by Adelman reprinted in this volume.] Though I admire Adelman's essay, I differ with her conclusion, which maintains that "Macbeth is a recuperative consolidation of male power" (p. 111). Another thoughtful recent reading of the play is offered by Jonathan Goldberg in "Speculations: *Macbeth* and Source," *Post-Structuralist Readings of English Poetry*, ed. Richard Machin and Christopher Norris (Cambridge: Cambridge University Press, 1987). "The hypermasculine world of *Macbeth* is haunted," writes Goldberg, "by the power represented by the witches; masculinity in the play is directed as an assaultive attempt to secure power, to maintain success and succession, at the expense of women" (p. 52). Yet Goldberg too reads the witches, and Mary Queen of Scots, "the figure that haunts the patriarchal claims of the *Basilikon Doron*" (p. 53), as woman, as female, rather than as the emblems of a disquieting gender undecidability (bearded women; woman as head of state).

The presence of gender anxiety and its contiguity to border crossings and boundary transgressions has been evident from the opening moments of the play, when the three witches, the weird sisters, gloatingly plot their revenge upon the sailor's wife through their designs upon her husband, the "master o' the Tiger." The witches, who physically exhibit signs of their gender undecidability, as Banquo notes ("You should be women,/ And yet your beards forbid me to interpret/That you are so" [1.3.45–47]), are in a sense pluralized, replicative dream-figures for Lady Macbeth. Both they and she whisper plots and hint at the glorious future for Macbeth, goading him on to "dare." We may remember also that Medusa, whose name means "the Queen," was originally one of three. Wherever Macbeth goes, to the castle or to the heath, he encounters the same powerful female presence that lures him to destruction.

As for the witches, their language early in the play is what we might now recognize as Medusa language, the language of gender undecidability and castration fear. "Like a rat without a tail" the First Witch will "do"; in glossing this zoological peculiarity the eighteenth-century editor George Steevens noted a belief of Shakespeare's time "that though a witch could assume the form of any animal she pleased, the tail would still be wanting, and that the reason given by some old writers for such a deficiency was, that though the hands and feet by an easy change might be converted into the four paws of a beast, there was still no part about a woman which corresponded with the length of tail common to almost all our four-footed creatures."[52] Again the woman comes up short—a Renaissance witch, it seems, could not even aspire to mimetic rathood, but instead had to content herself with a curtailed or foreshortened version of that condition. The gleeful assertion, "I'll drain him dry as hay" (1.3.18) may refer to unshakable thirst, a common affliction of sailors, but it is also plausibly a description of a man exhausted ("drained dry") by excessive sexual demands made upon him. "Sleep shall neither night nor day/Hang upon his penthouse lid . . . Weary sev'nnights, nine times nine,/Shall he dwindle, peak, and pine" (1.3.19–23).[53] The transgressive and usurping androgynous power of the witches seems to justify, indeed to invite, a reading of these lines as sexually invasive and demeaning; the drained husband will not, unlike the weird sisters, be capable of "doing." "Look what I have," the First Witch cries delightedly.

2 Witch: Show me, show me.
1 Witch: Here I have a pilot's thumb,
        Wrack'd as homeward he did come. *Drum within*

---

[52]Muir, ed., p. 12.
[53]In his notes on Shakespeare's sonnet 116, coincidentally another poetic narrative of marriage, a tempest, and a "wandering bark," Stephen Booth remarks that "many of the metaphors and ideas of this sonnet seem just on the point of veering off toward puerile joking about temporary abatement of female sexual desire." Booth situates the "puerile joking" and "preposterous teasing" (392) in the confident tone of the lover-poet; in *Macbeth* the tone is of course malevolent rather than erotic; dismissive, vengeful and vituperative rather than indulgent and affectionate—but the trope is a similar one. See also Booth's note on the word *bark* in Sonnet 80, line 7. *Shakespeare's Sonnets* (New Haven: Yale University Press, 1977), pp. 391–92.

3 Witch: A drum, a drum!
               Macbeth doth come.
               (26–31)

This dismembered "pilot's thumb" culminates the implicit narrative of sexual disabling and castration. The repetition of the word "come" to describe the progress of both Macbeth and the hapless "pilot" reinforces the metonymic association of the two figures, especially since Macbeth is also on his way home to be "wrack'd." (He uses the word in a similar context of storm and disaster just before his own decapitation at the play's close: "Blow wind, come wrack,/At least we'll die with harness on our back." [5.5.50–51].) Nor can we entirely ignore the possibility that "look what I have" can function as a gleeful, childlike announcement of sexual display. Just as the Medusa head incorporates the elements of sexual gazing (scopophilia) and its concomitant punishment, castration, so the First Witch's exhibition of a prize, coming as it does in the narrative just after the account of the "drained" sailor, invites a similar transgressive sight. The morphological similarity between thumb and phallus needs no elaboration, and the possession by the witches of a thumb/phallus as a fetishistic object would emphasize their ambiguous, androgynous character, shortly to be remarked by Banquo. The witches' chortling exchange, aptly described by Coleridge as exhibiting "a certain fierce familiarity, grotesqueness mingled with terror,"[54] introduces the entrance of Macbeth and Banquo, and marks Banquo's questions of them as appropriate descriptions of the uncanny:

> What are these
> So wither'd and so wild in their attire,
> That look not like th'inhabitants o' th' earth,
> And yet are on't? Live you? or are you aught
> That man may question? . . .
> You should be women,
> And yet your beards forbid me to interpret
> That you are so.
>   (1.3.39–47)

The "Medusa complex," if we may continue to call it that, persists throughout the play, from Macduff's horrified cry to the final scene. Macbeth's first act is to display a severed head. Even before the murder there is a muted anticipation of the myth, in an image that seems localized but will recur: Macbeth's curious insistence on the phenomenon of his hair standing on end as if it were alive. Learning that he is Thane of Cawdor, and therefore that the witches' other prophecies may come true, he contemplates the murder of Duncan and is terrified at the thought. "Why," he wonders aloud,

---

[54]Quoted in Frank Kermode, ed., *Four Centuries of Shakespearean Criticism* (New York: Avon Books, 1965), p. 537. From a report of a lecture given in Bristol in 1813.

> do I yield to that suggestion
> Whose horrid image doth unfix my hair
> And make my seated heart knock at my ribs,
> Against the use of nature?
>
> (1.3.134–37)

The word "horrid" comes from a Latin word meaning "to bristle with fear," and is used to mean "bristling, shaggy," throughout the Renaissance. Metaphorically, at least, Macbeth's hair stands on end, "unfixed" by the "horrible imaginings" that flood his mind. Significantly, his imagined physiological response occurs in a key passage about undecidability and the sensation of the uncanny. The "supernatural solicitings" are the text of transgressive doubt, when "nothing is but what is not."

Much later in the play he makes use of the same image, this time to emphasize not his emotional distraction but the numbness that has succeeded it. Hearing the distressful cry of women, he speculates on its source, but does not otherwise respond.

> I have almost forgot the taste of fears.
> The time has been, my senses would have cool'd
> To hear a night-shriek, and my fell of hair
> Would at a dismal treatise rouse and stir
> As life were in't. I have supp'd full with horrors.
>
> (5.5.9–13)

Notice "as life were in't." Hair that stands on end is occasionally mentioned elsewhere in Shakespeare, notably when Brutus beholds the ghost of Caesar and addresses it as a "monstrous apparition." "Art thou any thing?" he asks. "Art thou some god, some angel, or some devil,/That mak'st my blood cold, and my hair to stare?" (*Julius Caesar* 4.3.278–80). Never, however, does this figure appear with the imaginative intensity that it does in *Macbeth*. Occurring once near the beginning of the play and once near the end, the picture of the man with horrid, bristling hair frames the dramatic action in an oddly haunting way.

Like Brutus, Macbeth is also visited by the ghost of a man he has murdered, and that encounter provides the opportunity for another, more substantial evocation of the Medusa story. On this occasion Macbeth is the horrified onlooker, and the ghost of Banquo the instrument of his petrification.

The scene is the banqueting-hall, where the Scottish lords are gathering to feast with their new king. Macbeth has just learned of the successful murder of Banquo—"his throat is cut" (3.4.15). It is therefore with some complacency that he addresses the assembled lords, expressing the disingenuous hope that "the grac'd person of our Banquo" (3.4.40) is merely tardy rather than fallen upon "mischance" (42). But no sooner has he said these words than he turns to find the ghost of his old companion seated in the king's place. His shock is profound, and his language significant. In effect he is petrified, turned to stone.

Desperately he resolves to visit the weird sisters and compel them to show him the future. But when they do, it is only to present him with another Gorgon, one he will neither recognize nor interpret correctly. For the first apparition summoned by the witches is "an armed Head," prefiguring Macbeth's own ignoble decapitation. Had he read the apotropaic warning in the disembodied head, or in its words, his story might have ended differently. But his failure to "beware the Thane of Fife" (4.1.72), like his inability to comprehend the limits of his own power and knowledge, spells his doom. It remains for the Thane of Fife to transform him into yet another "new Gorgon," a warning sign to Scotland and to the audience of tragedy.

When Macduff confronts Macbeth on the field of battle, he offers, unwittingly, an explanation of the second apparition displayed by the witches, the bloody child. The apparition had proclaimed that "none of woman born/Shall harm Macbeth" (4.1.80–81) so that Macbeth departed confident of his safety. But now Macduff reveals that he "was from his mother's womb/Untimely ripp'd" (5.8.15–16). Macduff's Caesarean birth recalls the moment before the play began when, according to the sergeants' report, Macbeth "carv'd out his passage" (1.2.19) through the rebels and "unseam'd" Macdonwald "from the nave to th'chops" (22).[55] To be "not of woman born" is at least rhetorically to be exempt from the gender anxiety that so torments Macbeth—to be a man born only from a man. And the image of parthenogenesis suggested by this deliberately "paltering" phrase may also bring to mind the figure of Athena, the virgin war goddess, bearer of the Gorgon shield, who sprung full grown, armed and shouting from the head of her father, Zeus. Both of these births avoid the normal "passage" through the female body. Both avoid a disabling identification with the mother and with female weakness, empowering the figures thus begotten as appropriate emblems of retribution. Hearing this phrase—"from his mother's womb/Untimely ripp'd"— Macbeth's courage begins to fail. "I'll not fight with thee," he declares (22). "Then yield thee, coward," retorts Macduff,

> And live to be the show and gaze o' th' time!
> We'll have thee, as our rarer monsters are,
> Painted upon a pole, and underwrit,
> "Here may you see the tyrant."
>
> (5.8.23–27)

"Monster," a word which for the Renaissance carried the modern meaning of an unnatural being, also retained the force of its Latin root, *monere* (to warn) and hence meant a divine portent or sign. In Macduff's scenario the picture of Macbeth is to become an object lesson, a spectacle, a warning against tyranny, a

---

[55]Robert Watson describes the actions of several Shakespearean protagonists, Macbeth among them, as "enforcing their own rebirths by a sort of Caesarean section, carving out the opening through which the ambitious new identity appears" (Robert Watson, *Shakespeare and the Hazards of Ambition* [Cambridge, Mass.: Harvard University Press, 1984], p. 19). If recognized as a Caesarean operation, however, Macbeth's offstage action before the play begins encodes his own dramatic teleology, and thus insures the uncanny appropriateness of Macduff as the man who beheads him, also offstage, at the play's close.

figure for theater and for art. Like the head of Medusa, this painted figure would serve a monitory role, much in the manner of the dead suitors whose severed heads were to adorn the walls of Antioch in *Pericles*. Ultimately, however, taunted by so inglorious a fate, Macbeth decides to fight—and it is at this point that the next "new Gorgon" appears. Macbeth is slain, and in the next scene we find the stage direction, "Enter Macduff with Macbeth's head."

On the stage this is, or should be, an extremely disturbing moment. The head is presented to the spectators, both the onstage Scottish troops and the audience in the theater, and it is reasonable to suppose that before Macduff's speech of homage to Duncan's son, Malcolm ("Hail, King! for so thou art" [5.9.19]), there should be a brief silence. Even though this is a bloody play, and the soldiers are engaged in bloody battle, the sudden appearance of a severed head—and a recognizable one, at that—might give one pause. The audience, if not turned to stone, is at least likely to be taken aback. Macduff the avenging Perseus, Macbeth the horrified Medusa head, are presented as if in allegorical tableau. And since there is no stage direction that indicates departure, the bloody head of the decapitated king must remain onstage throughout all of Malcolm's healing and mollifying remarks. In his final speech he refers to "this dead butcher" (5.9.35), presumably with some sort of gesture in the direction of the head. However complete Malcolm's victory, however bright the future for Scotland under his rule, the audience is confronted at the last with a double spectacle; the new king and the old tyrant, the promising future and the tainted past.

Yet just as the head of Medusa became a powerful talisman for good once affixed to the shield of Athena, so the head of Macbeth is in its final appearance transformed from an emblem of evil to a token of good, a sign at once minatory and monitory, threatening and warning. Not in the painted guise foreseen by Macduff, but in its full and appalling reality, the head of the monster that was Macbeth has now become an object lesson in tyranny, a demonstration of human venality and its overthrow—"the show and gaze o' th' time."

The severed head, the gory locks of Banquo, and the armed head that appears as the witches' first apparition—all these have an iconographic congruence to the "new Gorgon" Macduff announced. But there is yet one more episode in the play which, to me at least, suggests associations with the Gorgon story, and which is, in its way, the most remarkable version of that story in the play. I refer to the final apparition displayed for Macbeth on the heath, at his importunate insistence. You will recall that the witches had told him to "seek to know no more" and that he had nonetheless insisted on an answer to his final question, "shall Banquo's issue ever/Reign in this kingdom?" (4.1.102–3). As we have seen, he threatens to curse them if they do not reply, and is answered by a chorus that makes plain that the ensuing vision is taboo, not to be gazed upon.: "Show!/Show!/Show!/Show his eyes, and grieve his heart;/Come like shadows, so depart" (4.1.107–11). Now there appear what the stage directions describe as *"A show of eight Kings, [the eighth] with a glass in his hand, and Banquo last."* Macbeth's anguished response is worth quoting in full because of its relevance to our line of inquiry:

> Thou art too like the spirit of Banquo; down!
> Thy crown does sear mine eyeballs. And thy hair,
> Thou other gold-bound brow, is like the first.
> A third is like the former. Filthy hags,
> Why do you show me this?—A fourth? Start, eyes!
> What, will the line stretch out to th' crack of doom?
> Another yet? A seventh? I'll see no more.
> And yet the eighth appears, who bears a glass
> Which shows me many more; and some I see
> That twofold balls and treble sceptres carry.
> Horrible sight! Now I see 'tis true,
> For the blood-bolter'd Banquo smiles upon me,
> And points at them for his. *[Apparitions vanish.]*
>   What? is this so?
> *1 Witch:*   Ay, sir, all this is so. But why
>   Stands Macbeth thus amazedly?
>
>   (112–26)

"Why stands Macbeth thus amazedly?" We could answer with the Doctor's words from the sleepwalking scene: "My mind she has mated, and amaz'd my sight." Notice Macbeth's words: "Sear mine eyeballs"; "start, eyes"; "horrible sight." Once again Macbeth is a man transfixed by what he has seen, once again in effect turned to stone. His murders have been for nothing; Banquo's sons will inherit the kingdom. This is his personal Gorgon, the sign of his own futility and damnation.

But the form of this particular apparition has more to tell us. The eighth king appears with "a glass," which shows us many more kings to come. A glass is a mirror—in the context of the scene a magic mirror, predicting the future, but as a stage prop quite possibly an ordinary one, borne to the front of the audience where at the first performance King James would have been seated in state. James, of course, traced his ancestry to Banquo, a fact which—together with his interest in witchcraft—may have been the reason for Shakespeare's choice of subject. The "glass" is another transgression of the inside/outside boundary, crossing the barrier that separates the play and its spectators.

Moreover, the word "glass" in Shakespeare's time meant not only "mirror" but also "model" or "example." Thus Hamlet is described as "the glass of fashion and the mould of form" (*Hamlet* 3.1.153); Hotspur as "the glass/Wherein the noble youth did dress themselves" (*2 Henry IV* 2.3.21), and King Henry V, in a variant of the figure, as "the mirror of all Christian kings" (*Henry V* 2. Prologue. 6). For the apparition of the eighth king to reflect such a "glass" (in the person of James I) with the glass he bears would therefore approximate in metaphorical terms the optical phenomenon of infinite regress when two mirrors face one another. Banquo's line would indeed "stretch out to th' crack of doom." Implicitly this trope is already present, since the king reflects all his ancestors. In this sense as well he is "a glass/Which shows [Macbeth] many more." James himself would later explicate this figure of the king as mirror in a speech to Parliament on 21 March, 1609:

Yee know that principally by three wayes yee may wrong a **Mirrour**.

First, I pray you, look not upon my Mirrour with a false light: which yee doe, if ye mistake, or mis-understand my Speach, and so alter the sence thereof.

But secondly, I pray you beware to soile it with a foule breath, and uncleane hands: I meane, that yee pervert not my words by any corrupt affections, turning them to an ill meaning, like one, who when hee hears the tolling of a Bell, fancies to himself, that it speakes those words which are most in his minde.

And lastly (which is worst of all) beware to let it fall or breake: (for glass is brittle) which ye doe, if ye lightly esteeme it, and by contemning it, conforme not your selves to my persuasions.[56]

What I would like to suggest here is that the reflecting glass or mirror in this scene is the counterpart of Perseus' reflecting shield, another transgression of the boundary between stage and reality. Perseus, we are told, was able to gaze on the reflection of Medusa without harm, although had he looked at her directly he would have been turned to stone. But the reflection or deflection of the dreadful image made it bearable. When the head was presented to Athena, and its image fixed on her aegis, it became a positive force, allied with the goddess and the virtues for which she stood. In the context of *Macbeth* the reflecting glass is the binary opposite of Macbeth's severed head: the glass is a happy spectacle demonstrating the long line of kings descended from Banquo, a line which James would doubtless hope to have "stretch out to th' crack of doom"; the head is a dismal spectacle signifying the end of a tyrant's solitary reign. Both are displaced versions of the Gorgon myth, "new Gorgons," since what horrifies Macbeth gratifies King James and the Jacobean audience. Indeed it may not be too extreme to suggest that James himself is the Athena figure here, to whom the head of the slain Macbeth is offered as a talisman and sign. The code of flattery which attended the theater of patronage would surely have allowed such a trope, and the apotropaic function of the severed head, warding off evil, would have been entirely consonant with the play's other compliment to English kings, the mention of the "healing benediction" (4.3.156)—the sovereign's ability to cure scrofula ("the evil") with the "king's touch," a custom which dated from the reign of Edward the Confessor, and was still in practice at the time of James I. Yet the fact that the "glass" transgresses the boundary of representation implies once again that tranquil containment is not possible without opening a new rift.

"There's no art To find the mind's construction in the face"

What is reflected in the mirror is thus, on the one hand, the king, and on the other hand, the sexually ambiguous head of the Medusa. There are in fact historical reasons why it should come as no surprise to find that gender undecidability in

[56]*Political Works*, p. 325.

Shakespeare is profoundly implicated in power. England had recently been ruled by a Queen who called herself a Prince, used the male pronoun in all her state papers, and was widely rumored to possess some of the anatomical features of the male sex. In a famous passage in her speech to her troops at Tilbury—when she appeared in the costume of an androgynous martial maiden—she declared:

> I know that I have the body but of a weak and feeble woman, but I have the heart and stomach of a king, and a king of England, too.[57]

Louis Montrose puts the matter of the queen's two bodies clearly when he remarks that "As the female ruler of what was, at least in theory, a patriarchal society, Elizabeth incarnated a contradiction at the very center of the Elizabethan sex/gender system."[58] "More than a man, and, in troth, sometimes less than a woman," as Cecil wrote to Harington.[59]

As for King James, he was known to have not only a wife but also male favorites. A preacher at St Paul's Cross spoke openly in a sermon about the King and "his catamites." Sir Walter Ralegh, discussing the King's special friend, the Duke of Buckingham, is reported to have said that royal favorites "were frequently commanded to uncomely, and sometimes unnatural, employments,"[60] and James himself wrote longingly to Buckingham as his "sweet child and wife," while expressing in his poems and letters his desire for "sweete bedchamber boyes."[61] "The love the king shewed," wrote Francis Osborne, "was as amorously conveyed, as if he had mistaken their sex, and thought them ladies."[62] Historically as well as dramatically, then, one can ask: was the Queen a man? Was the King a queen?

Elizabeth and James, in other words, themselves encoded boundary transgression at precisely the point of maximum personal and political power. This play marks the gender undecidability of monarchs. But if the curtain rises too soon on the bearded witches, revealing a scene of gender undecidability, is the final scene

---

[57]Paul Johnson, *Elizabeth I: A Study in Power and Intellect* (London: Weidenfeld & Nicolson, 1974), p. 320.

[58]Louis Montrose, "Shaping Fantasies: Figurations of Gender and Power in Elizabethan Culture," *Representations* 1 (Spring, 1983): 77.

> Queen Elizabeth was a cultural anomaly; and this anomalousness—at once divine and monstrous—made her powerful, and dangerous. By the skillful deployment of images that were at once awesome and familiar, this perplexing creature tried to mollify her subjects while enhancing her authority over them (p. 78).

[59]Sir Robert Cecil to Sir John Harington, 29 May 1603, printed in John Harington, *Nugae Antiquae*, 3 vols. (1779, rpt Hildesheim, 1968), 3, p. 264, quoted in Montrose, p. 78. Elizabeth, who had costumed herself as an Amazon queen, might well be represented as a Medusa, "at once divine and monstrous," by the generation after her death.

[60]Lawrence Stone, *The Causes of the English Revolution, 1529–1642* (London: Routledge & Kegan Paul. New York: Harper and Row, 1972), p. 89. Stone cites a number of further references, and remarks about "the widespread gossip about James's sexual tastes" that "the importance of these stories lies in the fact of their existence, not in their truth" (p. 158, n.112).

[61]Jonathan Goldberg, *James I and the Politics of Literature* (Baltimore: Johns Hopkins University Press, 1983), pp. 142–46; 269, n. 29.

[62]Francis Osborne, *Some Traditional Memorialls on the Raigne of King James I*, in *Secret History of the Court of James I*, ed. W. Scott (Edinburgh, 1811), I, pp. 274–76.

a restoration of decidability? Does Macbeth's brandished head apotropaically dismiss uncertainty, or reinscribe it? *That* is what remains uncertain. The attempts of feminists and others to reassign gender and power in *Macbeth* merely replicate the fundamental resistance we have seen in Freud, the refusal to regard the enigma as such, to gaze upon the head of the Medusa, to recognize the undecidability that may lie just beneath the surface of power—and perhaps of sexuality itself.

The word "apotropaic," so frequently associated with the power of the severed Medusa head, means "turning away" or "warding off," and derives from the same root as "trope," and also as Atropos, the third of the Moirai or Fates—Atropos whose name means the Inflexible or the Inexorable, she who cannot be turned away. Like the Gorgons, the Fates were three in number; they are represented in myth as old women, and probably originated not as abstract powers or destiny but as birth-spirits, telling the story of a child's future. The thread they spin, the tale or plot they weave, is the individual's destiny, the life line or the plot line. Atropos is variously described as spinning or singing, both creative arts, then as cutting the thread of life short. The Latin word *Fata* itself is probably an adaptation of the singular *fatum*, "that which is spoken." In fact, the Fates seem from the first to have been connected with narrative, and perhaps also with prophetic powers, as are Shakespeare's Weird Sisters. It is not entirely surprising, therefore, that an apotropaic object like the Medusa head, especially when represented in visual art or poetry, would have a doubled message to deliver, a message at once seductive and dangerous, enabling and disabling.

In its self-conception, in its stage history, in the doubleness of its final tableau, *Macbeth* seems almost paradigmatically to be a play that refuses to remain contained within the safe boundaries of fiction. It is a tragedy that demonstrates the refusal of tragedy to be so contained. As it replicates, it implicates. Things will not remain within their boundaries: sleepers and forests walk, the dead and the deeds return, the audience stares at forbidden sights. This is what the plot of *Macbeth* is about. Yet what is most uncanny about the play is perhaps that it is *both* apotropaic and atropic, *heimlich* and *unheimlich*, paltering with us constantly in a double sense. It is as though we too can in the end only cry, with Lady Macbeth's doctor, "A great perturbation in nature, to receive at once the benefit of sleep and do the effects of watching!" (5.1.9–11).

Macbeth and Witchcraft

Peter Stallybrass

For students of *Macbeth*, witchcraft[1] has always presented a problem. At the one extreme, we have scholars like T. A. Spalding and W. C. Curry who have unearthed some of the historical *minutiae* of medieval and Renaissance concepts of witchcraft;[2] at the other extreme, we have critics who accept the play's witchcraft only as a form of psychological symbolism. Since the publications of Keith Thomas's *Religion and the Decline of Magic* (1971) and Alan Macfarlane's *Witchcraft in Tudor and Stuart England* (1970),[3] the latter position has seemed less tenable. But this does not mean that we should return to the (admittedly useful) positivistic data-gathering of Spalding and Curry to understand the function of witchcraft in *Macbeth*. I see little point, for instance, in attempting to *classify* the Weird Sisters as witches or warlocks or norns (distinctions which were rarely observed by Tudor and Stuart witchcraft treatises or reports of trials). Such classifications tend to emphasize the exoticism of witchcraft beliefs without beginning to explain how such beliefs could ever have been held.

It is, indeed, worth emphasizing the "normality" of witchcraft beliefs. Although witchcraft accusations reached epidemic proportions in sixteenth- and seventeenth-century Europe, witchcraft beliefs are endemic in many societies. Their frequency, however, should not be taken as evidence for the truth of witchcraft (there is no proof, for instance, that "witches" eat their own children, cause sickness, plague or famine, or have sexual relations with devils) but as evidence of the social utility of such beliefs in a variety of societies. An adequate explanation of witchcraft, then, needs to have a double focus: on the one hand, it must describe

From John Russell Brown, ed. *Focus on Macbeth* (London: Routledge, 1982). Reproduced by permission of Routledge and the author.

[1]C. L'Estrange Ewen, in *Witchcraft and Demonianism: A Concise Account Derived from Sworn Depositions* (London: Heath, Cranton, 1933), p. 76, defines "true witchcraft" as "the joint accomplishments of spirit demons and their human converts." But Keith Thomas notes that "the term witchcraft was used loosely in Tudor and Stuart England, and was at one time or another applied to virtually every kind of magical activity or ritual operation that worked through occult methods" ("The Relevance of Anthropology to the Study of English Witchcraft," in *Witchcraft Confessions and Accusations*, ed. Mary Douglas [London: Tavistock Publications, 1970], p. 48).

[2]T. A. Spalding, *Elizabethan Demonology: An Essay in Illustration of the Belief in the Existence of Devils* (London: Charto and Windus, 1880) and W. C. Curry, *Shakespeare's Philosophical Patterns* (Baton Rouge: Louisiana State UP, 1937).

[3]For a valuable critique of their work, see E. P. Thompson, "Anthropology and the Discipline of Historical Context," *Midland History*, I (1972), pp. 41–55.

the actual beliefs and explain how they fit within a particular cosmology; on the other hand, it must take into account the *function* of such beliefs ("a myth provides a charter for action").[4]

Witchcraft beliefs are one way of asserting distinctions; they "sharpen definitions,"[5] as Mary Douglas puts it, including definitions of political and familial roles. They can be used, for instance, to account for the "unnatural" ambition of a rival or for the "unnatural" power of a woman. In doing so, such beliefs imply and legitimate their opposite, the "natural." In short, witchcraft beliefs are less a reflection of a real "evil" than a social construction from which we learn more about the accuser than the accused, more about the social institutions which tolerate/encourage/act on those accusations than about the activities of those people (in England, mainly women, mainly poor) who were prosecuted as witches. What Mary Douglas says of dirt could be said of witchcraft: it "is never a unique, isolated event" but rather "the by-product of a systematic ordering and classification . . . in so far as ordering involves rejecting inappropriate elements."[6] Witchcraft accusations are a way of reaffirming a particular order against outsiders, or of attacking an internal rival, or of attacking "deviance." Witchcraft in *Macbeth,* I will maintain, is not simply a reflection of a pre-given order of things: rather, it is a particular working upon, and legitimation of, the hegemony of patriarchy.

Witchcraft and Monarchy

The English government had, at least since 1300, been concerned with "witches"—"with sorcerers, because they might attempt to kill the king, with prophets (including astrologers) because they might forecast the hour of his death." The Duke of Buckingham, accused of treason in 1521, had been encouraged by a prophecy that he would be king, although he had been warned that the prophet, a Carthusian monk, "might be deceived by the devil." In 1558, Sir Anthony Fortescue was arrested for sorcery, having cast a horoscope which stated that the Queen "should not live passing the next spring," and in 1580, Nicholas Johnson was accused of "making her Majesty's picture in wax."[7] This last case was one of the factors in the passing of a new Act in 1580–81 which attacked the "divers persons wickedly disposed" who had "not only wished her Majesty's death, but also by divers means practised and sought to know how long her Highness should live, and who should reign after her decease, and what changes and alter-

---

[4]Malinowski, quoted by Philip Mayer, "Witches" in *Witchcraft and Sorcery,* ed. Max Marwick (Harmondsworth, England: Penguin Books, 1970), p. 48.

[5]Mary Douglas, Introduction to *Witchcraft Confessions and Accusations,* ed. Mary Douglas (1970), p. xxx.

[6]Mary Douglas, *Purity and Danger: An Analysis of Concepts of Pollution and Taboo* (London: Routledge and Kegan Paul, 1976), p. 35.

[7]George Lyman Kittredge, *Witchcraft in Old and New England* (Cambridge, Mass.: Cambridge UP, 1929), pp. 226, 229, and 260–61.

ations should thereby happen."[8] The Act went on to attack all those who, "by any prophecying, witchcraft, conjurations or other like unlawfull means whatsoever," attempted to harm the monarch or to meddle in her affairs. In England, then, there was already a clear connection between prophecy, witchcraft, and monarchy before James ascended the throne.

In Scotland, James was making his own connections. There is little evidence that he had an interest in witchcraft before 1590, but the sensational trials of that year changed his attitude. More than 300 witches were alleged to have met and confessions were extorted, with the aid of torture, which pointed to a conspiracy directed by the Earl of Bothwell against the king himself. James took an active part in the trial, and Agnes Samson's report of "the very words which passed between the King's Majesty and his Queen at Oslo in Norway the first night of their marriage" made him give "more credit to the rest."[9]

But if the trial triggered James's interest in witchcraft, we may suggest two possible determinants of the actual form his interest took. The first is, paradoxical though it may seem, his very desire to be in the intellectual vanguard. We need to remember that the witch craze was not the last fling of residual medieval "superstition," but, at least in part, the potent construction of some of the foremost intellectuals of the time, including Bodin. It may well be, as Christine Larner has suggested,[10] that it was James's attempt to keep up with intellectual developments on the Continent after his contact with scholars in Denmark in 1589 which first aroused his interest in witchcraft.

But if his interest was stimulated by Continental ideas, his new belief consolidated his pre-existing interest in the theory and practice of godly rule. If the King was God's representative on earth, then who could be a more likely victim of the devil's arts than he? In his early work on the Book of Revelations, James had associated the devil with Antichrist, in his guise of the Pope, but it was not difficult to imagine that the devil employed more than one agency. To suggest, then, that the monarchy was under demonic attack was to glorify the institution of monarchy, since that implied that it was one of the bastions protecting this world from the triumph of Satan. As Stuart Clark says, "demonism was, logically speaking, one of the presuppositions of the metaphysics of order on which James's political ideas ultimately rested."[11] Clark also shows how this kind of *antithetical* thinking is the logical corollary of *analogical* thinking. If kingship is legitimated by analogy to God's rule over the earth, and the father's rule over the family and the head's rule over the body, witchcraft establishes the opposite analogies, whereby the Devil

---

[8]"An Act against seditious words and rumours uttered against the Queen's most excellent Majesty" (23 Eliz., c. 2), quoted in *Witchcraft*, ed. Barbara Rosen, *Stratford-upon-Avon Library* 6 (1969), p. 56.

[9]*Newes from Scotland* (n.d.), sig. B2.

[10]"James VI and I and Witchcraft," in *The Reign of James VI and I*, ed. Alan G. R. Smith (London: Macmillan, 1973), pp. 74–90.

[11]Clark, *The Damned Art*, ed. Sydney Anglo (London: Routledge and Kegan Paul, 1977), pp. 156–57.

attempts to rule over the earth, and the woman over the family, and the body over the head.[12]

Henry Paul, in his important study of *Macbeth*,[13] argues in great detail for the indebtedness of the play to James's views on the nature of witchcraft and kingship. The play was performed before James and his father-in-law, the King of Denmark, at Hampton Court in 1606, and Paul argues that the play was shaped in important ways by royal patronage. But it is not demonstrable, in my view, that James's views (as set forth in his *Daemonologie*, for instance) were *sources* for the play, although they undoubtedly set ideological limits to it. In 1604, a play called *Gowrie*, performed by the King's Men, had been banned.[14] The play was presumably based on the Earl of Gowrie's attempt to murder James in 1600. Gowrie had been killed in the attempt, and on him had been found a bag "full of magicall characters, and words of inchantment, wherein, it seemed that he had put his confidence."[15] Whatever the reason for banning the play, the King's Men would have been unlikely to risk a second offensive play on the sensitive topics of the attack upon kings and the uses of the black arts.

But if James's ideas were not a source, they provide an analogue, sharing and partially determining the ideological terrain of *Macbeth*. Like James's works, *Macbeth* is constructed around the fear of a world without sovereignty. Similarly, Robert Bolton, preaching in 1621, attempted to legitimate sovereignty by constructing the imaginary horrors of a world without it:[16]

> Take Sovereignty from the face of the earth, and you turne it into a Cockpit. Men would become cut-throats and cannibals one unto another. Murder, adulteries, incests, rapes, robberies, perjuries, witchcrafts, blasphemies, all kinds of villainies, outrages, and savage cruelty, would overflow all Countries. We should have a very hell upon earth, and the face of it covered with blood, as it was once with water.

Macbeth *and Holinshed*

If it was the ascension of James to the English throne which suggested a play about Scottish history, and about James's own ancestry in particular, it is worth noting how Shakespeare utilized Holinshed, his main source for the play. To begin with, he simplified the outlines of the story to create a structure of clear antitheses. Holinshed's Duncan is a weak king, "negligent . . . in punishing

---

[12]Ibid., pp. 175–77.

[13]*The Royal Play of Macbeth* (New York: Macmillan, 1950).

[14]E. K. Chambers, *The Elizabethan Stage* (Oxford: Clarendon Press, 1923), I, p. 328. Chambers quotes a court gossip as saying, "I hear that some great councellors are much displeased with [*Gowrie*]."

[15]*Gowrie's Gonspiracie* (1600), in *The Harleian Miscellany* (London: R. Dutton, 1809), III, p. 86. See also Steven Mullaney, "Lying like Truth," *English Literary History*, 47 (1980), pp. 32–47. [Reprinted in this volume, pp. 61–73.]

[16]Quoted in William Lamont, *Godly Rule: Politics and Religion, 1603-60* (London: Macmillan, 1969), p. 49.

offenders,"[17] and unable to control the kingdom, whereas Shakespeare's Duncan is, as even Macbeth admits, "clear in his great office" (1.7.18). Holinshed's Macbeth has a legal right to the throne, since "by the old lawes of the realme, the ordnance was, that if he that should succeed were not of able age to take the charge upon himselfe, he that was next of bloud unto him should be admitted" (Holinshed, p. 172), whereas Shakespeare makes little of Macbeth's claim. Moreover, Shakespeare omits any reference to the "ten yeares in equall justice" during which Holinshed's Macbeth ruled after "the feeble and slouthfull administration of Duncane" (Holinshed, p. 173). Finally, Holinshed's Banquo is a party to Macbeth's plot to murder Duncan, whereas Shakespeare's Banquo is not.

What is striking about all these changes is that they transform dialectic into antithesis. Whereas Shakespeare's second historical tetralogy undoubtedly raises dialectical questions about sovereignty, *Macbeth* takes material eminently suitable for dialectical development (the weak ruler being overthrown by a ruler who establishes "equall justice") and shapes it into a structural antithesis. One reason for the shaping of the sources in this way was, no doubt, royal patronage. This meant, for instance, that Banquo, James's ancestor, had to be shown in a favourable light, and it may be that James's views on godly rule and on "the trew difference betwixt a lawfull, good King and an usurping Tyrant" were taken into account. Certainly, *Macbeth* differentiates as clearly as James's *Basilikon Doron* between the good king whose "greatest suretie" is his people's good will and the tyrant who builds "his suretie upon his peoples miserie."[18]

Holinshed's account, though, suggested another factor by which the tyrant might be distinguished from the godly ruler: his relation to witchcraft. For Holinshed describes how Macbeth "had learned of certaine wizzards" and had gained (false) confidence from a witch who told him "that he should never be slaine with man born of anie woman" (Holinshed, p. 175). But even over the issue of witchcraft, Holinshed is not entirely clear, because the crucial prophecies which embolden his Macbeth are made by "three women in strange and wild apparell, resembling creatures of elder world," and these women are later described as "either the weird sisters, that is (as ye would say) the goddesses of destinie, or else some nymphs or feiries, indued with knowledge of prophesie by their necromenti-call science" (Holinshed, pp. 171–72). It was probably these three women whom Dr Gwin transformed into the *Tres Sibyllae* who hailed James as King of Scotland and England in a performance presented to the king at Oxford on 27 August 1605.[19]

But for the Witches in *Macbeth* to have been presented as godly sibylls would have weakened the antithetical structure of the play. Only by making his Sisters

[17]Holinshed, *Chronicles of Scotland*, quoted in *Macbeth*, ed. Kenneth Muir, *The Arden Shakespeare* (London, 1972), p. 167. All quotations from Holinshed and from the play are taken from the Arden *Macbeth*.

[18]*Basilikon Doron*, in *The Political Works of James I*, ed. Charles H. McIlwain, Harvard Political Classics (Cambridge, Mass., 1918), pp. 18–19.

[19]Paul, *The Royal Play of Macbeth*, p. 163.

forces of darkness could Shakespeare suggest demonic opposition to godly rule. And here Shakespeare had to supplement Holinshed's account of Macbeth. For although the political effects of usurpation are suggested by Holinshed's account of how, after Macbeth murdered Banquo, "everie man began to doubt his owne life" (Holinshed, p. 174), there is little sense of the natural holocaust which Bolton saw as the logical outcome of the overthrow of sovereignty. For an image of a king's murder and the consequent turning of a country into "a very hell upon earth," Shakespeare had to turn back to Holinshed's account of Donwald's murder of King Duff, a murder which is itself the consequence of the King's execution of Donwald's kinsmen for conspiring with witches against him. Many of the horrifying events which follow Duff's death (the darkening of the sun, lightning and tempests, cannibalism amongst animals) reappear, more or less transformed, in *Macbeth*, reaffirming through antithesis the order which has been overthrown—the order of monarchy, of patriarchy, of the head, of "reason."

The Witches

"For Rebellion is as the sin of witchcraft" (I Samuel XV. 23). And the first two scenes of *Macbeth* present both witches and rebellion. But what kind of witches are they? In the first scene, we can note several aspects of them: they are connected with disorder in nature (not only thunder and lightning but also "fog and filthy air"); they are associated with familiars (Graymalkin and Paddock), the common companions of English witches but rarely mentioned in Scottish or Continental prosecutions; they can "hover"; they reverse moral values ("Fair is foul, and foul is fair") (1.1.11); they presumably foresee the future, since the third witch knows that the battle will be over by sunset. The third scene, though, shows more clearly what seems to be an ambiguity in the presentation of the Witches. On the one hand, they have features typical of the English village "witch," being old women, "wither'd" and with "choppy fingers" and "skinny lips." (Reginald Scot described English "witches" as "commonly old, lame, bleare-eied, pale, fowle, and full of wrinkles.")[20] Moreover, the second witch kills swine and the first witch pursues a petty vendetta, typical offences in English witch prosecutions. But, on the other hand, they are mysterious and "look not like th' inhabitants o' th' earth" (1.3.41), and they prophesy the future.

What is the function of this ambiguity? At one level, no doubt, it enabled Shakespeare to draw upon the common belief in an "evil" at work in the English countryside whilst never reducing the play's witches to village widows. But it was also structurally convenient because it established a double perspective on evil, allowing for the simultaneous sense of reduction in Macbeth as he becomes increasingly dependent on the "midnight hags" (4.1.48) and of his aspiration as, after "Disdaining Fortune" (1.2.17) in the battle, he attempts to

---

[20]Reginald Scot, *The Discoverie of Witchcraft*, ed. Montague Summers (London, 1930), p. 1.

grab hold of Providence itself. The double perspective operates throughout the play. On the one hand, Macbeth is reduced to the image of "a dwarfish thief" (5.2.22) before being literally reduced to the head which Macduff carries onto the stage. At this level, evil is conceptualized as eating up itself until nothing is left. But the conceptualization leaves no role for militant "good" (and therefore would not require the "great revenge" [4.3.214] of Malcolm and Macduff), and so the world of self-consuming evil is combined with a dualistic world in which both the Witches and Macbeth threaten to bring the world back to its first chaos or, as Bolton puts it, to create "a very hell upon earth," the hell of a world without sovereignty.

Lady Macbeth, the Witches, and Family Structure

The Witches open the play, but they appear in only the first and third scenes of the first Act. In the fifth and seventh scenes, the "temptress" is Lady Macbeth. In other words, scenes in which female figures champion evil alternate with public scenes (Duncan and news of the battle in scene 2; the honouring of Macbeth, Banquo, and Malcolm in scene 4; Duncan's reception at Macbeth's castle in scene 6). And the public scenes, with the exception of the last, are exclusively male. If this foregrounds the female figures, Lady Macbeth is also equated with the Witches in more specific ways. As Mark Rose says, "the third scene opens with the Witches alone, after which Macbeth enters and they hail him by his various titles. The fifth scene opens with Lady Macbeth alone, practising witchcraft. . . . And when Macbeth enters she, too, hails him by his titles."[21] Moreover, Lady Macbeth and the Witches are equated by their equivocal relation to an implied norm of femininity. Of the Witches, Banquo says:

> you should be women,
> And yet your beards forbid me to interpret
> That you are so.

> (1.3.45–47)

And Lady Macbeth invokes the "murth'ring ministers" (1.5.48) to unsex her.

The enticement of Macbeth both by the Witches and by his wife is briefly suggested in Holinshed's account of Macbeth, and in Holinshed's earlier account of Donwald's wife Shakespeare found a much expanded role given to a murderer's wife. But in neither account is any connection made between witchcraft and the murderer's wife. Again, we see the antithetical mode being strengthened in *Macbeth* by the development of analogies between "perverted femininity," witchcraft, and a world turned upside down. The analogy was not, of course, new, and it is notoriously enshrined in *Malleus Maleficarum* where

---

[21]Mark Rose, *Shakespearean Design* (Cambridge, Mass.: Harvard UP, 1972), p. 88.

Femina is derived from *Fe* and *Minus* "since [woman] is ever weaker to hold and preserve the faith."[22]

But it is important to note the shift of emphasis when Lady Macbeth "replaces" the witches. By this movement from the already damned to the secular world, the implications of the rejection of "womanhood" are made explicit. Whereas the witches are difficult to categorize at all within the implied norm, in 1.5, Lady Macbeth is shown in the very attempt of overthrowing a norm inscribed in her own body. "Remorse," "compunctious visitings of Nature," and the "milk" of "woman's breasts" (1.5.44–48) are established as the "feminine" virtues even as Lady Macbeth negates them. Indeed, because of the inscription of those virtues in Lady Macbeth, her relation to witchcraft is not as clear at the psychological as it is at the structural level. Although Lady Macbeth might say, like Joan la Pucelle, "I exceed my sex" (*1 Henry VI*, 1.2.90), her relation to witchcraft is never as explicit as Joan's. For Joan is not merely *accused* of being a "witch" and "damned sorceress" (3.2.38); her conjurings lead to the actual appearance of friends upon the stage.

Nevertheless, Lady Macbeth's invocation of the "murth'ring ministers" (1.5.48) as her children has particular resonance within the context of witchcraft, even if her ministers never appear. For her proclaimed role as mother/lover of the spirits implicitly subverts patriarchal authority in a manner typically connected with witchcraft. If the first Witch plans to come between a sailor and his wife in 1.3,[23] Lady Macbeth herself breaks the bond with her husband by suggesting both his metaphysical and physical impotence (he is not "a man" [1.7.49]) because he is unworthy of the respect due to a patriarch, because he is "a coward" (1.7.43), and, possibly, because, as we learn later, his is "a barren sceptre" (3.1.61). It is particularly ironic, then, that Macbeth says "Bring forth men-children only" (1.7.73). For the structural antitheses which the first act develops establish the relation between women, witchcraft, the undermining of patriarchal authority and sterility.

But how can the family be conceptualized if women are, literally, faithless? One way is to show that not all womanhood falls under the curse of witchcraft, and this is surely an important reason for the introduction of Lady Macduff in 4.2, a scene which has no base in Holinshed. Indeed, it is the destruction of this "ideal" family which leads to Macduff's revenge and the final dénouement. But Lady Macduff is introduced late in the play, and we have already been presented with another way out of the dilemma: a family without women—Duncan and his sons, Malcolm and Donalbain, Banquo and his son Fleance (at the end of the play, Siward and his son Young Siward). On the one hand, there are the (virtuous) families of men; on the other hand, there are the antifamilies of women. And here, the notorious question,

---

[22]Heinrich Krämer and Jacob Sprenger, *Malleus Maleficarum*, in *Witchcraft in Europe 1100–1700: A Documentary History*, ed. A. C. Kors and E. Peters (Philadelphia: U of Pennsylvania P, 1972), p. 121. James I answers the question of why there are twenty female witches to one male witch by affirming that "as that sexe is frailer than man is, so is it easier to be intrapped in these grosse snares of the Divell" (*Daemonologie* [London, 1603], pp. 43–44).

[23]The connection between the witches and sexuality is made by Dennis Biggins, "Sexuality, Witchcraft and Violence in *Macbeth*," *Shakespeare Studies*, ed. J. Leeds Barroll III, VIII, pp. 255–77.

"How many children had Lady Macbeth?" is not entirely irrelevant. For although Lady Macbeth says, "I have given suck" (1.7.54), her children are never seen on the stage, unlike the children of Duncan, Banquo, Macduff, and Siward. Are we not asked to accept a logical contradiction for the sake of a symbolic unity: Lady Macbeth is *both* an unnatural mother *and* sterile? This links her to the unholy family of the Witches, with their familiars and their brew which includes "Finger of birth-strangled babe" and the blood of a sow which has eaten its own litter (4.1.30 and 64–65). Like the Witches, Lady Macbeth and her husband constitute an "unholy" family, a family whose only children are the "murth'ring ministers."

The Development of Lady Macbeth and the Witches

I have been writing mainly of the ways in which the Witches and Lady Macbeth function in the first Act. But their functions are not constant throughout the play. Lady Macbeth is beginning to be developed into her own antithesis even before the murder takes place. "Nature" is reasserted through her in its most compelling guise—the Law of the Father which, in this society, founds and is founded by the Law of the King. Thus, Lady Macbeth says that she would have murdered Duncan herself "Had he not resembled/My father as he slept" (2.2.12–13). And in the last act, she is transformed from the pitiless instigator to murder to the guilt-ridden sleep-walker whose thoughts return to "the old man" who had "so much blood in him" (5.1.39). Curry interprets her sleep-walking as "demoniacal somnambulism."[24] But surely this is to miss the dramatic point, which is the reassertion of "the compunctious visitations of Nature" if only in sleep. Lady Macbeth's last words, indeed, are not of her own guilt but of the solicitous wife's care for her husband: "give me your hand. . . . To bed, to bed, to bed" (5.1.63–65). But the transformation of Lady Macbeth is used to affirm developmentally the antithetical structure. It operates as a specific closure of discourse within the binary opposition of virago (witch)/wife.

If Lady Macbeth's changing function is marked by psychological change, the Witches' changing function is marked by the changing function of their prophecies. Much has been made of the fact that the Witches speak equivocally, that they are, as Macbeth says, "imperfect speakers" (1.3.70). But the apparitions of the fourth act are progressively *less* equivocal, moving from the "armed head" to the "bloody child" to the "child crowned" to the "show of eight kings, the last with a glass in his hand" which shows Banquo's descendants stretched out "to th' crack of doom" (4.1.117). The Witches here, far from being "imperfect speakers," conjure up a vision whose truth is established by the presence of Banquo's descendant, James I. In this prophecy of the "good," dramatic fate (as yet incomplete) joins hands with completed political fate.

[24]Curry, *Shakespeare's Philosophical Patterns*, p. 89.

As with Lady Macbeth, then, so with the Witches: they are constructed so as to manifest their own antithesis. Cursed witches prophesy the triumph of godly rule. At one level, no doubt, this implies that even evil works providentially. As James himself had declared in the preface to *Daemonologie:*[25]

> For where the devilles intention in them is ever to perish, either the soule or the body, or both of them, that he is so permitted to deale with: God by the contrarie, drawes ever out of that evill glorie to himselfe.

But at another level, the association of the Witches with the workings of Providence is part of the process by which attention is focused upon Macbeth alone. In 1.1, the Witches are invoked by their familiars; in 1.5, Lady Macbeth invokes the spirits. But, in the third act, it is Macbeth, who had to be "invoked" to do the deed, who invokes the night to "Scarf up the tender eye of pitiful Day" (3.2.47). But Macbeth's conjunctions made even

> though the treasure
> Of nature's germens tumble all together,
> Even till destruction sicken
> (4.1.58–60)

lead to a future in which he, with his "fruitless crown" (3.1.60), has no place. At the end, his only "familiar" is "Direness, familiar to my slaughterous thoughts" (5.5.14).

The Development of the Play

The first act of the play is framed by images of witchcraft, rebellion, and murder. At the end of the second act, an old man describes a world turned upside down, in which owls kill falcons, horses revolt against men and cannibalize each other, and night strangles day. In 1.1, 1.3, 3.5, and 4.1, thunder sounds.[26] And in 3.5 and 4.1 Hecate, who, according to Jonson, "was believed to govern in witchcraft,"[27] appears. Indeed, 4.1, the last scene with the Witches, can be seen as the emblematic centre of the play, containing as it does both the vision of kings and the fullest display of the workings of the "secret, black, and midnight hags" (4.1.48). It is not my purpose to enter into the dispute about the authorship of the Hecate passages. Whether Shakespeare wrote them or not, they are perfectly in keeping with the structure of the play. Indeed, the dance of Hecate and the six

---

[25]*Daemonologie*, sig. A4.

[26]See *Daemonologie*, p. 46: "[Witches] can rayse stormes and tempests in the ayre, eyther upon Sea or land." For actual accusations, see L'Estrange Ewen, *Witchcraft and Demonianism*, p. 89: "in 1582, suspicion fell upon Joan Robinson as being responsible for a great wind which blew down a house, and Michael Trevisard (1601) caused the wind and weather to destroy the Mayor's new fold." But there is an obvious discrepancy between the limited destruction of these latter "witches" and the vision of a world turned upside down in *Macbeth*.

[27]Ben Jonson, *Selected Masques*, ed. S. Orgel (New Haven: Yale UP, 1970), p. 360.

Witches gives a concrete dramatization of the "deed without a name" (4.1.49) which reverses the whole order of "Nature." We need to imagine something like the Witches' dance in Jonson's *The Masque of Queens* (1609), which was[28]

> full of preposterous change, and gesticulation, but most applying to their property, who at their meetings, do all things contrary to the custom of men, dancing back to back and hip to hip, their hands joined, and making their circles backward, to the left hand, with strange fantastic motions of their heads and bodies.

In the rituals of Shakespeare's Witches, as of Jonson's, a Jacobean audience could contemplate the systematic undoing of the hierarchical ceremonies of speech, of cooking, of dancing.

It is also in Act 4, though, that the "prayers" for a "swift blessing" (3.6.47) which will restore those ceremonies begin to be answered by the discovery of medicines for "the sickly weal" (5.2.27). At the same time, the impotence of literal medicines is made explicit by two minor characters: the English doctor who admits the impotence of his art to cure scrofula, the Scottish doctor who admits the impotence of his art to cure "infected minds" ("More needs she the divine than the physician" [5.1.71]). The introduction of these characters should warn against any attempt to give too naturalistic an explanation of the play, since their function is largely to assert the dependence of physical health upon political and metaphysical order. Indeed, the only function of the English doctor is to dramatize the difference between his own weak art and the medicine of King Edward's "sanctity" (4.3.144). (The King's power to heal scrofula, a belief which originated with Edward I, was a useful piece of royal propaganda and, although James I was himself sceptical, he ultimately agreed to take part in the healing ceremony; its propaganda value may be suggested by the fact that Charles II touched 90,798 persons in nineteen years.[29]) Of course, King Edward offers Malcolm the practical aid of troops as well as the metaphysical aid of the "sundry blessings" which "hang about his throne" (4.3.158). But the "med'cines" of Malcolm's and Macduff's "great revenge" (4.3.214) are guaranteed and legitimated by a godly magic which surpasses "the great assay of art" (4.3.143).

Witchcraft, prophecy, and magic function in *Macbeth* as ways of developing a particular conceptualization of social and political order. Witchcraft is associated with female rule and the overthrowing of patriarchal authority which in turn leads to the "womanish" (both cowardly and instigated by women) killing of Duncan, the "holy" father who establishes both family and state. This in turn leads to the reversals in the cosmic order which the Old Man and Ross describe, and to the reversals in the patriarchal order, culminating in the killing of Lady Macduff and her son. The conclusion of the play reestablishes both the offended (and offending?[30]) father, a father, paradoxically, "not born of woman" (5.3.4) (does this imply

---

[28]Ibid., p. 92.

[29]Keith Thomas, *Religion and the Decline of Magic* (London: Weidenfeld and Nicolson, 1971), p. 193.

[30]Lady Macduff accuses her husband of lacking "the natural touch" (4.2.9).

that he is unnatural or untainted?[31]) and the offended son/king. And the Witches can simply disappear, their evil supplanted by the prophetic vision of Banquo's line and by the "heavenly gift of prophecy" and "miraculous work" (4.3.157 and 147) of a legitimate king.

Conclusion

This aspect of *Macbeth* as a work of cultural "ordering" could, of course, only make claims to "truth" within a cosmology which accommodated witchcraft beliefs. That cosmology was largely defined by the Bible. There are, indeed, interesting parallels between *Macbeth* and the story of Saul and the Witch of Endor in the Book of Samuel (I Samuel XXVIII), a text which was dealt with by nearly every Renaissance treatise on witchcraft. Jane Jack has explored this parallel in an important article, where she writes:[32]

> Like Saul, Macbeth hears from the witches the confirmation of what he most fears. The crisis of the story is the victory of the witches: the resolution of the story is the judgement passed on Macbeth at the end—the same judgement that is passed on Saul: "So Saul dyed for his transgression, that he committed against the word of the Lord, which he kept not, and in that he sought and asked consel of a familiar spirit" (glossed in Geneva version as a "witche and sorceress").

Jack goes on to assert the essentially religious tenor of *Macbeth*, a view which most critics of the play seem to hold. Murray, for example, maintains:[33]

> [*Macbeth*] is, if ever a poem were so, a *traditional Catholic Christian poem*, the vitality of which is rooted in an uncompromising medieval faith, and in a prescientific view of the nature of reality. Consequently it preserves in a tremendously powerful and well unified set of images one of the greatest forces in Western European culture, a force which, however alien it may seem to many of us today, we can afford neither to forget, nor to neglect, for it contains, and can still convey, much of the wisdom of human experience.

The "Christian" interpretation is, I believe, right in so far as it recognizes that *Macbeth* can only be understood in relation to a particular cosmology. But Murray, like Jack, attempts to separate religion from politics in a way which was totally foreign to sixteenth- and seventeenth-century thinking. For instance, the Fifth Commandment ("Honour thy father and thy mother"—but Sir Robert Filmer lopped off . . . "and thy mother"[34]) received new emphasis during this

---

[31]See Lucan, *Pharsalia*, 6, 554 ff.: "She [the witch] pierces the pregnant womb and delivers the child by an unnatural birth." Jonson quotes this passage in his commentary to *The Masque of Queens* (Ben Jonson, *Selected Masques*, p. 357).

[32]Jane H. Jack, "*Macbeth*, King James and the Bible," *English Literary History*, 22 (1955), pp. 182–83.

[33]W. A. Murray, "Why Was Duncan's Blood Golden?," *Shakespeare Survey*, 19 (1966), p. 43.

[34]Sir Robert Filmer, *Patriarcha and Other Political Works*, ed. Peter Laslett, Blackwell's Political Texts (Oxford, 1969), pp. 188, 269, 289.

period so as to give religious underpinnings to the patriarchal state.[35] Indeed, analogical thinking could be used not only to draw close parallels between the law of
Moses and the law of the State but also to collapse traditional distinctions. Thus, in
The Six Bookes of the Commonweale (1586), Bodin rejected Aristotle's distinction
between political and domestic hierarchy, claiming that the family "is the true
seminarie and beginning of every Commonweale."[36] Nor is it surprising that Bodin
also wrote an influential attack upon witchcraft, *Démonomanie des Sorciers*
(1580). If state and family were founded together, witchcraft founded the antistate
together with the antifamily. James I also made the connection between state and
family ("By the Law of Nature the King becomes a naturall Father to all his Lieges
at his Coronation"[37]) and he too saw witchcraft as the antithesis of both. If the family was theorized as the site of conflict between hierarchy and witchcraft, that was,
no doubt, because of its symbolic importance in early modern Europe when, as
Natalie Davis writes,[38]

> the nature of political rule and the newer problem of sovereignty were very much at
> issue. In the little world of the family, with its conspicuous tension between intimacy and
> power, the larger matters of political and social order could find ready symbolization.

Witchcraft, sovereignty, the family—those concepts map out the ideological terrain of *Macbeth,* a terrain which should be understood as a field of conflict, not a
"given."

I would argue, then, that Murray is wrong in attempting to collapse the present
moment of analysis back into the "eternity" of a past "wisdom." What, after all, are
those "well unified set of images," which give us "the wisdom of human experience," *about?* "Unreasoning womanhood," "eternal motherhood," mind as "a male
quality only," Murray tells us.[39] He points, I believe, to important elements in the
play, but he then requires that we *empathize* with its symbolic orderings without
reference of those orderings as embodying particular manoeuvres of *power.*

Those manoeuvres as they relate to "unreasoning womanhood" are spelled out
clearly enough in Krämer and Sprenger's *Malleus Maleficarum* (1486), the most
influential of all the Renaissance witchcraft treatises. In it, a section is dedicated to

[35]See Gordon J. Schochet, *Patriarchalism in Political Thought: The Authoritarian Family and Political Speculation and Attitudes Especially in Seventeenth Century England* (New York, 1975), pp. 37–98. For patriarchalism in the later part of the seventeenth century, see also James Daly, *Sir Robert Filmer and English Political Thought* (Toronto: U of Toronto P, 1979). It is worth noting that even More's *Utopia* is founded on the patriarchal family: see J. H. Hexter, *The Vision of Politics on the Eve of the Reformation* (New York: Basic Books, 1973), pp. 40–45.

[36]Jean Bodin, *The Six Bookes of a Commonweale,* trans. Richard Knolles (1606), reprinted, ed. Kenneth D. McRae, Harvard Political Classics (Cambridge, Mass.: Harvard UP, 1962), 1.2, p. 8. On the popularity of the *Six Bookes* in England, see Quentin Skinner, *The Foundations of Modern Political Thought* (Cambridge, 1978), II, p. 300.

[37]James I, *The Trew Law of Free Monarchies,* in *The Political Works of James I* (reprinted from the edition of 1606), intro. Charles H. McIlwain (Cambridge, Mass.: Harvard UP, 1918), p. 55.

[38]Natalie Z. Davis, "Women on Top: Symbolic Sexual Inversion and Political Disorder in Early Modern Europe," in *The Reversible World: Symbolic Inversion in Art and Society,* ed. Barbara B. Babcock (Ithaca: Cornell UP, 1978), p. 150.

[39]Murray, *op. cit.,* p. 39.

answering the question "Why Superstition is chiefly found in Women." The roots of witchcraft are there discovered to be in the very nature of women, a nature which includes her desire, following Eve, to betray mankind. "She is more carnal than a man"; "as she is a liar by nature, so in her speech she stings while she delights us"; "her heart is a net, and her hands are bands. He that pleaseth God shall escape from her; but he that is a sinner shall be caught by her"; "can he be called a free man whose wife governs him . . . ? I should call him not only a slave, but the vilest of slaves, even if he comes of the noblest family"; "nearly all the kingdoms of the world have been overthrown by woman." (All of these statements have analogues in *Macbeth*.) In the *Malleus*, misogyny leads to the conclusion that "it is no matter for wonder that there are more women than men found infected with the heresy of witchcraft."[40] Krämer and Sprenger's advocacy of a programme of ruthless repression is a logical consequence of their fear of a supernatural power in the hands of the powerless. For who would the powerless direct their power against if not the powerful?

If Krämer's and Sprenger's beliefs were grounded in medieval Christian traditions, similar beliefs can be found in modern African societies which have been analysed by anthropologists attempting to understand the social functions of such beliefs. Esther Goody, for example, observes that amongst the Gonja in Ghana only women are punished for witchcraft, and she accounts for this by showing the relation between witchcraft and the prohibition against aggression amongst women, since they have been consigned to an exclusively nurturing role:[41]

> There are two regular characteristics of the female domestic role. First, in the role of mother, a woman is a focus of emotional ties. . . . Then, as wife, woman is defined as subordinate to her husband. Aggression, if permitted, would threaten both these characteristics. . . . And if a woman strikes her husband with a stirring stick . . . he will become impotent; aggression in a woman's role renders a man powerless—it cannot be permitted.

A woman's refusal to be subordinated, then, is often accounted for by witchcraft. Similarly, Max Gluckman notes that[42]

> In Nupe the evil witches who kill are women. . . . Nadel seeks to answer why. He finds a striking conflict between the roles which, ideally, women ought to play and that many women in fact do. Ideally, a Nupe woman should be a good wife, subservient to her husband, bearing him many children, and staying at home to care for them and their father. In reality, a great deal of trade is in the hands of women.

Women seem to be particularly vulnerable to witchcraft accusations in patrilineal, patrilocal societies, where women are cut off from their own kin and expected to merge their interests with those of their husbands' kin.

[40]*Malleus Maleficarum*, pp. 120, 126, 127, 124, 124, 127.

[41]Esther Goody, "Legitimate and Illegitimate Aggression in a West African State," in *Witchcraft Confessions and Accusations*, ed. Mary Douglas, p. 241.

[42]Max Gluckman, "Moral Crises: Magical and Secular Solutions," in *The Allocation of Responsibility*, ed. Max Gluckman (Manchester: Manchester UP, 1972), p. 19.

Two versions of how women operate in this kind of situation are constructed in *Macbeth*. Lady Macduff submerges her interests in her husband's, and when he flees she is totally defenceless; Lady Macbeth actively pursues her husband's interests, but only those interests which separate him from his kin. In the latter case, this leads to Macbeth's murder of his cousin, to the isolation of the husband with his "dear wife" (3.2.36), cut off from "honour, love, obedience, troops of friends" (5.3.25), and finally, to the total isolation of Macbeth in the field of battle. But the play, concentrating increasingly on Macbeth himself as it develops, does not analyse the position of women; rather, it mobilizes the patriarchal fear of unsubordinated woman,[43] the unstable element to which Krämer and Sprenger attributed the overthrow of "nearly all the kingdoms of the world," to which the Gonja and the Nupe attribute witchcraft.

I am not proposing to conflate the imaginary society of *Macbeth* with Gonja or Nupe society. But I am arguing for the *general* relevance of anthropological and sociological models of the relation between witchcraft beliefs and structures of political and social dominance. We need such models, I believe, if we are to analyse, rather than repeat, the terms of the play itself. What I have attempted to show here is the use of witchcraft as a form of ideological closure within *Macbeth*, a returning of the disputed ground of politics to the undisputed ground of "Nature."

But the play is not, of course, *about* witchcraft, nor does the threat of the Biblical "Thou shalt not suffer a witch to live" (Exodus, 22.18) hang over *Macbeth* as it hangs over *The Witch of Edmonton* (1621), for instance. And it cannot be said that the witches in *Macbeth* provide the only explanatory element in the play. If their prophecies provide one motive for the killing of a king, the radical instability of the concept of "manliness" is sufficient to precipitate the deed. But it would be misleading to interpret this overdetermination as a *conflict* between supernatural and natural modes of explanation, since, within the cultural context, there was no necessity to choose between those modes. (For example, Mother Sawyer in *The Witch of Edmonton* is at first abused as a witch merely because, as she complains, "I am poor, deform'd and ignorant" [2.1.3]; but the fact that she is presented sympathetically as a scapegoat—the natural explanation—is not seen as contradicting the fact that she becomes a witch—the supernatural explanation—and therefore presumably "deserves" her death.) Nevertheless the coexistence of those modes suggests that the structural closures which I have been examining do not preclude a problematic relation between "highly" and "holily" (1.5.20–21).

---

[43]A fear which, in Davenant's version of *Macbeth*, Lady Macbeth herself is made to share:

You were a man
And by the Charter of your sex you should
have govern'd me.
                              (4.4.62–64)

Christopher Spencer, *Davenant's Macbeth* (New Haven: Yale UP, 1961), p. 132.

Lady Macbeth's Barren Sceptre

Carol Rutter with Sinead Cusack

Sinead Cusack graduated to Lady Macbeth from an apprenticeship in RSC takeovers—moving into parts created by other actresses—and a confident coming-of-age in a succession of major roles: Celia, Portia, Kate, Beatrice. She doesn't hold with glorifying her profession: in her terms, acting is not a mystery but a craft, and her roles emerge very practically out of the stuff of daily life. When she talks about her working methods, she moves rapidly from general observation to specific roles.

Early in the 1986 Stratford season, Sinead Cusack told the director of *Macbeth*, Adrian Noble, that some elements in the role of Lady Macbeth would be problematic for her.

He said, "What do you mean?" and I said, "I've just given birth! I have another baby. I'm going to find that area of her very difficult . . ." He told me not to worry, but I was very worried, because every time I came to that line "I have given suck, and know/How tender 'tis . . ."—I can't say it even now—I thought, "I'm never going to be able to speak that line. Not while I'm nursing my own baby." You're always left a bit raw after having a baby; I felt very vulnerable, and I was worried about that element coming into play too much in Lady Macbeth, but in fact I was able to incorporate that rawness into my own performance.

Indeed, the idea of maternity came close to the centre of her performance and the whole production. Sinead had strong images of Lady Macbeth and her relationship with Macbeth.

"I wanted people to see someone who had warmth and fecundity; I liked the idea of her hair being fair. I didn't see her as a very clever woman—she is a grasper of opportunity.

She knows she has Macbeth in thrall and she can make him do anything. And yet she has no knowledge of the hell that she's letting loose in his mind and his life, and what he will become. Never for a second does she have a notion of that."

In fact, she had begun imagining her Lady Macbeth when she was still a teenager:

The extract "Lady Macbeth's Barren Sceptre" from *Clamorous Voices: Shakespeare's Women Today* by Carol Rutter et al., edited by Faith Evans, first published in Great Britain by The Women's Press Ltd, 1988, 34 Great Sutton Street, London EC1V ODX, reprinted on pages 119–133, is used by permission of The Women's Press.

from about the age of fifteen, when I first read the play. I wanted to play her very young because I had a sense of a Lady Macbeth I had never seen. I wanted her to be young, very beautiful, and to have a sort of amorality, a complete ignorance of right and wrong, the sort of blinkered vision of a child who grabs what it wants with no thought of the consequence. I wanted a woman in white. That vision lived with me throughout my twenties, but no one asked me to play it. I hadn't the craft or the skills, and anyway no one had that view of the role. It was traditionally played by someone older. In black.

It wasn't until she was in her late thirties—ironically, too old to qualify for the part in her fantasy, but now mature enough in her craft to attempt it—that she was offered Lady Macbeth opposite Jonathan Pryce. The character she had outlined in her head, however, still survived virtually intact.

I told Adrian about this vision of mine and we thought how we might bring an element of it to bear. One of the things I was adamant about right from the beginning was that the first view you would have of the Macbeths would be of a successful, blessed couple. I wanted the audience to be drawn to them right from the beginning of the play. Macbeth—a poet, warrior, philosopher, an extraordinary man of vision, adored by everyone around him. They all speak of him in hushed tones. Married to this beautiful woman. Macbeth and his wife are the golden couple—like the Kennedys—who have everything.

Everything, that is, except one thing: they have no children.

Lady Macbeth says, "I have given suck . . ." So where is that baby? What happened to their child? I'm not certain who asked the question first or whether we all had the idea simultaneously, but as we explored it in rehearsal, we decided that the Macbeths had had a child and that the child had died. The line can be interpreted differently, but that's the interpretation we chose, and as the idea grew it seemed to have a beautiful logic.

So as rehearsals progressed, it was this bleak biological datum—"He hath no children"—that began to focus the tragedy. *Macbeth* became not so much a political tragedy of multiple betrayal as a domestic drama, the destruction of a marriage. Lacking children, the Macbeths' energies re-directed themselves into obsessions that travestied creativity: they killed other people's children, turning their kingdom into a wasteland. But when they discovered what it meant to hold a barren sceptre, their childlessness doubly mocked them. There could be no success without succession.

The image of the lost child became the most potent reference point in Noble's production. First suggested in a blood-smeared child rescued from the battlefield in the opening scene, it reappeared in other bloody children: the one who rises from the witches' cauldron, the one who "from my mother's womb untimely ripped"—Macduff— bleeds Macbeth at the end.

This Macbeth liked having children around. He liked children's games. The witches' apparitions were children, seductive in white nightgowns, playing blind man's bluff with the kneeling king on the floor, giggling their predictions into his ear, then circling him in an endless procession of Banquo's future issue. These same white-gowned children then became Macduff's ambushed family. One of them sat on the floor playing with the assassin's bootstraps before he was picked up and stabbed.

Sinead felt that such images found a contemporary expression for the evil that the play is exploring. The abuse of children is the ultimate taboo, the death of a child the ultimate grief.

That sort of loss, the loss of a child, is so huge, so massive, that it can either draw you closer together or separate you, or it can turn the need for a child into an obsessive need for something else. If you've lost a child and there are no more children, you either leave the man or you become obsessive about the man and about his happiness and security. That's the avenue I chose to go up as Lady Macbeth—that she had turned, not in on herself, but completely in on him.

Marital claustrophobia became a key image of the production as a whole.

But Adrian and I didn't really talk about the play until the eve of the first rehearsal. That wasn't a good idea. I kept asking to be involved in discussions; Jonathan Pryce was allowed to participate but not me. I wanted to talk to the designer, Bob Crowley—but that didn't happen either. Eventually we had a meeting in London and I was shown the set model and costume designs.

There it was—my nightmare! I was dressed in black, the set was a black box. Macbeth was in black. I thought, "This is it, this is the production I didn't want to be in." They said, "What do you want?" and I said, "I want to be in white, or anything but black. Don't predispose the audience right from the beginning of the play to the tragedy and horror and evil. That'll come. But let it come."

Sinead won on the dress. She played Lady Macbeth in green. ("They wouldn't countenance white.") She first appeared not as the black widow spider of theatre tradition but as a slight green figure with a broad halo of fair hair.

She changed her mind about the black box. She came to see it as "an inspired piece of design" that "helped us as actors because it had a wonderful theatrical sense." It began as a battlefield, impaled with a thicket of torn battle standards, across which three shuffling hags picked their way, rolling over corpses, salvaging from under one that live but blood-soaked child. When, at the end of the battle sequence, these flags were struck by Duncan's victorious army, the black box became Dunsinane, an emptied-out space that seemed vast because it contained only the small figure of Lady Macbeth. For Sinead, the place seemed double.

That first entrance, when I walked on stage and I had those black walls around me, I could feel I was actually on the battlements of the castle—I had a very strong sense of that, I always brought it on with me—but at the same time I could have been in one of those small stone rooms that are found in Scottish castles.

Bob Crowley's set often had this paradoxical sense of seeming to double as something else. It was an illusionist's box where any number of conjuror's tricks might defeat the eye. Doors suddenly appeared, stairs shot out of flush walls. Then the walls themselves began to move. The Macbeths' world got smaller and smaller until it felt like a coffin.

Pryce played Macbeth as a man who lurched from hero to madman to clown, first armour-plated and draped in black tartan, then bizarrely clerical, finally clownish, ending up in huge boots and slack stockings. He rolled up his shirt-sleeves before killing Duncan.

Sinead's Lady Macbeth marked her journey to confusion with equivalent land-marks: sensual, intimate with her husband before the murder; rigid behind a cos-metic mask after the coronation; transformed into a demented child in the sleep-walking scene. Her first entrance (1.5) was restless, almost fugitive. She was clutching a letter, the one in which Macbeth reports the witches' prediction. She was looking for somewhere to read it alone.

The decision you have to make about the letter is whether she's read it before, whether it's a letter she's had clasped to her bosom for some time. After trying out various things, I came to the conclusion that she had just been handed the letter, and that she'd headed for that particular space in order to read it. It was interest-ing how we arrived at that isolation. There are other choices, you know. It doesn't have to be as isolated as we made it, and it certainly doesn't have to be as still as we made it.

During rehearsal I was experimenting all over the place. I couldn't say the lines without moving. I was using my hands, my body, I was all over the stage. At one point I sat in front of a mirror and daubed lipstick all over my face, but I still found I couldn't simply say the lines: I hadn't got the courage. And then finally one day Adrian said, "Just cut out all of that, just stand in the middle of the stage and say them," and I found it very difficult indeed.

In Sinead's performance the words of the letter tumbled out. Her eyes could scarcely keep pace with her mouth, which seemed already to know what the letter contained:

> They met me in the day of success, and I have learned by the perfectest report they have more in them than mortal knowledge. When I burned in desire to question them further, they made themselves air, into which they vanished . . . these Weird Sisters saluted me, and referred me to the coming on of time with, "Hail, king that shalt be."

When she reads that letter it's almost uncanny for her, because she thinks, "This supernatural news that he's giving me about these three sisters is confirming some-thing that I had already envisioned, that we had already talked about." The letter is almost familiar to her. *That experience with the Weird Sisters—almost as if she knew it would happen. It's as if suddenly everything comes right. Macbeth ought to be Duncan's successor. There was no blood succession in Scotland, the crown was not handed on to the son automatically. Macbeth was the natural heir. They had talked about his succession.*

Had they discussed the murder of Duncan? I don't think they had. But they had talked about Macbeth being King.

Her own view, the one she'd always held, was that if he wasn't named successor by Duncan then the way through would be to kill. Suddenly, there's the letter with its supernatural news—and the whole universe is endorsing her view, saying to her, "You're right, your vision is correct, and here's the proof." The idea is familiar because she's been through it all in her head already. And here it is: "You're on the right track. You have every right to this. He deserves it."

Macbeth is a capable killer. His reported soldiership in scene 2 proves that. But can he murder?

She knows that where he's weak is in the honour stakes. He's got too much honour. So he's a little bit susceptible, his honour might take away his courage at the crucial moment of murder.

Lady Macbeth was strong enough for both. In the first half of her first soliloquy she weighed up her husband, tapping the folded letter against her palm:

Glamis thou art, and Cawdor, and shalt be
What thou art promised. Yet do I fear thy nature:
    . . . What thou wouldst highly
That wouldst thou holily, wouldst not play false,
And yet wouldst wrongly win.

Lady Macbeth's naïve assessment of her husband's nature constantly stunned Sinead when she detached herself from the role and looked at the character.

She has this extraordinary seeming knowledge of him, that he may not be able to do it: if she did but know! And it's only seeming knowledge because Lady Macbeth has no real knowledge of what he will become. She lacks imagination.

She was musing in the soliloquy, musing about him. The actual acceptance of killing, and the acceptance of Duncan being killed, had already taken place in her mind. But murder—that sort of killing was against everything Macbeth believes in. He is an "honourable man." She's on to him so fast: how will I persuade him? How will I deal with it? How will I kill . . . It seemed to me at this point in this scene that the murderer is going to be her. She will kill.

And then it happens again. Another of those supernatural markers drops her way, as if confirming her route. A messenger enters. "The King comes here tonight." She can't believe her ears. "Thou'rt mad to say it!" Sinead's Lady Macbeth was instantly alert.

The minute she sees the opening she says, "Now we do it. Now's the perfect time— everything is right. Duncan is being given to us on a plate."

But then a new misgiving shook her. Would *she* be strong enough? Lady Macbeth dismissed the messenger. Vulnerable and alone, she began to pray:

> Come, you spirits
> That tend on mortal thoughts, unsex me here
> And fill me from the crown to the toe top-full
> Of direst cruelty . . . Come to my woman's breasts
> And take my milk for gall, you murdering ministers.

Sinead saw the speech as a bargain struck with those "murdering ministers": she was willing to renounce her sexuality, her erotic power over Macbeth, in exchange for that other power, the kind that comes with a crown.

In rehearsal one of the areas we explored was their sexual obsession. Sexually he was totally dependent on her. He needed that sex in order to reassure himself of his own values, his own strength. And she knows, she knows she can play on that. She knows she can get him to do things because of that. And she uses it.

In the soliloquy she is saying, "I will throw away my sexuality, I will give it up, I will never enjoy those areas again, I will never have children again—if I can have this. It's a bargain I've made with the devil. In order to achieve this for him, I will deny my self."

Yet the pernicious bargain was more, it was an admission of vulnerability.

Lady Macbeth knows that she loves Macbeth. She knows that she has tenderness and vulnerability where he is concerned. She knows that that is her weakness, that she is capable of love. Love of a child, love of a man. So now, when all the signs are saying, "The time is right," and pointing her the way she must urge him to go, she says, "I can't do it. I've got to get help from outside. I can't do it on my own because my love will let me be weakened into letting him fail." She invokes the spirits to make her strong. Not "unsex me"—make me an un-woman, a pseudo-man; but "unsex me"—make me invulnerable to love. And then Macbeth walks on stage and she plays the old games.

Pryce's Macbeth materialised behind her, out of a black hole at the back.

I didn't see him; I felt him. What we wanted was for him to be completely silent but for her to know that he's there by a kind of kinetic energy they both react to. (How did I know he was there? That isn't mysterious—Jonathan pants on stage.)

The effect was of two white faces eerily superimposed on one another while their bodies, miles apart, recoiled as if from a physical shock. That physical energy became transferred to the words, all those interweaving half-lines.

We became locked into each other's language:

Macbeth:	My dearest love,
	Duncan comes here tonight.
Lady Macbeth:	And when goes hence?
Macbeth:	Tomorrow, as he purposes.
Lady Macbeth:	O never
	Shall sun that morrow see!

We felt that there was a kind of synchronicity between them. It's as if they're in tune with each other's minds. They're so enmeshed, the couple. When they grow apart, at the end of the murder scene, you find that they're talking different languages, but here they both know what they are talking about. So we didn't kiss on the greeting—"My dearest love"—we decided to face the business first. After "Never/Shall sun that morrow see!" it's as if the kiss is a confirmation of both their thoughts, a physical sealing of a compact. The way Jonathan played it, it's as if Macbeth needed to be enclosed by her, in order to be able to deal with the idea, to encompass it. He clung to me like the lines cling to each other.

And then Lady Macbeth says, "He that's coming/Must be provided for." It's an amazing line. She's going to play hostess to Duncan at Dunsinane, and "provide" is what gracious hostesses always do. It's a wonder of a line to play because the reverberations do the acting for you, make the audience go "Aaaagh!"

"Provided for" here means murdered, and the poise of her euphemism marks her detachment. Not from her husband—they left the scene "hanging on to each other"—but from the killing. "You notice she never actually says, 'kill.' " The Macbeths would never be closer than in that exit.

In the following scene (1.6) they were already unaccountably apart. Duncan arrives at Dunsinane, but Macbeth is not at the door to greet him. For Lady Macbeth, playing hostess,

that was very awkward . . . Both should have been there. But he's not. She apologises, and Duncan makes a joke of it, but it is a departure from protocol that is noted. She's covering up for him. She knows he can't face that ceremony because of what he is about to do. So she substitutes for him, with great eloquence and ritual. And we never see Macbeth with Duncan again.

Sinead considers the direction of this scene "inspired." Duncan's battle-weary men, still grimy with blood and dirt, were slumped against the castle walls, waiting.

All those rough soldiers were lying around, and then this woman swept through them in a green dress and a red shawl. To those men she was like a vision, a drink of

*water in the desert. I felt very strongly that the scene had to be beautiful, and she had
to look welcoming, to highlight the horror of what she was doing—and all those men
had to react to her, either sexually or as if to a mother, but all of them had to react.*

They did. Men who looked dead came alive, and followed her into Dunsinane.

Sinead's view of Lady Macbeth as society hostess came to the fore in the following scene (1.7), when her husband failed her yet again. Dinner was being
served somewhere off stage. *Again* Macbeth had departed from protocol.

*Very, very badly. We're supposed to be entertaining the King at a banquet in
his honour, and Macbeth left Duncan, he left the King, and to cap it all, he didn't
come back! Imagine—he gets up and leaves and people think, oh, it's a phone call
or he's gone to have a pee, but fifteen, twenty minutes elapse, and the King is sitting there . . . That's frivolous, but if you put it in a modern context—the Kennedys
again—you can see how much it mattered.*

In fact, Macbeth had fled, seeking refuge where he could hammer things out:
"If it were done when 'tis done, then 'twere well/It were done quickly." But what
if it's not done when it's done; what if that is only the beginning?

Lady Macbeth pursued him. This time it was she who materialised out of the
doorway behind, blocking all the light that had flooded through it from the banqueting hall, condensing it into a grotesque shadow. Her question "Why have you
left the chamber?" was not looking for an answer but for a fight.

*She has to get him. She knows she has to strengthen his resolve. So she goads him as
far as she can, sexually and in all kinds of ways. "Was the hope drunk?" "Art thou
afeard?" Are you a man? Is this all you're worth? She uses everything! Every weapon.*

*But as I was saying the words, part of me was also silently appealing to him,
soothing him, as if he were a child: "I know what you're going through, and I don't
want you to be going through it." But she herself found the strength from somewhere (maybe those "murdering ministers" stepped in!) not to take him in her
arms and say, "Hush, hush, it's all right, you needn't do it."*

Because he *has* to do it; there is a higher purpose. Macbeth covered his head
with his arms to block out the relentless noise, then lashed out: he slapped her
hard across the mouth. It stunned her, but she continued her verbal battering:

*She goes on and on and on, and finally when she sees that her clever tongue, her
sexuality, her goading, nothing is going to work on him—then she pulls out the one
area that she's never used, the secret area of the child . . .*

*The slap—for the Macbeths that moment was nothing. That slap was part of
our natural physicality. Jonathan did hit me every night, and made the unfortu-
nate mistake of saying so in the press, and someone wrote in saying, "Why is she
such a wimp to take it?" But the scene was such that I believe if we'd done a fake*

slap, we would have destroyed that electric current of violence between us. I shouldn't admit these things because actors should be able to fake slaps very easily and still be able to keep the mood, but I was convinced we wouldn't be able to sustain that extraordinary power if we were doing a fake number. I much preferred a stinging slap every night. Technically Jonathan is very clever and I think only on three occasions did he get me on the jawbone, but mostly it was absolutely flat on and it would sting for a minute and then it was gone.

The slap was a step in a process of escalation. But it was not the critical moment. The critical moment was what came next, the area she'd never used, the secret area of the child. "I have given suck, and know/How tender 'tis to love the babe that milks me." But she would have "dashed the brains out, had I so sworn as you/Have done to this." What she says about the baby, and his reaction to it, is completely divorced from their natural exchange. The use of the baby—that was the worst, that was the real sin. And that's when he knows how much she wants this for him, when he understands the sacrifice that she's making. And that's when he grabbed her, held her, and they were both crying.

His response to his barren wife was a bit of a joke: "Bring forth men-children only!" He was trying to regain control. He was using black humour to restore things to some kind of equilibrium.

Pryce's Macbeth constantly faced crisis with clowning. Later, the role would trap him, but for now, he saw the immediate future, the murder, as a huge joke. What a joke it would be to smear Duncan's servants with his blood! They left the scene laughing, but sharing the joke meant sharing the job.

And while Macbeth was about it, Lady Macbeth was alone again on stage.

She is very frightened. She says, "The doors are open." She sees what he is doing, not actually, but in her mind; she is imagining it as it happened and she's beginning to fracture. The line, "Had he not resembled/My father as he slept, I had done't," shocks her. She's trying to hang on. And then she hears a noise, and she goes to the stairs, and then he erupts from the chamber. Panic, panic, panic! She doesn't understand what he's talking about—the language is coming apart! She says to him,

Lady Macbeth:	Did you not speak?		
Macbeth:		When?	
Lady Macbeth:			Now.
Macbeth:			As I descended?
Lady Macbeth:	Ay.		
Macbeth:	Hark.		

And then she sees the blood. Now in that moment when she sees the blood, something happens to her gut. For her, the sight is horrible. It shocks her, the reality of it. She has imagined the killing, but people who have visions are often shocked by the reality when it comes. When she faces the blood on his hands it's like a blow to the stomach. And then she gets over it. As an actress I tried to show just a little click in my brain that I could store up to use and refer back to later when I had blood on my own hands.

After that we began talking different languages. We who had needed to touch each other all the time grew distant. When he had killed, neither of us wanted to touch the other.

She tried to follow him, tried to understand.

She's saying, "What do you mean, you heard voices?" She's trying to make it practical: well, of course, "There are two lodged together," that's why you heard the voices saying a prayer. And he says, "I could not say 'amen,'" and she says, "Consider it not so deeply": it doesn't matter. But she realises he's gone somewhere that she doesn't understand; she can't bring him back. It's as if she's seeing him drifting, drifting, she's trying to pull him back, but he won't come.

Because she's been frightened by seeing the blood, she can't bring her usual power to bear. I wanted to touch him, but he drew away. We couldn't do what we were used to doing. For the first time in our lives. We weren't touching. And she's panicking.

Then she sees that he's brought the daggers! God—he was so stupid! I shrieked at him. That was the Irish fishwife in me. But he wouldn't take them back. So I did. Trying to make it practical. She went up those stairs—she rubbed her hands in Duncan's blood—and the woman who came down those stairs was a child. She was stretching out her hands like a child—half guilty, half defiant.

The fingers were splayed, the shoulders slightly hunched, the eyes feverish, the intonation a child's.

Something's clicked in her brain. Again, she's taken too much. It was a character shift. I don't know where it came from—stretching out the hands like a child—but it was a great help to me for her descent into the murky areas below.

This gesture, which Sinead would repeat in the sleepwalking scene in Act 4, marked the crossroads. From now on, Lady Macbeth was different: the wife of the murderer became Queen of Scotland. And as Queen, Sinead did wear black.

The next time we see her she has been crowned and she is dressed in full regalia, in a black velvet dress, tightly corseted, a Tudor cape up to her ears, a ruff that came right up to her chin, and the crown on top. When I had to put on those huge heavy robes I thought I'd never be able to bear the weight—it was amazing to stand there bowed down by those clothes. It was a great design point. It's a play that's constantly talking about borrowed robes.

I was very keen that the softness we had seen in her first scene—the hair, the warm make-up, the ruffles down her back—should be gone. After the coronation I wanted her to be very constricted—her hair pulled back, her skin almost stretched across her cheek-bones, whitened, and with blood-red lipstick on—I hadn't worn lipstick before. It was a cover-up, saying, "Now I am the Queen, and I will look like the Queen," while at the same time she was disintegrating inside. From that point onwards she is keeping the façade up—and the façade is magnificent.

There was more killing to be done but Lady Macbeth had no stomach for it.

In rehearsal we discussed endlessly whether she knew Macbeth was going to kill Banquo, and we came to the conclusion that indeed she did, and she didn't want him to do it. She had switched strategies entirely. Her view was, "Look, we've got it. You're King! It doesn't matter whether they suspect, you're inviolate. We cannot be touched!"

But she knows he's contemplating the next one, and she thinks, "No, no, it's getting out of hand, don't take that further step . . ."

Macbeth and Lady Macbeth have a little scene (3.2) just after he has organised Banquo's murder. She starts the scene with a servant, asking him to tell the King she'd like to speak with him. And then, alone, she says, "Naught's had, all's spent,/Where our desire is got without content." It's so poignant and so bewildered. She's saying, "I've got everything I wanted for him, and he's got everything he ever wanted, but we have no contentment. Why?" She doesn't understand. She hasn't faced any of the realities—there's just this blind, blinkered vision of what life is going to be.

"How now, my Lord? Why do you keep alone," her line to Macbeth when he entered, was very plaintive; it meant, "Why don't you love me any more?" She knows that not only has she lost his love, she has lost her power as well, power to change him or to comfort him. Without him loving her, she can't do anything for him. Or with him. She knows it—he's drifting, drifting, and she can't follow.

And he's frightening her now, too. He's talking of more killing. He says, "Thou know'st that Banquo and his Fleance lives." That's when she knows he's going to kill again, and that he's going to kill Fleance, he's going to kill the child.

They had completely reversed roles now. Lady Macbeth needed no more. She didn't care about what was out there, she had what she wanted—for him. But he needs to secure his position now, and keep his paranoia at bay by killing off anyone who's suspicious. And she knows he's going to kill the child! It's excruciating . . .

But then, just for a moment, it looked as if everything was going to be all right. He came very close to me—"Come, seeling night,/Scarf up the tender eye of pitiful day"—and he passed his hand across my face, and we were about to kiss, and she thought, "It's going to be all right! Thank God! He wants to kiss me!"

And we're getting closer, and it's going to be all right, and then the maniac reared his head. He suddenly shouted, "Waaaaww!" and I jumped. It was horrible, horrible. And then he smeared all my lipstick across my face. He put his hand in my mouth and yanked down my jaw, mocking a kiss. It was a travesty of the embrace, of how it used to be. He was throwing their sexuality back in her face, saying, "That no longer has power in my life," scoffing at her with that bark of a laugh. His mania was staggeringly dangerous and she was terrified, terrified. And deeply hurt. Lost.

By the end of the banquet, two scenes later, Lady Macbeth knew that the marriage was over. The scene (3.4) was set on a narrow strip along the front of the stage, across its entire width.

A bit of the stage rose up; a white sheet covered it: that was our "table." Macbeth was at one end and Lady Macbeth was at the other and all the Thanes were sitting with their backs to the audience. We did the gracious bit—"Everybody have a nice time"—and then Macbeth went berserk! He suddenly shouted, "Which of you have done this?" Nobody knew what he was talking about.

And then we were having this terrible row, the King and Queen, right in the middle of the Thanes. Normally directors set the argument to the side.

The embarrassment of all those people watching . . . awful! She was trying to cut the others out, trying to stop him and he was going on and on, he just didn't see them, didn't care about them. It was the most embarrassing thing you could imagine for a wife. She was saying through clenched teeth, "Don't do this here, please, let's get out," trying to ease him out, "let's do it somewhere else, just don't do it in front of them!"

Because the Thanes' backs were to the audience, everything was cast on our two faces. I could sense them, their embarrassment, their suspicion, watching to see him incriminate himself.

Lady Macbeth saw her husband on the brink of madness and, despite her façade, knew that she was there too. Unlike him, though, she didn't see Banquo's ghost.

It was terribly dangerous, because I didn't know what he was talking about!

At the end of the banquet scene I remember sitting watching him across that table—we couldn't have been farther apart, and there's such a lot of time for Lady Macbeth to watch him in the scene—watching, and knowing that in my attempt to give him what I believed he wanted, I had unleashed a monster. He was completely gone from me and he would never come back. It was a feeling of absolute hopelessness. It was complete loss.

In one of his convulsive gestures, lunging at a spectre no one else could see, Macbeth had pulled the table-cloth off the table. Then he sat stiffly, his Thanes having scattered in disarray, trying to repair the damage by smoothing out the table-cloth.

It was so banal, that gesture of setting the table again! That's what I liked about our production. Again and again we were allowed as actors to not be those huge tragic figures but sometimes to be terribly domestic, terribly mundane, so that it brought the level of that evil into an area we all know.

The Macbeths were once again alone. Physically, though, they were estranged, polarised at opposite ends of the table. Macbeth had been changed by killing and he no longer needed her.

She's been replaced by this sort of mania, this paranoia. She says at the end of the scene, "You lack the season of all natures, sleep." I put my hand through his hair. It was the first time he'd let me touch him since the murder, and he took my hand and he held it to his face in agony. *Then he just dropped it: "Come, we'll to sleep." As if he'd said, "Right," like clapping up a bargain on some livestock, "let's go to bed." The way Jonathan played that line was wonderful! So threatening. That's when she realised the full extent of his madness.*

And she recoiled from the word "sleep" because it wasn't a natural continuation of the touch. In the normal run of things, if we'd touched in that way we would indeed have gone to bed. But the way he said it I knew we wouldn't be going to bed to love each other, there wouldn't be a natural continuation of any gentleness: that would never happen again. What he went on to say was even worse: "My strange and self-abuse/Is the initiate fear that wants hard use." That is, "I need more, I've got to have more, I want more killing." "We are yet but young in deed" wasn't weary or desperate. It was apologetic. He meant, "Look, I'm sorry about what happened at the banquet. I was feeling a bit shaky, and the reason I fell apart was that, actually, I haven't had enough practice, that's all. I'll get better." But he'd left her behind. He'd gone. Literally. He walked off stage.

Lady Macbeth followed behind. The witches—the director shifted a scene here—were coming on, picking up bits of the ruined banquet to use for their cauldron scene. She saw them. She looked at them, and then she looked away as if to say, "No, I'm not seeing that," and exited. There was no shock or recoil. It was just the meshing of two worlds.

Or the unhinging of a mind. The separate exits marked their divorce, took them into different worlds. Macbeth sought out other women—he went to the witches—while Lady Macbeth went mad. And although the play itself broadens out, as the scene shifts to England and follows Malcolm's march on Scotland, Macbeth's walls were closing in and Lady Macbeth's world had shrunk to a single room where she walked in her sleep and played out, night after night, the murder of Duncan.

For the actress, there is now a long off-stage wait, until 5.1.

I would go to my dressing room and have a great time—a strong cup of tea, a fag— and then I messed myself up. People hated the way I looked in the sleepwalking scene and I don't give a tuppenny! I loved it.

I had on this gown of white cotton, almost like a hospital gown, and then I had Macbeth's jumper on—the one he'd worn under his armour: she'd been sleeping in it. I wanted to give the impression that she'd been in that nightgown for a long time, that she wasn't dressing during the day, and the nightgown was soiled. And then one day in rehearsal—it's ridiculous how these things happen, they have no logic to them—Adrian said to me, "Tuck the nightie up into your knickers, I think you're going to paddle in the sea." Of course—washing her hands!

I'm a sleepwalker myself. Once when I was a child my parents were having a party; at about eleven o'clock I emerged from my bedroom and I walked through the hallway into the garden and took off my nightie. I dug a hole in the garden and I buried my nightdress. And then I went back to bed. My parents told me that my sleepwalking was characterised by speed. I was very busy in my sleep, and I found that a great help, coming down fast, in the sleepwalking scene. I felt that her particular brand of unrest would be those frantic little devil-thoughts that you can't knock out of your mind, devil-thoughts that keep coming back—about blood, about blood. You know when you're panicking, frantically panicking, and these little shooting thoughts are hitting you and getting embroiled and all mixed up in your head and you can't stop the voices, you can't stop the sounds: that's the sort of unrest I pictured her as having, and that's certainly the way the sleepwalking speech is written—erratic, disjointed.

What I found I had to do in rehearsal was to clarify absolutely in my head what each of those thoughts reminded me of, what situations they were pictures of. It's terribly easy to generalise madness or unrest or panic into one long blur, but you have to isolate each single thought so that it's absolutely clear to you where the picture—where those words—comes from. It took me ages and ages to do that.

I ran down the stairs and then I turned and I held out my hands—it was that same spasmodic child gesture from after the murder when I showed Macbeth Duncan's blood on my hands—only it wasn't Macbeth standing there, it was my gentlewoman and the physician. I saw Macbeth. As I thrust out my hands to display the blood to him, the candle slipped out of my hand and my woman caught it, but I was already walking forward. I knelt and starting putting stuff all over my face. I was looking in a mirror and making myself up to be Queen. To be the very, very beautiful Queen.

Then I was rubbing, rubbing. "Yet here's a spot." "Out, damned spot!" Each of those angle turns in the speech was a new picture. "One: two"—the clock strikes, she's hearing the bell she signalled Macbeth with when everything was "provided"—"why then,'tis time to do't." And we've got to do it. The next thought that came—"Hell is murky!"—was utterly bereft. She was using loss, the loss of him, the loss of the child. Without him she didn't know where to go. Hell is murky and she's lost her way; she doesn't know the way through.

Then all the old gestures began to echo what had gone before. "Fie, my lord, fie! A soldier and afeard?" was very prim; "What need we fear . . . none can call our power to accompt" was irritable and steely together—one can imagine that she said many times, "We are untouchable!" But the next picture pushes in—talk about untouchable! "Yet who would have thought the old man to have had so much blood in him?" I was looking at Duncan's body again. Those Scottish castles have lots of very small stone rooms. It was easy to imagine one of those little bedchambers covered in blood from wall to wall.

I played a madness in this scene that I don't think has been there in other productions. It was a mind that had disintegrated into shards—that's how I imagined her—rather than a retrospective, reflective consideration of my life. I couldn't play that option. I tried a few times in rehearsals, but it didn't work. I felt this desolate child saying, "We can do it—we can—no we can't—I've lost him. I've lost him!" A mind in shards.

On the "Oh! Oh! Oh!" I collapsed on the floor. But then I pulled myself together, in queenly fashion, took my little pot of carmine, made up my lips with that queen-red lipstick, put my carmine away, looked down at my hand—and saw blood on my fingers! It was the carmine, but I saw Duncan's blood! I went berserk then and began scrabbling in the earth. I tried to rub the blood off the floor, but then the floor suddenly shot out—a plank in the boards shot forward—and this place was turning into a gallery built over hell!

Technically, one of the things I found useful was the idea that when the plank shot out, I had my battlement: I walked forward, out on the battlement, and I was going to throw myself over! That was the moment when I was going to kill myself—only I couldn't, and I retreated, pulling myself together, saying, "Wash your hands; put on your nightgown."

And then that last line, "I tell you yet again, Banquo's buried, he cannot come out on's grave." Adrian Noble gave me a note on that line: she's saying, "No— please—this can't be happening," she's trying to persuade herself, to hold their madness at bay. It's an absolute panic attack. She's shaking. "Don't say he's come out of his grave, because if we admit to that one, we're lost."

But that's exactly what she was, lost, and these are Lady Macbeth's last lines in the play. The ravaged sleepwalker, showing only the vestiges of the golden girl she had been, recalled the witches' paradox, "Fair is foul and foul is fair," for the beauty was defaced, and, in winning, Lady Macbeth lost everything. The murderer ended up a suicide. For Sinead Cusack, the end of Lady Macbeth's play was "Lonely. So lonely. Utter desolation. I couldn't have done it in my twenties."

Escaping the Matrix: The Construction of Masculinity in *Macbeth* and *Coriolanus*

Janet Adelman

Just before Lear rushes out into the storm, he prays to the absent gods to "touch [him] with noble anger,/And let not women's weapons, water-drops,/Stain [his] man's cheeks" (2.4.278–80): threatened by the "mother" within (2.4.56), he attempts to mobilize manly anger against her. But Lear cannot sustain his anger; and in the end, after his great rage has passed, he dissolves mercifully into relationship with the mother he has made of Cordelia. The drive toward masculine autonomy diverted in him is in effect deflected onto Edmund, who becomes the standard-bearer for masculinity as he orders Cordelia's death; and it is resurrected in Macbeth and Coriolanus, each of whom similarly constructs his exaggerated and blood-thirsty masculinity as an attempt to ward off vulnerability to the mother.[1] For the cannibalistic witch-mothers Lear finds in Goneril and Regan are resurrected in Lady Macbeth and Volumnia; and fatherless, these sons are terribly subject to their power. The initially defining act for both of them thus turns on re-imagining the origin of masculine selfhood: both Macbeth's early victory over Macdonwald and the conquest of Corioli that gives Coriolanus his name figure the

From Janet Adelman, *Suffocating Mothers: Fantasies of Maternal Origin in Shakespeare's Plays, "Hamlet" to "The Tempest"* (New York: Routledge, Chapman and Hall, 1992), pp. 130–64. Reproduced by permission of Johns Hopkins Press, Routledge, and the author. The original footnotes have been renumbered and shortened with the author's permission.

[1]The chapter from which this essay was taken combines two previous essays (on *Coriolanus* in 1978; on *Macbeth* in 1985). Though each of those essays dealt with the construction of a rigid male identity as a defense against overwhelming maternal power, they did so in slightly different terms. The differences between them reflect what I have learned from a group of critics engaged with feminism and object-relations psychoanalysis between 1978 and 1985: especially Richard Wheeler, Madelon Gohlke Sprengnether, Coppélia Kahn, Carol Neely, Peter Erickson, Murray Schwartz, and David Wilbern. For the specific connections between *Macbeth* and *Coriolanus*, see especially Gohlke ("'I Wooed Thee with My Sword': Shakespeare's Tragic Paradigms," reprinted in this volume, pp. 46–60), Kahn (*Man's Estate: Masculine Identity in Shakespeare* [Berkeley: U of California P, 1981], pp. 151–92), and Wheeler (*Shakespeare's Development and the Problem Comedies* [Berkeley: U of California P, 1981], pp. 203–13), each of whom notes that the plays share a common concern with establishing a defensive masculinity; in particular, Kahn's chapter title—"The Milking Babe and the Bloody Man in *Coriolanus* and *Macbeth*"—indicates the similarity of our arguments. Linda Bamber also analyzes the two plays together but interprets their similarity differently: for her, the absence of a true feminine Other in both plays prevents the development of true manliness in their heroes (*Comic Women, Tragic Men: A Study of Gender and Genre in Shakespeare* [Stanford, Calif.: Stanford UP, 1982], pp. 20, 91–107).

decisive masculine act as a bloody rebirth, replacing the dangerous maternal origin through the violence of self-creation. For both heroes, as for Troilus, heroic masculinity turns on leaving the mother behind. Or on seeming to leave her behind: for both plays construct the exaggerated masculinity of their heroes simultaneously as an attempt to separate from the mother and as the playing out of her bloodthirsty will; both enact the paradox through which the son is never more the mother's creature than when he attempts to escape her.

Maternal power in *Macbeth* is not embodied in the figure of a particular mother (as it is in *Coriolanus*); it is instead diffused throughout the play, evoked primarily by the figures of the witches and Lady Macbeth. Largely through Macbeth's relationship to them, the play becomes (like *Coriolanus*) a representation of primitive fears about male identity and autonomy itself, about those looming female presences who threaten to control one's actions and one's mind, to constitute one's very self, even at a distance. When Macbeth's first words echo those we have already heard the witches speak—"So foul and fair a day I have not seen" (1.3.38); "Fair is foul, and foul is fair" (1.1.11)—we are in a realm that questions the very possibility of autonomous identity. As with Richard III, the maternal constitutes the suffocating matrix from which he must break free; and as with Richard, his solution will be to hew his way out with a bloody axe.[2]

This fantasy of escape in fact haunts *Macbeth*. In its last moments, as Macbeth feels himself increasingly hemmed in by enemies, the stage resonates with variants of his repeated question, "What's he,/That was not born of woman?" (5.7.2–3; for variants, see 5.3.4, 6; 5.7.11, 13; 5.8.13, 31). Repeated seven times, Macbeth's allusion to the witches' prophecy—"none of woman born/Shall harm Macbeth" (4.1.80–81)—becomes virtually a talisman to ward off danger; even after he has begun to doubt the equivocation of the fiend (5.5.43), mere repetition of the phrase seems to Macbeth to guarantee his invulnerability. And as he repeats himself, his assurance seems to turn itself inside out, becoming dependent not on the fact that all men are, after all, born of woman but on the fantasy of escape from this universal condition.[3] The duplicity of Macbeth's repeated question—its capac-

---

[2]See Adelman, *Suffocating Mothers* (New York: Routledge, 1992), pp. 1–10 for suffocation and the caesarean solution in *Richard III*. In his classic preoedipal account of the failure of differentiation in *Macbeth*, David B. Barron associates the cutting and breaking imagery throughout the play with Macbeth's attempt to "cut his way out of the female environment which chokes and smothers him"; he notes that the choking/suffocating/smothering images find their realization in the witches' "birth-strangled babe" ("The Babe That Milks: An Organic Study of *Macbeth*," originally published in 1960 and reprinted in *The Design Within*, ed. M. D. Faber [New York: Science House, 1970], p. 268). For similar preoedipal readings of the play, see Marvin Rosenberg's *The Masks of Macbeth* (Berkeley: U of California P, 1978), pp. 81–82, 270–72, and especially Kahn's *Man's Estate*, pp. 151–55, 172–92, Wheeler's *Shakespeare's Development*, pp. 144–49, and David Willbern's "Phantasmagoric *Macbeth*," *English Literary Renaissance* 16 (1986): 520–49.

[3]Oddly, this fantasy is present in the report of the Earl of Gowrie's attempt to kill King James in 1600, a report that may have influenced Shakespeare in *Macbeth*. James Weimis of Bogy, testifying in 1600 about the earl's recourse to necromancy, reported that the earl thought it "possible that the seed of a man and woman might be brought to perfection otherwise then by the *matrix* of the woman" ("Gowries Conspiracie: A Discoverie of the unnaturall and vyle Conspiracie, attempted against the

ity to mean both itself and its opposite—carries such weight at the end of the play, I think, because the whole of the play represents in very powerful form both the fantasy of a virtually absolute and destructive maternal power and the fantasy of absolute escape from this power; I shall argue in fact that the peculiar texture of the end of the play is generated partly by the tension between these two fantasies. For if the unsatisfactory equivocation through which Macduff defeats Macbeth seems to suggest that no man is not born of woman, the play nonetheless re-imagines autonomous male identity only through the ruthless excision of all female presence, its own peculiar satisfaction of the witches' prophecy.

In *Macbeth,* as in *Hamlet,* the threat of maternal power and the crisis it presents for individuated manhood emerge in response to paternal absence; once again, the death of the father figures the fall into the maternal realm. But if in *Hamlet* Shakespeare constructs this fall as the death of the ideally masculine father, here he constructs a revised version in which the fall is the death of the father as ideally androgynous parent. For Duncan initially seems to combine in himself the attributes of both father and mother: he is the center of authority, the source of lineage and honor, the giver of name and gift; but he is also the source of all nurturance, planting the children to his throne and making them grow. He is the single source from which all good can be imagined to flow, the source of a benign and empowering nurturance, the opposite of that imaged in the witches' poisonous cauldron and Lady Macbeth's gall-filled breasts. Such a father does away with any need for a mother: he is the image of both parents in one, threatening aspects of each controlled by the presence of the other.[4] When he is gone, "The wine of life is drawn, and the mere lees/Is left this vault to brag of" (2.3.93–94): nurturance itself is spoiled, as all the play's imagery of poisoned chalices and interrupted feasts implies. In his absence male and female break apart, the female becoming merely helpless or merely poisonous and the male merely bloodthirsty; the harmonious relation of the genders imaged in Duncan fails.

Or so the valorizing of Duncan suggests. But in fact masculinity and femininity are deeply disturbed even before his death; and he himself seems strikingly absent before his death. Heavily idealized, this ideally protective father is nonetheless largely ineffectual: even while he is alive, he is unable to hold his kingdom together, reliant on a series of bloody men to suppress an increasingly successful series of rebellions.[5] The witches are already abroad in his realm; they in fact constitute our introduction to that realm. Duncan, not Macbeth, is the first person to

Kings Maiesties Person at Sanct-Iohnstoun, upon Twysday the Fifth of August, 1600," in *A Selection from the Harleian Miscellany* [London: C. and G. Kearsley, 1793], p. 196).

[4]David Sundelson (*Shakespeare's Restorations of the Father* [New Brunswick, N.J.: Rutgers UP, 1983], p. 3), Harry Berger, Jr. ("The Early Scenes of *Macbeth*: Preface to a New Interpretation," *English Literary History* 47 [1980]: 26–28), and Willbern ("Phantasmagoric *Macbeth*," pp. 522–23) all see Duncan as an androgynous parent.

[5]Many commentators note that Shakespeare's Duncan is less ineffectual than Holinshed's; others note the continuing signs of his weakness. See especially Harry Berger's brilliant account of the structural effect of Duncan's weakness in defining his (and Macbeth's) society ("The Early Scenes of *Macbeth*," pp. 1–31).

echo them ("When the battle's lost and won" [1.1.4]; "What he hath lost, noble Macbeth hath won" [1.2.69]). The witches' sexual ambiguity terrifies: Banquo says of them, "You should be women,/And yet your beards forbid me to interpret / That you are so" (1.3.45–47). Is their androgyny the shadow-side of the King's, enabled perhaps by his failure to maintain a protective masculine authority? Is their strength a consequence of his weakness? . . . Banquo's question to the witches may ask us to hear a counter-question about Duncan, who should be man. For Duncan's androgyny is the object of enormous ambivalence: idealized for his nurturing paternity, he is nonetheless killed for his womanish softness, his childish trust, his inability to read men's minds in their faces, his reliance on the fighting of sons who can rebel against him. Macbeth's description of the dead Duncan—"his silver skin lac'd with his golden blood" (2.3.110)—makes him into a virtual icon of kingly worth; but other images surrounding his death make him into an emblem not of masculine authority but of feminine vulnerability. As he moves toward the murder, Macbeth first imagines himself the allegorical figure of Murder, as though to absolve himself of the responsibility of choice. But the figure of murder then fuses with that of Tarquin:

> wither'd Murther,
> . . . thus with his stealthy pace,
> With Tarquin's ravishing strides, towards his design
> Moves like a ghost.
>
> (2.1.52–56)

These lines figure the murder as a display of male sexual aggression against a passive female victim: murder here becomes rape; Macbeth's victim becomes not the powerful male figure of the king but the helpless Lucrece. Hardened by Lady Macbeth to regard maleness and violence as equivalent, that is, Macbeth responds to Duncan's idealized milky gentleness as though it were evidence of his femaleness. The horror of this gender transformation, as well as the horror of the murder, is implicit in Macduff's identification of the king's body as a new Gorgon ("Approach the chamber, and destroy your sight/With a new Gorgon" [2.3.70–71]). The power of this image lies partly in its suggestion that Duncan's bloodied body, with its multiple wounds, has been revealed as female and hence blinding to his sons: as if the threat all along was that Duncan would be revealed as female and that this revelation would rob his sons of his masculine protection and hence of their own masculinity.[6]

In *King Lear*, the abdication of protective paternal power seems to release the destructive power of a female chaos imaged not only in Goneril and Regan but also in the storm on the heath. Macbeth virtually alludes to Lear's storm as he

---

[6]Wheeler sees the simultaneously castrated and castrating Gorgon-like body of Duncan as the emblem of the world Macbeth brings into being (*Shakespeare's Development*, p. 145); I see it as the emblem of a potentially castrating femaleness that Macbeth's act of violence reveals but does not create. For an interesting counter-reading, see Marjorie Garber ("Macbeth: The Male Medusa," reprinted in this volume, pp. 74–103).

approaches the witches in Act 4, conjuring them to answer though they "untie the winds, and let them fight/Against the Churches," though the "waves/Confound and swallow navigation up," though "the treasure/Of Nature's germens tumble all together,/Even till destruction sicken" (4.1.52–60; see *King Lear*, 3.2.1–9). The witches merely implicit on Lear's heath have become in *Macbeth* embodied agents of storm and disorder, and they are there from the start. Their presence suggests that the paternal absence that unleashes female chaos (as in *Lear*) has already happened at the beginning of *Macbeth*. That absence is merely made literal in Macbeth's murder of Duncan at the instigation of female forces: from the start, this father-king cannot protect his sons from powerful mothers, and it is the son's—and the play's—revenge to kill him, or, more precisely, to kill him first and love him after, paying him back for his excessively "womanish" trust and then memorializing him as the ideal androgynous parent.[7] The reconstitution of manhood becomes a central problem in the play in part, I think, because the vision of manhood embodied in Duncan has already failed at the play's beginning.

The witches constitute our introduction to the realm of maternal malevolence unleashed by the loss of paternal protection; as soon as Macbeth meets them, he becomes (in Hecate's probably non-Shakespearean words) their "wayward son" (3.5.11). This maternal malevolence is given its most horrifying expression in Shakespeare in the image through which Lady Macbeth secures her control over Macbeth:

> I have given suck, and know
> How tender 'tis to love the babe that milks me:
> I would, while it was smiling in my face,
> Have pluck'd my nipple from his boneless gums,
> And dash'd the brains out, had I so sworn
> As you have done to this.
>
>   (1.7.54–59)

This image of murderously disrupted nurturance is the psychic equivalent of the witches' poisonous cauldron; both function to subject Macbeth's will to female forces. For the play strikingly constructs the fantasy of subjection to maternal malevolence in two parts, in the witches and in Lady Macbeth, and then persistently identifies the two parts as one. Through this identification, Shakespeare in effect locates the source of his culture's fear of witchcraft in individual human history, in the infant's long dependence on female figures felt as all-powerful: what

---

[7]Many commentators, following Freud, find the murder of Duncan "little else than patricide" ("Those Wrecked by Success," *The Standard Edition of the Complete Psychological Works of Sigmund Freud*, ed. James Strachey [London: The Hogarth Press, 1957], vol. 14, p. 321); see, for example, Rabkin (Norman Rabkin, *Shakespeare and the Problem of Meaning* [Chicago: U of Chicago P, 1981], pp. 106–9), and Watson (Robert N. Watson, *Shakespeare and the Hazards of Ambition* [Cambridge, Mass.: Harvard UP, 1984], esp. pp. 85–88, 98–99). By emphasizing the degree to which Duncan is absent even before his murder, I mean to suggest the extent to which maternal power—including the power to incite parricide—is a consequence as well as a cause of paternal absence.

the witches suggest about the vulnerability of men to female power on the cosmic plane, Lady Macbeth doubles on the psychological plane.

Lady Macbeth's power as a female temptress allies her in a general way with the witches as soon as we see her. The specifics of that implied alliance begin to emerge as she attempts to harden herself in preparation for hardening her husband: the disturbance of gender that Banquo registers when he first meets the witches ("you should be women/And yet your beards forbid me to interpret/That you are") is played out in psychological terms in Lady Macbeth's attempt to unsex herself. Calling on spirits ambiguously allied with the witches themselves, she phrases this unsexing as the undoing of her own bodily maternal function:

> Come, you Spirits
> That tend on mortal thoughts, unsex me here,
> And fill me, from the crown to the toe, top-full
> Of direst cruelty! make thick my blood,
> Stop up th' access and passage to remorse;
> That no compunctious visitings of Nature
> Shake my fell purpose, nor keep peace between
> Th' effect and it! Come to my woman's breasts,
> And take my milk for gall, you murth'ring ministers.
> (1.5.40–48)

In the play's context of unnatural births, the thickening of the blood and the stopping up of access and passage to remorse begin to sound like attempts to undo reproductive functioning and perhaps to stop the menstrual blood that is the sign of its potential.[8] The metaphors in which Lady Macbeth frames the stopping up of remorse, that is, suggest that she imagines an attack on the reproductive passages of her own body, on what makes her specifically female. And as she invites the spirits to her breasts, she reiterates the centrality of the attack specifically on maternal function: needing to undo the "milk of human kindness" (1.5.17) in Macbeth, she imagines an attack on her own literal milk, its transformation into gall. This imagery locates the horror of the scene in Lady Macbeth's unnatural abrogation of her maternal function. But latent within this image of unsexing is the horror of the maternal function itself. Most modern editors follow Johnson in glossing "take my milk for gall" as "take my milk in exchange for gall," imagining in effect that the spirits empty out the natural maternal fluid and replace it with the unnatural and poisonous one. But perhaps Lady Macbeth is asking the spirits to take her milk *as* gall, to nurse from her breasts and find in her milk their sustaining poison. Here the milk itself is the gall; no transformation is nec-

---

[8]Despite some over-literal interpretation, Alice Fox and particularly Jenijoy La Belle usefully demonstrate the specifically gynecological references of "passage" and "visitings of nature," using contemporary gynecological treatises: see Fox ("Obstetrics and Gynecology in *Macbeth*," *Shakespeare Studies* 12[1979]: 129) and La Belle (" 'A Strange Infirmity': Lady Macbeth's Amenorrhea," *Shakespeare Quarterly* 31 [1980]: 382) for the identification of "visitings of nature" as a term for menstruation; see La Belle (p. 383) for the identification of "passage" as a term for the neck of the womb.

essary. In these lines, Lady Macbeth focuses the culture's fear of maternal nursery—a fear reflected, for example, in the common worries about the various ills (including female blood itself) that can be transmitted through nursing and in the sometime identification of colostrum as witch's milk.[9] Insofar as her milk itself nurtures the evil spirits, Lady Macbeth localizes the image of maternal danger, inviting the identification of her maternal function itself with that of the witch. For she here invites precisely that nursing of devil-imps so central to the current understanding of witchcraft that the presence of supernumerary teats alone was often taken as sufficient evidence that one was a witch.[10] Lady Macbeth and the witches fuse at this moment, and they fuse through the image of perverse nursery.

It is characteristic of the play's division of labor between Lady Macbeth and the witches that she, rather than they, is given the imagery of perverse nursery traditionally attributed to witches. The often-noted alliance between Lady Macbeth and the witches constructs malignant female power both in the cosmos and in the family; it in effect adds the whole weight of the spiritual order to the condemnation of Lady Macbeth's insurrection. But despite the superior cosmic status of the witches, Lady Macbeth seems to me finally the more frightening figure. For Shakespeare's witches are an odd mixture of the terrifying and the near-comic. Even without consideration of the Hecate scene (3.5) with its distinct lightening of tone and its incipient comedy of discord among the witches, we may begin to feel a shift toward the comic in the presentation of the witches: the specificity and predictability of the ingredients in their dire recipe pass over toward grotesque comedy even while they create a (partly pleasurable) shiver of horror. There is a distinct weakening of their power after their first appearances: only in 4.1 do we hear that they themselves have masters (1.63). The more Macbeth claims for them, the less their actual power seems: even their power over the storm—the signature of maternal malevolence in *King Lear*—is eventually taken from them. By the time Macbeth evokes the cosmic damage they can wreak (4.1.50–60), we have already felt the presence of such damage, and felt it moreover as issuing not from the

---

[9]See Janet Adelman, *Suffocating Mothers: Fantasies of Maternal Origin in Shakespeare's Plays, "Hamlet" to "The Tempest"* (New York: Routledge, Chapman and Hall, 1992), pp. 130–64. Chapter 1 (pp. 4, 7, and notes 12, 13, and 28) for these ills; and see Samuel X. Radbill for the identification of colostrum with witch's milk ("Pediatrics," in *Medicine in Seventeenth Century England*, ed. Allen G. Debus [Berkeley: U of California P, 1974], p. 249). The topic was of interest to King James, who claimed to have sucked his Protestantism from his nurse's milk; his drunkenness was also attributed to her (see Henry N. Paul, *The Royal Play of Macbeth* [New York: The Macmillan Company, 1950], pp. 387–88).

[10]Many commentators on English witchcraft note the unusual prominence given to the presence of the witch's mark and the nursing of familiars; see, for example, Barbara Rosen's introduction to her collection of witchcraft documents (*Witchcraft* [London: Edward Arnold, 1969], pp. 29–30). She cites contemporary documents on the nursing of familiars, e.g., on pp. 187–88 and 315; the testimony of Joan Prentice, one of the convicted witches of Chelmsford in 1589, is particularly suggestive: "At what time soever she would have her ferret do anything for her, she used the words 'Bid, Bid, Bid, come Bid, come Bid, come suck, come suck, come suck'" (p. 188). Katherine Mary Briggs quotes a contemporary (1613) story about the finding of a witch's teat (*Pale Hecate's Team* [New York: Arno Press, 1977], p. 250).

witches but from a divinely sanctioned nature firmly in league with patriarchal order. The witches' displays of thunder and lightning, like their apparitions, are merely childish theatrics compared to what we have already heard: the serious disruptions of natural order—the storm that toppled the chimneys and made the earth shake (2.3.53–60), the unnatural darkness in day (2.4.5–10), the cannibalism of Duncan's horses (2.4.14–18)—are the horrifying but reassuringly familiar signs of God's displeasure, firmly under His—not their—control. Partly because their power is thus circumscribed, nothing the witches say or do conveys the presence of awesome and unexplained malevolence in the way that Lear's storm does. Even the process of dramatic representation itself may diminish their power: embodied, perhaps, they lack full power to terrify; "Present fears"—even of witches—"are less than horrible imaginings" (1.3.137–38). They tend thus to become as much containers for, as expressions of, nightmare; to a certain extent, they help to exorcise the terror of female malevolence by localizing it.

The witches may of course have lost some of their power to terrify through the general decline in witchcraft belief. Nonetheless, even when that belief was in full force, these witches would have been less frightening than their Continental sisters, their crimes less sensational. For despite their numinous and infinitely suggestive indefinability, insofar as they are witches, they are distinctly English witches; and most commentators on English witchcraft note how tame an affair it was in comparison with witchcraft belief on the Continent.[11] The most sensational staples of Continental belief from the *Malleus Maleficarum* (1486) on—the ritual murder and eating of infants, the attacks specifically on the male genitals, the perverse sexual relationship with demons—are missing or greatly muted in English witchcraft belief, replaced largely by a simpler concern with retaliatory wrongdoing of exactly the order Shakespeare points to when one of his witches announces her retaliation for the sailor's wife's refusal to share her chestnuts.[12] We may hear an echo of some of the Continental belief in the hint of their quasi-sexual attack on the sailor with the uncooperative wife (the witches promise to "do and do and do," leaving him drained "dry as hay") and in the infanticidal contents of the cauldron, especially the "finger of birth-strangled babe" and the blood of the sow

---

[11]For their "Englishness," see Peter Stallybrass, "*Macbeth* and Witchcraft," p. 109 in this volume. Alan Macfarlane's important study of English witchcraft, *Witchcraft in Tudor and Stuart England* (New York: Harper and Row, 1970), frequently notes the absence of the Continental staples: if the witches of Essex are typical, English witches do not fly, do not hold Sabbaths, do not commit sexual perversions or attack male potency, do not kill babies (see pp. 6, 160, and 180, for example).

[12]Macfarlane finds the failure of neighborliness reflected in the retaliatory acts of the witch the key to the social function of witchcraft in England; see *Witchcraft in Tudor and Stuart England*, especially pp. 168–76, for accounts of the failures of neighborliness—very similar to the refusal to share chestnuts—that provoked the witch to act. James Sprenger's and Heinrich Kramer's *Malleus Maleficarum* (trans. Montague Summers [New York: Benjamin Blom, 1970]) is the *locus classicus* for Continental witchcraft beliefs: for the murder and eating of infants, see pp. 21, 66, 99, and 100–101; for attacks on the genitals, see pp. 47, 55–60, and 117–19; for sexual relations with demons, see pp. 21, 112–14. Or see Reginald Scot's convenient summary of these beliefs (*The Discoverie of Witchcraft* [London, 1584; reprinted, with an introduction by Hugh Ross Williamson, Carbondale: Southern Illinois UP, 1964], p. 31).

"that hath eaten/ Her nine farrow." The cannibalism that is a staple of Continental belief may be implicit in the contents of that grim cauldron; and the various eyes, toes, tongues, legs, teeth, livers, and noses (indiscriminately human and animal) may evoke primitive fears of dismemberment close to the center of witchcraft belief. But these terrors remain largely implicit. For Shakespeare's witches are both smaller and greater than their Continental sisters: on the one hand, more the representation of English homebodies with relatively small concerns; on the other, more the incarnation of literary or mythic fates or sybils, given the power not only to predict but to enforce the future. But the staples of Continental witchcraft belief are not altogether missing from the play: for the most part, they are transferred away from the witches and recur as the psychological issues evoked by Lady Macbeth in her relation to Macbeth. She becomes the inheritor of the realm of primitive relational and bodily disturbance: of infantile vulnerability to maternal power, of dismemberment and its developmentally later equivalent, castration. Lady Macbeth brings the witches' power home: they get the cosmic apparatus, she gets the psychic force. That Lady Macbeth is the more frightening figure—and was so, I suspect, even before belief in witchcraft had declined—suggests the firmly domestic and psychological basis of Shakespeare's imagination.

The fears of female coercion, female definition of the male, that are initially located cosmically in the witches thus find their ultimate locus in the figure of Lady Macbeth, whose attack on Macbeth's virility is the source of her strength over him and who acquires that strength, I shall argue, partly because she can make him imagine himself as an infant vulnerable to her. In the figure of Lady Macbeth, that is, Shakespeare rephrases the power of the witches as the wife/mother's power to poison human relatedness at its source; in her, their power of cosmic coercion is rewritten as the power of the mother to misshape or destroy the child. The attack on infants and on the genitals characteristic of Continental witchcraft belief is thus in her returned to its psychological source: in the play these beliefs are localized not in the witches but in the great central scene in which Lady Macbeth persuades Macbeth to the murder of Duncan. In this scene, Lady Macbeth notoriously makes the murder of Duncan the test of Macbeth's virility;[13] if he cannot perform the murder, he is in effect reduced to the helplessness of an infant subject to her rage. She begins by attacking his manhood, making her love for him contingent on the murder that she identifies as equivalent to his male potency: "From this time /Such I account thy love" (1.7.38–39); "When you durst do it, then you were a man" (1.7.49). Insofar as his drunk hope is now "green and pale" (1.7.37), he is identified as emasculated, exhibiting the symptoms not only of hangover but also of the green-sickness, the typical disease of timid young virgin women. Lady Macbeth's argument is, in effect, that any signs of the

---

[13]In an early essay that has become a classic, Eugene Waith established the centrality of definitions of manhood and Lady Macbeth's role in enforcing Macbeth's particularly bloodthirsty version, a theme that has since become a major topos of *Macbeth* criticism ("Manhood and Valor in Two Shakespearean Tragedies," *ELH* 17 [1950]: 262–73).

"milk of human kindness" (1.5.17) mark him as more womanly than she; she proceeds to enforce his masculinity by demonstrating her willingness to dry up that milk in herself, specifically by destroying her nursing infant in fantasy: "I would, while it was smiling in my face,/Have pluck'd my nipple from his boneless gums,/And dash'd the brains out" (1.7.56–58). That this image has no place in the plot, where the Macbeths are strikingly childless, gives some indication of the inner necessity through which it appears. For Lady Macbeth expresses here not only the hardness she imagines to be male, not only her willingness to unmake the most essential maternal relationship; she expresses also a deep fantasy of Macbeth's utter vulnerability to her. As she progresses from questioning Macbeth's masculinity to imagining herself dashing out the brains of her infant son, she articulates a fantasy in which to be less than a man is to become interchangeably a woman or a baby,[14] terribly subject to the wife/mother's destructive rage.

By evoking this vulnerability, Lady Macbeth acquires a power over Macbeth more absolute than any the witches can achieve. The play's central fantasy of escape from woman seems to me to unfold from this moment: for if Macbeth's bloodthirsty masculinity is partly a response to Lady Macbeth's desire, in effect an extension of her will, it simultaneously comes to represent the way to escape her power. We can see the beginnings of this process in Macbeth's response to her evocation of absolute maternal power. Macbeth first responds by questioning the possibility of failure ("If we should fail?" [1.7.59]). Lady Macbeth counters this fear by inviting Macbeth to share in her fantasy of omnipotent malevolence: "What cannot you and I perform upon/Th' unguarded Duncan?" (1.7.70–71). The satiated and sleeping Duncan takes on the vulnerability that Lady Macbeth has just invoked in the image of the feeding, trusting infant; Macbeth releases himself from the image of this vulnerability by sharing in the murder of this innocent. In his elation at this transfer of vulnerability from himself to Duncan, Macbeth imagines Lady Macbeth the mother to infants sharing her hardness, born in effect without vulnerability; in effect, he imagines her as male and then reconstitutes himself as the invulnerable male child of such a mother:

> Bring forth men-children only!
> For thy undaunted mettle should compose
> Nothing but males.
>
> (1.7.73–75)

Through the double pun on *mettle/metal* and *male/mail*, Lady Macbeth herself becomes virtually male, composed of the hard metal of which the armored male is made. Her children would necessarily be men, composed of her male mettle,

---

[14]Lady Macbeth maintains her control over Macbeth through 3.4 by manipulating these categories: see 2.2.53–54 (" 'tis the eye of childhood/That fears a painted devil") and 3.4.57–64 ("Are you a man? . . . these flaws and starts . . . would well become/A woman's story"). In his response to Banquo's ghost, Macbeth invokes the same categories and suggests their interchangeability: he dares what man dares (3.4.98); if he feared Banquo alive, he could rightly be called "the baby of a girl" (3.4.105).

armored by her mettle, lacking the female inheritance from the mother that would make them vulnerable. The man-child thus brought forth would be no trusting infant; the very phrase "men-children" suggests the presence of the adult man even at birth, hence the undoing of childish vulnerability. The mobility of the imagery—from male infant with his brains dashed out, to Macbeth and Lady Macbeth triumphing over the sleeping, trusting Duncan, to the all-male invulnerable man-child—suggests the logic of the fantasy: only the child of an all-male mother is safe. We see here the creation of a defensive fantasy of exemption from the woman's part: as infantile vulnerability is shifted to Duncan, Macbeth creates in himself the image of Lady Macbeth's hardened all-male man-child; his murder of Duncan thus becomes the sign of his distance from the infant whom Lady Macbeth could destroy, the sign of the mettle that composes him.

Macbeth's temporary solution to the infantile vulnerability and maternal malevolence revealed by Lady Macbeth is to imagine Lady Macbeth the all-male mother of invulnerable infants and to imagine himself as such an infant, in effect doing away with vulnerability by doing away with the female site of origin. The final solution, both for Macbeth and for the play itself, though in differing ways, is an even more radical excision of the female site of origin: it is to imagine a birth entirely exempt from women, to imagine in effect an all-male family, composed of nothing but males, in which the father can be fully restored to power. Overtly, of course, the play denies the possibility of this fantasy: Macduff carries the power of the man not born of woman only through the equivocation of the fiends, their obstetrical joke that quibbles with the meaning of "born" and thus confirms circuitously that all men come from women after all. Even Macbeth, in whom, I think, the fantasy is centrally invested, knows its impossibility: his false security depends exactly on his common-sense assumption that everyone is born of woman. Nonetheless, I shall argue, the play curiously enacts the fantasy that it seems to deny: punishing Macbeth for his participation in a fantasy of escape from the maternal matrix, it nonetheless allows the audience the partial satisfaction of a dramatic equivalent to it. The equivocating ending of *Macbeth* seems to me to play out this dual process of repudiation and enactment, uncreating any space for the female even while it seems to insist on the universality of maternal origin.

The witches prophesy invulnerability for Macbeth insofar as all men are born of women:

> Be bloody, bold, and resolute: laugh to scorn
> The power of man, for none of woman born
> Shall harm Macbeth.

(4.1.79–81)

But the prophecy has the immediate force of psychic relevance for Macbeth in part because it so perfectly fits with the fantasy constructions central to 1.7: even as it depends on the vulnerability of all others, it ambiguously constructs Macbeth as exempt from this vulnerability. For the witches here invite Macbeth to make himself into the bloody and invulnerable man-child he has created as a defense against maternal malevolence in 1.7. The creation of this man-child is recalled by the apparition of the Bloody Child that accompanies the witches' prophecy: the apparition alludes at once to the bloody vulnerability of the infant destroyed in fantasy by Lady Macbeth and to the bloodthirsty masculinity that seems to promise escape from this vulnerability, the bloodiness the witches urge Macbeth to take on. The doubleness of the image thus epitomizes exactly the doubleness of the prophecy itself, which constructs Macbeth's invulnerability in effect from the vulnerability of maternal origin in all other men. Macbeth does not question this prophecy, even after the experience of Birnam Wood should have taught him better, partly because it so perfectly meets his needs: in encouraging him to "laugh to scorn / The power of man," the prophecy seems to grant him exemption from the condition of all men, who bring with them the liabilities inherent in their birth. As Macbeth carries the prophecy as a shield onto the battlefield, his confidence in his own invulnerability increasingly reveals his sense of exemption from the universal human condition. Repeated seven times, the phrase "born to woman" with its variants begins to carry for Macbeth the meaning "vulnerable," as though vulnerability itself were the taint deriving from woman; his own invulnerability comes therefore to stand as evidence for his exemption from that taint. This is the subterranean logic of Macbeth's words to Young Siward immediately after Macbeth has killed him.

> Thou wast born of woman:—
> But swords I smile at, weapons laugh to scorn,
> Brandish'd by man that's of a woman born.
> (5.7.11–13)

Young Siward's death becomes in effect proof that he was born of woman; and in the logic of Macbeth's psyche, his own invulnerability is the proof that he was not. The "but" records this fantasied distinction: it constructs the sentence, "You, born of woman, are vulnerable; but I, not born of woman, am not."

Insofar as this is the fantasy embodied in Macbeth at the play's end, it is punished by the equivocation of the fiends: the revelation that Macduff derives from woman, though by unusual means, musters against Macbeth all the values of ordinary family and community that Macduff carries with him. Macbeth, "cow'd" by the revelation (5.8.18), is forced to take on the taint of vulnerability; the fantasy of escape from the maternal matrix seems to die with him. But although this fantasy is punished in Macbeth, it does not quite die with him; it continues to have a curious life of its own in the play, apart from its embodiment in him. Even from the beginning of the play, the fantasy has not been Macbeth's alone: as the play's most striking bloody man, he is in the beginning the bearer of this fantasy for the all-male community that depends on his bloody prowess. The opening scenes strikingly construct male and female as realms apart; and the initial descriptions of Macbeth's battles construe his prowess as a consequence of his exemption from the taint of woman.

In the description of his battle with Macdonwald, what looks initially like a battle between loyal and disloyal sons to establish primacy in the father's eyes is oddly transposed into a battle of male against female:

> Doubtful it stood;
> As two spent swimmers, that do cling together
> And choke their art. The merciless Macdonwald
> (Worthy to be a rebel, for to that
> The multiplying villainies of nature
> Do swarm upon him) from the western isles
> Of Kernes and Gallowglasses is supplied;
> And Fortune, on his damned quarrel smiling,
> Show'd like a rebel's whore: but all's too weak;
> For brave Macbeth (well he deserves that name),
> Disdaining Fortune, with his brandish'd steel,
> Which smok'd with bloody execution,
> Like Valour's minion, carv'd out his passage,
> Till he fac'd the slave;
> Which ne'er shook hands, nor bade farewell to him,
> Till he unseam'd him from the nave to th' chops,
> And fix'd his head upon our battlements.
>
> (1.2.7–23)

The two initially indistinguishable figures metaphorized as the swimmers eventually sort themselves out into victor and victim, but only by first sorting themselves out into male and female, as though Macbeth can be distinguished from Macdonwald only by making Macdonwald functionally female. The "merciless Macdonwald" is initially firmly identified; but by the time Macbeth appears, Macdonwald has temporarily disappeared, replaced by the female figure of Fortune, against whom Macbeth seems to fight ("brave Macbeth, . . . Disdaining Fortune, with his brandish'd steel"). The metaphorical substitution of Fortune for Macdonwald transforms the battle into a contest between male and female; in effect, it makes Macbeth's claim to his name—"brave Macbeth"—contingent on his victory over the female. We are prepared for this transformation by Macdonwald's sexual alliance with the tainting female, the whore Fortune; Macbeth's identification as valor's minion redefines the battle as a contest between the half-female couple Fortune/Macdonwald and the all-male couple Valor/Macbeth. Metaphorically, Macdonwald and Macbeth take on the qualities of the unreliable female and the heroic male; Macbeth's battle against Fortune turns out to be his battle against Macdonwald because the two are functionally the same. Macdonwald, tainted by the female, thus becomes an easy mark for Macbeth, who demonstrates his own untainted manhood by unseaming Macdonwald from the nave to the chops: simultaneously castrating and performing a caesarian section on him, Macbeth remakes Macdonwald's body as female, revealing what his alliance with Fortune has suggested all along.

In effect, then, the battle that supports the father's kingdom plays out the creation of a conquering all-male erotics that marks its conquest by its triumph over a feminized body, simultaneously that of Fortune and Macdonwald. Hence, in the double action of the passage, the victorious unseaming happens twice: first on the body of Fortune and then on the body of Macdonwald. The lines descriptive of

Macbeth's approach to Macdonwald—"brave Macbeth . . . Disdaining Fortune, with his brandish'd steel,/. . . carv'd out his passage"—make that approach contingent on Macbeth's first carving his passage through a female body, like Richard III hewing his way out (*3 Henry VI*, 3.2.181). The language here perfectly anticipates Macduff's birth by caesarian section, revealed at the end of the play: if Macduff is ripped untimely from his mother's womb, Macbeth here manages in fantasy his own caesarian section,[15] carving his passage out from the unreliable female to achieve heroic male action, in effect carving up the female to arrive at the male. Only after this rite of passage can Macbeth meet Macdonwald: this act of aggression toward the female body, with its accompanying fantasy of self-birth, marks Macbeth's passage to the contest that will define his maleness partly by attributing tainted femaleness to Macdonwald. For the all-male community surrounding Duncan, then, Macbeth's victory is allied with his triumph over femaleness; self-born, he becomes invulnerable, "lapp'd in proof" (1.2.55) like one of Lady Macbeth's armored men-children. Even before his initial entry into the play, that is, Macbeth becomes the bearer of the shared fantasy that secure male community depends on the prowess of the man not born of woman, the man who can carve his own passage out, the man whose very maleness is the mark of his exemption from maternal origin and the vulnerabilities that are its consequence.

Ostensibly, the play rejects the version of manhood implicit in the shared fantasy of the beginning. Macbeth himself is well aware that his capitulation to Lady Macbeth's definition of manhood entails his abandonment of his own more inclusive definition of what becomes a man (1.7.46); and Macduff's response to the news of his family's destruction insists that humane feeling is central to the definition of manhood (4.3.221). Moreover, the revelation that even Macduff had a mother sets a limiting condition on the fantasy of a bloody masculine escape from the maternal matrix and hence on the kind of manhood defined by that escape. Nonetheless, even at the end, the play enables one version of the fantasy that heroic manhood is exemption from the female even while it punishes that fantasy in Macbeth. The key figure in whom this double movement is vested at the end of the play is Macduff; the unresolved contradictions that surround him are, I think, marks of ambivalence toward the fantasy itself. In insisting that mourning for his family is his right as a man, he presents family feeling as central to the definition of manhood; and yet he conspicuously leaves his family vulnerable to destruction when he goes off to offer his services to Malcolm. The play moreover insists on reminding us that he has inexplicably abandoned his family: both Lady Macduff and Malcolm question the necessity of this abandonment (4.2.6–14, 4.3.26–28), and the play never allows Macduff to explain himself. This unexplained abandonment severely qualifies Macduff's force as the play's central exemplar of a healthy manhood that can include the possibility of relationship to women: the play seems to vest diseased familial relations in Macbeth and the possibility of healthy ones in

---

[15] I am specifically indebted to Willbern's reading of the caesarian implications of the unseaming from nave to chops ("Phantasmagoric *Macbeth*," pp. 528–29).

Macduff; and yet we discover dramatically that Macduff has a family only when we hear that he has abandoned it. Dramatically and psychologically, he takes on full masculine power only as he loses his family and becomes energized by the loss, converting his grief into the more "manly" tune of vengeance (4.3.235); the loss of his family here enables his accession to full masculine action even while his response to that loss insists on a more humane definition of manhood. The play here pulls in two directions; and it then reiterates this doubleness by vesting in Macduff its final fantasy of exemption from woman. The ambivalence that shapes the portrayal of Macduff is evident even as he reveals to Macbeth that he "was from his mother's womb/Untimely ripp'd" (5.8.15–16): the emphasis on untimeliness and the violence of the image suggest that he has been prematurely deprived of a nurturing maternal presence; but the prophecy construes just this deprivation as the source of Macduff's strength. The prophecy itself both denies and affirms the fantasy of exemption from women: in affirming that Macduff has indeed had a mother, it denies the fantasy of male self-generation; but in attributing his power to his having been untimely ripped from that mother, it sustains the sense that violent separation from the mother is the mark of the successful male. The final battle between Macbeth and Macduff thus replays the initial battle between Macbeth and Macdonwald. But Macduff has now taken the place of Macbeth: he carries with him the male power given him by the caesarian solution, and Macbeth is retrospectively revealed as Macdonwald, the woman's man.

The doubleness of the prophecy is less the equivocation of the fiends than Shakespeare's own equivocation about the figure of Macduff and about the fantasy vested in him in the end. For Macduff carries with him simultaneously all the values of family and the claim that masculine power derives from the unnatural abrogation of family, including escape from the conditions of one's birth. Moreover, the ambivalence that shapes the figure of Macduff similarly shapes the dramatic structure of the play itself. Ostensibly concerned to restore natural order at the end, the play bases that order upon the radical exclusion of the female. Initially construed as all-powerful, the women virtually disappear at the end. Increasingly cribbed and confined by the play, Lady Macbeth's psychic power and subjectivity are increasingly written out of it. At first a source of terror, she increasingly becomes the merely helpless wife, alienated from her husband's serious business, pleading with him to come to bed, cooperatively dying offstage in her separate sphere, amidst a cry of women. Even when she is at the center of the stage, her own subjectivity is denied her: the broken object of others' observation in the sleep-walking scene, she has become entirely absent to herself. By the end, she is so diminished a character that we scarcely trouble to ask ourselves whether the report of her suicide is accurate or not. At the same time, the witches who are her avatars disappear from the stage and become so diminished in importance that Macbeth never alludes to them, blaming his defeat only on the equivocation of their male masters, the fiends. Even Lady Macduff exists only to disappear.

With the excision of all the female characters, nature itself can in effect be reborn male. The bogus fulfillment of the Birnam Wood prophecy emphasizes the extent to which the natural order of the end depends on this excision of the female. Critics sometimes see in the march of Malcolm's soldiers bearing their green branches an allusion to the Maying festivals in which participants returned from the woods bearing branches, or to the ritual scourging of a hibernal figure by the forces of the oncoming spring.[16] The allusion seems to me clearly present; but it serves I think to mark precisely what the moving of Birnam Wood is not. Malcolm's use of Birnam Wood is a military maneuver. His drily worded command (5.4.4–7) leaves little room for suggestions of natural fertility or for the deep sense of the generative world rising up to expel its winter king; nor does the play later enable these associations except in a scattered and partly ironic way. These trees have little resemblance to those in the Forest of Arden; their branches, like those carried by the apparition of the "child crowned with a tree in his hand" (4.1.86), are little more than the emblems of a strictly patriarchal family tree. This family tree, like the march of Birnam Wood itself, is relentlessly male: Duncan and sons, Banquo and son, Siward and son. There are no daughters and scarcely any mention of mothers in these family trees. We are brought as close as possible here to the fantasy of family without women.[17] In that sense, Birnam Wood is the perfect emblem of the nature that triumphs at the end of the play: nature without generative possibility, nature without women. Malcolm tells his men to carry the branches to obscure themselves, and that is exactly their function: insofar as they seem to allude to the rising of the natural order against Macbeth, they obscure the operations of male power, disguising them as a natural force; and they simultaneously obscure the extent to which natural order itself is here reconceived purely as male.[18]

[16]See, for example, Goddard (Harold Goddard, *The Meaning of Shakespeare* [Chicago: U of Chicago P, 1951], pp. 520–21); John Holloway (*The Story of the Night* [London: Routledge and Kegan Paul, 1961], p. 66); Rosenberg (*Masks of Macbeth*, p. 626); and Watson (*Shakespeare and the Hazards of Ambition*, pp. 89, 106–16). Even without sensing the covert presence of a vegetation myth, critics often associate the coming of Birnam Wood with the restoration of spring and fertility. Only Bamber demurs: in her account Birnam Wood rises up in aid of a male alliance, not as the Saturnalian disorder of the Maying rituals (*Comic Women*, p. 106). My view coincides with hers.

[17]As Wheeler notes, the description of Malcolm's saintly mother makes him "symbolically the child of something approximating virgin birth" (*Shakespeare's Development*, p. 146)—in effect another version of the man not quite born of woman. The fantasy of escape from maternal birth and the creation of all-male lineage would probably have been of interest to King James, whose problematic derivation from Mary, Queen of Scots, must occasionally have made him wish himself not born of (that particular) woman, no matter how much he was publicly concerned to rehabilitate her image. See Jonathan Goldberg's account of James's complex attitude toward Mary (*James I and the Politics of Literature* [Baltimore, Md.: The Johns Hopkins UP, 1983], pp. 11–17, 25–26, and 119) and his later speculations on Mary and the fantasy of parthenogenesis in *Macbeth* ("Speculations: *Macbeth* and Source," in *Shakespeare Reproduced: The Text in History and Ideology*, ed. Jean E. Howard and Marion F. O'Connor [New York and London: Methuen, 1987], p. 259).

[18]Although neither Berger nor Stallybrass discusses the function of Birnam Wood specifically, I am indebted here to their discussions of the ideological function of the play's appeal to cosmology in the service of patriarchy, Berger seeing it as "a collective project of mystification" (Harvy Berger, "Text Against Performance in Shakespeare: The Example of *Macbeth*," in *The Forms of Power and the Power of Forms in the Renaissance*, ed. Stephen Greenblatt, *Genre* 15 (1982): 64), Stallybrass as "a returning of the disputed ground of politics to the undisputed ground of Nature" ("*Macbeth* and Witchcraft," pp. 104–118 in this volume).

If we can see the fantasy of escape from the female in the play's fulfillment of the witches' prophecies—in Macduff's birth by caesarian section and in Malcolm's appropriation of Birnam Wood—we can see it also in the play's psychological geography. The shift from Scotland to England is strikingly the shift from the mother's to the father's terrain. Scotland "cannot/Be call'd our mother, but our grave" (4.3.165–66), in Rosse's words to Macduff: it is the realm of Lady Macbeth and the witches, the realm in which the mother *is* the grave, the realm appropriately ruled by their bad son Macbeth. The escape to England is an escape from their power into the realm of the good father-king and his surrogate son Malcolm, "unknown to woman" (4.3.126). The magical power of this father to cure clearly balances the magical power of the witches to harm, as Malcolm (the father's son) balances Macbeth (the mother's son). That Macduff can cross from one realm into the other only by abandoning his family suggests the rigidity of the psychic geography separating England from Scotland. At the end of the play, Malcolm returns to Scotland mantled in the power England gives him, in effect bringing the power of the fathers with him: bearer of his father's line, unknown to woman, supported by his agent Macduff (himself empowered by his own special immunity from birth), Malcolm embodies utter separation from women and as such triumphs easily over Macbeth, the mother's son.

The play that begins by unleashing the terrible threat of destructive maternal power and demonstrates the helplessness of its central male figure before that power thus ends by consolidating male power, in effect solving the problem of masculinity by eliminating the female. The play's recuperative consolidation of masculinity answers the maternal threat unleashed and never fully contained in *Hamlet* and *King Lear:* here, maternal power is given its most virulent sway and then handily abolished. In the end, we are in a purely male realm, founded—as Prospero's will be—on the excision of maternal origin; here, mothers no longer threaten because they no longer exist. But this solution is inherently unstable: the ending of *Coriolanus* will undo the ending of *Macbeth,* bringing back the mother with a vengeance.

The central psychological concerns of *Macbeth* are reiterated in *Coriolanus:* once again, masculinity is constructed in response to maternal power, and in the absence of a father; and once again, the hero attempts to recreate himself through his bloody heroics, in fantasy severing the connection with his mother even as he enacts the ruthless masculinity that is her bidding. "Bring forth men-children only!/For thy undaunted mettle should compose/Nothing but males" (1.7.73–75), Macbeth tells Lady Macbeth in response to her fantasy of infanticide; and Coriolanus initially seems to be the incarnation of this invulnerable "man-child" (*Coriolanus,* 1.3.17), the child who sucks only valiantness from the mettle/metal of his mother's breast (*Coriolanus,* 3.2.129). But as in *Macbeth,* his very pose as self-sufficient man-child marks his subjection to his mother: even more insistently than *Macbeth, Coriolanus* problematizes the construction of heroic masculinity, locating its source in the deprivation that is the maternal signature in both plays.

Maternal malevolence is never as horrific in *Coriolanus* as in *Macbeth*: *Coriolanus* localizes and domesticates the power of the witches and Lady Macbeth in the literal relation of mother and son. But although Volumnia does not make stews out of body parts or threaten to dash Coriolanus's brains out while he is nursing, her less melodramatic disruptions of the feeding situation give her a power over her son that is the psychic equivalent of theirs: "framed" (5.3.63) by her equation of starvation and masculinity, he becomes the man her fancy builds (2.1.198). By failing to feed him enough, she makes hunger the sign of his vulnerability, creating him as a virtual automaton who cannot tolerate his own ordinary human neediness and who thus is compelled to act out needs he can neither understand nor satisfy. Under her tutelage, any acknowledgment of need—starting with the acknowledgment that he, like the crowd he so despises, needs food—threatens to undermine his masculine autonomy, in effect returning him to the maternal breast from which he could never get enough. But finally self-starvation is no solution to the problem of human vulnerability; in the end, it returns him to the same place of deprivation. Framed by maternal insufficiency, Coriolanus can never successfully wean himself from what he has never truly had:[19] thrusting him out, Volumnia binds him to her. Despite his efforts at self-creation, this exiled son is utterly unable to separate from his mother; thus in the end he turns on Rome and his mother in an outraged attempt to stabilize his identity by eradicating his deprivation at its source. In its violence, his return takes on the configuration of a failed separation ritual, a final desperate attempt to separate himself from his mother by destroying her, forging a new name for himself in the fires that will burn Rome.

Coriolanus begins in the landscape of maternal deprivation. It was written during a period of rising corn prices and the accompanying fear of famine; in May 1607, "a great number of common persons"—up to five thousand, Stow tells us in his *Annales*—assembled in various Midlands counties, including Shakespeare's own county of Warwickshire, to protest the acceleration of enclosures and the resulting food shortages.[20] Shakespeare rewrites the popular uprising in Plutarch to make it reflect the contemporary threat: in Plutarch the people riot because the Senate refuses to control usury; in Shakespeare they riot because they are hungry. And if the specter of a multitude of hungry mouths, ready to rise and demand their own, is the exciting cause of *Coriolanus*, the image of the mother who has not fed her children enough is at its center. One does not need the help of a psychoanalytic approach to notice that Volumnia is not a nourishing mother. Her attitude toward food is nicely summed up when she rejects Menenius's invitation to a consolatory dinner after Coriolanus's banishment: "Anger's my meat: I sup upon

---

[19]See D. W. Winnicott on weaning: weaning goes well if "the baby really has had something to be weaned from" (*The Child, the Family, and the Outside World* [Harmondsworth: Penguin Books, 1964], p. 80).

[20]John Stow, *Annales* (London, 1631), p. 890.

myself/And so shall starve with feeding" (4.2.50–51). We might suspect her of having been as niggardly in providing food for her son as she is for herself, or rather suspect her of insisting that he too be self-sufficient, that he feed only on his own anger; and indeed, he is apparently fed only valiantness by her ("Thy valiantness was mine, thou suck'st it from me" [3.2.129]). He certainly has not been fed the milk of human kindness: when Menenius later tells us that "there is no more mercy in him than there is milk in a male tiger" (5.4.28–29), he seems to associate Coriolanus's lack of humanity not only with the absence of any nurturing female element in him but also with the absence of mother's milk itself.[21] Volumnia takes some pride in the creation of her son, and when we first meet her, she tells us exactly how she's done it: by sending him to a cruel war at an age when a mother should not be willing to allow a son out of the protective maternal circle for an hour (1.3.5–15). She elaborates her creation as she imagines herself mother to twelve sons and then kills all but one of them off: "I had rather had eleven die nobly for their country, than one voluptuously surfeit out of action" (1.3.24–25). To be noble is to die; to live is to be ignoble and to eat too much. If you are Volumnia's son, the choice is clear.

But the most telling—certainly the most disturbing—revelation of Volumnia's attitude toward feeding comes some twenty lines later, when she is encouraging Virgilia to share her own glee in the thought of Coriolanus's wounds: "The breasts of Hecuba/When she did suckle Hector, look'd not lovelier/Than Hector's forehead when it spit forth blood/At Grecian sword contemning" (1.3.40–43). Blood is more beautiful than milk, the wound than the breast, warfare than peaceful feeding. But this image is more disturbing than these easy comparatives suggest. It does not bode well for Coriolanus that the heroic Hector doesn't stand a chance in Volumnia's imagination: he is transformed immediately from infantile feeding mouth to bleeding wound. For the unspoken mediator between breast and wound is the infant's mouth: in this imagistic transformation, to feed is to be wounded; the mouth becomes the wound, the breast the sword. The metaphoric process suggests the psychological fact that is, I think, at the center of the play: the taking in of food is the primary acknowledgment of one's dependence on the world, and as such, it is the primary token of one's vulnerability. But at the same time as Volumnia's image suggests the vulnerability inherent in feeding, it also suggests a way to fend off that vulnerability. In her image, feeding, incorporating, is transformed into spitting out, an aggressive expelling; the wound once again becomes the mouth that spits "forth blood/At Grecian sword contemning." The wound spitting blood thus becomes not a sign of vulnerability but an instrument of attack.

Volumnia's attitudes toward feeding and dependence are echoed perfectly in her son. Coriolanus persistently regards food as poisonous (1.1.177–78,

---

[21]Menenius' words point to the rigid and ferocious maleness so prized by Rome. See Phyllis Rackin, "*Coriolanus*: Shakespeare's Anatomy of *Virtus*," *Modern Language Studies* 13 (1983): 68–79, for the denial of female values in the play as a consequence of the Roman overvaluation of valor as the chiefest virtue. Rackin's analysis of the ways in which the traditionally female images of food, harvesting, and love are turned to destructive purposes throughout the play is particularly revealing.

3.1.155–56); the only thing he can imagine nourishing is rebellion (3.1.68–69, 116). Among the patricians, only Menenius is associated with the ordinary consumption of food and wine without an allaying drop of Tiber in it, and his distance from Coriolanus can be measured partly by his pathetic conviction that Coriolanus will be malleable—that he will have a "suppler" soul (5.1.55)—after he has had a full meal. But for Coriolanus, as for his mother, nobility consists precisely in *not* eating: he twice imagines starving himself honorably to death before asking for food, or anything else, from the plebians (2.3.112–13; 3.3.89–91).

Coriolanus incorporates not only his mother's attitude toward food but also the transformations in mode implicit in her image of Hector. These transformations— from feeding to warfare, from vulnerability to aggressive attack, from incorporation to spitting out—are at the center of Coriolanus's character and of our responses to him; for the whole of his masculine identity depends on his transformation of his vulnerability into an instrument of attack, as Menenius suggests when he tells us that each of Coriolanus's wounds "was an enemy's grave" (2.1.154–55). Cominius reports that Coriolanus entered his first battle a sexually indefinite thing, a boy or Amazon (2.2.91), and found his manhood there: "When he might act the woman in the scene, / He prov'd best man i'th'field" (2.2.96–97). The rigid masculinity that Coriolanus finds in war becomes a defense against acknowledgment of his neediness; he nearly succeeds in transforming himself from a vulnerable human creature into a grotesquely invulnerable and isolated thing. His body becomes his armor (1.3.35, 1.4.24); he himself becomes a weapon "who sensibly outdares his senseless sword, / And when it bows, stand'st up" (1.4.53–54), or he becomes the sword itself: "O me alone! Make you a sword of me!" (1.6.76). His whole life becomes a kind of phallic exhibitionism, devoted to disproving the possibility that he is vulnerable.[22] In the transformation from oral neediness to phallic aggression, anger becomes his meat as well as his mother's; Volumnia's phrase suggests not only his mode of defending himself against vulnerability but also the source of his anger in the deprivation imposed by his mother. We see the quality of his hunger and its transformation into aggression when, after his expulsion from Rome, he tells Aufidius, "I have . . . / Drawn tuns of blood out of thy country's breast" (4.5.99–100). Fighting here, as elsewhere in the play, is a poorly concealed substitute for feeding (see, for example, 1.9.10–11; 4.5.191–94, 222–24); and the unsatisfied ravenous attack of the infant on the breast provides the motive force for warfare. The image allows us to understand the ease with which Coriolanus turns his rage toward his own feeding mother, Rome.[23]

---

[22]For discussions of Coriolanus' phallic identification and its consequences, see Robert J. Stoller, "Shakespearean Tragedy: *Coriolanus*," *Psychoanalytic Quarterly* 35 (1966): 263–74; and Emmet Wilson, Jr., "Coriolanus: The Anxious Bridegroom," *American Imago* 25 (1968): 224–41. In "An Interpretation of Shakespeare's *Coriolanus*," *American Imago* 14 (1957): 407–35, Charles J. Hofling sees Coriolanus as a virtual embodiment of Reich's phallic-narcissistic character. Each of these analysts finds Coriolanus's phallic stance to some extent a defense against passivity (see Stoller, pp. 267, 269–70; Wilson, *passim;* Hofling, pp. 421, 424).

[23]David B. Barron sees Coriolanus's oral frustration and his consequent rage as central to his character. See "*Coriolanus*: Portrait of the Artist as Infant," *American Imago* 19 (1962): 171–73. This essay anticipates mine in some of its conclusions and many of its details of interpretation.

Thrust prematurely from dependence on his mother, forced to feed himself on his own anger, Coriolanus refuses to acknowledge any neediness or dependency: for his entire sense of himself depends on his being able to see himself as a self-sufficient creature. The desperation behind his claim to self-sufficiency is revealed by his horror of praise, even the praise of his general. The dependence of his masculinity on warfare in fact makes praise (or flattery, as he must call it) particularly threatening to him on the battlefield: flattery there, where his independence has apparently been triumphant, would imply that he has acted partly to win praise, that he is not self-sufficient after all; it would ultimately imply the undoing of his triumphant masculinity, and the soldier's steel would grow "soft as the parasite's silk" (1.9.45). The juxtaposition of soldier's steel and parasite's soft silk suggests both Coriolanus's dilemma and his solution to it: in order to avoid being the soft, dependent, feeding parasite, he has to maintain his rigidity as soldier's steel; that rigidity would be threatened were he to be "dieted/In praises sauc'd with lies" (1.9.51–52). (The same fears that underlie Coriolanus's use of this image here are brought home to him by Aufidius's charges at the end of the play: that he broke "his oath and resolution, like/A twist of rotten silk" [5.6.95–96]; that he "whin'd and roar'd away" the victory [5.6.98]; that he is a "boy of tears" [9.6.101].)

The complex of ideas that determines Coriolanus's response to praise also determines the rigidity that makes him so disastrous as a political figure. As he contemptuously asks the people for their voices and later gives up his attempt to pacify them, the language in which he imagines his alternatives reveals the extent to which his unwillingness to ask for the people's approval, like his abhorrence of praise, depends on his attitude toward food: "Better it is to die, better to starve,/Than crave the hire which first we do deserve" (2.3.112–13); "Pent to linger/But with a grain a day, I would not buy/Their mercy at the price of one fair word" (3.3.89–91). Asking, craving, flattering with fair words are here not only preconditions but also equivalents of eating: to refuse to ask is to starve; but starvation is preferable to asking because asking, like eating, is an acknowledgment of one's weakness, one's dependence on the outside world. "The price is, to ask it kindly" (2.3.75), but that is the one price Coriolanus cannot pay. When he must face the prospect of revealing his dependence on the populace by asking for their favor, his whole delicately constructed masculine identity threatens to crumble. In order to ask, a harlot's spirit must possess him; his voice must become as small as that of a eunuch or a virgin minding babies; a beggar's tongue must make motion through his lips (3.2.111–18). Asking, then, like susceptibility to praise, would undo the process by which he was transformed on the battlefield from boy or woman to man. That he imagines this undoing as a kind of reverse voice change suggests the extent to which his phallic aggressive pose is a defense against collapse into the dependent oral mode of the small boy. And in fact, Coriolanus's own use of language constantly reiterates this defense. Instead of using those linguistic modes that acknowledge dependence, Coriolanus spits out words, using them as weapons. His invective is in the mode of Hector's wound, aggressively spitting forth blood: it is an attempt to deny vulnerability by making the very area of vulnerability into the means of attack.[24]

Coriolanus's abhorrence of praise and flattery, his horror lest the people think that he got his wounds to please them (2.2.147–50), his insistence that he be given the consulship as a sign of what he is, not as a reward (1.9.26), his refusal to ask—all are attempts to claim that he is *sui generis*. This attitude finds its logical conclusion in his desperate cry as he sees his mother approaching him at the end:

> I'll never
> Be such a gosling to obey instinct, but stand
> As if a man were author of himself
> And knew no other kin.
> (5.3.34–37)

The gosling obeys instinct and acknowledges his kinship with mankind; but Coriolanus will attempt to stand alone. (Since his manhood depends exactly on this phallic standing alone, he is particularly susceptible to Aufidius's taunt of "boy" after he has been such a gosling as to obey instinct.) The relationship between Coriolanus's aggressive pose and his attempts to claim that he is *sui generis* is most dramatically realized in the conquest of Corioli; it is here that Coriolanus most nearly realizes his fantasy of standing as if a man were author of himself. For the scene at Corioli represents a glorious transformation of the nightmare of oral vulnerability ("to th'pot" [1.4.47], one of his soldiers says as he is swallowed up by the gates) into a phallic adventure that both assures and demonstrates his independence. Coriolanus's battlecry as he storms the gates sexualizes the scene: "Come on;/If you'll stand fast, we'll beat them to their wives" (1.4.40–41). But the dramatic action itself presents the conquest of Corioli as an image not of rape but of triumphant rebirth: after Coriolanus enters the gates of the city, he is proclaimed dead; one of his comrades delivers a eulogy firmly in the past tense ("Thou wast a soldier/Even to Cato's wish" [1.4.56–57]); then Coriolanus miraculously reemerges, covered with blood (1.6.22), and is given a new name. For the assault on Corioli is both a rape and a rebirth: the underlying fantasy is that intercourse is a literal return to the womb from which one is reborn, one's own author.[25] The fantasy of self-authorship is complete when Coriolanus is given his new name, earned by his own actions.[26]

[24]In his discussion of Coriolanus's cathartic vituperation, Kenneth Burke suggests that invective is rooted in the helpless rage of the infant. See "*Coriolanus*—and the Delights of Faction," *Hudson Review* 19 (1966): 200.

[25]To see Corioli as the mother's womb here may seem grotesque; the idea becomes less grotesque if we remember Volumnia's own identification of country with mother's womb just as Coriolanus is about to attack another city (see discussion elsewhere in this essay). Wilson (Emmett Wilson, Jr., "Coriolanus: The Anxious Bridegroom," *American Imago* 25[1968]: 224–41) suggests that the attack on Corioli represents defloration—specifically, that it expresses the equation of coitus with damaging assault and the resultant dread of a retaliatory castration.

[26]The force of this new name is partly corroborated by Volumnia, who delights in reminding her son of his dependence on her: she has trouble learning his new name from the start (2.1.173) and eventually associates it with the pride that keeps him from pity for his family (5.3.170–71).

But despite the boast implicit in his conquest of Corioli, Coriolanus has not in fact succeeded in separating himself from his mother; even the very role through which he claims independence was designed by her—as she never tires of pointing out ("My praises made thee first a soldier" [3.2.108]; "Thou art my warrior:/I holp to frame thee" [5.3.62–63]). In fact, Shakespeare underlines Volumnia's point by the placement of two central scenes. In 1.3, before we have seen Coriolanus himself as a soldier, we see Volumnia first describe her image of her son on the battlefield and then enact his role: "Methinks I see him stamp thus, and call thus:/'Come on you cowards, you were got in fear/Though you were born in Rome'" (1.3.32–34). This marvelous moment suggests not only the ways in which Volumnia herself lives through her son, but also the extent to which his role is her creation. For when we see him in the next scene, acting exactly as his mother had predicted, we are left with the impression that he is merely enacting her enactment of the role that she has imagined for him.

That Coriolanus is acting under Volumnia's direction even in the role that seems to ensure his independence of her helps to explain both his bafflement when she suddenly starts to disapprove of the role she has created ("I muse my mother/Does not approve me further" [3.2.7–8]) and his eventual capitulation to her demand that he shift roles, here and at the end of the play. For his manhood is secure only when he can play the role that she has designed, and play it with her approval. He asks her, "Why did you wish me milder? Would you have me/False to my nature? Rather say I play/The man I am" (3.2.14–16). But "I play the man I am" cuts both ways: in his bafflement, Coriolanus would like to suggest that there is no distance between role and self, but he in fact suggests that he plays at being himself, that his manhood is merely a role. Given that Volumnia has created this dilemma, her answer is unnecessarily cruel, but telling: "You might have been enough the man you are,/With striving less to be so" (3.2.19–20). Volumnia is right: it is the intensity and rigidity of Coriolanus's commitment to his masculine role that make us suspect the intensity of the fears that this role is designed to hide, especially from himself. For the rigidity of the role and the tenuousness of the self that it protects combine to make acknowledged play-acting of any kind terrifying for Coriolanus, as though he can maintain the identity of self and role, and hence his integrity, only by denying that he is able to assume a role. Because he cannot acknowledge the possibility of role playing, Coriolanus must respond to his mother's request that he act a new role as a request that he be someone other than Coriolanus. When he finally agrees to take on the role of humble supplicant, he is sure that he will act badly (3.2.105–6), and that he will lose his manhood in the process (3.2.111–23).

The fragility of the entire structure by which Coriolanus maintains his claim to self-sufficient manhood helps to account for the violence of his hatred of the plebeians. For Coriolanus uses the crowd to bolster his own identity: he accuses them of being exactly what he wishes not to be. He does his best to distinguish himself from them by emphasizing his aloneness and their status as multitude as the very grounds of their being.[27] Throughout, he associates his manhood with his isolation, so that "Alone I did it" (5.6.116) becomes a sufficient answer to Aufidius's charge that he is a boy. Hence the very status of the plebeians as crowd reassures him that they are not men but dependent and unmanly things, merely children—a point of view that Menenius seems to confirm when he tells the tribunes: "Your abilities are too infant-like for doing much alone" (2.1.36–37). His most potent image of the crowd is as an appropriately infantile common mouth (3.1.22, 155) disgustingly willing to exhibit its neediness. Coriolanus enters the play identified by the plebeians as the person who is keeping them from eating (1.1.9–10); indeed, one of his main complaints about the plebeians is that they say they are hungry (1.1.204–7). Coriolanus himself has been deprived of food, and he seems to find it outrageous that others should not be. His position here is like that of the older brother who has fought his way into manhood and who is now confronted by an apparently endless group of siblings—"my sworn brother the people" (2.3.95), he calls them—who still insist on being fed by mother Rome, and whose insistence on their dependency threatens the pose of self-sufficiency by which his equilibrium is perilously maintained. To disclaim his own hunger, Coriolanus must therefore disclaim his kinship with the crowd; "I would they were barbarians—as they are, /. . . not Romans—as they are not" (3.1.236–37). But the formulation of the disclaimer itself reveals the very tensions that it is designed to assuage. Insofar as he wishes the people non-Roman, he acknowledges their Romanness; but this acknowledgment of kinship must immediately be denied by the assertion that they are in fact not Roman. The very insistence on difference reveals the fear of likeness.

But the multitudinous mouth of the crowd is horrifying to Coriolanus not only insofar as it threatens to reveal his own oral neediness to him but also insofar as it makes the nature of his vulnerability uncomfortably precise. In this hungry world, everyone seems in danger of being eaten. The crowd suspects the senators of cannibalistic intentions: "If the wars eat us not up, they will; and there's all the love they bear us" (1.1.84–85). Since Coriolanus twice dismisses them as ignoble food ("quarry" [1. 1. 197]; "fragments" [1.1.221]), their fears seem not entirely without basis. But Coriolanus thinks that, without the awe of the Senate, the crowd would "feed on one another" (1.1.187). Given their choice, the tribunes would naturally enough prefer that the "present wars devour" Coriolanus (1.1.257) instead of the populace. The people's belief that the death of Coriolanus would allow them to have corn at their own price (1.1.9) is eventually sustained by the plot, insofar as Coriolanus opposes the giving of corn gratis (3.1.113–17). But at the start of the play, we are not in a position to understand the logic behind their association between killing Coriolanus and an unlimited food supply; and in the context of all the cannibalistic images, the mysterious association seems to point toward a fan-

---

[27]And so does Shakespeare. In Plutarch, Coriolanus is accompanied by a few men both when he enters the gates of Corioli and when he is exiled from Rome. Shakespeare emphasizes his isolation by giving him no companions on either occasion.

tasy in which the people, rather than the wars, will devour Coriolanus.[28] Menenius explicates this fantasy:

> *Menenius:*   Pray you, who does the wolf love?
> *Sicinius:*   The lamb.
> *Menenius:*   Ay, to devour him, as the hungry plebeians would the noble Martius.
>
>   (2.1.6–9)

And in the third act, as the people begin to find their teeth and rise against Coriolanus, his images of them as mouths begin to reveal not only his contempt for their hunger but also his fear of his own oral vulnerability, fear of being bitten, digested, pecked at: "You being their mouths, why rule you not their teeth?" (3.1.35); "How shall this bosom multiplied digest / The senate's courtesy?" (3.1.130–31); "Thus we debase / The nature of our seats, . . . / . . . and bring in / The crows to peck the eagles" (3.1.134–38). The fear of being eaten that lies just below the surface in these images is made explicit when Coriolanus tells Aufidius that the people have "devour'd" all of him but his name (4.5.77).

The crowd, then, is both dependent, unmanly, contemptible—and terrifyingly ready to rise up and devour Coriolanus. Through his portrayal of the crowd, Coriolanus can manage to dismiss the specter of his own hunger and insist on his identity as an isolated and inviolable thing ("a thing / Made by some other deity than nature" [4.6.91–92], as Cominius says). But he cannot dismiss the danger that exposure to their hunger would bring. His absolute horror of the prospect of showing his wounds to win the consulship depends partly, I think, on the complex of ideas that stands behind his characterization of the crowd. In Plutarch, Coriolanus shows his wounds; in Shakespeare, the thought is intolerable to him and, despite many promises that he will, he never does. For the display of his wounds would reveal his kinship with the plebeians in several ways: by revealing that he has worked for hire (2.2.149) as they have (that is, that he and his deeds are not *sui generis* after all); by revealing that he is vulnerable, as they are; and by revealing, through the persistent identification of wound and mouth, that he too has a mouth, that he is a dependent creature. Moreover, the exhibition of his wounds to the crowd is impossible for Coriolanus partly because his identity is sustained by exhibitionism of another sort. Coriolanus is right in believing that he must not "stand naked" (2.2.137) before the crowd, asking for their approval; for this standing naked would reverse the sustaining fantasy by which he hoped to "stand / As if a man were author of himself" (5.3.35–36). For the phallic exhibitionism of Coriolanus's life as a soldier has been designed to deny the possibility of kinship

---

[28]In his suggestive essay on the people's voices in *Coriolanus*, Leonard Tennenhouse notes that "Coriolanus, the child denied love in the service of patrician ideals, is perceived by the mob as the one who denies. The mysterious source of the cannibalistic rage directed against him is the recognition by the plebeians that he would withhold from them what the patrician mother would withhold from her son—nurturance and thus life itself" ("*Coriolanus:* History and the Crisis of Semantic Order," *Comparative Drama* 10 [1976]: 335).

with the crowd; it has served to reassure him of his potency and his aggressive independence, and therefore to sustain him against fears of collapse into the dependent mode of infancy. To exhibit the fruits of his soldiership as the emblems not of his self-sufficiency but of his vulnerability and dependence, and to exhibit them precisely to those whose kinship he would most like to deny, would transform his chief means of defense into a proclamation of his weakness: it would threaten to undo the very structure by which he lives. And finally, insofar as he would expose himself as vulnerable and dependent by displaying his wounds, he would invite the oral rage of the crowd to satisfy itself on him. "If he show us his wounds and tell us his deeds, we are to put our tongues into those wounds and speak for them" (2.3.5–8), the Third Citizen says; his grotesque image suggests that the sweet licked by the multitudinous tongue (3.1.155–56) would be "sweet" Coriolanus himself (3.2.107).

During the first part of the play, Coriolanus uses his opposition to the crowd to define himself and to fend off his vulnerability. But after the exile from Rome, this source of definition fails, and Coriolanus turns toward his old enemy Aufidius to confirm himself. For if Coriolanus has throughout defined himself by opposition, he has defined himself by likeness as well; from the beginning, we have watched him create a mirror image of himself in Aufidius. As soon as he hears that the Volsces are in arms, Coriolanus announces the terms of his relationship with Aufidius: "I sin in envying his nobility;/And were I anything but what I am,/I would wish me only he" (1.1.229–31). But the noble Aufidius is Coriolanus's own invention, a reflection of his own doubts about what he is, an expression of what he would wish himself to be. Shakespeare takes pains to emphasize the distance between the Aufidius we see and the Aufidius of Coriolanus's imagination. The Aufidius invented by Coriolanus seems designed to reassure Coriolanus of the reality of his own male grandeur by giving him the image of himself; his need to create a man who is his equal is in fact one of the most poignant elements in the play and helps to account for his tragic blindness to his rival's true nature as opportunist and schemer. Immediately after Coriolanus has imagined himself Aufidius, he allows us to see the extent to which he is dependent on Aufidius for his self-definition in a nearly prophetic confession: "Were half to half the world by th' ears, and he/Upon my party, I'd revolt to make/Only my wars with him" (1.1.232–34). Later, the Coriolanus who shrinks violently from the praise of others eagerly solicits news of Aufidius's opinion of him; and his oddly touching "Spoke he of me?" (3.1.12) reveals the extent to which he needs to see himself in Aufidius's eyes. As he approaches Antium after the exile, he pauses to reflect on the strangeness of his actions but succeeds only in suggesting that the issue driving him from Rome and toward Aufidius is a "trick not worth an egg" (4.4.21), as though for the moment the fact of his union with Aufidius is more important than the circumstances that drove him to it. His attempt to explain his actions begins and ends with the image of friends "who twin, as 'twere, in love/Unseparable" (4.4.15–16), who "interjoin their issues" (4.4.22). The movement of this soliloquy reveals the fantasy of twinship underlying his relationship with Aufidius both as foe and as friend.

The union with Aufidius is for Coriolanus a union with an alter ego; it represents a flight from the world of Rome and his mother toward a safe male world. Devoured in all but name by Rome (4.5.77), Coriolanus enters Antium afraid of being eaten: he fears that the Volscian wives will slay him with spits (4.4.5) and tells the Third Servingman that he has dwelt "i'th'city of kites and crows" (4.5.43), a city of scavengers. (That this city is both the wilderness and Rome itself is suggested by Coriolanus's echo of his earlier peril, the crows who will peck the eagles [3.1.138].) Here, far from Rome, Coriolanus at last allows his hunger and his vulnerability to be felt, and he is given food. He presents himself to Aufidius during a great feast, from which he is initially excluded: "the feast smells well, but I/Appear not like a guest" (4.5.5–6). But here in Antium, the play moves toward a fantasy in which nourishment may be safely taken because it is given by a male, by a father-brother-twin rather than a mother. Coriolanus is finally taken into the feast. In the safe haven provided by his mirror image, he will not be devoured; instead, he will eat. Aufidius's servants give us the final development of this fantasy:

> *First Servant:*   . . . Before Corioles he scotched him and notched him like a carbonado.
> *Second Servant:*   And he had been cannibally given, he might have broiled and eaten him too.
>
> (4.5.191–94)

The scene moves, then, from hunger and the fear of being eaten to an image of Coriolanus triumphantly eating Aufidius. Since his mother will not feed him, Coriolanus will find in Aufidius the only nourishment that can sustain him; and insofar as Aufidius is his alter ego, he, like his mother, will sup on himself.

When Coriolanus is banished from Rome, he responds with an infantile fantasy of omnipotent control: "I banish you!" (3.3.123). He then attempts to ensure the reality of his omnipotence by wishing on his enemies exactly what he already knows to be true of them: "Let every feeble rumour shake your hearts!/. . . Have the power still/To banish your defenders" (3.3.125–28). Few curses have ever been so sure of instantaneous fulfillment. Having thus exercised his rage and assured himself of the magical power of his invective, Coriolanus finally makes his claim to true independence: "There is a world elsewhere!" (3.3.135). His encounter with Aufidius is an attempt to create this world, one in his own image; but even the union with Aufidius leads ultimately back to Rome and his mother. For Coriolanus's rage, like his hunger, is properly directed toward his mother; though it is deflected from her and toward the plebeians and Volscians for much of the play, it finally returns to its source. For Rome and his mother are finally one:[29] in exiling

---

[29]Donald A. Stauffer, in *Shakespeare's World of Images* (New York: W. W. Norton, 1949), p. 252, points out that Rome is less *patria* than *matria* in this play; he discusses Volumnia as a projection of Rome, particularly in 5.3. Virtually all psychoanalytic critics comment on the identification of Volumnia with Rome.

Coriolanus, Rome reenacts the role of the mother who cast him out. Although in his loving farewell his family and friends are wholly distinguished from the beast with many heads, by the time he has returned to Rome they are no more than a poor grain or two that must be consumed in the general fire (5.1.27). (Even in his loving farewell we hear a note of resentment when he consoles his mother by telling her: "My hazards still have been your solace" [4.1.28].) As he approaches Rome, the devouring populace becomes indistinguishable from his loving mother. But Menenius has already pointed toward the fantasy that identifies them:

> Now the good gods forbid
> That our renowned Rome, whose gratitude
> Towards her deserved children is enroll'd
> In Jove's own book, like an unnatural dam
> Should now eat up her own!
> (3.1.287–91)

The cannibalistic mother who denies food and yet feeds on the victories of her sweet son stands at the darkest center of the play, where Coriolanus's oral vulnerability is fully defined. Here, talion law reigns: the feeding infant himself will be devoured; the loving mother becomes the devourer. In this dark world, love itself is primitive and dangerous: both the First Citizen and Menenius suggest that here, to be loved is to be eaten (1.1.84–85; 2.1.6–9).

Coriolanus's return to Rome is not ultimately a return to his mother; it is rather a last attempt to escape her love and its consequences. If Coriolanus can make himself a new name, forged in the fires of burning Rome (5.1.14–15), he can construct a new identity independent of his mother: an identity that will demonstrate his indifference to her, his separation from her. For he can stand as author of himself only by destroying his mother. The return to Rome is an act of retaliation against the mother on whom he has been dependent, the mother who has cast him out. But it is at the same time an acting out of the child's fantasy of reversing the roles of parent and child, so that the life of the parent is in the hands of the omnipotent child. The child becomes a god, dispensing life and death (5.4.24–25): becomes in effect the author of his mother, so that he can finally stand alone.

But Coriolanus can sustain neither his fantasy of self-authorship nor his attempt to realize a godlike omnipotent power. And the failure of both leaves him so unprotected, so utterly devoid of a sense of self that, for the first time in the play, he feels himself surrounded by dangers. The capitulation of his independent selfhood before his mother's onslaught seems to him to require his death, and he embraces that death with a passivity thoroughly uncharacteristic of him:

> O my mother, mother! O!
> You have won a happy victory to Rome;
> But for your son, believe it, O, believe it,
> Most dangerously you have with him prevail'd,
> If not most mortal to him. But let it come.
> (5.3.185–89)

Volumnia achieves this happy victory partly because she makes the dangers inherent in his defensive system as terrifying as those it is designed to keep at bay. Her last confrontation with her son is so appallingly effective because she invalidates his defenses by threatening to enact his most central defensive fantasies, thereby making their consequences inescapable to him.

The very appearance of his mother, coming to beg him for the life of her city and hence for her own life, is an enactment of his attempt to become the author of his mother, his desire to have power over her. He has before found her begging intolerable (3.2.124–34); when she kneels to him here, making the role reversal of mother and child explicit (5.3.56), he reacts with an hysteria that suggests that the acting-out of this forbidden wish threatens to dissolve the very structures by which he orders his life:

> What's this?
> Your knees to me? to your corrected son?
> Then let the pebbles on the hungry beach
> Fillip the stars. Then let the mutinous winds
> Strike the proud cedars 'gainst the fiery sun,
> Murd'ring impossibility, to make
> What cannot be, slight work!
>
> (5.3.56–62)

At first sight, this speech seems simply to register Coriolanus's horror at the threat to hierarchy implied by the kneeling of parent to child. But if Coriolanus were responding only—or even mainly—to this threat, we would expect the threatened chaos to be imaged as high bowing to low; this is in fact the image we are given when Volumnia first bows to her son as if—as Coriolanus says— "Olympus to a molehill should / In supplication nod" (5.3.30–31). But Coriolanus does not respond to his mother's kneeling with an image of high bowing to low; instead, he responds with two images of low mutinously striking at high. The chaos imaged here is not so much a derivative of his mother's kneeling as of the potential mutiny that her kneeling seems to imply: for her kneeling releases the possibility of his mutiny against her, a mutiny that he has been suppressing all along by his exaggerated deference to her. His response here reveals again the defensive function of his hatred of the mutinous and leveling populace:[30] the violence of his images suggests that his mother's kneeling has forced him to acknowledge his return to Rome as a rising up of the hungry and mutinous forces within himself. With her usual acumen, Volumnia recognizes the horror of potential mutiny in Coriolanus's response and chooses exactly this moment to assert, once again, his dependence on her: "Thou art my warrior" (5.3.62).

---

[30]Participants in the Midlands uprising were commonly called "levelers," in startling anticipation of the 1640s. See, for example, Stow [*Annales*, p. 890].

Coriolanus's forbidden wish to have power over his mother was safe as long as it seemed impossible. But now that protective impossibility itself seems murdered, and he is forced to confront the fact that his wish has become a reality. Nor are the hungry and mutinous forces within him content to murder only an abstract "impossibility": the murderousness of the image is directed ultimately at his mother. And once again, Volumnia makes Coriolanus uncomfortably clear to himself: after she has enacted his terrifying fantasy by kneeling, she makes it impossible for him to believe that her death would be merely an incidental consequence of his plan to burn Rome. For she reveals exactly the extent to which his assault is on both. Her long speech builds to its revelation with magnificent force and logic. She first forces him to see his attack on his country as an attack on a living body by accusing him of coming to tear "his country's bowels out" (5.3.103). Next, she identifies that body as their common source of nurture: "the country, our dear nurse" (5.3.110). Finally, as she announces her intention to commit suicide, she makes absolute the identification of the country with herself. After she has imagined him treading on his country's ruin (5.3.116), she warns him:

> Thou shalt no sooner
> March to assault thy country than to tread—
> Trust to't, thou shalt not—on thy mother's womb
> That brought thee to this world.
> (5.3.122–25)

The ruin on which Coriolanus will tread will be his mother's womb—a warning accompanied by yet another assertion of his dependence on her as she recalls to him the image of himself as a fetus within that womb.

If Coriolanus's mutinous fantasies are no longer impossible, if his mother will indeed die as a result of his actions, then he will have realized his fantasy of living omnipotently without kin, without dependency. In fact this fantasy, his defense throughout, is articulated only here, as he catches sight of his mother (5.3.34–37), and its expression is the last stand of his claim to independence. Throughout this scene, Volumnia has simultaneously asserted his dependence on her and made the dangers inherent in his defense against that dependence horrifyingly clear; and in the end, it is the combination of her insistence on his dependency and her threat to disown him, to literalize his fantasy of standing alone, that cause him to capitulate. Finally, he cannot "stand/ As if a man were author of himself/And knew no other kin"; he must become a child again, a gosling, and admit his neediness. The presence of his own child, holding Volumnia's hand, strengthens her power over him. For Coriolanus seems to think of his child less as his son than as the embodiment of his own childhood and of the child that remains within him; even when we are first told about the son, he seems more a comment on Coriolanus's childhood than on his fatherhood. The identification of father and child is suggested by Coriolanus's response as he sees wife, mother, and child approaching: "My wife comes foremost; then the honour'd mould/Wherein this trunk was fram'd, and in her hand/The grandchild to her blood" (5.3.22–24). Here Coriolanus does not acknowledge the child as his and his wife's: he first imagines himself in his mother's womb and then imagines his child as an extension of his mother. Even Coriolanus's language to Menenius as he earlier denies his family reveals the same fusion of father and son: "Wife, mother, child, I know not" (5.2.80), he says, in a phrase that suggestively identifies his own mother as the mother of the child and the child he attempts to deny as himself. Volumnia had once before brought Coriolanus to submission by reminding him of himself as a suckling child (3.2.129); now virtually her last words enforce his identification with the child that she holds by the hand: "This fellow had a Volscian to his mother;/ His wife is in Corioles, and his child/ Like him by chance" (5.3.178–80). But at the same time that she reminds him of his dependency, she disowns him by disclaiming her parenthood; she exacerbates his sense of himself as a child, and then threatens to leave him—as he thought he wished—alone. And as his fantasy of self-sufficiency threatens to become a reality, it becomes too frightening to sustain. Just as his child entered the scene holding Volumnia's hand, so Coriolanus again becomes a child, holding his mother's hand.

In *Macbeth,* the fantasy of caesarian self-birth is the answer to the mother's power over her feeding infant: if vulnerability comes of having a mother, the solution is to be self-born, not born of woman. Although *Macbeth* punishes this fantasy in Macbeth himself, its creation of an all-male lineage and landscape keeps the caesarian solution available for its audience. *Coriolanus* enacts, exposes, and then punishes the fantasy of self-authorship much more ruthlessly than *Macbeth*: though Coriolanus begins as Macbeth's heroic "man-child," he ends fully subject to the place of origin and to the mortality that place entails. In the end, neither Coriolanus nor *Coriolanus* can sustain the fantasy that he is motherless, the author of himself.

Initially, the play seems to grant Coriolanus the status he desires: renamed by his self-birth at Corioli, he apparently escapes the condition of his natural birth, becoming "Jove's statue" (2.1.264), "a thing/ Made by some other deity than nature,/ That shapes man better" (4.6.91–93). His determination to forge a new name in the fires that burn Rome plays out the logic of this escape: his renaming now will be the explicit sign of his destruction of the maternal body, the "country" that is simultaneously Rome and his mother's womb. But it is the work of the play's ending to demonstrate that he has not been made by some other deity than nature, hence to demonstrate his subjection to the "mother's womb/ That brought [him] to this world" (5.3.124–25). In fact the fantasy of self-authorship emerges explicitly only *in extremis,* only at the moment that marks its limitation—immediately after Coriolanus himself sees his mother approaching and identifies her, not by name or familial position, but as "the honour'd mould/ Wherein this trunk was fram'd" (5.3.22–23). The fantasy of escape itself is the sign of his subjection: at the very moment that Coriolanus would stand alone, he is returned to the "natural" place of origin. Unable finally to destroy that place in himself, he must capitulate to it; and in the bleak psychological landscape of this play, this capitulation means his death.

At the moment of capitulation, the ending of *Coriolanus* undoes the ending of *Macbeth*: if *Macbeth* enacts the severing of maternal connection, *Coriolanus* brutally displays the failure of this attempt. If maternal power is excised from Scotland, it is triumphant in Rome—and its triumph inevitably means the failure of male autonomy, the death of the male self. "O mother, mother!/What have you done?" (5.3.182–83): Coriolanus is killed in Antium immediately after Volumnia is triumphantly welcomed to Rome; the action of *Coriolanus* in fact construes her triumph as his death. If Macbeth dies fighting, heroically mantled in his own self-sufficiency, Coriolanus dies helpless and unarmed, his multiply-penetrated body the sign of his mother's presence in him. The ending of *Coriolanus* thus revises the ending of *Macbeth* without offering any relief from its bleak alternatives. Between them, the two plays enact the logic of a terrible either/or: either the excision of the female or the excision of the male, either the death of the mother or the death of her son.

And with these two plays, Shakespeare's tragic art itself seems to have come to an impasse. Both plays deny us the traditional comforts of tragic theater; both protagonists die in terrible isolation, still in flight from the contamination that relationship to the female would bring. Moreover, both plays constitute the theatrical itself as the realm of disturbance: if both figure maternal presence as devastating to the masculine identity of the son, both strikingly figure theater as allied with this dangerous female presence. This figuration seems to me to shape the dramaturgy of the two plays: taken together, they constitute a theatrical doing and undoing, engaging their audiences theatrically in the central psychological dilemmas of their protagonists as they play out in their own dramaturgy first the dangers of merger with the female and then the recoil into an exaggerated autonomy.

The loss of masculine autonomy that is the psychological threat of *Macbeth* everywhere infects that play's dramaturgy: for the play's audience as for its hero, distinctions between inner and outer fail as discrete objects blur and fuse, overwhelmed by their own boundary instability. "Rapt" by the "horrid image" of Duncan's murder (1.3.57, 135), Macbeth is driven to enact it in the world; under the guidance of the witches who speak the voice of his own horrible imaginings, "be it thought and done" (4.1.149) becomes less his wish than his fate, as though he were doomed to have the firstlings of his heart become the firstlings of his hand (4.1.147–48). As in a dream, the images of his own desires and fears are projected outward into the world, so that he meets fantasy-versions of himself again and again: in the traitor to whom he clings (1.2.8), the bloody child arising from the witches' cauldron, the man not born of woman, perhaps especially in the final desolate landscape, emptied of generative potential. And except for the English interlude, the play insists that we share in his claustrophobic and phantasmagoric space:[31] meeting the witches that are ambiguously inside and outside

---

[31]If the boundary between inner and outer is dangerous for Hamlet, it is virtually nonexistent for Macbeth. I borrow the word "phantasmagoric" from David Willbern in order to register my debt to his rich exploration of these issues (see "Phantasmagoric *Macbeth*," esp. pp. 532–35); but Willbern's imagined audience is less claustrophobically engaged with Macbeth than mine is (pp. 535–40, 549). Although Macbeth's response to maternal threat is crucially inflected by his gender, I do not distinguish between male and female in imagining an audience trapped inside his head: much of the primary fantasy material

of Macbeth, seeing the dagger that both is and is not a dagger of his mind, we do not know where we are, whose voice we hear, any more than Macbeth knows whose voice cries out "Sleep no more!" (2.2.34). This is the dramaturgy of the witches' cauldron, where function is smothered in surmise (1.3.141). And though the spectacular theater of the witches' cauldron ends in the vision of a triumphant male lineage (4.1.106–11), this spectacle nonetheless marks the space of the theatrical itself as female in origin: it erupts from the witches' cauldron as the play erupts from their first words, materializing as though called forth by them.

For *Macbeth*, participation in the theatrical means participation in the witches' realm; in the end, in the chastened realm of Malcolm, even theater must be robbed of its magic. When Malcolm commands his troops to carry the boughs of Dunsinane's trees, he simultaneously appropriates the "natural" and exposes the devices of the witches' theater, in effect ruining their theatrical effect by showing us the stage hands moving the props. Under his rule, the theater of spectacle is exorcised, and we are firmly on the ground of the literal, where objects stay themselves. And this antitheatrical territory is, I think, the ground upon which *Coriolanus* stands. In *Coriolanus* there are no supernatural beings, blurring boundaries by calling up their fantastic spectacles; this play, like Malcolm, seems deliberately to refuse what *Macbeth* constitutes as the theatrical.

Casting the theatrical as the feminine, Coriolanus himself refuses to participate in it: spectacle is for him the sign of boundary confusion, a dangerously feminizing self-exposure; acting is the province of the harlot, the eunuch, the virgin minding babies (3.2.112–15). Refusing theater, Coriolanus will not act for applause: he refuses to show himself to us as he refuses to show his wounds to the populace, as though he feared that we too would find him feminized by the display. Insisting on his own rigid integrity, Coriolanus enforces ours: if Macbeth invites our dangerous merger, Coriolanus courts our alienation, dismantling the relationship between actor and audience. Excluded by his exclusion of the theatrical, we are in effect denied our roles as spectators to his tragic scene. And this work of exclusion is carried out by the whole play, not simply by its protagonist; throughout, *Coriolanus* replicates in its audience Coriolanus's own isolation, his own claim to self-authorship. If the dramaturgy of *Macbeth* characteristically threatens boundaries, smothering function in its female element, the dramaturgy of *Coriolanus* characteristically reinforces boundaries, walling in cities and individuals. If the metamorphically fluid language of *Macbeth* works to merge and blur distinctions, incarnadining "the multitudinous seas," "Making the green one red" (2.2.61–62), the metallic language of *Coriolanus* works to define and separate, to limit, almost as rigidly as Coriolanus himself does.

---

of the play seems to me to derive from infantile vulnerabilities prior to fixed gender organization. The ungendered nature of this material may in fact make the ending of the play particularly bleak for women, who are positioned inside Macbeth's fantasy for much of the play but then are written out of its resolution. (For a very powerful account of gendered reading and cross-gender identification in *Macbeth*, see Madelon Sprengnether's "Reading as Lady Macbeth," in *Women's Re-visions of Shakespeare*, ed. Marianne Novy [Urbana: U of Illinois P, 1990], pp. 227–41.)

In this world of isolates, we too become isolates, as rigid and separate as Coriolanus himself is.

The association of the theatrical with the feminine in both *Macbeth* and *Coriolanus* threatens to dismantle theater altogether: if Malcolm diminishes its effects by mastering and displaying its props, Coriolanus refuses to act and refuses us our role as spectators. Winnicott suggests that play can happen only in the transitional space established by trust in the good-enough mother;[32] here, in the absence of such trust, rigid autonomy seems the only antidote to terrifying boundary instability, and there can be no play. Shakespeare's capacity to re-imagine play, to turn toward the new theatrical art of the romances, will depend in part on his re-imagining the relationship of theater to the maternal; as Antony is re-created in the spacious theater of Cleopatra's imagination, Shakespeare will move beyond the impasse of *Macbeth* and *Coriolanus* into a region where play once more becomes possible.

[32]See the essays collected in D. W. Winnicott, *Playing and Reality* (London: Tavistock Publications, 1971), especially "Transitional Objects and Transitional Phenomena," pp. 1–25. My understanding of Winnicott and of Shakespeare has been deeply influenced by Schwartz, whose wonderfully rich reading of Shakespeare through Winnicott (Murray Schwartz, "Shakespeare through Contemporary Psychoanalysis," in *Representing Shakespeare: New Psychoanalytic Essays*, eds. Murray Schwartz and Coppélia Kahn [Baltimore: Johns Hopkins UP, 1980], pp. 21–32) traces the loss and recovery of play space in his tragedies and romances; the fullest Winnicottian reading of *Macbeth* is Willbern's brilliant account of the play's violations of this space ("Phantasmagoric *Macbeth*").

"Who Does the Wolf Love?" *Coriolanus* and Interpretations of Politics

Stanley Cavell

Something that draws me to *Coriolanus* is its apparent disdain of questions I have previously asked of Shakespearean tragedy, taking tragedy as an epistemological problem, a refusal to know or to be known, an avoidance of acknowledgment, an expression (or imitation) of skepticism. Coriolanus's refusal to acknowledge his participation in finite human existence may seem so obviously the fact of the matter of his play that to note it seems merely to describe the play, not at all to interpret it. It may be, however, that this lack of theoretical grip itself proposes a moral, or offers a conclusion, namely that *Coriolanus* is not exactly to be understood as a tragedy, that its mystery—supposing one agrees to something like a mystery in its events—will be located only in locating its lack or missing of tragedy, hence its closeness to tragedy.

But systematically to pursue this possibility would require—from me—following out a sense that this play presents a particular interpretation of the problem of skepticism as such (skepticism directed toward our knowledge of the existence of others), in particular an interpretation that takes skepticism as a form of narcissism. This interpretation does not in itself come to me as a complete surprise since a book I published a few years ago—*The Claim of Reason*—begins with an interpretation of Wittgenstein's *Philosophical Investigations* that takes his move against the idea of a private language (an idea that arises in his struggle against skepticism) as a move against a kind of narcissism, a kind of denial of an existence shared with others; and my book ends with a reading of *Othello* as a depiction of the murderous lengths to which narcissism must go in order to maintain its picture of itself as skepticism, in order to maintain its stand of ignorance, its fear or avoidance of knowing, under the color of a claim to certainty.[1] What surprised me

From Stanley Cavell, *Disowning Knowledge in Six Plays of Shakespeare* (Cambridge: Cambridge UP, 1987). The postscript has been omitted here, and the notes shortened and renumbered. Essay first published in *Representations* 3 (1983): 1–20. © 1983 by the Regents of the University of California. Reproduced by permission of University of California Press and the author.

[1]For my discussion of *Othello*, see chapter 3 of *Disowning Knowledge: In Six Plays of Shakespeare* (Cambridge: Cambridge UP, 1987). Future reference to this edition will be included parenthetically in the text. The remarks on Sidney's tracts were introduced, expanded from an earlier set on the subject, as a result of an exchange with Stephen Greenblatt.

more in *Coriolanus* was its understanding of narcissism as another face of incestuousness, and of this condition as one in which language breaks down under one's sense of becoming incomprehensible, of the sense of oneself as having lost the power of expression, what I call in *The Claim of Reason* the terror of inexpressiveness; together with the thoroughness with which Narcissus's fate is mirrored in the figure of Coriolanus, a figure whose every act is, by that act, done to him so perfectly that the distinction between action and passion seems to lose its sense, a condition in which human existence becomes precarious, if perhaps transcendable. I mention these connections with the philosophical issue of skepticism not because I pursue them further in the essay to follow but only to attest my conviction that a work such as a play of Shakespeare's cannot contribute the help I want from it for the philosophical issues I mention unless the play is granted the autonomy it is in one's power to grant, which means, seen in its own terms. What does this mean? What is a play of Shakespeare's? I shall try to say something about these questions.

Something else also draws me. The way I have been understanding the conflicts the play engenders keeps sending me back over paths of thought that I believe many critics have found to be depleted of interest, or conviction; three paths, or branches of paths, in particular: (1) those that look in a Shakespearean play for something like an idea of theater, as it were for the play's concept of itself; (2) those that sense Christian stirrings and murmurings under the surface of the words; and (3) even those paths of thought that anticipate something you might call the origins of tragedy in religious ritual. I am, I suppose, as drawn to critical paths that others find empty as some poets are to words that others find flat. But to say fully why one is drawn to a work, and its work of interpretation, can only be the goal of an interpretation; and the motive of an interpretation, like what one might call the intention of the work it seeks, exists fully only in its satisfaction.

I expect, initially, general agreement on two facts about *Coriolanus*. First, compared with other Shakespearean tragedies this one lacks what A. C. Bradley called "atmosphere" (in his British Academy lecture on the play, the decade after his *Shakespearean Tragedy*). Its language, like its hero, keeps aloof from our attention, as withdrawn, austere, as its rage and its contempt permit. Second, the play is about the organization of the body politic and about how that body is fed, that is, sustained. I expect, further, that readers from opposed camps should be willing to see that the play lends itself equally, or anyway naturally, to psychological and to political readings: Both perspectives are, for example, interested in who produces food and in how food is distributed and paid for. From a psychological perspective (in practice this has in recent years been psychoanalytic) the play directs us to an interest in the development of Coriolanus's character. From a political perspective the play directs us to an interest in whether the patricians or the plebeians are right in their conflict and in whether, granted that Coriolanus is unsuited for political leadership, it is his childishness or his very nobility that unsuits him.

In the critical discussions I have read so far, the psychoanalytic perspective has produced more interesting readings than the political. A political reading is apt to become fairly predictable once you know whose side the reader is taking, that of the patricians or that of the plebeians; and whose side the reader takes may come down to how he or she sees Menenius's fable of the organic state, the parable of the belly, and upon whom we can place the blame for Coriolanus's banishment. If few will consider it realistic to suppose that Coriolanus would have made a good political leader, fewer will deny that in losing him the city has lost its greatest hero and that this loss is the expression of a time of crisis in the state. It is a time of famine in which the call for revolt is made moot by the threat and the fact of war and invasion, followed by a time in which victory in the war, and bitterness over its conduct, creates the call for counterrevolt by the state's defender and preserver. In such a period of crisis everyone and no one has good arguments, everyone and no one has right on their side. In Aufidius's great description of Coriolanus at the end of Act 4 he summarizes as follows:

> So our virtues
> Lie in th' interpretation of the time, . . .
> One fire drives out one fire; one nail, one nail;
> Rights by rights falter, strengths by strengths do fail.
> (4.7.49–50, 54–55)

One might say that just this division of fire and right is the tragedy, but would that description account for the particular turns of just these events, as distinct from the losses and ironies in any revolutionary situation? Even the most compelling political interpretation—in my experience this is given in Bertolt Brecht's discussion with members of his theater company of the opening scene of the play[2]—seems to have little further to add, in the way of interpretation, once it makes clear that choosing the side of the plebeians is dramatically and textually viable. This is no small matter. It shows that Shakespeare's text—or what we think of as Shakespeare's humanity—leaves ample room for distinctions among the "clusters" of citizens, and it shows the weight of their common position in opposition to that of the patricians. And I take this in turn to show that the politics of the play is essentially the politics of a given production, so that we should not expect its political issues to be settled by an interpretation of what you might call "the text itself."

Exactly the power of Brecht's discussion can be said to be its success in getting us *not* to interpret, not, above all, to interpret food, but to stay with the opening fact of the play, the fact that the citizens of Rome are in revolt because there is a famine (and because of their interpretation of the famine). They and their families are starving and they believe (correctly, for all we know) that the patricians are hoarding grain. Not to interpret this means, in practical or theatri-

---

[2]See Bertolt Brecht, *Collected Plays*, vol. 9, ed. Ralph Manheim and John Willett (New York: Methuen, 1973), pp. 378–94.

cal terms, that we come to see that this cluster is of human beings, individual human beings, who work at particular trades and who live in particular places where specific people await news of the outcome of their dangerous course in taking up arms. This fact of their ordinary humanity is the most impressive fact that can be set against the patricians' scorn of them—a fact that ought not to be visible solely to a Marxist, a fact that shows up the language of the leaders as mysterious and evasive, as subject to what one may think of as the politics of interpretation.

Yet we also feel that the pervasive images of food and hunger, of cannibalism and of disgust, do mean something, that they call upon us for some lines of interpretation, and that the value of attending to this particular play is a function of the value to individual human beings of tracing these lines.

Psychoanalysts naturally have focused on the images of food and feeding that link Coriolanus and his mother. In a recent essay, " 'Anger's My Meat': Feeding, Dependency, and Aggression in *Coriolanus*,"[3] Professor Janet Adelman has given so clear and fair an account of some two decades of psychoanalytic interpretations of food and feeding in the play, in the course of working out her further contributions, that I feel free to pick and choose the lines and moments bearing on this aspect of things that serve my somewhat different emphases.

Twice Volumnia invokes nursing. Early she says to Virgilia, rebuking her for worrying about her husband:

> The breasts of Hecuba
> When she did suckle Hector, look'd not lovelier
> Than Hector's forehead when it spit forth blood
> At Grecian sword, contemning.
> (1.3.40–43)

And in her first intercession with her son:

> Do as thou list.
> Thy valiantness was mine, thou suck'st it from me,
> But owe thy pride thyself.
> (3.2.128–30)

Both invocations lead one to think what it is this son learned at his mother's breast, what it is he was fed with, particularly as we come to realize that both mother and son declare themselves to be starving. It is after Coriolanus's departure upon being banished, when Menenius asks Volumnia if she'll sup with him, that she comes out with

> Anger's my meat: I sup upon myself
> And so shall starve with feeding.
> (4.2.50–51)

---

[3]In *Representing Shakespeare*, ed. Murray Schwartz and Coppélia Kahn (Baltimore: Johns Hopkins UP, 1980), and reproduced as the first part of Adelman's essay in this book, pp. 134–67.

As Coriolanus mocks and resists the ritual of asking for the people's voices, his being keeps revolting, one time as follows:

> Better it is to die, better to starve,
> Than crave the hire which first we do deserve.
>   (2.3.112–13)

I say that mother and son, both of them, *are* starving, and I mean throughout, always, not just when they have occasion to say so. I take Volumnia's vision of supping upon herself not to be a picture simply of her local anger but of self-consuming anger as the presiding passion of her life—the primary thing, accordingly, she would have to teach her son, the thing he sucked from her, of course under the name of valiantness. If so, then if Volumnia and hence Coriolanus are taken to exemplify a Roman identification of virtue as valor, they should further be taken as identifying valor with an access to one's anger. It is "in anger, Juno-like," godlike, that Volumnia laments (4.2.52–53); and it is this anger that the tribune Sicinius is remarking as, in trying to avoid being confronted by her, he says, "They say she's mad" (4.2.9). Along these lines, I emphasize Coriolanus's statement about deserving rather than craving not as

> *Better* it is to *die,* better to *starve,*
> Than crave . . .

as if he is asserting the rightness of a particular choice for the future; but as

> Better it is to die, *better* to starve,
> Than crave . . .

as if he is reaffirming or confessing his settled form of (inner) life. I expect that the former is the more usual way of emphasis, but I find it prejudicial.

Coriolanus and Volumnia are—I am taking it—starvers, hungerers. They manifest this condition as a name or a definition of the human, like being mortal. And they manifest this as a condition of insatiability (starving by feeding, feeding as deprivation). It is a condition sometimes described as the infiniteness of desire, imposing upon the finiteness of the body. But starving for Volumnia and her son suggests that this infiniteness is not the cause of human insatiability but is rather its effect. It is the effect not of an endless quantity, as though the self had, or is, endless reserves of desire; but of an endless structure, as though desire has a structure of endlessness. One picture of this structure is given by Narcissus for whom what is longed for is someone longing, who figures beauty as longing. Starving by feeding presents itself to Coriolanus as being consumed by hunger, and his words for hungering are desiring and craving. And what he incessantly hungers for is . . . not to hunger, not to desire, that is, not to be mortal. Take the scene of interview by the people:

Coriolanus:	You know the cause, sir, of my standing here?
Third Citizen:	We do, sir; tell us what hath brought you to't.
Coriolanus:	Mine own desert.

> Second Citizen: Your own desert?
> Coriolanus: Ay, but not mine own desire.
> Third Citizen: How, not your own desire?
> (2.3.66–72)

If you desire to be desireless, is there something you desire? If so, how would you express it; that is, tell it; that is, ask for it? Coriolanus's answer to this paradox is to become perfectly deserving. Since to hunger is to want, to lack something, he hungers to lack nothing, to be complete, like a sword. My speculations here are an effort to do justice to one's sense of Coriolanus as responding not primarily to his situation with the plebeians, as if trapped by an uncontrollable disdain; but as responding primarily to his situation with himself, as befits a Narcissus, trapped first by an uncontrollable logic. Although I shall come to agree with Plutarch's early observation or diagnosis in his *Life of Caius Martius Coriolanus* that Coriolanus is "altogether unfit for any man's conversation," I am in effect taking this to mean not that he speaks in anger and contempt (anger and contempt are not unjustifiable) but that whereas under certain circumstances he can express satisfaction, he cannot express desire and to this extent cannot speak at all: The case is not that he will not ask for what he wants but rather that he can want nothing that he asks. His solution amounts, as both patricians and plebeians more or less note, to becoming a god. What god? We have to get to this.

Let us for the moment continue developing the paradox of hungering. To be consumed by hunger, to feed upon oneself, must present itself equally as being fed upon, being eaten up. (To feed means both to give and to take nourishment, as to suckle means both to give and to take the breast.) So the other fact of Coriolanus's and Volumnia's way of starving, of their hunger, is their sense of being cannibalized.[4]

The idea of cannibalization runs throughout the play. It is epitomized in the title question I have given to these remarks: "Who does the wolf love?" (2.1.6). Menenius asks this of the tribunes of the people at the opening of Act 2. One of them answers, with undeniable truth: "The lamb." And Menenius, ever the interpretive fabulist, answers: "Ay, to devour him, as the hungry plebeians would the noble Martius." The other tribune's answer—"He's a lamb, indeed, that baes like a bear"—does not unambiguously deny Menenius's interpretation. The shock of the interpretation is of course that it is from the beginning the people, not the patricians, and least of all Coriolanus, who are presented as lambs, anyway as food for patrician wolves. In Menenius's opening effort to talk the people out of revolt he declares that "The helms o' th' state . . . care for you like fathers" (1.1.76), to which the First Citizen replies, "Care for us? . . . If the wars eat us not up, they will; and there's all the love they bear us" (1.1.78, 84–85). This fantasy is borne out

---

[4]"There seems to be some question whether one's knowing oneself is something active, something one does . . . or rather something one suffers, something that happens to one" (Stanley Cavell, *The Claim of Reason: Wittgenstein, Scepticism, Morality and Tragedy* [Oxford: Clarendon Press, and New York: Oxford UP, 1979], p. 352).

when the general Cominius speaks of Coriolanus's coming to battle as to a feast (1.9.10). And the idea of the warrior Coriolanus feeding on a weaker species may be raised again in the battle at Corioli in his threat to any soldier who holds back, "I'll take him for a Volsce,/And he shall feel mine edge" (1.4.28–29), allowing the suggestion of his sword as a piece of cutlery. The idea of an ungovernable voraciousness is furthered by Volumnia's association of her son with his son's tearing apart a butterfly with his teeth. On the other hand, when Coriolanus offers himself to Aufidius at Antium he expresses his sense of having been devoured, with only the name Caius Martius Coriolanus remaining, devoured by "the cruelty and envy of the people" (4.5.75). And Menenius, whose sense of justice is constricted, among other things by his fear of civil disorder, is accurate in his fears, in the consequences they prophesy for Rome, and he will repeat his vision of civil cannibalism:

> Now the good gods forbid
> That our renowned Rome, whose gratitude
> Towards her deserved children is enroll'd
> In Jove's own book, like an unnatural dam
> Should now eat up her own!
>   (3.1.287–91)

All readers of this aspect of the play will recognize in this description of Rome as potentially a cannibalistic mother an allusion to Volumnia; and the identification of Volumnia and Rome is enforced in other ways, not least by Volumnia herself when in the second and final intercession scene she says to her son:

> . . . thou shalt no sooner
> March to assault thy country than to tread
> —Trust to't, thou shalt not—on thy mother's womb
> That brought thee to this world.
>   (5.3.122–25)

It is very much to the point to notice that in Menenius's vision of Rome as an "unnatural dam" an identity is proposed between a mother eating her child and a mother eating herself: If Rome eats up all Romans there is no more Rome, for as one of the tribunes asks, "What is the city but the people?" (3.1.198).

The paradox and reciprocity of hungering may be found registered in the question "Who does the wolf love?" If the question is asking for the object of the wolf's affection, the more nearly correct grammar would seem to be "Whom does the wolf love?"[5] But this correctness (call it a patrician correctness, a refinement in which the plebeians apparently do not see the good) would rule out taking the question also in its opposite direction, grammatically strict as it stands, namely as asking whose object of affection the wolf is. (Who does love the wolf?) The answer

---

[5]This point was emphasized by Professor Harry Berger in his remarks introducing an earlier version of this essay, which was delivered at Stanford University in 1985.

given directly, "The lamb," does not rule out either direction, but as the ensuing discussion demonstrates, the direction will be a function of what or whom you take the lamb to be, hence what the wolf. Both directions, the active and the passive constructions of the play's focal verbs, are operative throughout the action. I have mentioned this explicitly in the cases of feeding and suckling. But it is, I find, true less conspicuously, but pertinently, in such an odd moment as this:

> *Coriolanus:*   Let them hang.
> *Volumnia:*   Ay, and burn too.
> (3.2.23–24)

One of the functions in providing Volumnia with this amplification here strikes me as suggesting her sense of the inevitable reflexiveness of action in their Rome: Are hanging and burning actions done to someone, or something "they" are, or will be, doing?

The circle of cannibalism, of the eater eaten by what he or she eats, keeps being sketched out, from the first to the last. You might call this the identification of narcissism as cannibalism. From the first: At the end of Coriolanus's first long speech he says to the citizens:

> You cry against the noble Senate, who
> (Under the gods) keep you in awe, which else
> Would feed on one another.
> (1.1.187–89)

And at the last: Rome devouring itself is the idea covered in the obsessive images of Coriolanus burning Rome. It was A. C. Bradley again who at the end of his British Academy lecture pointed out the sudden and relentless harping, principally after the banishment, on the image of fire, of Rome burning. Bradley makes nothing further of the point, but it is worth noting, in view of the theme of starving and cannibalism, that fire in this play is imagined under the description of it as *consuming* what it burns.

You may say that burning as a form of revenge is Coriolanus's projection onto Rome of what he felt Rome was doing to him. This cannot be wrong, but it so far pictures Coriolanus, in his revenge, to be essentially a man like Aufidius, merely getting even; the picture requires refining. Suppose that, as I believe, in Coriolanus's famous sentence of farewell, "I banish you!" (3.3.123), he has already begun a process of consuming Rome, incorporating it, becoming it. Then when the general Cominius tried in vain to plead with him to save Rome, and found him to be sitting "in gold, his eye/Red as 'twould burn Rome" (5.1.63–64), he somewhat misunderstood what he saw. He took Coriolanus to be contemplating something in the future whereas Coriolanus's eye was red with the present flames of self-consuming. Consuming the literal Rome with literal fire would accordingly only have been an expression of that self-consuming. Thus would the city understand what it had done to itself. He will give it—horribly—what it deserves. Thus is the play of revenge further interpreted.

These various understandings of cannibalism all illustrate the ancient sentiment that man is wolf to man. (The Roman Plautus, to whom Shakespeare is famously indebted, is credited with being the earliest namable framer of the sentiment. A pertinent modern instance occurs in Brecht's *Threepenny Opera.*) But the question "Who does the wolf love?" has two further reaches which we must eventually consider. First, there is the repetition of the idea that devouring can be an expression of love. Second, if, as I think, there is reason here to take the image of the wolf as the figure of the mythical animal identified with Rome, the one who suckled the founders of Rome (Volumnia is the reason), there is reason to take the lamb it is said to love (or that loves it) as the mythical animal identified with Christ.

Before this, I should make explicit a certain way in which the account of Coriolanus's motivation I have been driving at is somewhat at odds with the direction of psychoanalytic interpretation summarized and extended by Janet Adelman.[6] She understands Coriolanus's attempt to make himself inhumanly independent as a defense against his horror of dependence, and his rage as converting his wish to be dependent against those who render him so. A characteristic turn of her argument consists of a reading of some lines I have already had occasion to quote:

> The breasts of Hecuba
> When she did suckle Hector, look'd not lovelier
> Than Hector's forehead when it spit forth blood
> At Grecian sword, contemning.

Adelman reads as follows:

> Blood is more beautiful than milk, the wound than the breast, warfare than peaceful feeding. . . . Hector is transformed immediately from infantile feeding mouth to bleeding wound. For the unspoken mediator between breast and wound is the infant's mouth: in this imagistic transformation, to feed is to be wounded; the mouth becomes the wound, the breast the sword. . . . But at the same time as Volumnia's image suggests the vulnerability inherent in feeding, it also suggests a way to fend off that vulnerability. In her image, feeding, incorporating, is transformed into spitting out, an aggressive expelling; the wound once again becomes the mouth that spits. . . . The wound spitting blood thus becomes not a sign of vulnerability but an instrument of attack. (p. 131; p. 152 in this volume)

This is very fine and it must not be denied. But the transformation of Hector's mouth into a wound must not in turn deny two further features of these difficult lines. First, when Hector contemns Grecian swords, he is also to be thought of as fighting, as wielding a sword, so the mouth is transformed into, or seen as, a cutting weapon: The suckling mother is presented as being slashed by the son-hero, eaten by the one she feeds. Suffering such a fantasy would constitute some of Volumnia's more normal moments. Second, the lines set up an equation between a mother's milk and a man's blood, suggesting that we must understand the man's

---

[6]In the essay cited in note 3.

spitting blood in battle not simply as attacking but equally, somehow, as providing food, in a male fashion. But how? Remember that Coriolanus's way to avoid asking for something, that is, to avoid expressing desire, is by what he calls deserving the thing. His proof of desert is his valiantness, so his spitting blood in battle is his way of deserving being fed, that is to say, being devoured, being loved unconditionally. (War and feeding have consistently been joined in the words of this play. A plebeian says: "If the wars eat us not up, they will" [1.1.85–86]. And Cominius: Coriolanus "cam'st thou to . . . this feast, having fully dined before" [1.9.10–11]; but again Cominius does not get the connection complete.) To be fed by Volumnia is to be fed *to* her. But since the right, or effective, bleeding depends (according to the equation of blood and milk) upon its being a form of feeding, of giving food, providing blood identifies him with his mother. His mother's fantasy here suggests that the appropriate reciprocation for having nourished her son is for him to become her, as if to remove the arbitrariness in her having been born a woman; and since it is a way of putting her into the world it is a way of giving birth to her. Her son's companion fantasy of reciprocation would be to return Rome's gift, to nurse Rome with the valiantness he sucked from it.

This fantasy produces contradictions that are a match for the fury of contradictions one feels in Coriolanus's position (for example, between the wishes for dependence and for independence). For he can only return his nourishment if Rome—taken as the people—deserves it. Hence the people's lack of desert entails his lack of desert, entails that he cannot do the thing that acquires love; he is logically debarred from reciprocating. The fact that he both has absolute contempt for the people and yet has an absolute need for them is part of what maddens him. (This implies again that I cannot understand Coriolanus's emotions toward the people as directed simply to, say, their cowardice, their being poor fighters. I am taking it that he needs their desert for, so to speak, private reasons as much as public.) The other part of what maddens him is that neither the people nor his mother—neither of the things that mean Rome—will understand his position. Neither understands that his understanding of his valiantness, his virtue, his worth, his deservingness, is of himself as a provider, and that this is the condition of his receiving his own sustenance. (This assumes that he shares his mother's fantasy of the equation of milk and blood—as if there is nothing in her he has not taken in.) The people, precisely on the contrary, maddeningly accuse him of *withholding* food; and his mother precisely regards his heroism purely as toughness, devoid of tenderness; or pure fatherhood devoid of motherhood; and as deserving something more than acknowledging what he provides, more than the delicate balance of his self-account, as if being made consul were indeed something more. ("Know, good mother,/I had rather be their servant in my way/Than sway with them in theirs" [2.1.200–202].) In these misunderstandings they have both already abandoned him, weaned him, before the ritual of being made consul comes to grief and he is formally banished. This prior rejection, not just once but always, inherently, would allow the understanding of his anger as his mother interprets anger, that is, as lamentation ("Anger's my meat . . . lament as I do,/In anger, Juno-like"). We may not contradict her interpretation, though we may interpret it further. We might go on to interpret it as depression.

I might characterize my intention in spelling out what I call these fantasies as an attempt to get at the origin of words, not the origin of their meaning exactly but of their production, of the value they have when and as they occur. I have characterized something like this ambition of criticism variously over the years, and related it to what I understand as the characteristic procedure of ordinary language philosophy. . . . And do my spellings-out help? Do they, for example, help comprehend Coriolanus's subsequent course—how he justifies his plan to burn Rome and how he is talked out of his plan by his mother? It is not hard to encourage oneself in the impression that one understands these things. To me they seem mysteries. I shall sketch the answers I have to these questions and then conclude by indicating how these answers serve to interpret our relation to this play, which means to me, to understand what a Shakespearean play is (as revealed in this instance).

I pause, in turning to these questions, to make explicit an issue that at any time may nag our consciousness of the play. The mother relation is so overwhelmingly present in this play that we may not avoid wondering, at least wondering whether we are to wonder, what happened to the father. The play seems to me to raise this question in three ways, which I list in decreasing order of obviousness. First, Menenius is given a certain kind of fatherly role, or a role as a certain kind of father, but the very difficulty of conceiving of him as Coriolanus's real father, which is to say, as Volumnia's husband and lover, keeps alive our imagination of what such a figure might look like. Second, Coriolanus's erotic attachment to battle and to men who battle suggests a search for the father as much as an escape from the mother. This would afford an explanation for an otherwise, to me, insufficiently explained use in the play of the incident from Plutarch's Life in which Coriolanus asks, exhausted from victorious battle, that a man in the conquered city of Corioli be spared slavery on the ground that Coriolanus had "sometime lay at the poor man's house," a man whose name Coriolanus discovers he has forgotten. The vagueness of the man's identity and Coriolanus's expression of confusion in the Shakespeare—distinct differences from the occurrence of the incidents in Plutarch—suggest to my mind that the unnamed figure to whom Coriolanus wishes to provide reparation is, vaguely, transiently, an image of his father.[7]

Third, and so little obvious as to be attributable to my powers of hallucination, Coriolanus's effort at mythological identification as he sits enthroned and

---

[7]This is not meant as an alternative to but as an extension of the fine perception in the last note to Act 1, scene 9, by the editor of the Arden edition (Philip Brockbank) that "One name is found in the scene and another is lost." My thought is that both are names held by Caius Martius Coriolanus. I suppose I am influenced in this thought by a further change Shakespeare makes in Plutarch's characterization of the man. In Plutarch Coriolanus speaks of the man as "an old friend and host of mine"; it is at the analogous moment in Shakespeare that Coriolanus speaks of the man as one at whose house he lay. The opening words of Plutarch's Life are "The house of the Martians," where "house" of course means "family," a phrase and passage employed by Shakespeare at the end of Act 3 where the tribunes invoke Coriolanus's biological descent as if to their sufficient credit for having considered it but to Coriolanus's insufficient credit for election to consul.

entranced before Rome is an effort—if one accepts one stratum of description I shall presently give of him—to come unto the Father. (I shall not go into the possibilities here, or fantasies, that a patrician matron is simultaneously father-mother, or that, in replacing his father, he becomes his own father.)

I was about to ask how we are to grasp Coriolanus's return and his change of heart. My answer depends on plotting a relation between him and the other sacrificial lamb I have mentioned, the lamb of God, Christ. I say plotting a relation between the figures, not at all wishing to identify them. I see Coriolanus not so much as imitating Christ as competing with him. These are necessarily shadowy matters and although everything depends on accuracy in defining this relation all I can do here is note some elements that will have to figure in the plotting.

Earlier I spoke of Coriolanus's solution to the paradox of hungering not to hunger, of wanting not to want, of asking not to ask, as one of becoming a god. Now we may see that Christ is the right god because of the way he understands his mission as providing nonliteral food, food for the spirit, for immortality; and because it is in him that blood must be understood as food. If one is drawn to this as a possibility, one may find surprising confirmation for it in certain of Coriolanus's actions and in certain descriptions of his actions. (I am not interested in claiming that Coriolanus is *in some sense* a scapegoat, the way perhaps any tragic hero is; but in claiming that he is a specific inflection of *this* scapegoat.)

First his actions, two especially. First is his pivotal refusal to show his wounds. I associate this generally with the issue of Christ's showing his wounds to his disciples, in order to show them the Lord—that is, to prove the Resurrection—and specifically with his saying to Thomas, who was not present at the first showing and who made seeing the wounds a condition of believing, that is, of declaring his faith, "Thomas, because thou hast seen me, thou believest: blessed are they that have not seen, and have believed" (John 20:29). (Thomas would not believe until he could, as he puts it and as Jesus will invite him to, "put mine hand into his side"; Aufidius declares the wish to "wash my fierce hand in's heart" [1.10.27]. I make no further claims on the basis of this conjunction; I can see that some good readers may feel that it is accidental. I do claim that good reading may be guided, or inspired, by the overexcitement such conjunctions can cause.) The second action is the second intercession, in which Volumnia, holding her son's son by the hand, together with Virgilia and Valeria appears to Coriolanus before Rome. I take this to invoke the appearance, while Christ is on the cross, of three women whose names begin with the same letter of the alphabet (I mean begin with M's, not with V's), accompanied by a male he loves, whom he views as his mother's son (John 19:25–27). (Giving his mother a son presages a mystic marriage.)

I do not suppose that one will be convinced by these relations unless one has antecedently felt some quality of—what shall I say?—the mythic in these moments. This is something I meant in calling these relations "shadowy matters": I meant this not negatively but positively. It is a way to understand Volumnia's advice to Coriolanus that when he makes his appeal to the people he act out the meaning of his presence:

> . . . for in such business
> Action is eloquence, and the eyes of th'ignorant
> More learned than the ears.
>
> (3.2.75–77)

I accept this as advice Shakespeare is giving to his own audience, a certain hint about why the words of this particular play may strike one as uncharacteristically ineloquent.

The second source of confirmation for Coriolanus's connection with the figure of Christ lies, I said, in certain descriptions of his actions. I specify now only some parallels that come out of Revelation. In that book the central figure is a lamb (and there is also a dragon), and a figure who sits on a special horse and on a golden throne, whose name is known only to himself, whose "eyes were as a flame of fire," and who burns a city that is identified as a woman; it is, in particular, the city (Babylon) which in Christian tradition is identified with Rome. And I associate the opening of Coriolanus's opening diatribe against the citizens, in which he rebukes their wish for "good words" from him—glad tidings—accusing them of liking "neither peace nor war," with the message Christ dictates to the writer of Revelation: "I know thy works, that thou art neither cold nor hot; . . . Therefore, because thou art luke warm, and neither cold nor hot, it will come to pass that I shall spew thee out of my mouth" (Revelation 3:15–16). (An associated text from Plutarch would be: "So Martius, being a stowte man of nature, that never yelded in any respect, as one thincking that to overcome allwayes, and to have the upper hande in all matters, was a Token of magnanimities, and of no base and fainte corage, which spitteth out anger from the most weake and passioned parte of the harte, much like the matter of an impostume: went home." Whatever the ambiguities in these words, the general idea remains, indelibly, of Coriolanus's speech, when angry, as being the spitting forth of the matter of an abscess.[8] This play about food is about revoltedness and disgust. *Coriolanus* and Revelation are about figures who are bitter, disgusted by those whom they have done good, whose lives they have sustained.)

Conviction, or lack of it, in these relations is something one has naturally to assess for oneself. Granted that they are somehow at work, they work to make comprehensible what Coriolanus's identification with the god is (they are identified as banished providers of spiritual food) and what his justification for destruc-

---

[8]I quote from North's translation of Plutarch's biography of Coriolanus, which is given in an appendix to the Arden edition of *Coriolanus* (London: Methuen, 1976). The "impostume" passage occurs on p. 133.

Coriolanus's sense of disgust with the people is more explicitly conveyed by Shakespeare through the sense of their foul smell than of their foul taste. Shakespeare does use the idea of spitting twice: once, as cited, to describe Hector's forehead bleeding in battle, and the second time in Coriolanus's only scene of soliloquy, disguised before Aufidius's house: "Then know me not;/Lest that thy wives with spits, and boys with stones,/In puny battle slay me" (4.4.4–6)—so that both times spitting is linked with battle and with food. As I have implied, I understand Coriolanus's vision of his death in Antium at the hands of wives and boys as a prophecy of the death he actually undergoes there, spitted by the swords of strange boys.

tion is (the people lack faith and are to suffer judgment) and why he changes his mind about the destruction. It is, I think, generally felt that his mother prevails with him by producing human, family feeling in him, in effect showing him that he is not inhuman. This again cannot be wrong, but first of all he has his access of family feeling the moment he sees the four figures approaching (a feeling that does not serve to carry the day), and second, his feeling, so conceived, does not seem to me to account for Coriolanus's words of agony to his mother as he relents and "Holds her by the hand silent."

> O mother, mother!
> What have you done? Behold, the heavens do ope,
> The gods look down, and this unnatural scene
> They laugh at. O my mother, mother! O!
> You have won a happy victory to Rome;
> But, for your son, believe it, O, believe it,—
> Most dangerously you have with him prevail'd,
> If not most mortal to him. But let it come.
>   (5.3.182–89)

(I say these are words of agony, but so far as I recall, no critic who cites them seems to find them so. I feel here especially at a disadvantage in never having been at a performance of *Coriolanus*. But I find on reading this passage, or rather in imagining it said [sometimes as by specific actors; Olivier, of course, among them, and the young Brando], that it takes a long time to get through. Partly that has to do with the fact of the repetition of words in the passage; partly with the specific words that are repeated, "O," "mother," and "believe it." It has further to do, I feel sure, with my uncertainty about how long the silences before and within this speech are to be held—a speech that may be understood as expressing the silence with which this son holds, and then relinquishes, his mother's hand. Suppose we try imagining that he does not relinquish her hand until just before the last sentence, "But let it come"—as if what is to come is exactly expressive of their separating, or, say, that of Rome from Rome. Then how far do we imagine that he goes through the imagining of what is to come, and how long would the imagining take, before he takes upon himself the words that invite its coming?) What it means that she may be "most mortal" to him cannot be that he may be killed—the mere fact of death is hardly what concerns this man. He must mean somehow that she has brought it about that he will have the wrong death, the wrong mortality, a fruitless death. Has she done this by showing him that he has feelings? But Christ, even by those who believe that he is the Lord, is generally held to have feelings. Coriolanus's speech expresses his agonized sense that his mother does not know who he is, together with an agonized plea for her belief. She has deprived him of heaven, of, in his fantasy, sitting beside his father, and deprived him by withholding her faith in him, for if she does not believe that he is a god then probably he is not a god, and certainly nothing like the Christian scenario can be fulfilled, in which a mother's belief is essential. If it were his father who sacrificed him for the city of man then he could be a god. But if it is his mother who sacrifices him he is not a god. The logic of his situation, as well as the psychology, is that he cannot sacrifice himself. He can provide spiritual food but he cannot make himself into food, he cannot say, for example, that his body is bread. His sacrifice will not be redemptive; hence one may say his tragedy is that he cannot achieve tragedy. He dies in a place irrelevant to his sacrifice, carved by many swords, by hands that can derive no special nourishment from him. It is too soon in the history of the Roman world for the sacrifice to which he aspires and from which he recoils.

And perhaps it is too late, as if the play is between worlds. I know I have been struck by an apparent incorporation in *Coriolanus* of elements from Euripides's *Bacchae,* without knowing how or whether a historical connection is thinkable. Particularly, it seems to me, I have been influenced in my descriptions by feeling under Coriolanus's final plea to his mother the plea of Pentheus to his mother, outside the city, to see that he is her son and not to tear him to pieces. The *Bacchae* is about admitting the new god to the city, present in one who is returning to his native city, a god who in company with Demeter's grain brings nourishment to mankind, one who demands recognition in order to vindicate at once his mother's honor and his being fathered by Zeus; the first in the city to acknowledge his divine descent are two old men. My idea is that Coriolanus incorporates both raging, implacable Dionysus and raging, inconstant Pentheus and that Volumnia partakes both of the chaste yet god-seduced Semele and of the mad and murderous Agave. Volumnia's identifying of herself with Juno (specifically, with Juno's anger) may thus suggest her sensing herself as the cause of her curse. It is not essential to my thought here that Shakespeare knew of Euripides's play. It is enough to consider that he knew Ovid's account of Pentheus's story and to suppose that he took the story as Euripides had, as about the kind of son (one unable to express desire) to whom the failure of his mother's recognition presents itself as a sense of being torn to pieces.

What is the good of such a tragedy of failed tragedy? Which is to ask: What is this play to us? How is it to do its work? This is the question I have been driving at and now that it is before us I can only state flatly, without much detail, my provisional conclusions on the topic.

They can by now be derived from certain considerations about Menenius's telling of the parable of the belly in the opening scene of the play. Every reader or participant has to make something of this extended, most prominently placed event. Until recent times most critics have assumed that Menenius is voicing a commonplace assumption of the times in which Shakespeare wrote and one that represents Shakespeare's view of the state—the state as a hierarchical organism, understandable on analogy with the healthy, functioning body. It is my impression that recent critics have tended not to dwell on the fable, as though the conservative way is the only way to take it and as though that vision is no longer acceptable, or presentable. But this seems to me to ignore what I take to be the three principal facts about Menenius's telling of the tale, the facts, one may say, of the drama in the telling. (1) The tale has competing interpretations. What the first citizen calls its "application" is a *question.* He and Menenius joke about whether the people or the patricians are better represented by the belly. (2) The tale is about food, about its distribution and circulation. (3) The tale is told (by a patrician) to citizens who are in the act of rising in revolt against a government they say is deliberately starving them; hence the patrician can be said to be giving them words *instead* of food. The first mystery of the play is that this seems to work, that the words stop the citizens, that they stop to listen, as though these citizens are themselves willing, under certain circumstances, to take words for food, to equate them.

Coriolanus's entrance at the end of the argument over the application of the fable confirms this equation of words and food: He has from the early lines of the play been identified as the people's chief enemy, here in particular as chief of those who withhold food; and his opening main speech to them, after expressing his disgust by them, is to affirm that he does withhold and will go on withholding "good words" from them. Accordingly every word he speaks will mean the withholding of good words. He will, as it were, have a sword in his mouth. There are other suggestions of the equation of words and food in the play (for example, the enlivening of the familiar idea that understanding is a matter of digesting) but this is enough for me, in view of my previous suggestions, to take the equation as part of the invocation of the major figure of our civilization for whom words are food. The word made flesh is to be eaten, since this is the living bread. Moreover, the parables of Jesus are characteristically about food, and are always meant as food. The words/food equation suggests that we should look again at Volumnia's intercession speeches, less for their content than for the plain fact of their drama, that they are much the longest speeches Coriolanus listens to, that they cause his mother to show him her undivided attention and him to give her his silence; he is as if filled up by her words. It pleases me further to remember that Revelation also contains a vision of words that are eaten: There is a book the writer swallows that tastes as sweet as honey in the mouth but bitter in the belly (10:10), as if beauty were the beginning of terror, as in, for example, a play of Shakespeare's.

My conclusion about the working of the play, about what kind of play it is, adds up then as follows. I take the telling of the parable of the belly as a sort of play-within-the-play, a demonstration of what Shakespeare takes his play—named for Coriolanus—to be, for *Coriolanus* too is a tale about food, with competing interpretations requiring application, told by one man to a cluster, call this an audience, causing them to halt momentarily, to turn aside from their more practical or pressing concerns in order to listen. Here is the relevance I see in the fact that the play is written in a time of corn shortages and insurrections. The fact participates not just in the imagery of the play's setting, but in the question of the authority and the virtue of portraying such a time, at such a time, for one's fellow citizens; a question of the authority and the virtue in being a writer. I see in

Shakespeare's portrayal of the parable of the belly a competition (in idea, perhaps in fact) with Sir Philip Sidney's familiar citing of the tale in his *Defence of Poetry,* or a rebuke of it.[9] Sidney records Menenius's application of the tale as having "wrought such effect in the people, as I never read that only words brought forth but then, so sudden and so good an alteration; for upon reasonable conditions a perfect reconcilement ensued." But in casting his partisan, limited Menenius as the teller of the tale, and placing its telling at the opening of the play, where we have minimal information or experience for judging its events, Shakespeare puts into question both the nature of the "alteration" and the "perfection" of the reconciliation. Since these are the two chief elements of Sidney's defense of poetry, this defense is as such put into question; but hence, since Shakespeare is nevertheless giving his own version of the telling of the fable, making his own story about the circulation of food, he can be understood as presenting in this play his own defense of poetry (more particularly, of plays, which Sidney particularly attacks). It is in this light noteworthy that Sidney finds "Heroical" poetry to be most "[daunting to] all back-biters," who would "speak evil" of writing that presents "champions . . . who doth not only teach and move to a truth, but teacheth and moveth to the most high and excellent truth" (p. 131). But since "the image of such worthies" as presented in such works "most inflameth the mind with desire to be worthy" (p. 131), and since *Coriolanus* is a play that studies the evil in such an inflammation, Shakespeare's play precisely questions the ground of Sidney's claim that "the Heroical . . . is not only a kind, but the best and most accomplished kind of Poetry" (p. 131).

What would this play's defense of poetry be; I mean how does it direct us to consider the question? Its incorporation of the parable of the belly I understand to identify us, the audience, as starvers, and to identify the words of the play as food, for our incorporation. Then we have to ask of ourselves, as we have to ask of the citizens: Why have we stopped to listen? That is, what does it mean to be a member of this audience? Do we feel that these words have the power of redemption for us?

They are part of an enactment of a play of sacrifice; as it happens, of a failed sacrifice. And a feast-sacrifice, whether in Christian, pre-Christian, Nietzschean, or Freudian terms, is a matter of the founding and the preserving of a community. A community is thus identified as those who partake of the same body, of a common victim. This strikes Coriolanus as our being caught in a circle of mutual partaking, incorporating one another. And this is symbolized, or instanced, by speaking the same language. A pervasive reason Coriolanus spits out words is exactly that they *are* words, that they exist only in a language, and that a language is meta-

[9]Sir Philip Sidney, "The Defence of Poesy," in *Sir Philip Sidney: Selected Poetry and Prose*, ed. Robert Kimbrough, 2nd ed. (Madison, Wi.: U of Wisconsin P, 1983), p. 126. Future references to this edition will be included parenthetically in the text. The remarks on Sidney's tracts were introduced, expanded from an earlier set on the subject, as a result of an exchange with Stephen Greenblatt.

physically something shared, so that speaking is taking and giving in your mouth the very matter others are giving and taking in theirs.

It is maddeningly irrelevant to Coriolanus which party the belly represents. What matters to him is that, whoever rules, all are members, that all participate in the same circulation, the same system of exchange, call it Rome; that to provide civil nourishment you must allow yourself to be partaken of. This is not a play about politics, if this means about political authority or conflict, say about questions of legitimate succession or divided loyalties. It is about the formation of the political, the founding of the city, about what it is that makes a rational animal fit for conversation, for civility. This play seems to think of this creation of the political, call it the public, as the overcoming of narcissism, incestuousness, and cannibalism; as if it perceives an identity among these relations.

In constructing and contesting with a hero for whom the circulation of language is an expression of cannibalism, *Coriolanus* takes cannibalism as symbolic of the most human of activities, the most distinctive, or distinguished, of human activities. (Sidney cites the familiar conjunction: "Oratio, next to Ratio, . . . [is] the greatest gift bestowed upon mortality" [p. 134].) Coriolanus wishes to speak, to use words, to communicate, without exchanging words; without, let us say, reasoning (with others); to speak without conversing, without partaking in conversation. Here is the conversation for which he is unfit; call it civil speech. Hence I conceive *Coriolanus* to be incorporating Montaigne's interpretation of literal cannibalism as more civilized than our more sophisticated—above all, more pervasive—manners of psychological torture, our consuming others alive.[10] Montaigne's "On Cannibals" is more specifically pertinent to this play: its story of a cannibal prisoner of a cannibal society valorously taunting his captors by reminding them that in previous battles, when he had been victorious over them, he had captured and eaten their ancestors, so that in eating him they will be consuming their own flesh—this is virtually the mode in which Coriolanus addresses himself to the Volscians in putting himself at their mercy. And more variously pertinent: The essay interprets cannibalism as revenge; and it claims (in one of those moods of measured hilarity) that when three men from a cannibal society visited Rouen and were asked what they found most amazing about the ways of Montaigne's countrymen, one of their responses was as follows (I shall not comment on it but quote in Frame's translation):

> Second (they have a way in their language of speaking of men as halves of one another), they had noticed that there were among us men full and gorged with all sorts of good things, and that their other halves were beggars at their doors, emaciated with hunger

---

[10]Finding the words/food representation so compelling, I am ignoring here the path along which the circulation of words also registers the circulation of money (as in "so shall my lungs/Coin words" [3.1.76–77]; and in "The price is, to ask it kindly" [2.3.77]). The sense of consuming as expending would relate to Coriolanus's frantic efforts to deny that his actions can be recompensed ("better to starve than crave the hire"—for example, of receiving voices *in return*). Money depends upon the equating of values; Coriolanus, on their lack of equation, on measurelessness, pricelessness.

and poverty; and they thought it strange that these needy halves could endure such an injustice, and did not take the others by the throat, or set fire to their houses.[11]

Within the experience of such a vision of the circulation of language a question, not readily formulatable, may press for expression: To what extent can Coriolanus (and the play that creates him and contests with him) be understood as seeing his salvation in silence? The theme of silence haunts the play. For example, one of Coriolanus's perfectly cursed tasks is to ask for "voices" (votes) that he exactly wishes not to hear. Again, the words "silent" and "silence" are beautifully and mysteriously associated, once each, with the women in his life: with his wife ("My gracious silence, hail!" [2.1.174]); and with his mother ("He holds her by the hand silent" [5.3.183]). Toward both, the word of silence is the expression of intimacy and identification; but in his wife's case it means acknowledgment, freedom from words, but in a life beyond the social, while in his mother's case it means avoidance, denial, death, that there is no life beyond the social. The ambiguities here are drilled through the action of the play by the repeated calls "Peace, peace"—hysterical, ineffective shouts of this particular word for silence. The play literalizes this conventional call for silence by implying that speech is war, as if this is the reason that both words and war can serve as food. But the man for war cannot find peace in peace—not merely because he, personally, cannot keep a civil tongue in his head, but because a tongue is inherently uncivil (if not, one hopes, inveterately so). Silence is not the absence of language; there is no such absence for human beings; in this respect, there is no world elsewhere.

Coriolanus cannot imagine, or cannot accept, that there is a way to partake of one another, incorporate one another, that is necessary to the formation rather than to the extinction of a community. (As he cannot imagine being fed without being deserving. This is his precise reversal of Christ's vision, that we cannot in ourselves deserve sustenance, and that it is for that reason, and in that spirit, that we have to ask for it. Thus is misanthropy, like philanthropy, a certain parody of Christianity.) The play *Coriolanus* asks us to try to imagine it, imagine a beneficial, mutual consumption, arguing in effect that this is what the formation of an audience is. (As if *vorare* were next to *orare*.)

It seems to me that what I have been saying demonstrates, no doubt somewhat comically, the hypothesis of the origin of tragedy in religious ritual—somewhat comically, because I must seem rather to have deflated the problem, implying that whether the hypothesis is true depends on what is meant by "tragedy," what by "origin," and which ritual is in mind. I have, in effect, argued that if you accept the words as food, and you accept the central figure as invoking the central figure of the Eucharist, then you may accept a formulation to the effect (not that the play is the ritual of the Eucharist, but to the effect) that the play celebrates, or aspires to, the same fact as the ritual does, say the condition of community. Eucharist means

---

[11]See *The Complete Essays of Montaigne*, trans. Donald Frame (Stanford: Stanford UP, 1976), p. 159.

gratitude, precisely what Coriolanus feels the people withhold from him. This is another way to see why I am not satisfied to say that Coriolanus is enraged first of all by the people's cowardice. Perhaps one may say that to Coriolanus their cowardice means ingratitude. As for the idea of origin, we need only appeal to Descartes's idea that the origin of a thing is the same thing that preserves it. What preserves a tragedy, what creates the effect of a certain kind of drama, is the appropriation by an audience of this effect, our mutual incorporation of its words. When the sharing of a sacrifice is held on religious ground, the ritual itself assures its effectiveness. When it is shifted to aesthetic ground, in a theater, there is no such preexisting assurance; the work of art has to handle everything itself. You might think of this as the rebirth of religion from the spirit of tragedy. A performance is nothing without our participation in an audience; and this participation is up to each of us.

To enforce the necessity of this decision to participate (a decision which of course has its analogue for the individual reader with the script in his or her hands) is the way I understand the starkness of the words of this play, their relative ineloquence, their lack of apparent resonance. The play presents us with our need for one another's words by presenting withholding words, words that do not meet us halfway. It presents us with a famine of words. This way of seeing it takes it to fulfill a prophecy from the Book of Amos (8:12): "Behold, the days come, saith the Lord God, that I will send a famine in the land, not a famine of bread, nor a thirst for water; but of hearing the words of the Lord."

Coriolanus and the Expansion of City Liberties

Leah S. Marcus

In *Coriolanus,* as in *Measure for Measure,* a city dominates the stage but this time the city is Rome, a much more familiar locus for English Renaissance audiences than Vienna. We might expect the Rome of *Coriolanus* to be associated with the "unlocalized" code of Roman law. But the city in this play is not the Rome of empire—it is the Rome of the early republican period, a Rome which is, like early Jacobean London, expanding out to incorporate the suburban areas around it, and is, like Jacobean London, dominated by fierce civic pride and clamor for the preservation of local autonomy. In Parliament and in London, political leaders disgruntled with James's tendencies toward absolutism looked to republican Rome for alternatives to government by royal prerogative. For his part, James muttered aloud about the contemporary English "Tribunes" who stirred up sentiment against him. *Coriolanus* is overlaid with a language of civic "liberties and franchises" which does not occur in Shakespeare's sources, but which carries strong topical reverberations with the jurisdictional battles in Shakespeare's London. In this play—perhaps four years after *Measure for Measure*—local law and privilege win out against the more global and arbitrary claims of absolutism.

The figure of Caius Martius Coriolanus cannot readily be equated with James I or with any other specific contemporary offender against the "freedoms" of London. But he is associated with abuses of local authority like those which the City of London was contesting in the early Stuart period, whether the transgressors against civic ordinance were agents of the king or aristocrats sheltered by the royal dispensing power. In *Coriolanus,* through the person of the arrogant, isolated warrior, royal and aristocratic privilege is symbolically banished from a city whose political divisions make it readily comparable to London. Coriolanus is a figure who would have been far more at home within a climate of empire than in Rome of the Republic. He, like the Tarquins in *Lucrece,* is a violator of civic liberties. And he, like them, is cast off. As a result of his inability to function within the turbulent republican system "within the wall," he is banished "without," turned

From Leah S. Marcus, *Puzzling Shakespeare: Local Reading and Its Discontents* (Berkeley: Univ. of California Press, 1988), 202–11. The original footnotes have been renumbered. © 1988 The Regents of the University of California. Reprinted by permission of the University of California and the author.

into a scapegoat whose expulsion both makes possible and bears witness to the expansion of the city and its "liberties."

Coriolanus is one of the folio plays that does not exist in an earlier printed version. Like some of the others, it is so laden with highly charged topical materials that we may be tempted to speculate it was withheld from earlier publication for that reason alone. The usual date assigned to it is 1608, and the usual basis for the dating is the strong correlation between the grain riots which open the play and the grain rioting that year and the year before in England. In some ways, the civil disorders of the play are closer to the English situation in 1607–8 than to that of the early Roman Republic. According to the standard classical sources, the dearth in Rome had been caused by the peasants' failure, amid the throes of political upheaval, to plant their crops as usual. In *Coriolanus*, by contrast, the gods made the dearth, or at least a significant part of it. As in the English famine in 1607 and 1608, disastrous weather is to blame, along with hoarding of produce by some institutions and individuals. In the Midlands, where the worst rioting took place, "Levellers" tore down hedges and filled up ditches that enclosed land which had once been held in common. They saw themselves quite clearly as defending their ancient "liberties" against a new breed of aristocratic encroachment. It was a rural version of the familiar London conflict between the city's customary rights and "walled off" enclaves of special privilege—royal, courtly, ecclesiastical—which were surrounded by the city but immune from its jurisdiction.[1]

In London, too, dearth and hoarding were acute problems in the famine of 1608. There was some rioting; the problem of supply was compounded by a long-standing jurisdictional dispute between the London Corporation and officials of

---

[1] Among the many recent studies of *Coriolanus*, I am particularly indebted to E. C. Pettet, "*Coriolanus* and the Midlands Insurrection of 1607," *Shakespeare Survey* 3 (1950): 34–42; the extensive discussion of topicality in Geoffrey Bullough, ed., *Narrative and Dramatic Sources of Shakespeare*, 5 (New York: Columbia Univ. Press, 1964), 456–60; Clifford Chalmers Huffman, *Coriolanus in Context* (Lewisburg, Pa: Bucknell Univ. Press, 1971); W. Gordon Zeeveld, "'*Coriolanus*' and Jacobean Politics," *Modern Language Review* 57 (1962): 321–34; and Janet Adelman's psychoanalytic study of the climate of hunger in the play, " 'Anger's My Meat': Feeding, Dependence, and Aggression in *Coriolanus*," 1978; reprinted in *Representing Shakespeare: New Psychoanalytic Essays*, ed. Murray M. Schwartz and Coppélia Kahn (Baltimore: Johns Hopkins Univ. Press, 1980), 129–49. [This essay forms a part of "Escaping the Matrix," the Adelman essay reprinted here.] My brief analysis intersects Adelman's at several points. I am suggesting a political dimension for her analysis of phallic aggression and hunger.

I am also indebted to Stuart Kurland, whose work in manuscript presented at Midwest MLA, 1986, helped get me thinking about the play, and to Jonathan Dollimore, *Radical Tragedy: Religion, Ideology and Power in the Drama of Shakespeare and His Contemporaries* (Chicago: Univ. of Chicago Press, 1984), 218–30; Jonathan Goldberg, *James I and the Politics of Literature* (Baltimore: Johns Hopkins Univ. Press, 1983), 186–93, 202; Leonard Tennenhouse, "*Coriolanus*: History and the Crisis of Semantic Order," 1977; reprinted in *Selected Essays on Renaissance Drama*, ed. Clifford Davidson (New York: AMS, 1985); Kenneth Burke, "*Coriolanus*—and the Delights of Faction," in *Essays in Shakespearean Criticism*, ed. James L. Calderwood and Harold E. Toliver (Englewood Cliffs, N.J.: Prentice-Hall, 1970), 530–47; James L. Calderwood, "*Coriolanus*: Wordless Meanings and Meaningless Words," also in *Essays in Shakespearean Criticism*, 548–59; and Stanley Cavell's amplification and reinterpretation of Adelman in terms of the politics of the gift and cycles of nurturance and anality, " 'Who does the wolf love?' *Coriolanus* and Interpretations of Politics," 1984; reprinted in this volume (pp. 168–87).

the court—particularly the Warders of the Tower of London, where foodstuffs arriving by water were unloaded—over who had the right to collect customs on the cargo and distribute it. The shortages inevitably made the conflict more pressing. In the play, the arrogant Coriolanus incites the hatred of the Roman rioters by insisting that the grain supply be kept out of their hands: they have not done the state sufficient service to "deserue Corne gratis" (TLN 1822).[2] So strongly is he identified with the withholding of food that the citizens assume they have only to do away with him to achieve abundance: "Let vs kill him, and wee'l haue Corne at our own price" (TLN 13–14). Coriolanus's rigid stance recapitulates the attitude of court officials in London who claimed the special privilege of receiving and distributing foodstuffs in violation of the customs of the city. Some Tower officials even took it upon themselves to exact their own private percentage of every cargo unloaded, much to the prejudice of the shipmen, who lost their profit and began taking their produce elsewhere, and of the public, who ended up paying higher prices.[3] In the Rome of *Coriolanus*, as in contemporary London, hunger is rampant, but hunger for civic respect pinches worse: the touchy citizens regard flagrant violation of their local "laws" and customs as a crime almost more heinous than any other.

What the citizens want most is precisely what Coriolanus refuses to give them. If there is any one precipitating cause behind his rejection as consul, it is his inability to act within what the aristocrats scoffingly refer to as the citizens' "rotten Priuilege, and Custome" (TLN 882). As Mark Kishlansky has observed, the portrayal of civic election in the "Rome" of *Coriolanus* has no prototype in the play's classical sources; instead, it accurately replicates the process of English parliamentary selection or of wardmote selection to the London Common Council.[4] In order to be elected consul, Coriolanus can be chosen by acclamation, but must also observe ancient civic ritual, which he would prefer to "o'erleap." He must don the robe of humility, ask individual citizens for their votes according to the "Custome of Requests," and show his wounds to the assembled populace. With poor grace, he manages to perform the "Custome of Requests," but he cannot bring himself to show his wounds. That too is a departure from Shakespeare's classical sources—in

---

[2]Throughout this essay I will be referring to the Norton Facsimile edition of *The First Folio of Shakespeare*, ed. Charlton Hinman (New York: Norton, 1968). I have kept folio spellings but have silently expanded contractions and changed stage directions from italics to roman when quoted in isolation. References to the texts of the plays are indicated by "through line number" (TLN) in my text.

[3]See the series of interesting encounters recorded in *Analytical Index to the Series of Records Known as the Remembrancia . . . AD 1579–1664* (London: Francis & Co., 1878), 426–34. In a petition to Queen Elizabeth, the mayor, aldermen, and commonalty of the City of London had protested that the city enjoyed sole right to the "survey, search, assay, examination, weighing, and trying of all kinds of goods, merchandize, victuals, etc." brought to the city either by land or water (p. 436). In 1603 some of the London guilds also complained about wrongs done by His Majesty's purveyors (p. 94).

[4]Mark S. Kishlansky, *Parliamentary Selection: Social and Political Choice in Early Modern England* (Cambridge: Cambridge Univ. Press, 1986), 3–9. Although Kishlansky's attack on the "Whig" interpretation of the early modern electoral process has aroused controversy among historians, he convincingly demonstrates that a locus of tension in *Coriolanus* is the breakdown of a traditional system by which a candidate's selection is validated by popular acclamation, but in which that acclamation is actively invoked through the candidate's "courting" of the people.

Plutarch, Coriolanus shows his wounds.[5] The seemingly minor alteration focuses attention on the aristocrat's contempt for the "rotten," dusty customs of the city. He has been amply advised that "the People must haue their Voyces,/Neyther will they bate one iot of Ceremonie" (TLN 1360–61), but it is precisely the idea of "the People" as possessing a voice and identity apart from his own that he cannot stomach. To show them his wounds would be to grant them a kind of authority over his secret vulnerability, demean him to their level, "vnbuild the Citie" and "lay all flat," bring the "Roofe to the Foundation,/And burie all" (TLN 1908–17). The fastidiously specific procedures which the citizens insist upon in the name of their ancient privileges are, for Coriolanus, both inconsequential and outrageous, an opening into chaos.

Throughout the play, Coriolanus's arrogant assumption that he can freely override the "liberties and franchises" of the city is interpreted by Roman citizens and tribunes in terms of the language of Stuart absolutism. Coriolanus has "resisted laws" and would "winde" himself "into a power tyrannical," "affecting one sole Throne without assistance." The tribunes charge that he "would depopulate the city, & be euery man himself" (TLN 1995). That feared engulfment of identity is very much like the obliteration of autonomy and local meaning associated in London with the menacing claims of empire. At one point during the civic tug of war, a brief riot erupts as the "peoples Magistrates" attempt to arrest Coriolanus but are beaten off by the aristocrats. That conflict closely mimics the undignified skirmishes of the streets of Jacobean London in which local JPs were prevented from making an arrest by royal marshals claiming higher jurisdiction. Finally Coriolanus is expelled as a tyrant and "Enemy to the People" through the same city gates he had earlier entered in triumph. In *Measure for Measure* a public trial earns the duke the right to marry and reclaim his city; in *Coriolanus*, a public trial issues in "divorce" and estrangement, the hero's perpetual banishment "without the wall." Even as the city rejects him, Coriolanus almost comically banishes the city (TLN 2411)—as though its monuments and topography can be uprooted as easily as he.

The charges against Coriolanus are, of course, not altogether justified. The vacillating citizens on their own appear willing to affirm him as consul, but they are inflamed against him by their tribunes, who need to vanquish the contemptuous aristocrat in order to protect their own authority. Coriolanus's monumental narcissism may or may not have specifically imperial ambition behind it (in terms of Roman history, such ambition might have been anachronistic in the early republican period). But his martial specialty, reflected in his honorific surname Coriolanus, is highly threatening to the concept of civic liberties. He excels in the solitary penetration of walled cities—Corioles, Antium. War in the play is a "Ravisher" of cities and he is its phallic agent, daring to penetrate alien walls alone, threatening to invade even his "mother city" Rome in an act which would "treade" on his "Mothers wombe/That brought thee to this world" (TLN 3478–80). As in

---

[5]Geoffrey Bullough, ed., *Narrative and Dramatic Sources of Shakespeare*, 5: 518.

Lucrece and *Measure for Measure,* there is a strong link between political autocracy and sexual conquest. For Coriolanus, the citizens and their quaint claims to authority "within the wall" are incomprehensible, inchoate, achieving definition only insofar as they are dominated with the sword from without.

In interesting ways, *Coriolanus* recasts the emerging Renaissance preoccupation with personal and political authorship. Coriolanus strives to be "author of himself" in much the same way that Renaissance writers—even the Stuart monarch—were beginning to claim authorship as a way of overriding the endless, protean multiplicity of "local" meaning. Coriolanus perceives the people as pieces, scabs, fragments; he is a unity, self-identical, self-contained like a sword. He is frequently associated with the gods; at the height of his fleeting popularity after the victory over Corioles, the nobles bend to him as to "*Ioues* statue" (TLN 1196)—unalterable, impervious, like marble. If he is to earn the consulship, the citizens demand that he participate in a civic pageant of which he is not sole "author." Like England's James I, he is but a reluctant performer—"It is a part that I shall blush in acting"—and finally refuses to participate in a ritual of which he will not be the controlling focus. His preferred form of civic pageantry is the military triumph to the sound of trumpets, centering gloriously upon himself "crown'd with an Oaken Garland, with Captaines and Souldiers, and a Herauld" (TLN 1061–63). He can only relate to the citizens from a Jove-like eminence apart, and cannot imagine a form of civic government which is not an aristocratic hegemony. "when two Authorities are vp,/Neither Supreame; How soone Confusion/May enter 'twixt the gap of Both, and take/The one by th'other" (TLN 1803–6). His formulation is a strong justification for absolutism. Brutus complains, "You speak a'th' people, as if you were a God,/To punish; Not a man, of their Infirmity" (TLN 1773–74). At one point the hero appears to take on a composite identity, like a Stuart monarch: "as if that whatsoeuer God, who leades him,/Were slyly crept into his humane powers" (TLN 1138–39). A god, Jove-like, self-created, partaking of the "sacred body" of kingship—the language surrounding Coriolanus is the language of Stuart power, particularly as refracted through the complaints of contemporaries who found it threateningly excessive.

To view the play's political conflict from the perspective of civic liberties is to gain a somewhat more sympathetic view of the Roman citizens and their leaders than is often brought out in performance. On stage, as in recent critical analysis, the tense balance between the plebeians and the aristocrat can tilt either way, depending on how sympathetically either flawed entity is presented. We need, as usual, to assume that there could have been an almost equal flexibility in Renaissance performance, depending on place and circumstance. One of the play's characters muses that "Our Vertue,/Lie in th'interpretation of the time" (TLN 3140–41): there could scarcely be a better epigraph for the nature of topicality itself and its capacity to take on different colorations as a result of even slight adjustments of character and dramatic action. As recent performances have shown, a powerful lead actor can easily move the major locus of the play's conflict away from the political and toward the personal and psychological. To the extent that the tragedy in performance focuses on the plight of Coriolanus alone, his dilemma becomes an entrapment between two ideas of the city: between the volatile Rome of the citizens and the demanding Rome of Volumnia, cruel nurturant. In London, 1608, however, there were special factors that would have moved the play back toward the locus of political conflict which I have suggested here. In that year, in addition to the problems we have already seen recapitulated in the play, there was a landmark victory for the city and its liberties.

The most important circumstance linking *Coriolanus* topically to the year 1608 (or a little before or after) has scarcely surfaced in discussions of the play. In 1608, after much parleying back and forth, James I granted London a new charter which rescinded some of the abuses aired in the play and gave the city increased authority over several of the enclaves within it which had traditionally been exempt from its jurisdiction. The dark scenario of empire was not unfolding in London according to the direst expectations of its citizens in 1603 and 1604. Instead, even as the clashes between rival officials continued, James I was increasingly inclined to make accommodation with the city's franchises and liberties and with the "Tribunes of the People." He acted partly out of increasing recognition of London's sensitivity to the issue, but much more out of a financial embarrassment which the city could do much to repair. The monarch was "hungry" too: many of the parliamentary debates in the period before *Coriolanus* focused on matters of royal supply. Two years later in the Parliament of 1610, Menenius's Parable of the Belly and the Members came up in debate in connection with the matter of royal supply. According to contemporary report, James's "price" for the new London charter was funds to build a new royal banqueting house—again, as in *Coriolanus*, the issue of abundant foodstuffs is balanced against civic respect.[6]

The new London charter gave the city greatly increased jurisdiction over Blackfriars, Whitefriars, West Smithfield, and the precincts of Duke's Place. Perhaps more important, it gave London justices of the peace the right to act in

---

[6]I am indebted for the reference to the 1610 Parliament to Annabel Patterson, personal communication, June 17, 1986. The Fable of the Belly and the Members, of course, came up regularly in political discourse. See, for example, the aftermath of the Essex affair, in which the fable was used to argue that citizens have to support their prince lest all be slaughtered, *Calendar of State Papers Domestic, Elizabeth I*, 5: 405 (Feb.? 1600); and for another example within a Roman Catholic context, Camden's *Remaines* as excerpted in Geoffrey Bullough, ed., *Narrative and Dramatic Sources of Shakespeare*, 5: 551–52.

On the monetary connection between banqueting and city "liberty," see E. K. Chambers, *The Elizabethan Stage* (Oxford: Clarendon Press, 1923), 2: 480. For parliamentary debates over supply and purveyance, see, for example, R. C. Munden's discussion, "James I and 'the growth of mutual distrust': Kings, commons and reform, 1603–4," in Kevin Sharpe, ed., *Faction and Parliament: Essays in Early Stuart History* (Oxford: Clarendon Press, 1978), 43–72; Wallace Notestein, *The House of Commons 1604–1610* (New Haven: Yale Univ. Press, 1971), 96–106, 186–210; and W. Gordon Zeeveld, "'Coriolanus' and Jacobean Politics," 324–34. The phrase "Tribunes of the People" and references to the "head" and the "members" were used frequently during the debates to refer to members of the House of Commons who took the populist side against purveyance.

criminal matters without hindrance by other keepers of the peace or royal ministers. No longer, if the charter was observed, would there be the inglorious spectacle in the London streets of local officials trying to make an arrest but finding themselves detained by royal marshals instead. The charter also reaffirmed London's customary control over shipping and unloading of boats on the Thames; in theory at least, the citizens and the London Corporation now had the control of foodstuffs within their own hands. Last but not least, the charter explicitly stated that the liberties it guaranteed to London superseded royal proclamations to the contrary. It was an important victory for the city, an official guarantee of an end to some of the worst inroads by absolutist government against London's precious liberties and franchises.[7]

Samuel Taylor Coleridge once remarked, with reference to *Coriolanus*, on the "wonderful philosophic impartiality in Shakespeare's politics."[8] It is true that the play identifies serious flaws on both sides of the Roman civic conflict. Coriolanus's massive arrogance is balanced off against the vacillation of the Roman citizens, who display little of the steadiness and "civility" they will need if they are to execute the political functions granted them in theory through the election of their own tribunes as well as the military functions they have taken on themselves through their banishment of the warrior. But the play does not end impartially. It is a tragedy for the aristocrat, a victory for the citizens, despite the Volscian forces massed threateningly outside the walls. Coriolanus, who has contemned the citizens as scraps, meaningless pieces, is himself reduced to little more, cut down by multiple stab wounds within the boundaries of an enemy city. Having refused his part in civic pageantry while alive, he is doomed to fulfill it in death: when his body is carried through the streets of Antium, he finally shows his wounds to a group of gazing citizens. As Janet Adelman's keen analysis has pointed out, the isolate Coriolanus does not permit audience sympathy: his very nature "insists that we keep our distance." The play "separates and limits" rather than permitting resolution and reconciliation.[9] In that sense, *Coriolanus* effects a more complete "divorce" between the city and the aristocracy than that worked in contemporary London, where the bargain struck between monarch and city over the new 1608 charter preserved a measure of reciprocity. In the play, the conflict is implacable, cast in extreme form. The Enemy of the People has been destroyed; Rome has been made militarily vulnerable as a result; but her precious "liberties and franchises" remain intact and the cornerstone of her future greatness has been laid. For republican Rome, as for its enemy Aufidius, the death of Coriolanus becomes

[7]The text of the 1608 charter is printed in *The Historical Charters and Constitutional Documents of the City of London*, rev. ed., ed. Walter de Gray Birch (London: Whiting & Co., 1887), 139–50. For an account of the charter's limitations, see Valerie Pearl, *London and the Outbreak of the Puritan Revolution: City Government and National Politics, 1625–43* (London: Oxford Univ. Press, 1961), 27–33. Needless to say, despite the new royal guarantees, the royal encroachments continued.

[8]Cited from *Coleridge's Shakespearean Criticism*, ed. Thomas Middleton Raysor (London: Constable, 1930), 1: 89.

[9]Adelman, " 'Anger's My Meat' " in *Representing Shakespeare*, ed. Murray M. Schwartz and Coppélia Kahn, 144–45.

a source of new invigoration: "therefore shall he dye,/And Ile renew me in his fall" (TLN 3703–4).

In critical analysis or performance of *Coriolanus,* it is easy enough to take sides for or against the aristocrat. From the perspective of localization, however, what the play *does* is more important: it enacts a civic victory like the expansion of London authority; it does so by casting out a symbolic representative of the artificial constraints imposed on the city from above. Coriolanus is a direct threat to city liberties, but also an externalization of the self-contempt and collective self-disparagement which would keep the city down, perhaps even diminish its capacity for local pride and identity by encouraging the inroads of imperial ideology and making the citizens "of no more Voyce/Then Dogges" (TLN 1618–19). The 1608 *Coriolanus* invites Londoners to don a robe of humility of their own and wear it more productively than Coriolanus—see their own weaknesses as a group reflected in their Roman counterparts so that they can cast off their unsettled, fragmented factionalism and prepare themselves for increased political autonomy. In a sense, the citizens are invited to assume as part of their new "Authoritie" a new sense of "authorship" over their collective political actions. What will thereby be created is, of course, an urban entity which moves toward an imperialist potential of its own—toward the vision of Dryden's *Annus Mirabilis* a half century later, in which the city itself becomes empress, glorious, conquering Imperia. But that is another story. What concerns us here is the earlier stage which is delineated in *Coriolanus:* the city casts off a privilege that overrides its own, an "unlocalized" law by which civic identity is eroded. *Coriolanus* turns *Measure for Measure* on its head.

The play can also be seen as creating a space for itself—for the genre of Jacobean tragedy—out of the expulsion of the aristocrat from the city. Coriolanus has refused his part in civic pageantry "within the wall." As a result of his contempt for the "liberties" and "charters" of Rome and its "violent, testy magistrates," he is banished without—to the place of the London stage, just outside the city's jurisdiction. Thereafter, the language he uses in describing his predicament becomes increasingly theatrical. As he tells his wife and mother from outside the gates of Rome, "Like a dull Actor now, I haue forgot my part,/And I am out, euen to a full Disgrace" (TLN 3390–91). He is condemned to "act" in his own tragedy in the "place of the stage" outside the city, since he will not conform to the demands of "custom" within it. We may be reminded of the fact that in ancient Athens the word *hubris* could refer either to overbearing pride or to an offense against the city deemed punishable by death.[10] The arrogant power and prerogative voided from the city convert to dramatic representation outside it: the play offers a recipe for the creation of Jacobean tragedy. Perhaps it is not mere happenstance that in the First Folio, *Coriolanus* is listed first among the tragedies. It marks out a "local" space for the others, displaying a mechanism by which the menace of aristocracy in London is transformed into a

---

[10]Kenneth Burke, "*Coriolanus*–and the Delights of Faction," 532.

safer mode of enactment outside it. Many Londoners feared the theater for its associations with arbitrary rule, its flouting of local ordinances and liberties. In *Coriolanus*, the enactment of tragedy—the self-imposed fall of a noble general—does not so much flout the laws and customs of the city as display their increasing power.

Antony and Cleopatra (c. 1607): *Virtus* under Erasure

Jonathan Dollimore

In Jonson's *Sejanus*, Silius, about to take his own life in order to escape the persecution of Tiberius, tells the latter: "The means that makes your greatness, must not come/In mention of it" (3.311–12). He is of course exposing a strategy of power familiar to the period: first there occurs an effacement of the material conditions of its possibility, second, a claim for its transcendent origin, one ostensibly legitimating it and putting it beyond question—hence Tiberius' invocation only moments before of "the Capitol,/. . . all our Gods . . . the dear Republic,/Our sacred Laws, and just authority" (3.216–18). In *Sejanus* this is transparent enough. In other plays—I choose for analysis here *Antony and Cleopatra* and *Coriolanus*—the representation of power is more complex in that we are shown how the ideology in question constitutes not only the authority of those in power but their very identity.

Staged in a period in which there occurred the unprecedented decline of the power, military and political, of the titular aristocracy, *Antony* and *Coriolanus*, like *Sejanus* before them, substantiate the contention that "'tis place,/Not blood, discerns the noble, and the base" (*Sejanus*, 5.1.11–12). Historical shifts in power together with the recognition, or at least a more public acknowledgement of, its actual operations, lead to the erasure of older notions of honour and *virtus*. Both plays effect a sceptical interrogation of martial ideology and in doing so foreground the complex social and political relations which hitherto it tended to occlude.

In his study of English drama in the seventeenth century C. L. Barber detects a significant decline in the presence of honour as a martial ideal and he is surely right to interpret this as due to changes in the nature and occupations of the aristocracy during that period. These included the professionalising of warfare and the increasing efficiency of state armies. The effect of such changes was that by the end of the seventeenth century there was considerably less scope for personal military initiative and military glory; honour becomes an informal personal code with an extremely attenuated social dimension.[1]

From Jonathan Dollimore, *Radical Tragedy: Religion, Ideology, and Power in the Drama of Shakespeare and His Contemporaries* (Durham, N.C.: Duke University Press, 1986), pp. 204–17. Reproduced by permission. The original footnotes have been restyled and renumbered.

[1]Charles Laurence Barber, *The Idea of Honour in the English Drama 1591–1700* (Gothemburg, Sweden: Elanders Boktr., 1957), pp. 269–79.

More recently, and even more significantly for the present study, Mervyn James has explored in depth the changing conceptions of honour between 1485 and 1642; most striking is his conclusion that there occurred "a change of emphasis, apparent by the early seventeenth century. . . [involving] . . . the emergence of a 'civil' society in which the monopoly both of honour and violence by the state was asserted."[2]

Such are the changes which activate a contradiction latent in martial ideology and embodied in two of Shakespeare's protagonists, Antony and Coriolanus. From one perspective—becoming but not yet residual—they appear innately superior and essentially autonomous, their power independent of the political context in which it finds expression. In short they possess that *virtus* which enables each, in Coriolanus's words, to "stand/As if a man were author of himself" (5.3.35–36). "As if": even as these plays reveal the ideological scope of that belief they disclose the alternative emergent perspective, one according to which Antony and Coriolanus are nothing more than their reputation, an ideological effect of powers antecedent to and independent of them. Even as each experiences himself as the origin and embodiment of power, he is revealed in the words of Foucault[3] to be its instrument and effect—its instrument because, first and foremost, its effect. Bacon brilliantly focusses this contradiction in his essay on martial glory: "It was prettily devised of Æsop: *The fly sate upon the axle-tree of the chariot wheel, and said, What a dust do I raise!*" Throughout Bacon's essay there is a dryly severe insistence on that fact which martial ideology cannot internally accommodate: "opinion brings on substance."[4] Such is the condition of Antony and Coriolanus, and increasingly so: as they transgress the power structure which constitutes them both their political and personal identities—inextricably bound together if not identical—disintegrate.

Virtus *and History*

Antony and Cleopatra anticipates the dawn of a new age of imperialist consolidation:

[2]Mervyn James, *English Politics and the Concept of Honour 1485–1642, Past and Present* Supplement 3, 1978 (Oxford: Past and Present Society, 1978), p. 2.

[3]Foucault conceives of power not as something possessed by subjects but as that which constitutes them; the individual is both the effect and the object of power:

> The individual is not to be conceived as a sort of elementary nucleus, a primitive atom, a multiple and inert material on which power comes to fasten or against which it happens to strike, and in doing so subdues or crushes individuals . . . The individual, that is, is not the *vis-a-vis* of power; it is, I believe, one of its prime effects. The individual is an effect of power, and at the same time, or precisely to the extent to which it is that effect, it is the element of its articulation. The individual which power has constituted is at the same time its vehicle.

See Michel Foucault, *Power/Knowledge*, ed. Colin Gordon (Brighton: Harvester, 1980), p. 98.

[4]Francis Bacon, *Essays*, introduction by Michael J. Hawkins (London: Dent, 1972), p. 158.

The time of universal peace is near.
Prove this a prosp'rous day, the three nook'd world
Shall bear the olive freely.

(4.6.5–7)

Prior to such moments heroic *virtus* may appear to be identical with the dominant material forces and relations of power. But this is never actually so: they were only ever coterminous and there is always the risk that a new historical conjuncture will throw them into misalignment. This is what happens in *Antony and Cleopatra;* Antony, originally identified in terms of both *virtus* and these dominant forces and relations, is destroyed by their emerging disjunction.

In an important book Eugene Waith has argued that "Antony's reassertion of his heroic self in the latter part of the play is entirely personal. What he reasserts is individual integrity . . . Heroism rather than heroic achievement becomes the important thing."[5] On this view Antony privately reconstitutes his "heroic self" despite or maybe even because of being defeated by circumstances beyond his control. I want to argue that the reverse is true: heroism of Antony's kind can never be "entirely personal" (as indeed Bacon insisted) nor separated from either "heroic achievement" or the forces and relations of power which confer its meaning.

The reader persuaded by the Romantic reading of this play is likely to insist that I'm missing the point—that what I've proposed is at best only true of the world in which Antony and Cleopatra live, a world transcended by their love, a love which "translineates man (sic) to divine likeness."[6] It is not anti-Romantic moralism which leads me to see this view as wholly untenable. In fact I want to argue for an interpretation of the play which refuses the usual critical divide whereby it is either "a tragedy of lyrical inspiration, justifying love by presenting it as triumphant over death, or . . . a remorseless exposure of human frailties, a presentation of spiritual possibilities dissipated through a senseless surrender to passion."[7] Nor do I discount the Romantic reading by wilfully disregarding the play's captivating poetry: it is, indeed, on occasions rapturously expressive of desire. But the language of desire, far from transcending the power relations which structure this society, is wholly in-formed by them.

As a preliminary instance of this, consider the nature of Antony's belated "desire" for Fulvia, expressed at news of her death and not so dissimilar to his ambivalent desire for Cleopatra (as the sudden shift of attention from the one to the other suggests):

Thus did I desire it:
What our contempts doth often hurl from us
We wish it ours again; the present pleasure,

---

[5] Eugene Waith, *The Herculean Hero in Marlowe, Chapman, Shakespeare and Dryden* (London: Chatto, 1962), p. 118.
[6] G. Wilson Knight, *The Imperial Theme* (London: Macmillan, 1965), p. 217.
[7] Derek Traversi, *An Approach to Shakespeare*, 3rd ed., 2 vols. (London: Hollis and Carter, 1969), II, p. 208.

By revolution low'ring, does become
The opposite of itself. She's good, being gone;
The hand could pluck her back that shov'd her on.
I must from this enchanting queen break off.
                                        (1.2.119–25)

True, the language of the final scenes is very different from this, but there too we are never allowed to forget that the moments of sublimity are conditional upon absence, nostalgic contemplation upon the fact that the other is irrevocably gone. As for present love, it is never any the less conditioned by the imperatives of power than the arranged marriage between Antony and Octavia.

Virtus *and* Realpolitik

In *Antony and Cleopatra* those with power make history yet only in accord with the contingencies of the existing historical moment—in Antony's words: "the strong necessity of time" (1.3.42). If this sounds fatalistic, in context it is quite clear that Antony is not capitulating to "Time" as such but engaging in *realpolitik,* real power relations. His capacity for policy is in fact considerable; not only, and most obviously, is there the arranged marriage with Octavia, but also those remarks of his which conclude the alliance with Lepidus and Caesar against Pompey:

[Pompey] hath laid strange courtesies and great
Of late upon me. I must thank him only,
Lest my remembrance suffer ill report;
At heel of that, defy him.
                                        (2.2.159–62)

In fact, the suggestion of fatalism in Antony's reference to time is itself strategic, an evasive displacing of responsibility for his impending departure from Cleopatra. As such it is parallelled later by Caesar when he tells the distraught Octavia,

Be you not troubled with the time, which drives
O'er your content these strong necessities,
But let determin'd things to destiny
Hold unbewail'd their way.
                                        (3.6.82–85)

The cause of her distress is divided allegiance between brother and husband (Caesar and Antony) who are now warring with each other. Caesar's response comes especially ill from one scarcely less responsible for her conflict than Antony; her marriage to the latter was after all dictated by his political will: "The *power* of Caesar, and/His *power* unto Octavia" (2.2.147–48; my italics). "Time" and "destiny" mystify power by eclipsing its operation and effect, and Caesar knows this; compare the exchange on Pompey's galley—*Antony:* "Be a child o' th' time./*Caesar:* Possess it, I'll make answer" (2.7.98–99). Caesar, in this respect, is reminiscent of

Machiavelli's Prince; he is inscrutable and possessed of an identity which becomes less fixed, less identifiable as his power increases. Antony by contrast is defined in terms of omnipotence (the more so, paradoxically, as his power diminishes): the "man of men" (1.4.72), the "lord of lords" (4.8.16).

In both *Antony and Cleopatra* and *Coriolanus* the sense of *virtus* (virtue) is close to "valour," as in "valour is the chiefest virtue" (*Coriolanus*, 2.2.82), but with the additional and crucial connotations of self-sufficiency and autonomous power, as in "Trust to thy *single virtue;* for thy soldiers /. . . have . . . / Took their discharge" (*King Lear,* 5.3.104–6; my italics). The essentialist connotations of "virtue" are also clearly brought out in a passage from *Troilus and Cressida* (1.2.29–30): "what hath mass or matter by itself / Lies rich in virtue and unmingled." In *Antony and Cleopatra* this idea of self-sufficiency is intensified to such an extent that it suggests a transcendent autonomy; thus Cleopatra calls Antony "lord of lords! / O *infinite virtue,* com'st thou smiling from / The world's great snare uncaught?" (4.8.16–18). Coriolanus is similarly described as proud, "even to the altitude of his virtue" (2.1.38). Against this is a counter-discourse, one denying that virtue is the source and ethical legitimation of power and suggesting instead that the reverse is true—in the words of Macro in *Sejanus,* "A prince's power makes all his actions virtue" (3.717). At the beginning of Act 3 for example Silius urges Ventidius further to consolidate his recent successes in war, so winning even greater gratitude from Antony. Ventidius replies that, although "Caesar and Antony have ever won / More in their officer than person" (3.1.16–17), an officer of theirs who makes that fact too apparent will lose, not gain favour. It is an exchange which nicely illustrates the way power is a function not of the "person" (3.1.17) but of "place" (3.1.12), and that the criterion for reward is not intrinsic to the "performance" (3.1.27) but, again, relative to one's placing in the power structure (cf. *Sejanus,* 3.302–5: "all best turns / With doubtful princes, turn deep injuries / In estimation, when they greater rise, / Than can be answered").

Later in the same act Antony challenges Caesar to single combat (3.13.20–28). It is an attempt to dissociate Caesar's power from his individual virtue. Enobarbus, amazed at the stupidity of this, testifies to the reality Antony is trying, increasingly, to deny:

> men's judgements are
> A parcel of their fortunes, and things outward
> Do draw the inward quality after them,
> To suffer all alike.
>
> (3.13.31–34)

In Enobarbus' eyes, Antony's attempt to affirm a self-sufficient identity confirms *exactly the opposite.* Correspondingly, Caesar scorns Antony's challenge with a simple but devastating repudiation of its essentialist premise: because "twenty times of better fortune" than Antony, he is, correspondingly, "twenty men to one" (4.2.3–4).

As effective power slips from Antony he becomes obsessed with reasserting his sense of himself as (in his dying words): "the greatest prince o' th' world, / The

noblest" (4.15.54–55). The contradiction inherent in this is clear; it is indeed as
Canidius remarks: "his whole action grows/Not in the power on't" (3.7.68–69).
Antony's conception of his omnipotence narrows in proportion to the obsessive-
ness of his wish to reassert it; eventually it centres on the sexual anxiety—an assertion of sexual prowess—which has characterised his relationship with both
Cleopatra and Caesar from the outset. He several times dwells on the youthfulness
of Caesar in comparison with his own age (e.g. at 3.13.20; 4.12.48) and is generally
preoccupied with lost youthfulness (e.g. at 3.13.192; 4.4.26; 4.8.22). During the
battle scenes of Acts 3 and 4 he keeps reminding Cleopatra of his prowess—mili-
taristic and sexual: "I will appear in blood" (3.13.174); "There's sap in't yet! The
next time I do fight,/I'll make death love me" (3.13.192–93); and:

> leap thou, attire and all,
> Through proof of harness to my heart, and there
> Ride on the pants triumphing.
>
> (4.8.14–16)

All this, including the challenge to single combat with Caesar, becomes an obsessive attempt on the part of an ageing warrior (the "old ruffian"–4.1.4) to reassert
his virility, not only to Cleopatra but also to Caesar, his principal male competitor.
Correspondingly, his willingness to risk everything by fighting on Caesar's terms
(3.7) has much more to do with reckless overcompensation for his own experienced powerlessness, his fear of impotence, than the largesse of a noble soul. His
increasing ambivalence towards Cleopatra further bespeaks that insecurity (e.g. at
3.12 and 4.12). When servants refuse to obey him he remarks, "Authority melts
from me"—but insists nevertheless "I am/Antony yet" (3.13.90–93): even as he is
attempting to deny it Antony is acknowledging that identity is crucially dependent
upon power. Moments later even he cannot help remarking the difference
between "what I am" and "what . . . I was" (3.13.142–43).

It is only when the last vestiges of his power are gone that the myth of heroic
omnipotence exhausts itself, even for him. In place of his essentialist fixedness,
"the firm Roman," the "man of steel" he once felt himself to be (1.4.43; 4.4.35),
Antony now experiences himself in extreme dissolution:

> That which is now a horse, even with a thought
> The rack dislimns, and makes it indistinct
> As water is in water . . .
>   Eros, now thy captain is
> Even such a body: here I am Antony,
> Yet cannot hold this visible shape
>
> (4.14.9–14)

Virtus, divorced from the power structure, has left to it only the assertion of a negative, inverted autonomy: "there is left us/Ourselves to end ourselves" (4.14.21–22).
And in an image which effectively expresses the contradiction Antony has been living out, energy is felt to feed back on itself: "Now all labour/Mars what it does;
yea, very force entangles/Itself with strength" (4.14.47–49). Appropriately to

this, he resolves on suicide only to bungle the attempt. The bathos of this stresses, uncynically, the extent of his demise. In the next scene it is compounded by Cleopatra's refusal to leave the monument to kiss the dying Antony lest she be taken by Caesar. Antony, even as he is trying to transcend defeat by avowing a tragic dignity in death, suffers the indignity of being dragged up the monument.

There is bathos too of course in Caesar's abruptly concluded encomium:

> Hear me, good friends—
> [*Enter an Egyptian*]
> But I will tell you at some meeter season.
> The business of this man looks out of him
> (5.1.48–50)

The question of Caesar's sincerity here is beside the point; this is, after all, an encomium, and to mistake it for a spontaneous expression of grief will lead us to miss seeing that even in the few moments he speaks Caesar has laid the foundation for an "official" history of Antony. First we are reminded that Caesar *is*—albeit regrettably—the victor. He then vindicates himself and so consolidates that victory by confessing to a humanising grief at the death of his "brother" (though note the carefully placed suggestion of Antony's inferiority: "the *arm* of mine own body" [5.1.45]; my italics). Caesar further vindicates himself by fatalising events with the by now familiar appeal to necessity, in this case "our stars, / Unreconcilable." Earlier Caesar had told Octavia that "The ostentation of our love. . . left unshown, / Is often left unlov'd" (3.6.52–53). Such is the rationale of his encomium, a strategic expression of "love" in the service of power. The bathos of these episodes makes for an insistent cancelling of the potentially sublime in favour of the political realities which the sublime struggles to eclipse or transcend. Actually, bathos has accompanied Antony throughout, from the very first speech of the play, the last three lines of which are especially revealing (Philo is speaking of Antony):

> Take but good note, and you shall see in him
> The triple pillar of all the world transform'd
> Into a strumpet's fool. Behold and see.
> (1.1.11–13)

The cadence of "triple pillar of all the world" arches outward and upward, exactly evoking transcendent aspiration; "transformed" at the line end promises apotheosis; we get instead the jarringly discrepant "strumpet's fool." Cynical, perhaps, but Philo's final terse injunction—"Behold and see"—has prologue-like authority and foresight.

After Antony's death the myth of autonomous *virtus* is shown as finally obsolescent; disentangled now from the prevailing power structure, it survives as legend. Unwittingly Cleopatra's dream about Antony helps relegate him to this realm of the legendary, especially in its use of imagery which is both Herculean and statuesque: "His legs bestrid the ocean; his reared arm/Crested the world" (5.2.82–83). Cleopatra asks Dolabella if such a man ever existed or might exist; he answers: "Gentle Madam, no." Cleopatra vehemently reproaches him only to qualify instantly her own certainty—"But if there be nor ever were one such"—thereby, in the hesitant syntax, perhaps confirming the doubts which prompted the original question.

His legs bestrid the ocean: in dream, in death, Antony becomes at last larger than life; but in valediction is there not also invoked an image of the commemorative statue, that material embodiment of a discourse which, like Caesar's encomium, skilfully overlays (without ever quite obscuring) obsolescence with respect?

Honour and Policy

If the contradiction which constitutes Antony's identity can be seen as a consequence of a wider conflict between the residual/dominant and the emergent power relations, so too can the strange relationship set up in the play between honour and policy. Pompey's reply to Menas' offer to murder the triumvirs while they are celebrating on board his (Pompey's) galley is a case in point:

> Ah, this thou shouldst have done,
> And not have spoke on't. In me 'tis villainy:
> In thee 't had been good service. Thou must know,
> 'Tis not my profit that does lead mine honour:
> Mine honour, it. Repent that e'er thy tongue
> Hath so betray'd thine act. Being done unknown,
> I should have found it afterwards well done,
> But must condemn it now.
>
> (2.7.73–80)

Here honour is insisted upon yet divorced from ethics and consequences; the same act is "villainy" or "service" depending on who performs it; ignorance of intent to murder is sufficient condition for approving the murder after the event.

Elsewhere in the play we see these inconsistencies resolved in favour of policy; now honour pretends to integrity—to be thought to possess it is enough. Once again it is a kind of political strategy which takes us back to Machiavelli's *The Prince*. Antony tells Octavia: "if I lose mine honour/I lose myself" (3.4.22–23). Octavia has of course been coerced into marriage with Antony to heal the rift (now reopened) between him and Caesar, her brother. So, for Antony to speak to her of honour seems hypocritical at least; when, however, Antony goes further and presents himself as the injured party ready nevertheless to forego his revenge in order to indulge Octavia's request that she be *allowed* to act as mediator— "But, as you requested,/Yourself shall go between's" (3.4.24–25)—the honour in question is shown to be just another strategy in his continuing exploitation of this woman.

When Thidias is persuading Cleopatra to betray Antony and capitulate to Caesar, honour is now a face-saving strategy for *both* sides; because she "embraced" Antony through fear, says Caesar, he construes the scar upon her honour as "constrained blemishes,/Not as deserv'd." Cleopatra quickly concurs: "He [Caesar] is a god, and knows/What is most right. Mine honour was not yielded,/But conquer'd merely" (3.13.59–62).

In Enobarbus we see how policy aligns positively with realism and judgement. He, like Philo at the outset of the play, Ventidius in 3.1 and the soldier in 3.7 who urges Antony not to fight at sea, occupies a role in relation to power very familiar in Jacobean tragedy: he possesses an astuteness characteristic of those removed from, yet involved with and dependent upon—often for their very lives—the centre of power; his is the voice of policy not in the service of aggrandisement so much as a desire for survival. So, for example, we see in 3.6 Enobarbus attempting to dissuade Cleopatra from participating in the war and Antony from fighting on Caesar's terms. Failing in the attempt, Enobarbus leaves Antony's command but is struck with remorse almost immediately. Since he left without his "chests and treasure" (4.5.8) we are, perhaps, to presume that material gain of this kind was not his motive. Enobarbus, like Antony, comes to embody a contradiction; the speech of his beginning "Mine honesty and I begin to square" (3.13.41) suggests as much, and it becomes clear that he has left his master in the name of the "judgement" which the latter has abdicated but which is integral still to his, Enobarbus', identity as a soldier. Yet equally integral to that identity is the loyalty which he has betrayed.

The extent of people's dependence upon the powerful is something the play never allows us to forget. Cleopatra's beating of the messenger in 2.5 is only the most obvious reminder; a subtler and perhaps more effective one comes at the end of the play when Cleopatra attempts to conceal half her wealth from Caesar. In the presence of Caesar she commands Seleucus, her "treasurer," to confirm that she has surrendered all; "speak the truth, Seleucus" she demands and, unfortunately for her he does, revealing that she has kept back as much as she has declared. Cleopatra has ordered him "Upon his *peril*" (5.2.142) to speak the truth (i.e. lie) while he, with an eye to Caesar, replies that he would rather seal his lips "than to my *peril*/Speak that which is not." Here, truth itself is in the service of survival. Cleopatra, outraged, finds this unforgivable; for servants to shift allegiance is, in her eyes (those of a ruler) "base" treachery (5.2.156). The play however, in that ironic repetition of "peril" (my italics) invites an alternative perspective: such a shift is merely a strategy of survival necessitated precisely by rulers like her. Yet doubly ironic is the fact that while Seleucus is described as a "slave, of no more trust/Than love that's hir'd" (5.2.153–54) her own deceit is approved by Caesar as the "wisdom" (5.2.149) appropriate to one in her position. Elsewhere Caesar speaks in passing of the "much tall youth" (2.6.7) that will perish in the event of war; Octavia speaks of the consequence of war between Caesar and Antony being as if "the world should cleave, and that slain men/Should solder up the rift" (3.4.31–32; cf. 3.13.180–81; 4.12.41–42; 4.14.17–18). It is a simple yet important truth, one which the essentialist rhetoric is never quite allowed to efface: to kiss away kingdoms is to kiss away also the lives of thousands.

Sexuality and Power

Those around Antony and Cleopatra see their love in terms of power; languages of possession, subjugation and conspicuous wealth abound in descriptions of the people. More importantly, Antony and Cleopatra actually experience themselves in the same terms. Antony sends Alexas to Cleopatra with the promise that he will "piece/Her opulent throne with kingdoms. All the East/(Say thou) shall call her mistress" (1.5.45–47). Later Caesar describes the ceremony whereby that promise was honoured, a ceremony aiming for an unprecedented *public* display both of wealth and power: "Cleopatra and himself in chairs of gold/Were publicly enthron'd"; Antony gives to Cleopatra the stablishment of Egypt and makes her "Absolute Queen" of Syria, Cyprus and Lydia. "This in the public eye?" inquires Maecenas; "I' th' common showplace" confirms Caesar (3.6.4–12). Cleopatra for her part sends twenty separate messengers to Antony. On his return from Egypt Enobarbus confirms the rumour that eight wild boars were served at a breakfast of only twelve people, adding: "This was but as a fly by an eagle: we had much more monstrous matter of feast, which *worthily deserved noting*" (2.2.185, my italics).

Right from the outset we are told that power is internal to the relationship itself: Philo tells us that Antony has been subjugated by Cleopatra (1.1.1–9) while Enobarbus tells Agrippa that Cleopatra has "pursed up" (i.e. pocketed, taken possession of) Antony's heart (2.2.190). As if in a discussion of political strategy, Cleopatra asks Charmian which tactics she should adopt in order to manipulate Antony most effectively. Charmian advocates a policy of complete capitulation; Cleopatra replies: "Thou teachest like a fool—the way to lose him!" (1.3.10). Antony enters and Cleopatra tells him: "I have no power upon you," only then to cast him in the role of treacherous subject: "O, never was there queen/So mightily betrayed! Yet at the first/I saw the treasons planted" (1.3.23–26). Whatever the precise sense of Cleopatra's famous lines at the end of this scene—"O my oblivion is a very Antony,/And I am all forgotten"—there is no doubt that they continue the idea of a power struggle: her extinction is coterminous with his triumph.

Attempting to atone for his departure, Antony pledges himself as Cleopatra's "soldier, servant, making peace or war,/As thou affects" (1.3.70). This is just one of many exchanges which shows how their sexuality is rooted in a fantasy transfer of power from the public to the private sphere, from the battlefield to the bed. In 2.5 Cleopatra recalls with merriment a night of revelry when she subjugated Antony and then engaged in cross-dressing with him, putting "my tires and mantles on him, whilst/I wore his sword Philippan" (2.5.22–23). Inseparable from the playful reversal of sexual roles is her appropriation of his power, military and sexual, symbolised phallically of course in the sword. Later Antony takes up the sword-power motif in a bitter reproach of Cleopatra for her power over him; here he sees her as his "conqueror" (3.11.66, and compare 4.14.22–23). Another aspect of the power- sexuality conjunction is suggested in the shamelessly phallic imagery which the lovers use: "Ram thou thy fruitful tidings in mine ears,/That long time have been barren" (2.5.24–25), although again Cleopatra delights in reversing the roles (as at 2.5.10–15).

Here then is another aspect of the contradiction which defines Antony: his sexuality is informed by the very power relations which he, ambivalently, is prepared to sacrifice for sexual freedom; correspondingly, the heroic *virtus* which he wants to reaffirm in and through Cleopatra is in fact almost entirely a function of the power structure which he, again ambivalently, is prepared to sacrifice for her.

Ecstasy there is in this play but not the kind that constitutes a self-sufficient moment above history; if *Antony and Cleopatra* celebrates anything it is not the love which transcends power but the sexual infatuation which foregrounds it. That infatuation is complex: ecstatic, obsessive, dangerous. Of all the possible kinds of sexual encounter, infatuation is perhaps the most susceptible to power—not just because typically it stems from and intensifies an insecurity which often generates possessiveness and its corollary, betrayal, but because it legitimates a free play of self-destructive desire. In Antony's case it is a desire which attends and compensates for the loss of power, a desire at once ecstatic and masochistic and playing itself out in the wake of history, the dust of the chariot wheel.

The Politics of Display
and the Anamorphic Subjects
of *Antony and Cleopatra*

Heather James

> Then, world, thou hast a pair of chaps, no more,
> And throw between them all the food thou hast,
> They'll grind the one the other.

$$(3.5.13–15)^1$$

Criticism of *Antony and Cleopatra,* like the play itself, has tended to divide into oppositional camps dedicated to politics and sexual love respectively. From the earliest accounts of the historical Antony and Cleopatra and their place in Rome's transformation into an imperial government, sexuality and politics have been inextricably bound together as opposites. In the most authoritative classical version, the *Aeneid,* the conflictual relationship between the two achieves its most paradoxical form in the words Aeneas uses to abandon Dido. Speaking of his duty to the unfounded Rome, Aeneas conflates the values that the epic has hitherto treated as oppositional: *"hic amor, haec patria est"* ("There is my love, there my country") (4.347). With these words, Vergil acknowledges the empire's readiness to institutionalize its vision of the ideal citizen as a subject modelled on the empire's own centralized and repressive character. The proposition that there is no difference between *amor* and *Roma,* at first wholly counter-intuitive, provisionally yields an ideal of patriotic love capable of harnessing disruptive erotic desires.

A modern forum for the struggle of sexual and political concerns which caused the fictional Aeneas to leave Dido and the historical Antony to follow Cleopatra is to be found in the debate between Jonathan Dollimore and Carol Thomas Neely. As exponents of cultural materialism and Anglo-American feminism, they respectively appropriate and repossess the languages of sexuality and gender for the purposes of narrowly political analysis on the one hand, and feminist, psychoanalytic,

Previously unpublished. Reproduced with the permission of the author.

[1]All references to *Antony and Cleopatra* are from the Arden edition, ed. M. R. Ridley (London: Methuen & Co., 1954).

and characterological study on the other.[2] The debate, whose particulars I defer for later discussion, at first appears to turn on questions of priority—i.e., whether concerns with politics or with sexuality and subjectivity matter more to the play—but actually revolves around the more troubling question of whether sexuality *per se* is even relevant to *Antony and Cleopatra.* Dollimore proposes a restricted model of politics as a master discourse able to absorb all representations in its own interpretive terms. As metaphors for an essentially political discourse, sexuality, subjectivity, and gender become so many effects as opposed to material causes of events in the play.

The following essay seeks to retie *Antony and Cleopatra's* concerns with sexuality and politics into a "knot intrinsicate" and, more generally, to argue that sexuality, gender, and a refurbished notion of character should be reconsidered as indispensible terms of—not arbitrary metaphors for—political questions in the emergent Roman empire of the play, in Jacobean England, and in the Shakespearean theater. Since dramatic representations are at times taken to replicate the perspectives found in classical sources (an older assumption) or the vested interests of Jacobean court politics (a newer one), I stress here the potential independence of the theater from inherited or politically dominant positions. In the following pages, I propose to investigate the relationship of Antony and Cleopatra to the conventions and fictions through which they are recognized and constituted as exemplary types. I argue that Antony and Cleopatra assume increasingly self-conscious positions in relation to the ideologically charged conventions and legends 1) to which Octavian seeks to reduce them within the play and 2) through which the Jacobean audience would respond to them as classical exemplars relevant to Jacobean social and political concerns. Through readings of Cleopatra's disruptive relation to Petrarchan conventions and the challenge that both lovers issue to the authoritative *Aeneid,* I finally argue for a working model of politics that can account for the characters' *resistance* to constitutive codes, whether literary or political, Roman or Jacobean. The *effect* of character has the potential to illuminate political functions of the Shakespearean theater that are obscured by the reductions of Antony and Cleopatra to political allegories.

I

Let him forever go, let him not—Charmian,
Though he be painted one way like a Gorgon,
The other way's a Mars.

(2.5.115–17)

---

[2]Jonathan Dollimore, "Shakespeare, Cultural Materialism, Feminism and Marxist Humanism," *New Literary History* 21, no. 3 (Spring 1990): 471–94, presents a lively response to the critique of Carol Thomas Neely, "Constructing the Subject: Feminist Practice and the New Renaissance Discourses," *English Literary Renaissance* 18 (1988): 5–18.

These are the startling lines Shakespeare's Cleopatra speaks when she finally accepts the truth of the messenger's report that Antony has entered into a political marriage with Octavia and thus betrayed her. Cleopatra describes him as a perspective painting which presents two distinct images interchangeably, depending on the position of the viewer. For Janet Adelman, one of the few critics to note Cleopatra's perspective, the image of Antony as both Gorgon and Mars encapsulates the play's thematic and structural concern with judgment.[3] Her account of the epistemological and ideological functions of *Antony and Cleopatra*'s dramatic structure and characterization remains the most illuminating view to date, and it is within the general context she has established that I wish to situate my comments on the peculiarities of Cleopatra's perspective image. Since the image of Antony oscillates specifically between the female Gorgon of myth and the Roman god of war, it is one of the more striking instances of the play's notorious "gender trouble": the perspective image yokes together extreme versions of both genders, and thus calls on us to reconsider, from Cleopatra's point of view, the variously anxious and exuberant exchange of gender identities that characterizes the love affair of Antony and Cleopatra.[4] Because Cleopatra is the speaker, the image grants us a rare opportunity to view the gender trouble without jaundiced and moralizing commentary from the Romans. My immediate concern, however, is what it means for Cleopatra, who is consistently identified with feminine artifice, to use an artistic image to express her divided response to Antony. The perspective image and Shakespeare's choice of speaker have a great deal to teach us about the status of Cleopatra as a character, as well as her relation to gender norms and to the conventions, simultaneously political and literary, with which we evaluate the play's legendary figures.

The most startling feature of Cleopatra's perspective image is that it superimposes on the martial and divine Antony the image of a Gorgon. Although there were three Gorgon sisters, the significant one was Medusa. In what might be called her prehistory, Medusa was raped by Poseidon in the temple of Athene, who exacted the punishment which made her notorious: she was transformed into a snaky-haired monster who was either so beautiful or so hideous that she turned to stone all who beheld her. Perseus, with the aid of Athena, approached the Gorgon by looking in his shield, and successfully decapitated her—and in the form

[3]Janet Adelman, *The Common Liar: An Essay on Antony and Cleopatra* (New Haven: Yale University Press, 1973), p. 24.

[4]For discussions of the play's "gender trouble," see Janet Adelman, *Suffocating Mothers* (London: Routledge, 1992); Clare Kinney, "The Queen's Two Bodies and the Divided Emperor: Some Problems of Identity in *Antony and Cleopatra*," in eds. Anne Haselkorn and Betty Travitsky, *The Englishwoman in Print: Counterbalancing the Canon* (Amherst: University of Massachusetts Press, 1990); Theodora Jankowski, *Women in Power in the Early Modern Drama* (Urbana: University of Illinois Press, 1992); Jyotysna Singh, "Renaissance Antitheatricality, Antifeminism, and Shakespeare's *Antony and Cleopatra*," *Renaissance Drama* 41 (1989):77–90; Carol Thomas Neely, *Broken Rituals in Shakespeare's Plays* (New Haven: Yale University Press, 1985); Peter Erikson, *Patriarchal Structures in Shakespeare's Drama* (Berkeley: University of California Press, 1985); and Barbara Estrin, " 'Behind a Dream': Cleopatra and Sonnet 129," *Women's Studies* 9 (2) (1982):177–88.

of a truncated and snaky head she is best known. Medusa has obvious uses as a military weapon but, as the editors of the *Oxford Classical Dictionary* observe, she is even more popular as an apotropaic symbol—an image that causes a turning away in the viewer.[5] She appears pervasively in the Renaissance as a poetic trope for the stunning and decapacitating effects of female beauty. The Gorgon's emergence from Cleopatra's imagination poses the following question: what is she to Medusa, or Medusa to her? That is, what does the Gorgon signify to Cleopatra, and how does Cleopatra's appropriation of the Gorgon image relate to traditional uses of Medusa in poetry?

The image of the Gorgon is by no means incidental to the messenger scene that precedes it. Throughout the scene in which the messenger earns blows and curses for delivering his bad news, Cleopatra has gender transgression, male beauty, and the Gorgon's snaky locks on her mind. Early on, she tells the messenger that he should come "like a Fury crowned with snakes, / Not like a formal man" (2.5.40–41). Later she adds, "Hadst thou Narcissus in thy face, to me / Thou wouldst appear most ugly" in the same breath that she wishes Egypt were reduced to "a cistern for scaled snakes!" (2.5.95). In both cases, she employs mythological figures to blur gender distinctions. Narcissus' extraordinary beauty is accentuated by his liminal position between boy and man, and the ambiguity excites the imaginations and desires of men and women alike.[6] Cleopatra's earlier image is more overtly transgressive of gender boundaries. She superimposes on the messenger a virtual perspective painting: he is both an attractive man and a Fury crowned with snakes. The Eumenides, female personifications of revenge from the classical Underworld, appear to mortals either to visit revenge upon them or to coerce them into dire acts of revenge. The Furies at times do both: when they appear in fantasy to Dido, the fictional model for Cleopatra, the Furies not only drive her to madness and suicide as punishment for her illicit love affair with Aeneas, they also prompt her curse on Aeneas and Rome. Cleopatra's growing ambivalence toward Antony, the lover who repels and attracts her simultaneously, culminates in her perspective painting of him as both a gorgeous Mars and a harrowing Gorgon.

The Romans of *Antony and Cleopatra* would unanimously agree that Antony is, or was, a Mars. In the very first speech of the play, Philo bitterly reminisces about the former Antony, whose excesses took place on the battlefield and transformed him into a "plated Mars." The Romans would also accept the Medusa as an image for Cleopatra, Antony's "serpent of old Nile" (1.5.25). But any Roman would be

---

[5]N. G. L. Hammond and H. H. Scullard, *The Oxford Classical Dictionary*, second edition (Oxford at the Clarendon Press, 1970), under the listing "Gorgo," give a brief summary of the Medusa's history in the Classical period. Although she is working with the "male Medusa," which does not, I think, account for Cleopatra's image, Marjorie Garber provides a stimulating discussion of the Gorgon image in *Macbeth: Shakespeare's Ghost Writers: Literature as Uncanny Causality* (London: Methuen, 1987).

[6]In Ovid's account, *namque ter ad quinos unum Cephisius annum/addiderat poteratque puer iuvenisque videri:/multi illum iuvenes, multae cupiere puellae* ("Narcissus had reached his sixteenth year and might seem either boy or man. Many youths and many maidens sought his love"). *Metamorphoses* 3.351–53, trans. Frank Justus Miller (Cambridge: Harvard University Press, 1916).

astonished to hear the heroic commander compared to a Gorgon—even Caesar, who sneers at the Alexandrian Antony for being "not more manlike/Than Cleopatra; nor the queen of Ptolemy/More womanly than he" (1.4.5–7). The Gorgon/Mars image assumes a curiously nonjudgmental position on Antony and Cleopatra's practice of exchanging gender roles, a game that Caesar disdains and that Cleopatra laughingly celebrates at the beginning of the messenger scene: "I drunk him to his bed;/Then put my tires and mantles on him, whilst/I wore his sword, Philippan" (2.5.21–23). But the Medusa is not the appropriate mythological figure to illuminate transgressions of gender *per se.* Antony's sporadic willingness to "o'erflow the measure" of masculinity is not sufficient to explain Cleopatra's image. For this, we must turn to her uses in lyric poetry: the Medusa is the mythological creature who undergirds the poetics of desire in Petrarchan lyric.[7] The Medusa image is implicit throughout the *Rime Sparse,* in which the sight of Laura's beauty figuratively and repeatedly turns Petrarch to stone. At the end of the cycle of lyrics, Petrarch names the Medusa epiphanically in his poem to the Virgin, where he confesses, "Medusa et l'error mio m'an fatto un sasso/d'umor vano stillante" ("Medusa and my error have made me a stone dripping vain moisture," 366.111–12).[8]

When Cleopatra employs the image of the Medusa, she becomes the bearer of the desiring gaze, not its Petrarchan object. As a Mars, Antony ravishes and captivates her senses, and Cleopatra is unable to let him go forever. As a Gorgon, he turns her to stone, again through his physical attractions and her passionate desires. The Petrarchan gaze, however, was familiar to Jacobean audiences as the privilege of male subjects in literature. Conventionally, only beautiful women have the effect of the Medusa on the desiring man who beholds her and, conversely, only men desire beauty precisely in this way. Therefore, when Cleopatra uses the figure of the Medusa to express her ambivalence toward Antony, she does considerably more than anticipate literary traditions yet to come. When she adopts the Petrarchan stance and imagines Antony in the conventions used to describe the disabling effects of extreme feminine beauty, she disrupts powerful conventions through which early modern writers affirmed ideological norms of gender, desire, and masculine subjectivity.[9]

---

[7]See Robert M. Durling, *Petrarch's Lyric Poems,* and especially his comments on Petrarch's relationship to Ovid's *Metamorphoses* and Dante's *rime petrose,* which Durling includes in an appendix (Cambridge: Harvard University Press, 1976), and John Freccero, "Medusa: The Letter and the Spirit," *Dante: The Poetics of Conversion* (Cambridge: Harvard University Press, 1986).

[8]Petrarch's image adapts two lines of Lucretius' *De Rerum Natura: nonne vides etiam guttas in saxa cadentis/umoris longo in spatio pertundere saxa?* Petrarch uses allusion to delineate his own sense of sexual guilt, for he draws on the last two lines of Lucretius' notorious tirade against sexuality at the end of Book 4.

[9]Shakespeare delighted in "misusing" the blazon in ways which call into question the sexual and gender norms it typically reinforces. When Petruchio and Kate pretend to mistake Vincentio for a "young budding virgin," they tease him with an inventory of his cheeks, in which white and red war, and his starry eyes (*Shrew* 4.5.27–49). In *As You Like It,* Phebe falls in love with Ganymede/Rosalind, and immediately bursts into a lengthy blazon of his eye, leg, lip, and cheek, specifically admiring the feminine qualities of the supposed lad (3.5.109–35). All references are from *The Riverside Shakespeare,* gen. ed. G. Blakemore Evans (Boston: Houghton Mifflin, 1974).

The consequences of Cleopatra's image, then, are momentous, for she usurps the stance of the early modern male subject and disrupts the ideological privileges implicit in the Petrarchan conventions she uses. Reversing the conventions of gender assumed in the poetics of Petrarchan desire accomplishes two gains for *Antony and Cleopatra:* Shakespeare successfully makes Antony into an object of desire available to the audience and endows Cleopatra with the complex subjectivity associated with those who bear the desiring gaze and understand themselves as fundamentally divided by that desire. This feat does not merely reverse, but actually resuscitates Petrarchan poetics, whose resources were all but exhausted by 1607–8, when *Antony and Cleopatra* was written. In *Twelfth Night,* for example, Olivia parodies the cliche of the stony-hearted beloved, whose individual body parts receive minute praise in her abject lover's blazon:

> I will not be so hard-hearted; I will give out divers schedules of my beauty. It shall be inventoried, and every particle and utensil labell'd to my will: as, *item,* two lips, indifferent red; *item,* two grey eyes, with lids to them; *item,* one neck, one chin, and so forth (2.1.244–49).

Olivia herewith refuses to co-operate as a Petrarchan lady, but her form of rebellion is modest compared with that of the usurping Cleopatra. When an alluring woman is the Petrarchan speaker, not the object, Petrarchan poetics regains its rhetorical efficacy, which is the power to produce what Joel Fineman has called "subjectivity effects."[10] The central achievement of Petrarchism is the subjectivity effect it reserves for the male poet, whose interiority gains in depth and complexity in proportion to the abstraction and incoherence of the woman whose various beauties he praises and blames. To accomplish the poetic representation of the male subject, the woman's presence must be carefully restricted, and her body fragmented and dispersed: such is the strategy of a poetics whose hallmark is the blazon.[11] Cleopatra cannot give utterance to Petrarchan desire without exploding the most basic premises of Petrarchan convention.

Cleopatra's privileged moment of poetic activity and self-revelation comes at the end of an entire scene that dramatizes the extent to which Cleopatra herself is supremely anamorphic. Initially, her status as an outrageous stereotype of feminine impatience overpowers any sense of her interiority. Throughout the messenger scene, Cleopatra expends and misdirects her energies and thus reinforces the Roman sense of her as a *performance* of femininity rather than a living, breathing, and above all reflective, woman. As long as she rivets our attention to her perfor-

---

[10]Joel Fineman, "Shakespeare's *Will:* The Temporality of Rape," *Representations* 20 (Fall 1987): 25–76.

[11]Nancy J. Vickers, "Diana Described: Scattered Woman and Scattered Rhyme," ed. Elizabeth Abel, *Writing and Sexual Difference* (Chicago: University of Chicago Press, 1982). Although not concerned with Petrarch's representation of feminine beauty and its costs to female subjectivity, Thomas M. Greene, in *The Light in Troy* (New Haven: Yale University Press, 1982), provides an eloquent analysis of fallen Petrarchan consciousness. Fineman finds a characteristically Shakespearean model of subjectivity in the chiasmatic inversion of Petrarchan tropes, particularly of praise.

mance of female jealousy and rage, we are looking at Cleopatra from the outside and unlikely even to recognize that the scene does not encourage us to identify or sympathize with her as a suffering lover. She is all showy exterior—a comic, if negative, example of female incontinence.

Towards the end of the scene, however, Shakespeare suspends the comedy routine of the wildly impatient woman and has Cleopatra redirect her energies inward. She remarks, with no clear relevance to the dramatic plot, "In praising Antony I have dispraised Caesar" (108). She is thinking of Julius Caesar, her previous Roman lover, to whom she vastly prefers Antony. We may well wonder why her mind turns back to Julius Caesar and her slighting comparisons of him with Antony. What is significant is the dramatic effect created by Cleopatra's lapse in energy, her turn to her companions, and especially her introspection. When she begins to review her history and reproach herself, we are led to wonder what she is thinking, and to discover that we are sealed off from a consciousness we would like to know more about. For the first time in the scene, we gain partial access to her perspective and a vantage point from which to see her outrageous treatment of the messenger as a defense against her pain at Antony's betrayal. As long as she curses and "hales the messenger up and down," we forget that Antony has, in fact, betrayed her. Her history and self-consciousness become important to us as mysteries when she quietly berates herself.

Her unexpected recollection of Julius Caesar is characteristic of Shakespeare's strategic invocations of the three Roman commanders who have been Cleopatra's lovers. We are often reminded that Cleopatra regards her history with Pompey, Julius Caesar, and Antony quite differently from the Roman view, which censures and admires Cleopatra as the foreign, narcissistic temptress who sums up the "enigma of woman" in Sarah Kofman's phrase.[12] Shakespeare uses the Roman commanders, surprisingly, to point towards Cleopatra's perspective and personal history. At the end of 1.5, for example, Cleopatra recalls both "Broad-fronted Caesar" and "great Pompey," who "Would stand and make his eyes grow in my brow,/There would he anchor his aspect, and die/With looking on his life" (31–34)—an image which suggests that the Roman commanders generate the narcissistic love associated with Cleopatra. At such moments, Cleopatra is granted the privileged position, for a woman, of being "only" a subjective and epistemological Other, not the siren who stands for man's distracted imagination.

II

In the previous section I argued that when Cleopatra reveals Petrarchan desire, she revises the Petrarchan ideology of gender and subjectivity and, consequently, gains and revitalizes the subjectivity effects of Petrarchan poetics. This she accom-

[12]Sarah Kofman, *The Enigma of Woman: Woman in Freud's Writings*, trans. Catherine Porter (Ithaca: Cornell University Press, 1985).

plishes simply through her status as a kind of female love poet. And yet Cleopatra is not any woman. She is a queen and a legend, depicted in the play and in criticism as both a quintessential woman and a quintessential work of artifice.[13] Her power to disrupt Petrarchan poetics gains in force because she herself is pervasively defined as a consummate work of craft. She is an enchanting queen, great fairy, Thetis, witch, gipsy, a charm, and a spell to Antony and her audiences alike. A supremely artificial creature, she seems virtually to define womankind as artifice and proclaim herself a legendary source, not a mere instance, of literary temptresses. I will begin by tracing ways in which she is provisionally reduced to magnificent artifice within the play. Specifically, Cleopatra becomes a trope for feminine "infinite variety" that can be quantified as artistic, rhetorical, and sexual *copia*. Cleopatra, however, appropriates and disrupts her commodification as a trope. She exploits artistry, spectacle, and theatricality as self-representational materials in the exercise of her royal power.

Near the beginning of the play, Enobarbus describes her to the uneasy Antony as magnificent artwork. When Antony claims she is "cunning past man's thought," Enobarbus delivers a mock defense:

> Alack, sir, no, her passions are made of nothing but the finest part of pure love. We cannot call her winds and waters sighs and tears; they are greater storms and tempests than almanacs can report. This cannot be cunning in her; if it be, she makes a show'r of rain as well as Jove (1.2.144–49).

These "tear-floods" and "sigh-tempests" are Petrarchan and their debt to poetic convention denotes Cleopatra's artificiality: according to Enobarbus, her emotional hyperboles are both insincere and a pleasure to behold. In his parody of Cleopatra's Petrarchan mimicry, subjective depth is precisely what her displays eliminate. He implies, and Antony affirms, that she models desire for her beholders to interpret and internalize, but that her displays have little to do with "pure love."

Enobarbus complicates his picture of feminine artifice by comparing Cleopatra's seductive cunning to the arts of that divine philanderer, Jove. Jove's most artful and amorous shower was of gold, not rain, and in that form, he seduced Danäe. Interpreted by St. Augustine as a figure for the allure of rhetoric and fable, the tale was important to Petrarch and appears at the close of his famous *canzone delle metamorfosi*, song 23. After imagining himself successively metamorphosing into various figures from Ovid's *Metamorphoses*, Petrarch at last invokes Jove's shower as the success he can no longer hope to emulate.[14] Enobarbus, on the other

---

[13]Martin Spevack, *A New Variorum Edition of Antony and Cleopatra* (New York: Modern Language Association, 1990), records the responses of critics, starting with Swinburne, to "the woman of women, quintessential Eve" (p. 691).

[14]St. Augustine rails against the love of eloquence which leads human beings to understand, all too well, the appeal of Jove's adulteries and seductions in *Confessions* 1.16. He refers specifically to the scene in Terence's *Eunuchus,* in which a young man, Chaerea, rapes a woman and then rejoices in his exploit by recalling and describing a picture of Jove pouring himself in the lap of Danäe (*Eunuchus,* 3.5). Petrarch laments his inability either to gain his desires as Jove did or, following St. Augustine, to free himself from the love of rhetoric and Ovidian myth. For Song 23, see "Nel dolce tempo . . ." in *Petrarch's Lyric Poems: The "Rime Sparse" and Other Lyrics*, trans. and ed. Robert M. Durling (Cambridge: Harvard University Press, 1976), pp. 60–69.

hand, testifies to Cleopatra's ability to inhabit and reproduce the Ovidian world of change, myth, and flamboyant rhetoric. Unlike Petrarch, Cleopatra can make "a show'r of rain as well as Jove." Enobarbus' Cleopatra briefly emerges as a Petrarchan poet who fashions herself into a persuasive poem. At the last, Enobarbus furnishes a turn in his prose anti-sonnet: she is, he tells Antony, a "wonderful piece of work, which not to have been blest withal would have discredited your travel" (1.2.151–53). She is redeemed by the artifice to which she is simultaneously reduced.

Cleopatra is not, however, equivalent to the artistic conventions through which the play's men recognize her as Cleopatra. In his great set-piece, Enobarbus supplies the play's most sustained description and analysis of Cleopatra's paradoxical relationship to artwork:

> The barge she sat in, like a burnish'd throne
> Burn'd on the water: the poop was beaten gold;
> Purple the sails, and so perfumed that
> The winds were love-sick with them; the oars were silver,
> Which to the tune of flutes kept stroke, and made
> The water which they beat to follow faster,
> As amorous of their strokes. For her own person,
> It beggar'd all description: she did lie
> In her pavillion—cloth of gold, of tissue—
> O'er-picturing that Venus where we see
> The fancy outwork nature. On each side her,
> Stood pretty dimpled boys, like smiling Cupids,
> With divers-colour'd fans, whose wind did seem
> To glow the delicate cheeks which they did cool,
> And what they undid, did . . .
> Her gentlewomen, like the Nereides,
> So many mermaids, tended her i' the eyes,
> And made their bends adornings. At the helm
> A seeming mermaid steers: the silken tackle
> Swell with the touches of those flower-soft hands,
> That yarely frame the office. From the barge
> A strange invisible perfume hits the sense
> Of the adjacent wharfs. The city cast
> Her people out upon her; and Antony,
> Enthron'd i' the market-place, did sit alone,
> Whistling to the air; which, but for vacancy,
> Had gone to gaze on Cleopatra too,
> And made a gap in nature.
>   (2.2.191–218)

This rhetorical description—a virtual ecphrasis—sets up expectations that Cleopatra will be portrayed as a decorative object further embellished by the desiring gaze. In fact, the description, especially where Shakespeare diverges from North's Plutarch, reveals her to be a royal artisan who compels admiration and desire from beholders as part of her politics of display.[15]

This speech is a study in paradox, none more subtle than its equivocal handling of Petrarchan description. Enobarbus' rhetoric courts Petrarchan techniques of representing feminine beauty, but deflects them from Cleopatra herself: although the production around her elicits singular eloquence, her body seems to bereave her viewers and Enobarbus of words. The first lines blazon the abundant royalty surrounding her in the barge that imitates a "burnish'd throne," the poop of beaten gold, the silver oars, the sails of royal purple, and the flutes that accompany her triumph. Enobarbus then turns to Cleopatra's person, which, he tells us, "beggar'd all description." The phrase adapts the famous recognition of Narcissus, who exhausts himself in praise of his reflected image: *"inopem me copia fecit"* ("my rhetorical eloquence/physical beauty makes me poor"). After Enobarbus' conventional pause on the ineffability topos, we expect him to shift from Cleopatra's splendid wealth to her equally resplendent beauties. But he furnishes no elaborate description of the exotic Egyptian queen in a conventional head-to-toe *descriptio* or blazon itemizing especially dazzling body parts. Enobarbus is that unusual poet who literally means that a beautiful woman "beggars description."

Cleopatra's spectacle generates a surplus of desire in the viewers, who, if they look for a body to fix and ballast love, find an abundance in the dimples, smiles, delicate cheeks, eyes, and flower-soft hands Enobarbus mentions. However, these features expressly fail to constitute a blazon. Although standard Petrarchan items, they either do not belong to Cleopatra or, in the case of the cheeks and the eyes, they frustrate the rules of the blazon. Although Cleopatra "o'er-pictures" Venus, we hear a great deal more of the boy actors who play smiling Cupids and the gentlewomen who perform the parts of Nereides or mermaids. The cheeks belong to Cleopatra, but they misleadingly appear in the midst of a detailed account of the smiling and prettily dimpled boys who fan those "delicate cheeks." Once we have begun to visualize their smiles and dimples, we are more likely to flesh out our picture with the plump and ruddy cheeks of Cupids or *putti* than we are to start afresh with the cheeks of the elusive Cleopatra.

Eyes would be the centerpiece of a traditional description, for they are the hallmark of the Petrarchan blazon. But the eyes Enobarbus mentions create a stumbling block to aesthetic reconstruction: "Her gentlewomen, like the Nereides,/So many mermaids, tended her i' the eyes,/And made their bends adornings" (206–8). The scenario in North's Plutarch presents no difficulties:

---

[15]As Susanne Wofford points out to me, the ecphrasis describing Cleopatra comes from Plutarch but may well remind readers of Dido, who is clearly linked to rhetorical description in the *Aeneid*. In Book 1, Dido appears just at the end of the ecphrastic description of the Trojan war. Dido is first described in a highly pictorial simile to Diana leading her dancers, a simile Vergil adopts from the *Odyssey*'s nubile Nausicaa, and then presented, as if in a tableau, passing laws and assigning tasks. For both Shakespeare's Cleopatra and Vergil's Dido, ecphrasis establishes their erotic appeal and their political authority. For Dido alone, however, is the effect of paradox disabling.

"Her ladies and gentlewomen also, the fairest of them were appareled like the nymphs Nereides (which are the mermaids of the waters) and like the Graces, some steering the helm, others tending the tackle and ropes of the barge . . . "[16] Shakespeare obscures North's visual and rhetorical clarity by adding eyes which are curiously discontinuous with the spectacle and syntactically awkward. The eyes are unornamented, "nothing like the sun," or anti-Petrarchan because they are not "gemlike qualities the reader can string together into an idealized unity."[17] Cleopatra's eyes are doing something unimaginable in a Petrarchan lady: they are *watching*. As the Arden editor explains, Cleopatra's gentlewomen "waited in her sight, i.e., were not just a group of attendants in the background." When Shakespeare alters the duties of Cleopatra's attendants— North's gentlewomen "tend the tackle and ropes" while Shakespeare's more obscurely "tend her i' the eyes"—he foregrounds the Egyptian queen's eyes and, consequently, Cleopatra's status as royal spectator.

The alteration serves to distract attention from the persons and objects described in Cleopatra's theatrical display and to highlight the underdescribed Cleopatra and her distanced role as an observer. The shift is puzzling only if Cleopatra is taken to be the central object in an artistic display in which the viewer's experience is privileged. Shakespeare's Cleopatra, who watches the performance of her attendants' duties, is the central spectator of a masque-like display—equipped with musical, olfactory, and above all visual, enticements. In other words, Cleopatra on the barge functions like King James I at court performances of masques. As Stephen Orgel has shown, James I assumed a privileged position to gaze upon the masques: although it did not necessarily provide him with the best view of the spectacle, it foregrounded his royal figure, making him the chief spectator who, in turn, drew admiring gazes to himself.[18] Similarly, the artifice surrounding Cleopatra does not render her an artifact whose value is measured by such wealth, but instead testifies to her royal authority.

It is, I suggest, Cleopatra's royal status that makes her a paradoxically absent and omnipresent figure in her own masque. The success of her display depends on the audience's misrecognition of its basis in political strategy: if her politics of display are to match Stuart practices, her appearance should be perceived as a quasi-divine manifestation and interpreted in the light of the divine right to rule.

---

[16]I quote from Geoffrey Bullough, *Narrative and Dramatic Sources of Shakespeare* (London: Routledge & Kegan Paul and New York: Columbia University Press, 1975).

[17]I paraphrase John Freccero, who discusses the "radically fragmentary" intent of the Petrarchan technique of comparison, in which Laura's "virtues and her beauties are scattered like the objects of fetish worship." He argues that Laura's body must be reified, fragmented, and scattered in accordance to Petrarch's idolatrous poetics in "The Fig Tree and the Laurel: Petrarch's Poetics," *Literary Theory/Renaissance Texts*, eds. Patricia Parker and David Quint (Baltimore: The Johns Hopkins University Press, 1986), pp. 20–32.

[18]Stephen Orgel, *The Illusion of Power: Political Theater in the English Renaissance* (Berkeley: University of California Press, 1975). I thank Christopher Cobb, who encouraged me in my reading of Cleopatra's theatrical performance on the barge scene as a masque.

In fact, according to Enobarbus, the paradoxes of her display—which I take to emanate from her equivocal appearance as a consumable object and a pre-eminent subject—generate a near violation of the laws of physics. The air itself, "but for vacancy,/Had gone to gaze on Cleopatra too,/And made a gap in nature" (216–18). Her power, not her individual beauties, compels the desiring gaze. Cleopatra is a political artisan who shapes the Petrarchan gaze of her audience to reinforce her authority: she subjects her observers to the Petrarchan gaze, but refuses to be the satisfying Petrarchan object. She alone of all women "makes hungry where most she satisfies," another version of Narcissus' motto, *inopem me copia fecit*, because she has harnessed the energies of Petrarchan narcissism for her political advantage.

Although Enobarbus casts the description generally in the form of an anecdote about Cleopatra as an exotic sexual spectacle, he nonetheless supplies the material for a political analysis of her royal display. At the end of the speech, Enobarbus reveals that Cleopatra achieves a political conquest and that Antony is her trophy. Her politics of display are indebted to the quite different strategies of the Elizabethan and Jacobean courts. Her display and her oblique use of Petrarchan conceits recall the political techniques of Elizabeth I, who found that the language of Petrarchan desire was an effective means to represent her authority and to control ambitious statesmen.[19] In her use of the masque and its representation of her political apotheosis, however, Cleopatra's political strategies resemble those of James I rather than the more modest Elizabeth I. Exploiting Elizabeth's art of wooing and James' absolutism informs the odd duality of the barge scene, which represents Cleopatra's powers of seduction and subjugation. Enobarbus' speech concludes with the admission that the sexual and theatrical display is largely political and that in the competition of Egyptian and Roman powers, Cleopatra triumphs. Reclining in her burnished throne, the barge, Cleopatra overcomes Antony, who is "Enthron'd i' the market-place." She stages majesty to compete with Rome, or at least defer being annexed to it. The barge speech, like the messenger scene that soon follows, depicts Cleopatra as a Gorgon/Mars perspective: she is painted one way like a feminine artifact, the other way a woman whose power and interiority are more compelling than her attractive outside, to paraphrase Milton.

To test this reading of Cleopatra's politics of display, we might turn from Elizabethan and Jacobean court practices to evidence within the play itself. The most promising representations of her, and responses to her, are mostly to be found among the censorious but fascinated Romans who repeatedly solicit and

[19]See Arthur F. Marotti, " 'Love Is Not Love': Elizabethan Sonnet Sequences and the Social Order," *English Literary History* 49 (1982): 396–428, and Louis Adrian Montrose, " 'Shaping Fantasies': Figurations of Gender and Power in Elizabethan Culture," *Representations* 2 (1983): 61–94. Some recent criticism has argued for a close relationship of Cleopatra to the figure of Elizabeth. See Jankowski, op. cit. For an opposing argument that Cleopatra represents a censorious Jacobean perspective on Elizabethan rule, see Leonard Tennenhouse, *Power on Display: The Politics of Shakespeare's Genres* (London: Methuen, 1986), especially pp. 144–46.

narrate stories about her. Cleopatra poses a notorious problem of response and political utility to the Romans. I stress the latter point, because the Romans themselves find it imperative to treat Cleopatra as a sexual rather than a political threat. Pompey, for example, grows lyrical over Cleopatra's beauty only under specific conditions. In an apostrophe to the aging temptress, Pompey conjures those attractions he hopes will detain Antony in Egypt long enough for his own forces to gain control in Rome:

> but all the charms of love,
> Salt Cleopatra, soften thy wan'd lip!
> Let witchcraft join with beauty, lust with both,
> Tie up the libertine in a field of feasts,
> Keep his brain fuming . . .
>
> (2.1.20–24)

He invokes her fascinations only under heavy guard. First, Cleopatra must be cast as the romance enchantress closeting up Antony from the political world, and second, Pompey must insist upon his own skepticism, suggesting that, contrary to Enobarbus' famous assertion, her beauty will age and wither. But Pompey is not always so guarded about his interest in the legendary Cleopatra. Later, in the company of Antony and his men, he fishes for one of the most famous stories about her. "I have heard Apollodorus carried—" he begins, and Enobarbus completes his sentence, "A certain queen to Caesar in a mattress" (2.6.68–70). Pompey's responses to legends about Cleopatra reveal the extent to which Romans identify her attractions with the imaginative faculties themselves; they also suggest that Romans can only understand her sexuality as distracting and, therefore, as the siren call away from Roman duty. Pompey's views do not, of course, constitute proof that Cleopatra's powers of seduction are in any way antithetical to her political power. That may be his assumption, but we are not obliged to take the word of a man who proves to be a far from canny politician.

Pompey is not the only Roman to seek out ample descriptions of Cleopatra. Even Octavius Caesar's men prod for detailed accounts of the Egyptian queen at rather awkward moments: Maecenas and Agrippa pump Enobarbus for information immediately after Agrippa has negotiated the marriage of Antony to Octavia. With studied casualness, Maecenas observes that Cleopatra is "a most triumphant lady, if report be square to her." When Enobarbus obligingly mentions Antony's first meeting with Cleopatra on the river Cydnus, Agrippa pounces. He confirms the location—"There she appear'd indeed"—and then coyly hints for a more elaborate account of that spectacle: "or my reporter devis'd well for her" (2.2.189). These men have listened to gossip and the reports of their political informers, but when Enobarbus holds forth in the famous barge speech, they greedily devour his rhetoric for pleasure, not moralistic reproval. Enobarbus completes his luxurious account, and Agrippa enthusiastically bursts out with a rare Roman commendation for Cleopatra's prodigious sexuality and generativity: "Royal wench!/She made great Caesar lay his sword to bed;/He plough'd her, and she cropped" (2.2.226–28). Octavius Caesar's right-hand man can hardly contain his complex response to Cleopatra. His outburst is no locker room joke: he is ready, at this moment, to interpret Cleopatra's sexual and generative powers as a triumph over Roman militarism and, more astoundingly, to conceive of her sexuality as a complement to the warlike powers of "great Caesar." Compelling Caesar to turn his sword into a plow—an image of peace—does not emasculate Rome's greatest commander. Moreover, she is not defeated by pregnancy—Caesar's child is the harvest she made out of the Roman instrument of devastation. Thus, even Agrippa removes Cleopatra from the restraints of the temptress scenario. He recognizes, albeit obliquely, that she has power over Caesar as an explicitly "royal wench" who can combat and overcome Roman militarism. Her sexuality and generativity are versions of royal power—not disabling signs of feminine weakness.

The politics of display next appear in a scene which falls in the center of *Antony and Cleopatra* and deliberately revisits Enobarbus' description of Cleopatra on the barge. At the beginning of 3.6, an outraged Caesar describes to Agrippa the spectacle of Cleopatra, dressed as Isis, surrounded by her children, receiving kingdoms from Antony:

> I' the market-place, on a tribunal silver'd,
> Cleopatra and himself in chairs of gold
> Were publicly enthron'd, at the feet sat
> Caesarion, whom they call my father's son,
> And all the unlawful issue that their lust
> Since then hath made between them. Unto her
> He gave the stablishment of Egypt, made her
> Of lower Syria, Cyprus, Lydia,
> Absolute queen.
>
> *Maecenas*:   This in the public eye?
> *Caesar*:   I' the common show-place, where they exercise.
> His sons he there proclaim'd the kings of kings;
> Great Media, Parthia, and Armenia,
> He gave to Alexander; to Ptolemy he assign'd
> Syria, Cilicia, and Phoenicia: she
> In the habiliments of the goddess Isis
> That day appear'd, and oft before gave audience,
> As 'tis reported, so.
>
>   (3.6.3–19)

Caesar is offended on political rather than moral grounds. He is certainly prepared to poison Antony's reputation in Rome by stressing his opponent's choice publicly to acknowledge and display "the unlawful issue"of "their lust" and to do so in the "common show-place." But he is at best peripherally concerned with Antony's violations of decorum. Caesar recognizes clearly that Antony is not serving his pleasure but acting with political forcefulness.

In this scene, Antony publicly declares himself married to Cleopatra and bestows kingdoms upon her children and friends.[20] He does not fail to notice that those kingdoms are not his to give—on the contrary, his theater of bounty constitutes a public challenge to Caesar. As Caesar belatedly acknowledges to his men, he himself has provoked Antony's drastic measures. Taking financial advantage of Antony's assassination of Pompey, Caesar seized Pompey's goods and, to add insult to injury, refused to send any of the proceeds to Antony. He also deposed Lepidus, a grievous move he compounds by "detain[ing]/All his revenue" (3.6.29–30). Antony's Alexandrian theater presents an alternate center of power to the public: Caesar recognizes Antony's extravagant generosity in the marketplace as an imperialist challenge to counter Caesar's own acts. When Antony and Cleopatra "publicly enthrone" themselves on golden chairs placed on a silver tribunal, they establish a theatrical imitation of Rome, whose centrality they challenge.

Cleopatra is every inch the politician that Antony is. First, at their feet they prominently display "Caesarion, whom they call my father's son," Caesar reports with revulsion. Caesarion, the child of Cleopatra by Julius Caesar, is the centerpiece of the royal family's public display, because it is through him that the pair may lay claim to inheritance of the empire. Octavius Caesar's snarl over Caesarion's legitimacy proves him to be an astute reader of Antony and Cleopatra's royal iconography. He knows that the pair are presenting to the public an image of inheritance that seeks to eliminate him as the merely adoptive son of Julius Caesar. Upon the assassination of Julius, Octavius was introduced to Roman politics as the ally of Antony entirely because Julius' will named the mostly unknown youth as his adopted son and heir. Octavius understands that Antony and Cleopatra are staging a family portrait that emblematically suggests that they constitute the surer link to great Caesar: Antony assumes his old friend's place at the side of Cleopatra and adopts Julius' son, insistently named Caesarion. Finally, Octavius Caesar is fully aware that Antony and Cleopatra intend their audience of admirers and detractors to translate the politically ambitious family emblem into words and purvey the rhetorical description through all parts of the empire.

Second, Cleopatra appears in the "habiliments of the goddess Isis," a guise in which she "oft before gave audience." There is no mistaking the royal and political force of her choice to impersonate this goddess. To play-act Venus on the river Cydnus might be explained away as erotic frivolousness; to put on the dress of Isis is to appropriate the iconography of a powerful, many-named goddess whose religious jurisdiction extends far beyond Rome. Rome, in fact, is a

---

[20]In acknowledging his relationship with Cleopatra as a marriage and in publicly defining that marriage as a source of political power—an alliance with Egypt—the historical Antony set a precedent that Vergil presents as anti-Roman. Aeneas, of course, rejects Dido's view that they are married, insisting that he never held the torches of a bridegroom. It should be noted that Antony stood on firmer legal ground than did Aeneas: Romans accepted the common law marriage.

mere province to the ancient, multi-formed goddess. Cleopatra's use of Isis in her royal iconography is not lost on Caesar, who bitterly stresses that even before the marketplace display, she often "gave audience," presumably in her capacity as the judge and queen entitled to sit upon the silver tribunal and gold throne. She appears in an analogous position to Dido in her most powerful aspect as a queen, when Aeneas first sees her, giving laws to men, assigning tasks, and administering justice. When Vergil introduces her to Aeneas and the reader in a simile to Diana, the choice of the virgin goddess resounds with historical as well as tragic irony, for the historical Dido never met Aeneas. The chaste and powerful Dido makes a brief appearance in Vergil's poem before undergoing her metamorphosis into the tragic lover Vergil uses, among other things, to trivialize the political choices of the historical Antony and Cleopatra. Shakespeare's Cleopatra's choice of Isis, not Diana, underscores that her sexuality informs her political powers.

The marketplace scene is implicitly parallel to Enobarbus' earlier description of Cleopatra's spectacular political style, but in the latter case, the Romans are unable to privatize and eroticize her display. There is no way to exclaim of the marketplace display, "O rare for Antony!" (2.2.205) and thus use a man's amorous response to neutralize Cleopatra's royal appearance as Isis. Although the Romans recognize the political dimensions of Cleopatra's display, they are nonetheless still in a position to assimilate Enobarbus' description to the legend of Cleopatra, foreign temptress. The second episode, however, resolutely identifies theatrical spectacle, the use of the marketplace, and Cleopatra's sexuality as politically efficient strategies. Caesar himself recognizes the challenge, as we learn in the next scene when Cleopatra asks Enobarbus, "If not denounc'd against us, why should not we/Be there in person?" (3.7.5–7): Caesar recognizes her political authority and declares war on Cleopatra as well as Antony.

Caesar recognizes that gender ranks in the forefront of Cleopatra's politically subversive performances. He perceives the danger in a queen who can act more "manlike" than Antony and can stage herself as the goddesses Venus and Isis. Gender, the Egyptian queen insists, is a performance affirming or subverting political agendas: she can perform either as the goddess of love or as "the president of my kingdom" who can "Appear there [in battle] for a man" (3.7.17–18). Cleopatra asserts her right to "appear . . . for a man" in the face of Enobarbus' Roman-inflected gender anxiety: " 'tis said in Rome/That Photinus, an eunuch, and your maids/Manage this war" (13–15). Judith Butler's analysis of gender construction and its vulnerability to subversion is useful to an understanding of Cleopatra's sense of gender as a performance and a political strategy:

> gender is an identity tenuously constituted in time, instituted in an exterior space through a *stylized repetition of acts*. The effect of gender is produced through the stylization of the body and, hence, must be understood as the mundane way in which bodily gestures, movements, and styles of various kinds constitute the illusion of an abiding gendered self. . . . That gender reality is created through sustained social performances means that the very notions of an essential sex and a true or abiding masculinity or fem-

ininity are also constituted as part of the strategy that conceals gender's performative character and the performative possibilities for proliferating gender configurations outside the restricting frames of masculinist domination and compulsory heterosexuality.[21]

Butler's approach to gender illuminates the political strategy of Cleopatra's performances as "Cleopater," as the Egyptian queen is sometimes called when asserting her manly authority, and Cleopatra, who is skilled in the public performance of femininity in the extreme forms of Venus and Isis in order to consolidate her political authority. In the battle of Actium, however, her attempt to switch from a politics of display to military action proves to be a fatal error. A female prince had better "Appear . . . for a man" only in show, as Elizabeth did before her troops at Tilbury in 1588.

III

I have argued that Cleopatra establishes her subjective and political identities by subverting and exploiting the artistic conventions through which she is recognized and ideologically reconstructed by the Romans and by Shakespeare's audiences alike. Subversion and contestation are her methods for transvaluing the ideological institutions that seek to define her, whether they are the triumphs of Caesar, the fictions of Vergil, or the conventions of Petrarchism. "Vilest things/Become themselves in her, that the holy priests/Bless her, when she is riggish" (2.2.237–39) because she wrests control over the interpretive contexts for her representations and displaces the normally censorious meanings they produce. Cleopatra is capable of forcing praise even from the most negatively charged line in the *Aeneid*. In *Antony and Cleopatra*, the notoriously gynephobic utterance, *varium et mutabile semper/femina* (*Aeneid*, 4.569–570) ("Woman is a thing forever varying and changeful") is transformed to praise: *semper varium* becomes "infinite variety."[22] Shakespeare's Cleopatra is not simply a version of the legendary queen

---

[21]Judith Butler, *Gender Trouble: Feminism and the Subversion of Identity* (New York and London: Routledge, 1990), pp. 140–41.

[22]Shakespeare filters these contemptuous words from the *Aeneid* through Plutarch's celebratory description of feminine variety and change in Isis. In the *Moralia*, Plutarch remarks that "Isis is the feminine part of nature, apt to receive all generation, upon which occasion called she is by Plato the nurse and Pandeches, that is to say, capable of all. Yea and the common sort name her Myrionymus, which is as much to say, as having an infinite number of names, for that she receiveth all formes and shapes, according as it pleaseth that first reason to convert and turne her. Moreover, there is imprinted in her naturally a love of the first and principall essense, which is nothing else but soveraigne good, and it she desireth, seeketh, and pursueth after" (p. 1309). He later delivers a line that reads like a gloss on Shakespeare's "the holy priests/Bless her, when she is riggish": "according to the old tales, Isis was alwaies inamoured, and having pursued after it untill she enjoied the same, she afterwards became replenished with all goodnesse and beautie that here may be engendered" (p. 1318). I quote from the translation of Philemon Holland (London, 1603).

In Vergil's defense, critics rarely notice that Vergil by no means presents the misogynist words cited above as a divine oracle. He is careful to separate the second appearance of Mercury when he speaks these words from the first. Mercury's first visit is authorized by Jupiter, who supplies exact wording to

improved by Shakespeare's ability to exploit previous accounts. Her greatness partly comes from her unusual awareness of the conventions through which she is, and will be, constituted. She evades reduction to Petrarchism and theatrical display by turning them into self-representational strategies: like Coriolanus—but more successful—she wishes to be author of herself.[23]

The politics of display and the Petrarchan blazon, the two representational strategies I have discussed in relation to Cleopatra, figure prominently in the last two scenes of the play. When the lovers lose their battle against Caesar, they face, more than an immediate peril, a defeat that costs them control over their exemplary identities. *Antony and Cleopatra* features an unusual competition of theatrical and narrative representations which affect reputation and, consequently, shape the identities of the major characters. For example, as soon as Caesar hears that Antony and Cleopatra are presenting themselves as rulers of the known world, he seeks to undermine them by unleashing moralistic criticisms of Antony on the Roman populace. Not all such discursive practices are so crass, however. Myths of Isis or Hercules, genres such as lyric or epic, anecdotes about "a certain queen in a mattress" are pervasively used for ideological purposes and political contestation, whether overtly intended or not. While Antony and Cleopatra both understand that the emergent political ideology will refashion their reputations, the two meet their destinies and forcible crises of identity differently.

Cleopatra reveals her fear when she contemplates the Roman craftsmen who will carouse at her public display in Caesar's triumph:

>   mechanic slaves
> With greasy aprons, rules, and hammers shall
> Uplift us to the view. In their thick breaths,
> Rank of gross diet, shall we be enclouded,
> And forc'd to drink their vapor . . .
>   Saucy lictors
> Will catch at us like strumpets, and scald rhymers
> Ballad us out 'o tune. The quick comedians
> Extemporally will stage us, and present

---

the messenger. The second appearance of Mercury comes in Aeneas' dream, and the tone alters sharply from divine disgust at Aeneas to gynephobic fear of Dido. The second appearance is, I suggest, a Lucretian *simulacra* produced by Aeneas' anxious mind. See *De Rerum Natura*, where Lucretius describes the experience of anxiety *(anxius angor)* and visions produced by the tormented mind.

[23]In " 'So Unsecret to Ourselves': Notorious Identity and the Material Subject in Shakespeare's *Troilus and Cressida*," *Shakespeare Quarterly* 40 (1989): 413–40, Linda Charnes proposes a useful definition of identity slightly different from the Althusserian notion of being "subjected" to ideologies: "while 'subjectivity' does mean being subjected to determining forces it also implies the experience of undergoing a *relationship* to these forces. Subjectivity . . . means the individual's *experience* of his or her relationship to his or her 'identity' " (original italics). In the case of legendary characters, I might add, "identity" is often plural because it is literally prescribed by various ideologically biased accounts of such exemplary or notorious persons. Also see Timothy Hampton, *Writing from History: The Rhetoric of Exemplarity in Renaissance Literature* (Ithaca and London: Cornell University Press, 1990), who discusses the instability of the narrative mode of transmitting the life of an exemplar, and Leo Braudy, *The Frenzy of Renown: Fame and Its History* (Oxford: Oxford University Press, 1986).

> Our Alexandrian revels: Antony
> Shall be brought drunken forth, and I shall see
> Some squeaking Cleopatra boy my greatness
> I' the posture of a whore.
>
> (5.2.209–21)

Once Roman mechanics have built the theatrical scaffolding, Roman politicians will use ideological hammers and rules to reconstruct her "i' th' posture of a whore." The mechanic slaves, rhymers, and quick comedians will place her in low genres all the more humiliating because they travesty Cleopatra's spectacular form of rule and her transgressive relation to gender roles. She is particularly distressed at the prospect of being "subjected" to the Roman version of herself—an identity she would appear to confirm if she appeared before the crowds once again as chief spectator and spectacle, this time watching a mockery of her politics of display.[24] Cleopatra knows, moreover, that Caesar's triumph is only the beginning. The saucy lictors, rhymers, and comedians are low-class equivalents to the Augustan poets and historians who will also square her by their Roman rule.

Unlike Cleopatra, Antony does not anticipate Roman parodies of his heroic masculinity. Instead, he himself compulsively and hyperbolically acts out his future roles in a drastic crisis of identity. Despite the tendency of critics to see Cleopatra as discontinuous and erratic—that is, as a replica of anti-feminist versions of her gender—it is Antony who is most conspicuously and painfully divided among the various roles he is destined to play in future propaganda. When he perceives imminent disaster, for example, he bewilderingly adopts the role of Hercules furens, storming onstage to fulminate against the "triple-turn'd whore" he irrationally believes has betrayed him to Caesar. Antony wears "the shirt of Nessus" (4.12.43) when he internalizes the Roman view of Cleopatra as a calculating temptress. It is no coincidence that he comes to voice the very ideologies he fears will define both him and Cleopatra when they fail. Antony's crisis of identity is fundamentally *anticipatory* of the ideological accounts already setting in to construe his reputation in political and literary history.

Antony, as I will argue later, has a limited awareness that he, in his last moments, is succumbing to versions of himself that will support Augustan propaganda. We do not have to credit him with prescience, only a firm grasp of Roman ideas about public identity. Romans in *Antony and Cleopatra* delineate identity in terms of value-laden genres. Thus, Caesar himself stirringly invokes the formerly heroic Antony who abides in the laws of hard pastoral:

> Antony,
> Leave thy lascivious wassails. When thou once
> Was beaten from Modena, where thou slew'st
> Hirtius and Pansa, consuls, at thy heel
> Did famine follow, whom thou fought'st against,

---

[24]See *The Common Liar*, op. cit., especially the final section, where Adelman discusses the play's transvaluation of theatricality and with it, the ideological reductions of Antony and Cleopatra.

Though daintily brought up, with patience more
Than savages could suffer. Thou didst drink
The stale of horses, and the gilded puddle
Which beasts would cough at: thy palate then did deign
The roughest berry, on the rudest hedge;
Yea, like the stag, when snow the pasture sheets,
The barks of trees thou browsed. On the Alps
It is reported thou didst eat strange flesh,
Which some did die to look on: and all this—
It wounds thine honour that I speak it now—
Was borne so like a soldier, that thy cheek
So much as lank'd not.
                              (1.4.55–70)

Janet Adelman comments incisively on the "landscape of absolute deprivation" that, in Caesar's mind, "serves as the test of Antony's heroic masculinity."[25] To this account I would add that Caesar's general frame of reference for heroic deprivation is the genre of hard pastoral—the setting which nurtures the greatest of Roman heroes, such as Romulus and Remus. Hard pastoral specializes in rustic extremes, such as the "roughest berry, on the rudest hedge." Antony's ability to thrive in a landscape where men must "browse" like stags on the barks of trees proves that he inherited the rugged masculinity of Rome's forebears.[26] Further testimony to his illustrious heritage is that he, although "daintily brought up" can endure starvation better than savages and can eat "strange flesh" that others die to look on. Caesar uses more than hard pastoral tropes to depict Antony's brand of heroism: his tone is at least as nostalgic for the primary genres of Roman empire-building as it is for the heroic masculinity of Antony, who is made to seem painfully obsolescent. Such a man has little choice, in the emergent Roman bureaucracy, than to become an "old ruffian" and a dying lion, in the words of Caesar and Enobarbus, respectively.

Moreover, the implied model of identity construction will also inevitably induce a "most unnoble swerving" (3.11.50) from the self, since Antony cannot lead a life co-terminous with the codes of hard pastoral, georgic, and epic—the prized Roman genres. The course of Roman political history forbids such characterological integrity. Antony is doomed, then, "sometimes, when he is not Antony," to come "too short of that great property/Which still should go with Antony" (1.1.57–59). Antony himself experiences his failure of generic expectations as self-dissolution or anamorphosis:

Sometimes we see a cloud that's dragonish,
A vapour sometime, like a bear, or lion,
A tower'd citadel, a pendent rock,

[25]*Suffocating Mothers*, p. 179.
[26]Compare the upbringing of Cymbeline's two sons: their hearty physical exercise and regular doses of hard pastoral skepticism prepare them to defend their father in battle and be discovered as the lost heirs.

A forked mountain, or blue promontory
With trees upon 't, that not unto the world,
And mock our eyes with air. Thou hast seen these signs,
They are black vesper's pageants . . .
That which is now a horse, even with a thought
The rack dislimns, and makes it indistinct
As water is in water . . .
                              now thy captain is
Even such a body: here I am Antony,
Yet cannot hold this visible shape . . .

(4.14.2–14)

It is the Roman and not the Alexandrian Antony who fears self-loss through too many metamorphoses. In Egypt and under the influence of the theatrical Cleopatra, Antony is delighted to playact and even to exchange gender roles.

Antony's reference to "black vesper's pageants" may serve to acknowledge Cleopatra's reign over the metamorphic, unbounded, and theatrical world in which Antony is losing sight of his "visible shape": the evening star is Venus, the goddess of love so frequently associated with Cleopatra and Antony's evening star is "black" like Cleopatra, who is "with Phoebus' amorous pinches black" (1.5.28). Antony inevitably conceives of his self-dissolution in the terms Romans use to imagine Egypt: metamorphosis, fluid crossing of boundaries, theatricality. The entrance of Mardian the eunuch only reinforces Antony's momentary sense that he has been unmanned by Cleopatra, when in fact, he has been politically and generically undone by Caesar and time. His extravagant cry, "She has robb'd me of my sword," is affectingly foreshadowed by his sense of being made "indistinct/As water is in water" (4.14.10–11). His analogy recalls the Ovidian story, from the *Metamorphoses,* of Arethusa, a nymph who was transformed to a fountain in order to escape being raped, only to find that her would-be ravisher also turned himself to water to "mingle" his identity, story, and fortunes with hers entirely—to paraphrase Mardian's rejoinder to Antony's accusation.[27]

At the point of death, however, Antony is prepared to combat the versions of himself that will serve as negative exempla in the literature of the Roman imperial world. In a moment of magnificent self-awareness and assertion, Antony takes on Vergil's *Aeneid:*

Eros!—I come, my queen:—Eros!—Stay for me,
Where souls do couch on flowers, we'll hand in hand,
And with our sprightly port make the ghosts gaze:
Dido, and her Aeneas, shall want troops,
And all the haunt be ours. Come, Eros, Eros!

(4.14.50–54)

---

[27]Arethusa is also the name of one of the Hesperides; the two Arethusas may provide a link between the images of water and clouds, "black vesper's pageants."

One critic tests and rejects the possibility of "an Antony so ignorant of the *Aeneid* that he envisions Dido and her Aeneas united in death," and then goes on to explain the curious revision in terms of chronology:

> Antony speaks his lines on the field of Actium in 31 B.C. He cannot very well be misin-
> terpreting a poem that never saw the light of day until the author's death in 19 B.C.
> Antony, it would seem, is creating independently a version of a story that, from a strictly
> chronological point of view, has not yet been fixed in the canonical form we are familiar
> with from Vergil's *Aeneid*.[28]

This account has the attractions of historical accuracy and an Antony who resists the emergent Augustan ideology. The Antony I favor, however, is anachronistic and iconoclastic. Antony, as I see it, is partly aware of his presence on the Jacobean stage and more explicitly aware of the prismatic refractions of the legendary Antony that will constitute his "discontinuous identity" in literary history. That is, before attempting suicide, Shakespeare's Antony anticipates the Vergilian critique of his political and sexual choices and perceives that he has some shaping control over the ways in which readers will respond not to the historical Antony, but to Vergil's fiction. Antony's Elysium is not precisely Vergil's Underworld: it is the romantic fiction in which love (*amor*) takes precedence over the Roman empire (*patria* and *Roma*). Long after Rome has fallen, Antony and Cleopatra will pre-side, in fiction and in the Jacobean theater, over the Augustan Aeneas. Antony's choice to marry his queen and walk with her "hand in hand" will, he recognizes, affect the way "Dido and her Aeneas" exist in the imaginations of future genera-tions of readers.[29] The story of Dido will dominate over the story of empire-build-ing for many readers—who include Hamlet, Tamora, and Imogen in addition to troops of Vergilian imitators and translators and troops of real medieval and early modern readers such as St. Augustine (who claims he wept more for Dido than for his own soul), Chaucer, Shakespeare. Shakespeare's Antony, perhaps, takes credit for influencing readers' perspectives on Dido and Aeneas, the fictions Vergil shaped to criticize the historical Cleopatra and Antony.

Shakespeare grants Antony five magnificent lines of resistance to Caesar's ideological appropriation of him. Cleopatra, on the other hand, requires an entire act to fashion her alternate myths of selfhood. If Caesar attempts to reduce her to a puppet in his triumph, Cleopatra uses myth to escape. Myth, however, is not the unadulterated triumph it is sometimes thought to be: mytho-logical greatness is Cleopatra's compromise for failing to achieve imperial com-mand. Of her complex fictions, I will focus on her dream of Antony, the reverie she directs at Dolabella:

---

[28]Ronald R. MacDonald, "Playing Till Doomsday: Interpreting *Antony and Cleopatra*," *English Literary Renaissance* (1985): 78–99.

[29]It seems to me that Shakespeare's Antony is conflating the stories of Ovid's Orpheus and Eurydice and Vergil's Dido and Aeneas. In *Metamorphoses* 11.61–66, Orpheus is overjoyed to be reunited with Eurydice in death, and the two of them wander through the "blessed fields" (*per arva piorum*) of the Underworld side by side. Antony, of course, has reason to favor a mythological exem-plar who was unable to restrain his desire at the crucial moment.

> I dreamt there was an Emperor Antony.
> O such another sleep, that I might see
> But such another man! . . .

Dolabella: Most sovereign creature,—

Cleopatra: His legs bestrid the ocean, his rear'd arm
> Crested the world: his voice was propertied
> As all the tuned spheres, and that to friends:
> But when he meant to quail, and shake the orb,
> He was as rattling thunder. For his bounty,
> There was no winter in 't: an autumn 'twas
> That grew the more by reaping: his delights
> Were dolphin-like, they show'd his back above
> The element they lived in: in his livery
> Walk'd crowns and crownets: realms and islands were
> As plates dropp'd from his pocket.

Dolabella: Cleopatra!

Cleopatra: Think you there was, or might be such a man
> As this I dreamt of?

Dolabella: Gentle madam, no.

Cleopatra: You lie up to the hearing of the gods.
> But if there be, or ever were one such,
> It's past the size of dreaming: nature wants stuff
> To vie strange forms with fancy, yet to imagine
> An Antony were nature's piece, 'gainst fancy,
> Condemning shadows quite.

(5.2.76–100)

In her dream, possibly Cleopatra's greatest moment in the play, she achieves an amplification of selfhood—or subjectivity effects—by assuming and adapting the role of the desiring male poet for the final time. Dolabella is an ideal audience: although he claims not to believe in the hyperbolic portrait of the emperor Antony, he betrays Octavius' plans to exhibit the Egyptian queen in his triumph. His choice of loyalties discloses his astonishing investment in Cleopatra's fiction. An entranced reader, Dolabella falls in love with the Antony Cleopatra creates and with the Cleopatra who can create "such a man."

Of the various poetic techniques Cleopatra uses to recompose the heroic Antony, one is essential to the concerns of this essay: the blazon. At this point in the play, the Petrarchan blazon should stand out as a convention more honored in the distortion than the observance. I have argued that *Antony and Cleopatra* deploys the Petrarchan technique of itemizing female body parts in order to reveal its inadequacies in representing the royal Cleopatra. On only one occasion does Cleopatra adopt the normative uses of the blazon to contain the threat of female power by fragmenting her body: Cleopatra requires the messenger to return with a list of Octavia's individual traits—"bid him/Report the feature of Octavia; her years,/Her inclination, let him not leave out/The colour of her hair" (2.5.112–15). When it comes to representing her own person, however, Cleopatra avoids being itemized for visual and ideological purchase. As I argued earlier, Enobarbus' ecphrastic representation of Cleopatra on the barge reproduces the structure of a blazon while steadfastly repudiating its conventional function; and Cleopatra wields power by subjecting her beholders to the Petrarchan gaze of desire but refusing to be the Petrarchan object of desire. In her dream of Antony, she again employs and revises the blazon, singling out for admiration Antony's face, eyes, legs, "rear'd arm," and voice. But Cleopatra, the rare Shakespearean heroine to use the blazon to describe her beloved, does not fragment her imperial lover: she uses the blazon to reinforce our sense of his "bounty," out of which she reconstructs the heroic masculinity of an Antony whose identity has been fragmented and scattered by Roman opinion. In this, she is like Isis "wandering heere and there, gathering together the dismembered pieces" of Osiris' body, torn and mangled by his brother Typhon. "The report goes," Plutarch tells us, "that Isis found all other parts of Osiris body but only his privy member. . . . In sted of that natural part, she made a counterfet one, called Phallus, which she consecrated."[30] Through her cosmic blazon, Cleopatra restores Antony: in death he finally becomes the integrated, magnanimous hero who is spectrally present in the play in the memories of others and in rare moments of self-possession.[31]

IV

Cleopatra's transcendence is not from a historical Egyptian queen to a myth escaping the belittling contingencies of history and politics—although this is her ploy against Caesar's ideological rewriting of her as a whore and political travesty. Her great achievement is somewhat more modest: it is her transcendence over the artistic, Petrarchan, and ideological codes designed to objectify or depersonalize her on the one hand, and on the other, to disempower her politically. Cleopatra's subversive relationship to the conventions that mediate her historical representations and her politics of display suggest a need to re-evaluate the tendency in recent criticism to separate concerns with subjectivity from the political. More is lost than gained by defining politics in so restricted a fashion that sexuality evaporates into political concerns, the subject becomes only an anachronistically Freudian concept, and the most prestigious forms of politics to be found in a literary or dramatic text are topical, serendipitous traces of cultural practices only half-recognized by the author. I have sought to show that there is more than one form of politics in the world of *Antony and Cleopatra;* that sexuality and politics cannot be simply separated, opposed, or set in a stable hierarchical relationship; and that Cleopatra's characterological status cannot be extricated from the political discourses of the play.

---

[30]Plutarch, *Moralia*, trans. Philemon Holland (London, 1603), pp. 1309 and 1294.
[31]See Adelman, *The Common Liar*, op. cit., for a stimulating discussion of Cleopatra's role as Isis; see also Barbara J. Bono, *Literary Transvaluation: From Vergilian Epic to Shakespearean Tragicomedy* (Berkeley: University of California Press, 1984), who considers the Isis myth at greater length.

As stated at the outset of this essay, the critical trend to treat sexuality as the metaphorical register for an essentially political discourse has been defended by Jonathan Dollimore, who wishes to attend to "the way diverse social anxieties are displaced onto or into sexuality, to the interconnections between women's subordination and other kinds of subordination" (476).[32] Although tracing interconnections and displacements of this kind enables some exciting critical gains, Dollimore's leap from sexuality to politics is swift and wholly appropriative: "sexual desire," he asserts, is "the vehicle of politics and power" (486). This formula, applied to *Antony and Cleopatra,* means that sexuality is the triumphal cart on which Cleopatra's greatness is "boy'd" in the posture of a whore. For Dollimore, moreover, the cart doesn't belong to Caesar but to James I. He relates the play's sexual and ideological upheavals, particularly concerning honor and *virtus,* to Jacobean processes of cultural change. To this end, he cites the astonishing cry of Antony to Cleopatra, "leap thou, attire and all,/Through proof of harness to my heart, and there/Ride on the pants triumphing" (4.8.14–16)—in which political triumphs appear to be metaphors for sexual ones. Dollimore then hesitates between minimizing and excluding psychological and sexual interests in order to stress the "perhaps more pertinent" fact that

> in Jacobean England the warrior or martial ideal was in decline. The military leader identified by honor and courage was being disempowered, becoming obsolete as the state took over his powers, rather as the new political reality embodied in Caesar is displacing Antony (486–87).[33]

There are some very necessary steps missing in a statement like "a whole history informs Antony's sexuality" (487), in which "Antony" is allegorical and the "whole history" is limited to a portion of Jacobean history.

First of all, Dollimore omits characterological study as if anti-political by definition. There are no substantial grounds for feminist critics to take umbrage at Dollimore's subordination of women and sexuality to political discourse—as Carol Thomas Neely does—because he treats both sexes the same: as a political allegory for the discomfitted Jacobean warrior, Antony, too, is not a character and has no pertinent psychological and sexual concerns. The problem with Dollimore's analysis is that he associates "character" exclusively with the Freudian subject—as anachronistic and therefore irrelevant—and proceeds to organize sexuality and politics as an either/or proposition. There are, however, powerful models of subjective experience—some of which were of interest to Freud—available to early modern readers. Lucretius, for example, compares the fragile self to a broken vase allowing the soul to escape as clouds or smoke diffuse into air (*De Rerum Natura,* 3.434–36), an image strikingly similar to Antony's meditation on his own self-

---

[32]Jonathan Dollimore, "Shakespeare, Cultural Materialism, Feminism, and Marxist Humanism." See note 2.

[33]The relevant pages in *Radical Tragedy: Religion, Ideology, and Power in the Drama of Shakespeare and His Contemporaries* (Chicago: University of Chicago Press, 1984) are 204–17, reprinted in this volume pp. 197–207. The argument in "Shakespeare, Cultural Materialism, Feminism, and Marxist Humanism," from which I quote, is compressed from the earlier book.

dissolution. Classical authorities do not resolve questions about subjective constitutions. Instead, they generate multiple and competing versions which can, in the hands of a strong poet, delineate the early modern sense of the subject's construction in resistance to prevailing authorities. Thus *Antony and Cleopatra* might be said to pitch an Ovidian model of the metamorphic self against a Vergilian prescription for the proper citizen: the productive conflict between these models would explain the power of Antony's revision of the *Aeneid* in what he takes to be his last moments on earth. If the subject is defined by ideological institutions, we can often productively recognize those institutions by their literary co-ordinates (e.g., genre, rhetoric, allusion) and recognize the Shakespearean character in his or her relationship to the informing conventions. As my analysis of Cleopatra's usurpation of the privileged subjectivity effects of the Petrarchan male poet indicates, characterological status is by no means divorced from ideology and politics. Sexuality is too often pitted against political discourse, as if sex and politics were the competing images in a perspective painting.

The reading of Antony's threatened masculinity as a political allegory of the obsolescent Jacobean military involves a second, more surprising, omission: the scope of the play's engagement of history. While there is nothing inherently wrong with a resolutely topical reading of politics, a specifically Jacobean reading of the play can ill afford to overlook Roman political history. And matters of family and sexuality were, of course, of extreme interest to the political moment represented in *Antony and Cleopatra*. Augustus, the model of choice for James I, England's *novus Augustus*, found the repression of sexuality useful to the process·of fashioning a new political order.[34] Even Shakespeare's Antony exhibits awareness of the need to read and resist the *Aeneid*, the originary epic of empire-building. Antony's revision of Vergil insists that a political reading of the way Vergil's poem handles sexuality is preliminary to a reading of *Antony and Cleopatra*'s politics. The *Aeneid* not only launches *Antony and Cleopatra*'s investigations of fluid sexuality and gender roles but also attempts to establish their relation to the emergent imperialism of Augustus Caesar. As I noted earlier, Vergil actually invents the love affair between Dido and Aeneas, and does so to comment upon Antony and Cleopatra and to motivate the Punic wars with Carthage. In effect, he metaphorizes and genders nationalist and imperialist conflict.

Vergil's extraordinary choice to characterize the Punic wars in terms of gender and sexuality cannot, moreover, be explained in full by a model such as Dollimore's political allegory of sexuality. Vergil's choice responds to Rome's complicated history of morality laws and particularly Augustus' role in legislating sexuality. The relationship between sex and politics in the Roman world of emergent imperialism resists being placed easily into a hierarchy. According to Vergil's fic-

---

[34]Augustus Caesar strongly promoted a new morality among the Roman aristocracy and eventually succeeded in passing unpopular laws governing marriage. See Suetonius, *The History of Octavius Caesar Augustus* 34 and Propertius 2.7. For critical arguments on the subject, see Karl Galinsky, "Augustus' Legislation on Morals and Marriage" and Ronald Syme, *Roman Revolution* (Oxford: Oxford University Press, 1939, rpt. 1960).

tion, the first order of imperial business is to seek control over sexuality by transforming it into the metaphoric register of an essentially political discourse. By mis-
fortune rather than design, Dollimore's political allegory of sexuality curiously
replicates the move Vergil identifies with the imperialist drives of his poem.[35] It is
important to consider the reasons and the effects of Vergil's decision to trope and
gender politics in the *Aeneid*—and this is precisely what happens when he uses
the episode at Carthage to superimpose Octavian's war with Antony and Cleopatra
onto Rome's Punic wars with Carthage. One is struck by the irrelevance of the two
historical wars; the only party who stands to gain by the conflation is Augustus,
who can assimilate his personal war against Antony for supreme power—in addition to his morality laws—to the already existing and powerful model of the Punic
wars. For his part, Vergil gains a powerful metaphor for the imperialistic co-opta-
tion of citizens' identities, down to their very sexualities. Altogether, Augustan
political history significantly bears on the impulse of *Antony and Cleopatra's* political discourses to usurp the language of sexuality. The *Aeneid*, which plays a defining role in the "knot intrinsicate" of sex and empire, is the shadowy authority
behind the revisionist—not escapist—roles that Shakespeare's Antony and
Cleopatra play in response to the politics and the literary codes that attempt to
define their legendary identities and sexualities.

---

[35]Dollimore himself is not exhibiting imperialistic motives—he rightly bridles at Neely's designa-
tion of him as critically imperialistic in the above noted article. Given the historical circumstances
Shakespeare draws into the play, however, his method and axiom hardly have the subversive inflection
one associates with cultural materialism.

Theatre and the Space
of the Other
in *Antony and Cleopatra*

Ania Loomba

Negative Capability Reconsidered

The assumption of dominant Anglo-American criticism, that tragedy must arrive at "some comprehensive vision of the relation of human suffering to human joy" (Ribner, p. 1) and must lead via catharsis to moral certainty, was central in both bringing the privileged text to a closure and in institutionalising this by framing a hierarchical canon of "great" art. The exalted stature of Shakespearean drama, its affirmation of a moral (i.e. conservative) order and its movement towards a final and unquestionable truth are interdependent claims which are invoked to confirm one another (see also Heinemann, p. 203). On the other hand, Middletonian drama (for example) was dismissed as "not the highest kind of tragedy" because its protagonists do not arrive at any "recognition of truth" (Muir, pp. xiii–xiv). Truth-telling was an attribute of the Godlike and "detached" artist, and yet this criterion was selectively applied on a slanted principle: precisely what was celebrated as "negative capability" in the case of Shakespeare was dismissed as an "ironically detached unheroic view of life not attuned to the heroic passions of early tragedy" in the case of Middleton.

Bertolt Brecht has increasingly been used to re-read the plays of the period because he found a "complex, shifting, largely impersonal, never soluble" conflict, a "disconnectedness" of both structure and perspective that approximated to his own (p. 161) in what had been regarded as an omniscient authorial detachment. This has radical implications, not only for the reading of the plays, but for "democratising" the Renaissance canon, with its Shakespearean apex, for Brecht observed similar characteristics in at least twenty of Shakespeare's contemporaries.

Brecht's analysis was important also for focusing in a new and self-conscious way on structure and form as an aspect of textual meaning and perspective. The blurring of distinctions between comedy and tragedy had often been disparag-

From Loomba, Ania. *Gender, Race, Renaissance Drama* (Oxford: Oxford University Press, 1989). Reproduced by permission of Manchester University Press and the author. The original footnotes have been renumbered. The essay joins two sections that are separate in her book.

ingly noted by critics in relation to the plays of Middleton; *Women Beware Women*, for example, has been called an "unsuccessful attempt to create tragedy out of the materials and conventions of satiric comedy," its central theme "more appropriate to a broadside balladeer than the tragic poet" (Ornstein, p. 140). Brecht read such "impurities" in the context of the various ways in which Renaissance drama resisted artistic isolation into the world of make-believe. He noted that its language incorporated the speech of the beer-hall audiences; that daylight performances and open stages prevented hypnotic illusion, that the dramatisation of material familiar to the audience encouraged a critical approach; that the collective nature of the theatre companies and their life-style encouraged montage and epic construction which opposes the idea of drama as a self-sufficient microcosm. All this, says Brecht, led to a "naive surrealism," practised not only by Shakespeare but also by other dramatists of the period (see Heinemann, p. 209).

Robert Weimann has demonstrated that "the basis of Shakespeare's 'negative capability' is itself socio-historical," located partly in the "freedom, the detachment, and the imagination made available to him by the popular tradition in the theater" and partly in the fact that while older feudal values could already be questioned, those of capitalism "were not yet their *necessary alternative*"; the "myriad-mindedness" of Shakespeare's art is contextualised by Weimann in terms of the positioning of both artist and the playhouse (pp. 176–77), and is interwoven with the structural looseness of the plays. More recently, Jonathan Dollimore has elaborated the implications of the Brechtian connection by drawing upon Brecht's critical and dramatic approach to identify the materialist "realism" of Renaissance drama, its emphasis on discontinuity of form and character and its radical questioning of the philosophical and political status quo (*Radical Tragedy*; see also Heinemann, "How Brecht Read Shakespeare").

My own purpose here is to insert the dimension of gender more fully into such proto-Brechtian multiplicity and montage, and to suggest that the epic structure is at least partly derived from and closely related to the drama's interrogation of gender roles and patriarchal authority. Conversely, the non-teleological form itself becomes an important vehicle for resisting closure: it suggests, as Brecht claimed, the open-endedness of a situation—that if things could happen one way, they could also have happened in a totally different manner. Open-endedness in this sense does not connote a free-wheeling vaccuum: "true realism has to do more than just make reality visible on the stage . . . One has to be able to see the laws that decide how the processes of life develop" (*Brecht on Theatre*, p. 27).

An invocation of the sanctity of a linear and teleological structure was crucial for the colonial deployment of the Western canon. On the one hand, it ensured that questions of form and structure flooded (and still do) the examination papers, inviting the reader yet again to squeeze the text into a strait-jacket and to erase the possible fractures of experience in reading it. On the other, it imposed Western aesthetics (for example, the Aristotelian demarcation of tragedy from comedy) upon traditions, such as that of Indian drama (both classical and folk), which had acknowledged the intermingling of moods and genres. Westernised theatre groups, and imported British troupes (often playing melodramatic versions of Shakespeare) ensured the hegemony of such ideas in actual performance, and generations of actors were taught to forget the proto-Brechtian epic traditions of the Indian theatre.

Today there have been some efforts to revive such a heritage, and to enrich it by infusing it with contemporary relevance. This has included adaptations of Western drama; and when Habib Tanvir, for example, has performed Brecht's plays in the style of folk theatre from Chattisgarh, using the latter's actors and music, it has illustrated, among other things, the extent to which much Indian drama had worked on assumptions and techniques analogous to Brecht's. There is not the space here to consider the ways in which third world literatures, both traditional and modern, both writers unknown to the West and those who have become current objects of its gaze, like Rushdie, Márquez, and recently, Ghosh, step out from the model of linear time and space and transgress the dominant Western literary model. It may be said, however, that such a movement cannot be explained simply by analogies to Western rejections of linearity (such as those of Miller or Beckett) for it refers specifically to the disjunctures and complexities of a non-Western experience (see Datta, for example).

However, it will not do simply to demarcate the two either; for the refusal of a Western text to comply with the structural or ideological unity demanded of it by dominant criticisms is equally useful for questioning the preferred textual model. Hence to seize upon what Brecht saw as the "disconnectedness" of Renaissance drama is one way to contest its institutionalised usage as the barricade around a series of privileged positions. Finally, since the patriarchal gaze on women and the colonial one on its others is one-dimensional, because it aims both to obscure their depth and to deny their potential for mobility, we may usefully consider how montage, as a structural and thematic perspective, can challenge the dominant portrayals of women and other colonised peoples. At the same time, by identifying these perspectives and techniques as not exclusive to the hitherto privileged author or text and by bringing excluded ones into related focus, we may question the sanctity of the Western syllabus as it has been inherited and preserved by Indian departments of English..

Spatial Politics

Let us examine the effects of montage more closely by focusing on a text that is supposed to achieve tragic harmony. Three centuries of critical opinion, from Samuel Johnson onwards, has been preoccupied with "overcoming" the heterogeneous nature of both the form and the content of Shakespeare's *Antony and Cleopatra*: the focus has variously been on its disjointed structure, mingling of tragic and comic, flux in character; its divisions between private and public, male and female, high and low life; on what Danby has called the "dialectic" of

the text.[1] However, a correlation of these various binaries—the thematic oppositions, the broken structure, its treatment of fluid gender and racial identity—
has yet to be attempted. An "epic effect" has been noted, but in the classical
sense of the word (see Mark Rose, p. 2); we might more usefully employ the
term in its Brechtian sense to analyse these various schisms. "The continual
hurry of the action, the variety of incidents, and the quick succession of one
personage to another . . . the frequent changes of scene" (Johnson, quoted J. E.
Brown, p. 26) then emerge as contradicting the classical elevation of character
or teleological progression towards catharsis, as achieving a Brechtian alienation from character to posit a radical interrogation of the imperial and sexual
drama.

The geographical turbulence of the first three acts involves a redefinition of
femininity and of female space: patriarchal Rome contests Egyptian Cleopatra
for her geographical and sexual territory. Into the contest is woven the theme of
imperial domination. Dominant notions about female identity, gender relations
and imperial power are unsettled through the disorderly non-European woman.
These ideas appear to be reinstated as the quick shifts of scene are abandoned
in favour of a more orthodox climax at the end of the play, an apparent resolution of the dilemma. Whereas in the first three acts of the play there are twenty-
three changes of scene, and shifts of location within each as well, as the play
proceeds there is a change in the quality and quantity of movement: in Act 4
alone there are fifteen changes of locale, but all within Egypt. Act 5 contains
only two scenes, and both are confined to the area of Cleopatra's monument.
Alongside this, different characters strive to rise "above" their earlier turbulence and assert an inner unity of being. However, this harmony is precarious;
the manner of its achievement conveys the very opposite of a resolution and the
various sets of oppositions noted by critics are not subscribed to but eroded by
the play.

The issues of imperial expansion, political power and sexual domination are
dramatically compressed into spatial and geographical shifts and metaphors. The
almost cinematic movements—"panning, tracking, and playing with the camera"
(Danby, p. 197)—are designed to reveal the complexity of the terrain on which
men and women move as well as of their inner spaces. They penetrate into different aspects of power, which is at once something concrete—land, kingdoms,
wealth—and something relatively abstract—emotions, ideology, and sexuality.
Theatrical space is not just an inert arena but interacts with the texts' treatment of
social and psychological space.

Not only does the locale constantly shift, but in each setting we are reminded of
another. In Egypt, Rome is evoked, and vice versa. While leaving for Rome,

---

[1]L. C. Knights comments: "In *Macbeth* we are never in any doubt of our moral bearings. *Antony
and Cleopatra*, on the other hand, embodies different and apparently irreconcilable evaluations of the
central experience" (quoted J. R. Brown, *Antony and Cleopatra*, p. 172). Adelman; Belsey; Jardine;
Holloway; Mack; Markels; Mark Rose: and Rozett all emphasize different aspects of the heterogeneity
foregrounded by the play.

Antony tells Cleopatra: "thou, residing here, goes yet with me,/And I, hence fleeting, here remain with thee" (1.3.103-4). This is a common enough lovers' platitude
but it serves to remind us that in addition to the purely geographical shifts of terrain, there are also those of conceptual settings; the lovers' private world is constantly contrasted to the political space. Antony identifies the former with Egypt,
and in preferring it to Rome is trying to privatise love, to locate his relationship
with Cleopatra in a domestic arena. But he also attempts to expand this space so
that it excludes the other, threatening world of masculine politics, and crowds out
other concerns:

> *Cleopatra:*   I'll set a bourn how far to be belov'd.
> *Anthony:*   Then must thou needs finds out new heaven, new earth.
> (1.1.16–17)

This is what Donne's lovers are also trying to do as they seek ever more expansive
metaphors for their relationship and for each other: "She's all States, and all
Princes I"; their room becomes an "everywhere."

Roman patriarchy demonises Cleopatra by defining her world as private
(Antony is no longer a serious general by entering it); as female (Egypt robs
Antony and his soldiers of their manhood); and as barbaric (Antony is now a slave
of gypsies). But both Antony and Caesar are aware that Egypt is not merely a private space and that its female, non-European nature only intensifies its challenge
to imperial Rome:

> *Antony:*   My being in Egypt, Caesar
>   What was't to you?
> *Caesar:*   No more than my residing here at Rome
>   Might be to you in Egypt. Yet, if you there
>   Did practice on my state, your being in Egypt
>   Might be my question.
> (2.2.39–44)

Objective space is always invested with political or emotional connotations; as
Caesar indicates, Egypt is a place from which subversion can be practised, and as
such it can never be merely a lovers' retreat. Antony too courts Cleopatra with
territorial and political gifts: he will "piece/Her opulent throne with kingdoms; all
the East/ . . . shall call her mistress" (1.5.45–47). Caesar complains precisely of
this:

>   Unto her
> He gave the establishment of Egypt; made her
> of Lower Syria, Cyprus, Lydia,
> Absolute queen.
> (3.6.8–11)

Passionate as the relationship between Antony and Cleopatra is, "the language
of desire, far from transcending the power relations which structure this society, is
wholly informed by them" (Dollimore, *Radical Tragedy*, p. 203). These relations

are both sexual and racial. In the beginning Antony thinks he is in control of what he regards as the opposition between politics and pleasure; therefore he assumes that he can simultaneously possess the Roman matron Octavia through the legal bonding permitted by imperial patriarchy, and the oriental seductress Cleopatra, through a sexually passionate and "illicit" relationship:

> I will to Egypt;
> And though I make this marriage for my peace,
> I'th' East my pleasure lies.
>
> (2.3.39–41)

He alternately views Egypt as his retreat from Roman politics and a place to consolidate his bid for power. In short, he oscillates between Cleopatra's territory and Caesar's, both literally and otherwise. As the play proceeds he is no longer in command of such a divide: his position in both Rome and Egypt becomes unstable and manifests itself as a dislocation of personality: "I/Have lost my way for ever," "I have fled myself," "I have lost command" (3.10.3–4, 7, 23). "Authority melts from me," he cries, but like Faustus, the Duchess of Malfi, and Parolles, he invokes his lost "essential" self: "Have you no ears? I am/Antony yet" (3.13.90–93). Even as Antony complains that Caesar keeps "harping on what I *am*,/Not what he knew I *was*" (3.13.142-43; emphasis added), he is aware of the change in himself. Without power, without space, without Rome and without Cleopatra, Antony disintegrates.

It is important that Cleopatra's transformation into the "whore" and "witch" occurs precisely at this point: the language of what Antony perceives as a betrayal reduces Cleopatra's "infinite variety" to both patriarchal and racist stereotypes. Helen Carr has pointed out that "although the substitution of 'witch' for 'whore' as the primary image of the deviant woman signifies a greater degree of horror at the possibility of female sexuality, at the same time it represses the idea of a consciously sexual woman (the witch's fantasies are alien and evil intruders in her mind" (p. 51). Cleopatra, I have argued, is both: her sexuality is an aspect of her blackness and as such can only be erased later, when she herself adopts token Roman-ness. Whereas, in falling from Othello's favour, Desdemona became "begrim'd" and morally black and false to her true self, Cleopatra as the "foul Egyptian" only realises her "true" position as the complete outsider. As Antony perceives that he is only nominally the site of the conflict which is actually between Cleopatra and Caesar, the latent struggle for power between him and Cleopatra escalates. The metaphors for this three-way struggle become those of the land and the sea. Whether the fight should take place on the Roman element, the land, or Cleopatra's medium, the water, is at once a matter of military strategy and a measure of Antony's emotional and political affiliations. The erosion of the absolute space of love stems from his increasing perception of his own marginality, and Cleopatra's refusal to share her space. With all worlds being lost, Antony's vacillations cease, and so do the structural shifts. Such a movement is also dependent on the play's treatment of Cleopatra.

The Language of Patriarchy

The figure of Cleopatra is the most celebrated stereotype of the goddess and whore and has accommodated and been shaped by centuries of myth-making and fantasy surrounding the historical figure. In Shakespeare's representation of her, we can identify several different strands of contemporary meaning which intertwine with connotations attaching to her from earlier stories. My purpose in unravelling these is to suggest that Shakespeare does not simply indicate a stereotype but depicts it as constructed by various male perspectives in the play. . . . We can see how Renaissance politics and stagecraft shape Cleopatra's representation.[2]

Firstly, like Monticelso's characterisation of whores or Iago's view of Desdemona or the pronouncements of Flamineo, Bosola, Ferdinand, DeFlores and Alsemero, the construction of Cleopatra draws upon the medieval notion of the sexual appetite of women as rampant and potentially criminal: as the primordial sexual being she is also maledicted as "immoral," the "false soul" (4.12.25) and "a boggler" (3.13.110). Ellen Terry, one of the first actresses to play Cleopatra, believed that through her, Shakespeare had "told the truth about the wanton" (quoted Brown, *Antony and Cleopatra,* p. 54). Therefore she is simultaneously Isis and goddess as well as gypsy and "triple-turned whore" (4.12.13).

Secondly, Cleopatra's social status places her in a contradictory position. Status, wealth, class are refracted in their operation through the prism of gender, and do not work in the same way as for men. For example, in Middleton's *The Changeling,* Beatrice-Joanna thinks that she can buy DeFlores; her wealth gives her the illusion of power. But DeFlores, although literally her servant, is a man, and as such is beyond the reach of her class power. Soon he has her kneeling at his feet:

Beatrice:	Stay, hear me once for all; I make thee master
	Of all the wealth I have in gold and jewels;
	Let me go poor unto my bed with honour,
	And I am rich in all things.
DeFlores:	Let this silence thee:
	The wealth of all Valencia shall not buy
	My pleasure from me;
	Can you weep Fate from its determin'd purpose?
	So soon may you weep me.

(3.4.155–62)

Beatrice cannot simultaneously be a woman and have power over a man. Throughout the drama, women find the need to "appropriate masculine virtue" (see Belsey, pp. 183–84). Since femininity and power are increasingly incompatible, to be a woman in authority of any sort is necessarily to occupy an uneasy space.

As the "precious queen" Cleopatra is deified into the goddess Isis, recalling the attempts to depict Elizabeth I as the Virgin Queen, which fixed her visually as a

---

[2]Later in chapter 5 of *Gender, Race, Renaissance Drama,* I shall suggest that such a construction is then challenged and dismantled.

goddess and served to fill the iconographic vacuum created by the exit of Catholicism. Elizabeth needed, however, to reinforce her power by negating her femininity; she could only secure her status as ruler by "transcending" the limitations of her sex, i.e. by repudiating it: "I know I have the body of a weak and feeble woman, but I have the heart and stomach of a king, and of a king of England too" (Heisch, p. 55). Cleopatra similarly asserts:

> A charge we bear i'th' war,
> And as president of my kingdom, will
> Appear there for a man.
>   (3.7.16–18)

Despite this, both Elizabeth and Cleopatra evoke specifically Renaissance fears of female government; John Knox's *First Blast of the Trumpet against the Monstrous Regiment of Women* (1558) was directly addressed to Mary Tudor, but other queens—Mary, Queen of Scots, Margaret of Parma, Catherine de Medici, and Mary of Lorraine—contributed to the spectre of female government which it attacks. Ironically, such fears were heightened even as actual female authority in several spheres was dismantled. Evidence is available that women constituted a substantial part of medieval armies and often occupied leading positions within them (Hacker, pp. 643–71; Kelly, p. 86). Moreover, during the early Middle Ages, the queen had reigned as a royal partner, but as the state consolidated into a centralised authority, her political power dwindled into a ceremonious role, a token and a symbol of glamour. This was also emphasised by the prescriptions for female behaviour in medieval conduct books and in books such as Castiglione's *The Courtier* (1561). By 1656 Margaret Cavendish testified that "all heroic actions, public employments, powerful governments and eloquent pleadings are denied our sex in this age" (Kelly, p. 86).

The distinction made between warrior women and Amazons by Shepherd is useful here: like Elizabeth, Cleopatra enters the realm of androgyny, but unlike Elizabeth, who remained within the confines of female chastity, Cleopatra is more properly the Amazon who brings together patriarchal (and particularly Renaissance) fears of female government as well as sexual activity. Since women as lovers function as the private lives of men, their trespass into the public world of politics implies a dual identity, a changeability which also contributes to Cleopatra's construction as an inconstant and shifting being.

Thirdly, the idea of Cleopatra's dichotomous identity is elaborated in the images of her play-acting, dressing up, putting on disguises, planning and stage-managing her encounters with both Antony and Caesar. She is the supreme *actress*—theatrical, unruly and anarchic, whose "infinite variety" also derives from the roles she plays. Not only does she play the queen with theatrical grandeur and self-consciousness, she also assumes various other identities and becomes in turn masculine, or ultra-feminine, the jealous lover, the angry mistress, the penitent woman, and finally the Roman wife. Twice she makes specific references to disguise—once when she recalls wearing Caesar's armour (2.5.22–23) and again when she conjures up the image of a boy-actor impersonating her in Rome (5.2.213–20). She is as unpredictable as the theatre, and controls her audience at least partially by surprising them, as she does her lover by her changeability. But this last is misogynist Enobarbus's concept, and he conjures up the image of her seated in the barge to imply a scene meticulously executed to flaunt her beauty, power and glamour to Antony. The negative implications of this link with play-acting are derived from the precarious social position of popular theatre and the threat it posed to the status quo during this period (see Weimann, p. 172; Montrose, pp. 51–74; Dollimore, "Shakespeare, Cultural Materialism," p. 4). Hence the fears inspired by the duplicitous heroine are explicitly analogous to those generated by the theatre itself.

Fourthly, Cleopatra's play-acting specifically reverses gender roles; she not only wears Caesar's military attire but "put my tires and mantles" on Antony (2.5.22). Although cross-dressing is evident in translations of classical drama, of Greek romances and medieval stories, and in texts such as *Metamorphoses, Decameron, Orlando Furioso, Arcadia, The Faerie Queene*, and much stage comedy, its emergence as "a central Renaissance trope" (see Staton, pp. 79–89), one which was repeatedly interwoven with the themes of female rebellion in the drama and in the pamphlets on cross-dressing—*Haec-Vir, Hic-Mulier* and *Malde-Sacke*—can hardly be attributed to stage convention alone. As Jardine points out, dress emerges as a crucial signifier of sexual and social identity in the prescription and enforcement of elaborate and precise codes of dressing during the reign of both Elizabeth and James (pp. 141–42, 150). From indicting women's extravagant and lustful natures, satire against cross-dressing became specifically directed against their appropriation of male prerogatives. Monticelso in *The White Devil* identifies "Impudent bawds/That go in men's apparell" as among "the notorious offenders/Lurking about the City" (*The White Devil*, 4.1.56–57, 33–34). The female transvestite is seen to transgress into male territory and becomes a hermaphrodite, a monster who threatens sexual (and by implication all social) distinctions.[3]

Hence the fear that Cleopatra has the power to unman men echoes throughout the play, making explicit the threat posed by the monstrous woman to male power and authority. It is visually expressed by the images of cross-dressing. More generally this ties in with the usurping of male positions by any disorderly woman: Philo in the opening lines talks of Antony, "the triple pillar of the world transform'd/Into a strumpet's fool" (1.1.12–13). In the next scene Antony sees his great love as a bondage: "These strong Egyptian fetters I must break/Or lose myself in dotage" (1.2.113–14). Caesar too refers to the relationship as a reversal of gender roles:

> . . . he fishes, drinks and wastes
> The lamps of the night in revel; is not more manlike
> Than Cleopatra, nor the queen of Ptolemy
> More womanly than he.

> (1.4.4–7)

---

[3]The issue of cross-dressing has generated much recent discussion. See Montrose; Greenblatt; Jardine; Travitsky; Mary Beth Rose; and Clark.

This reversal is seen to compromise the masculinity of Antony's soldiers as well: Canidius comments, "So our leader's led/And we are women's men" (3.7.69–70) and Enobarbus warns Antony "Transform us not to women" (4.2.36). The fears posed by disguise, theatre, female government and sexuality thus flow into one another.

Finally, Cleopatra is the non-European, the outsider, the white man's ultimate "other." In *Othello*, colonialist, racist and sexist discourses are mutually dependent. Cleopatra embodies all the overlapping stereotypes of femininity and non-Europeans common in the language of colonialism. She is dangerous and snake-like, "the old serpent of the Nile" (1.4.25), the "serpent of Egypt" (2.7.26). On the one hand, she has a mysterious power over Antony, on the other he constantly reminds her that he found her "As a morsel cold upon/Dead Caesar's trencher," a "fragment/Of Cneius Pompey's" (3.13.116–18). The white man's love confers worth upon her, and she is made whole only by Antony's attentions. The recurrent food imagery reinforces her primitive appeal: she makes men hungry, she does not cloy their appetite (2.2.240-42); she is Antony's "Egyptian dish" (2.6.122), she is "salt Cleopatra" (2.1.21). She is the supreme actress, artifice herself, and simultaneously primitive and uncultivated.

The identification of Cleopatra with Egypt points to more than her status as its queen. In colonialist discourse, the conquered land is often explicitly endowed with feminine characteristics in contrast to the masculine attributes of the coloniser (see Hulme, pp. 17–32). All Egyptians, represented and symbolised by their queen, are associated with feminine and primitive attributes—they are irrational, sensuous, lazy and superstitious. Therefore Cleopatra's identification with a place conveys her power as ruler and also specifically identifies her as alien territory. The tensions between Rome as masculine and imperial and Egypt as its threatening "other" will be elaborated below. The images that cluster around Cleopatra are specifically Orientalist in nature: her waywardness, emotionality, unreliability and exotic appeal are derived from the stereotypes that Said identifies as recurrent in that discourse (p. 207).

In another context, Carr has described the metamorphosis of the opposition of virgin/whore into that of good wife/witch (p. 51). Cleopatra participates in both sets of dichotomies; she is "whore" as well as "witch" (4.12.13,47). Witches are both the projections of exaggerated patriarchal fears (Stallybrass, pp. 104–18 in this volume; Garrett, "Women and Witches") and also a colonial fantasy whereby the non-Christian outsider is connected to devilry. The episode with the soothsayer paves the way for a connection of all Egyptians and particularly Cleopatra with magic: she is an "enchantress," a "great fairy" (4.8.12) but of an alien variety—a "gypsy" (1.1.10; 4.12.28). So Pompey's desire, that "witchcraft join with beauty, lust with both" to charm Antony into inaction (2.2.22) clearly unites both patriarchal and racial implications of witchcraft. So Cleopatra emerges as the composite deviant, a "most monster-like" (4.12.6) "other" of the Roman patriarchal "self."

If Cleopatra's political being threatens patriarchy it also catalyses the contradictions within her, which are inherent in the position she occupies as a sexually active non-European female ruler. Although she is unique among the independent women in Renaissance drama, for she appears to command her own spaces, these are precariously constructed: as the ruler of Egypt her space is threatened by the expansionist designs of the Roman empire, and as a woman, by the contradictions of heterosexual love. Her insecurity, her fear of invasion—not just as a ruler, but also as a woman who is threatened even (or especially) by her lover—is evident in her physical stasis, her reluctance to move from her territory. However slippery, inconstant and variable Cleopatra may be, however she may threaten the boundaries between male and female, political and private worlds, she remains geographically stationary. She resents the intrusions of Roman messengers who remind her not only of Antony's wives, first Fulvia and then Octavia, but also of the imperial threat.

Cleopatra fluctuates between establishing her emotional and her political spaces: a vacillation without end for she cannot simultaneously occupy both. She finds it much harder to locate her own territory in relation to Antony than *vis-à-vis* Caesar. She can either function within the private life of a man, or enter politics as a honorary man and chaste woman, like Elizabeth. In any case it is a double bind. As "foul Egyptian" she will always stand outside Roman society: Antony can never fully trust her and will marry safe and obedient Roman women like Octavia to ensure his stability within that society. Her gender renders her politically unacceptable, her political status problematises her femininity, and her racial otherness troubles, doubly, both power and sexuality. To the extent that she acts as a ruler, she is perfectly comprehensible to Caesar: he even praises her for concealing her treasure from him; "nay, blush not, Cleopatra; I approve/Your wisdom in the deed" (5.2.148-49). But whereas he will not haggle over "things that merchants sold" (5.2.83), he refuses to grant her autonomy even in respect of her death.

The last act appears to "resolve" the various tensions of the play; the style now changes from montage and a mingling of comic and tragic to that of classical tragedy. It appears that Cleopatra is tamed; the wanton gypsy becomes Antony's wife, the queen is stripped to an essential femininity that attaches to all women irrespective of class: "no more but e'en a woman, and commanded/By such poor passion as the maid that milks/And does the meanest chares" (4.15.73–75). The variable woman is now "marble constant"; the witch gives way to the penitent goddess as Egypt tries to do "what's brave,/what's noble . . . after the high Roman fashion" (4.15.86-87).

Several aspects of this resolution serve to contradict its apparent implications. Firstly, Cleopatra is able to capitulate to Roman matrimony only after Antony has died, and when one aspect of her conflict has dissolved rather than being resolved. The prospect of sharing power with Antony no longer exists, and she begins to approximate the lovers in Donne's poems, or Antony's own earlier expressions of absolute emotion. After his death Antony can fill her world in a way that Antony alive could never be allowed to do:

> His face was as the heav'ns, and therein stuck
> A sun and moon, which kept their course and lighted

> The little O, the earth . . .
> His legs bestrid the ocean; his rear'd arm
> Crested the world.
>
> (5.2.79–83)

The poetry has been seen as sublime. Cleopatra's words display an effort to cloak personal and political loss in the language of a transcendental, eternal romance. Given the conditions of its utterance, the poetry reveals the politics of sublimation, rather than a transcendence of politics. Antony can now comfortably be called "husband" (5.2.285) without the risk to freedom that actual matrimony implies.

Cleopatra also lets her own fierce identification with Egypt slip for the first time. Literally, of course she still does not accept Caesar's Rome, which remains a threat:

> Shall they hoist me up,
> And show me to the shouting varletry
> Of censuring Rome? Rather a ditch in Egypt
> Be gentle grave unto me!
>
> (5.2.55–58)

But Rome was also Antony's space and as his wife she can adopt the "Roman fashion."

Secondly, if these moves reflect Cleopatra's contradictions, they are also strategic and constitute the unruly woman's last performances. Having lost power, it now becomes "paltry to be Caesar" (5.2.2); it is now time to speak of things other than power. Her suicide clouds her political defeat with mystic glamour and a show of autonomy. Her own body is the last "space" to be wrested from Roman control. The asp will bring her "liberty" in the absence of real territory. The maternal image of the snake at her breast tames her own earlier identification with the serpent, replacing the deadly Eastern inscrutability with a comprehensible version of the Madonna. Of course, *both* are patriarchal constructions of women. The first demonises the alien woman while the second seeks to domesticise her.

Till the end, Cleopatra attempts to maintain some vestiges of power even as she acknowledges Caesar as "the sole sir o'th' world" (5.2.119). It is only when every effort has failed that she has "immortal longings" (5.2.279). Without power "What should I stay—/In this vile world?" (5.2.311–12).

As Cleopatra achieves these false resolutions, the play also abandons the cinematic montage that so adequately expressed the discontinuity of character, the dialectic between inner and outer, political and personal, male and female spaces. The shifts of scene which conveyed both the vacillations of Antony and the unruly theatricality of Cleopatra give way to the elevation of the "Roman" suicides; to the conventional "climax" and the stock devices of formal drama, as patriarchal roles and divisions are apparently reinstated. If Cleopatra's fluid identity and play-acting demanded one kind of theatrical form, her new role as Antony's marble-constant wife employs the more classical technique. The Roman theatre takes over from the volatile Egyptian one. The closed space of the monument, the measured actions and tones, the slow, drawn-out scenes and the elevated language all tone down the fiery and unpredictable performances of the earlier Cleopatra. The narrative of masculinity and imperialism regains control but Cleopatra's final performance, which certainly exposes her own vulnerability, not only cheats Caesar but denies any final and authoritative textual closure.

Works Cited in this Essay

Adelman, Janet. *The Common Liar: An Essay on Antony and Cleopatra*. New Haven: Yale University Press, 1973.

Barker, Francis, et al., eds. *Europe and Its Others*. Vol. 2. Colchester: University of Essex, 1985.

Belsey, Catherine. *The Subject of Tragedy*. London and New York: Methuen, 1985.

Brecht, Bertolt. *Brecht on Theatre: The Development of an Aesthetic*, ed. and trans. John Willett. London: Eyre Methuen, 1964.

Brown, J. E. *The Critical Opinions of Samuel Johnson*. London: Russell, 1926.

Brown, John Russell, ed. *Antony and Cleopatra: A Casebook*. London: Macmillan, 1968.

Carr, Helen. "Woman/Indian: 'The American' and his Others," in Barker et al., eds., 1985.

Clark, Sandra. "*Hic Mulier/Haec Vir* and the Controversy over Masculine Women." *Studies in Philology* 82:2 (1985): 157–83.

Crane, Milton, ed. *Shakespeare's Art: Seven Essays*. Chicago: University of Chicago Press, 1973.

Danby, John F. "The Shakespearean Dialectic: An Aspect of *Antony and Cleopatra*." *Scrutiny* 16 (1949): 196-213.

Datta, P. K. Review of A. Ghosh's *The Circle of Reason*. *Social Scientist*, October 1986.

Dollimore, Jonathan. *Radical Tragedy: Religion, Ideology and Power in the Drama of Shakespeare and His Contemporaries*. Brighton: Harvester, 1983.

Dollimore, Jonathan. "Shakespeare, Cultural Materialism and the New Historicism," in Dollimore and Sinfield, eds., pp. 2–17.

Dollimore, Jonathan, and Sinfield, Alan, eds. *Political Shakespeare: New Essays in Cultural Materialism*. Manchester, England: Manchester University Press, 1985.

Greenblatt, Stephen. *Renaissance Self-Fashioning*. Chicago: University of Chicago Press, 1980.

Hacker, Barton. "Women and Military Institutions in Early Modern Europe: A Reconnaissance." *Signs* 6:4 (Summer 1981): 643–71.

Heinemann, Margot. "How Brecht Read Shakespeare," in Dollimore and Sinfield, eds., pp. 202–30.

Heisch, Alison. "Queen Elizabeth I and the Persistence of Patriarchy." *Feminist Review* no. 4 (1980).

Holloway, John. *The Story of the Night: Studies in Shakespeare's Major Tragedies*. London: Routledge, 1961.

Hulme, Peter. "Polytropic Man: Tropes of Sexuality and Mobility in Early Colonial Discourse," in Barker et al., eds., 1985.

Jardine, Lisa. *Still Harping on Daughters: Women in Seventeenth Century Drama*. Brighton: Harvester, 1983.

Kelly, Joan. *Women, History, Theory*. Chicago: University of Chicago Press, 1984.

Knox, John. *The First Blast of the Trumpet against the Monstrous Regiment of Women* (1558), ed. Edward Arber. Westminster: Archibald Constable, 1895.

Mack, Maynard. *"Antony and Cleopatra:* The Stillness and the Dance," in Milton Crane, ed., 1973.

Markels, Julian. *The Pillar of the World: Antony and Cleopatra in Shakespeare's Development*. Columbus: Ohio State University Press, 1968.

Montrose, Louis. "The Purpose of Playing: Reflections on a Shakespearean Anthropology." *Helios* no. 7 (1980): 51-74.

Muir, Kenneth, ed. *Thomas Middleton: Three Plays*. London: Dent, 1975.

Ornstein, Robert. *The Moral Vision of Jacobean Tragedy*. Madison: University of Wisconsin Press, 1965.

Ribner, Irving. *Jacobean Tragedy: The Quest for Moral Order*. London: Methuen, 1962.

Rose, Mark, ed. *Twentieth Century Interpretations of Antony and Cleopatra*. New Jersey: Prentice-Hall, 1977.

Rose, Mary Beth. "Women in Men's Clothing: Apparel and Social Stability in *The Roaring Girl*." *English Literary Renaissance* 14 (1984).

Rozett, Martha Tuck. "The Comic Structures of Tragic Endings: The Suicide Scenes in *Romeo and Juliet* and *Antony and Cleopatra*." *Shakespeare Quarterly* 36:2 (Summer 1985).

Said, Edward. *Orientalism*. London: Routledge, 1978.

Stallybrass, Peter. "*Macbeth* and Witchcraft," in John Russell Brown, ed. *Focus on Macbeth*. London: Routledge, 1982. Reprinted in this volume, pp. 104–18.

Staton, Shirley. "Female Transvestitism in Renaissance Comedy: 'A Natural Perspective That Is and Is Not.'" *Iowa State Journal of Research* 56 (1981): 79–89.

Travitsky, Betty. "The Lady Doth Protest: Protest in the Popular Writings of Renaissance Englishwomen." *English Literary Renaissance* 14:3 (1984).

Weimann, Robert. *Shakespeare and the Popular Tradition in the Theater*. Baltimore: Johns Hopkins University Press, 1978.

Antony and Cleopatra: Action as Imaginative Command

Michael Goldman

I

Most of Shakespeare's tragedies—*Romeo and Juliet* is perhaps the only arguable exception—are concerned, one way or another, with human greatness. Their heroes are larger than life and recognized as such by those around them. *Antony and Cleopatra*, however, differs from the rest of the tragedies in that it is centrally *about* greatness. The discussion of greatness is the activity to which the play's characters devote most of their time. In speech after speech, indeed scene after scene, they comment on each other's greatness—acknowledge it, praise it, measure it by various standards, are moved and changed by it, proclaim their own greatness, consider what greatness means. Love is also a subject of the play, of course. But the claim of the lovers—and even of their enemies—is that they are great lovers, no pair so famous, as Caesar says, and their language of love, particularly when quarreling and making up, is the language of fame, nobility, and superhuman comparison. They measure their passion against the scope and power of the universe and against all competitors, human, legendary, and divine. The competition knows no bounds, and there is no interest in second place, even in the hereafter.

Most critics of *Antony and Cleopatra* have recognized its concern with one aspect or another of greatness, but insufficient attention has been given to what the play conceives greatness to be. I would like to look into its definition of greatness not simply as an abstraction, but as a way of experiencing life, a sense of process that critically affects our sense of action. What I have called a definition of greatness might more accurately, if more awkwardly, be described as a concern with a certain kind of greatness and its way of acting upon the world. It seems to me to offer a clue to the play's dramatic unity and to some of the problems it presents for performers and critics—to the way Shakespeare moves his actors on the stage, to the kinds of action we are shown and not shown, and to the difficulties and rewards of the main parts.

From Goldman, Michael. *Acting and Action in Shakespearean Tragedy*, pp. 112–39. Copyright © 1985 by Princeton University Press. Reprinted by permission of Princeton University Press.

In *Antony and Cleopatra*, greatness is primarily a command over other people's imaginations. It depends on what people think of you and what you think of yourself. At the lowest level, it is style, effective self-dramatization; at the highest, it is a means of overcoming time, death, and the world. It is registered in the behavior of audiences, and a concern for greatness is reflected in a concern for audiences. The audience for greatness in *Antony and Cleopatra* is multiple: it is, first, the small group of people on stage at any time; second, the entire known world to whom Antony and Cleopatra constantly play and which seems always to regard them with fascination; it is also a timeless, superhuman audience, the heroes of history and legend and the gods themselves; finally, it is the audience of posterity, of whom we in the theater are a part. The play is very much aware that we have heard of its heroes before coming to the theater; their greatness, their ability to command imagination through time, has helped to draw us. When Cleopatra decides to stage her death—and it is a carefully planned spectacle—the immediate cause she cites is the prospect of an inadequate theatrical representation of her life, which will not do her justice but boy her greatness in the posture of a whore. And when Antony contemplates life after death with Cleopatra, he says that together they will make the "ghosts gaze" at them:

> Dido and her Aeneas shall want troops,
> And all the haunt be ours.
>
> (4.14.53–54)

Once more, it is the ability to command other imaginations that sets the seal on their greatness. Very closely associated with it, in this passage and throughout the play, is the ability to go beyond natural limit and thus to take on the transforming power of imagination itself.

Greatness, as Antony and Cleopatra possess it, is seen not as an aspect of one's deeds, nor even, primarily, as the potential for specific actions, but as a kind of emanation radiating from the two lovers across the civilized world and down through history. Even our first reference to Antony is not to his courage, strength, or martial skill, but to his eyes, "That o'er the files and musters of the war/Have glowed like plated Mars" (1.1.3–4). And this sense of greatness as a radiant attribute is felt in the spectacle with which we are immediately presented. The stage directions for the entrance that immediately follows read:

> *Flourish. Enter* ANTONY, CLEOPATRA, *her* LADIES, *the* TRAIN, *with* EUNUCHS *fanning her.*
>
> (1.1.10 s.d.)

One of the effects here, of course, is to place Antony amid the court of Egypt. There are no other Romans with him, so Antony is merely part of the entourage, part of the spectacle of Cleopatra's power which will add weight to Philo's description of him as a strumpet's fool. But the court is presented to us in its characteristic activity of *tending* Cleopatra, and this activity will catch our eye in the theater. Antony, Philo has said, has become the bellows and the fan to cool a gypsy's lust, and we immediately see Eunuchs fanning Cleopatra. The spectacle of the court of

Egypt actively tending Cleopatra occurs repeatedly in the text and is repeatedly referred to, most notably in Enobarbus' speech and in the preparations surrounding Cleopatra's death. And there are many natural opportunities for it which go unmarked in the stage directions. Very likely, it should happen whenever the Queen appears attended. It will certainly form part of the audience's enduring picture of Cleopatra. What can all this tending and fanning mean?

Enobarbus' speech, in its elaboration of the picture, offers a clue. First of all, as Enobarbus makes clear, the tending of Cleopatra is an activity which expresses and contributes to her greatness, especially in the sense of imaginative command. It does so by a battery of transformations—in which all the objects and persons that tend her pass beyond natural limit, and in which nature itself is transformed as if by a desire to worship Cleopatra. The barge is a throne and its perfume makes the winds lovesick; the water seems controlled by the flute music which establishes a rhythm for the silver oars; it seems amorous of their strokes. Next, we come to the tending and fanning proper:

> On each side her
> Stood pretty dimpled boys, like smiling Cupids,
> With divers-colored fans, whose wind did seem
> To glow the delicate cheeks which they did cool,
> And what they undid did. . . .
> Her gentlewomen, like the Nereides,
> So many mermaids, tended her i' th' eyes,
> And made their bends adornings.
>
> (2.2.203–10)

There is constant renewal here; every gesture of Cleopatra's attendants adds to her beauty, and they in turn seem to grow more beautiful in her presence. Her attendants seem like mythological creatures or works of art, but their superhuman loveliness is controlled, as everything in the speech is, by Cleopatra herself. Her nature goes beyond art:

> O'erpicturing that Venus where we see
> The fancy outwork nature.
>
> (202–3)

But if her nature goes beyond art, her art—as we have seen—commands nature. Cleopatra may beggar all description, but Enobarbus' powers of description have certainly been regally expanded by his subject. The effect of the spectacle of Cleopatra attended in her barge is to command both nature and imagination. She draws the city's people to her, commands Antony himself, and the spectacle *we* see—three hard-bitten campaigners chatting on an empty stage, one of them moved to sudden eloquence, the others listening raptly, urging him to go on— demonstrates how, even in Rome, she commands Enobarbus' imagination, too.

The constant renewal, the suggestion that the fanning both relieves and excites, reflects a characteristic of Cleopatra herself, who makes hungry where most she satisfies. Summing it up then, the spectacle of her appearances attended, with

their undulating movement, their splendor of dress, their warm focus on
Cleopatra, heightens our sense of the specific character of her greatness—its commanding, sun-like radiance, its power to transform all it touches, its self-renewing
fertility. We should note, too, if we wish to possess the design of the play, how the
significances of this spectacle—not only as generally transforming, but transforming of Roman things—are enriched for us over the whole course of the action. We
first see it, through Philo's eyes, as an example of a gypsy's lust—the gaudy, self-
indulgent world that has trapped and unmanned Antony. That perspective is
quickly challenged, however, and by the second act we see the spectacle from a
different Roman point of view in the surprising relish and richness of Enobarbus'
report. At the end of the play, the tending and adorning is part of the gallant,
ecstatic preparation by Cleopatra and her maids for death, and it continues after
she is dead—again a transformation, but an enhancing one, of something Roman,
the high Roman fashion of suicide.[1]

II

Critics have occasionally complained that *Antony and Cleopatra* is actionless,
but it is natural, given the play's notion of greatness, that so much of its on-stage
activity is taken up, not with direct combat or intrigue, say, things we normally
would think of as action, but with spectacle, praise—and reports. The play takes
unusual interest in reports, particularly reports about the great, and especially the
imaginative impact of reports both on the reporter and his audience. We think, of
course, of Enobarbus' report of Cleopatra. But there are also the play's many messengers and the reports that come to Caesar and Pompey early in the play. Caesar
is moved to an impassioned apostrophe to the absent Antony as news of Pompey's
strength mounts, and shortly afterward Pompey, having delivered a nicely parallel
invocation of Cleopatra's charms, turns from jaunty confidence to apprehension
and foreboding when he learns that Antony is on his way to Rome. These reactions
help to keep Antony in our thoughts while he is off-stage, and, more importantly,
measure his greatness by showing how thought of him dominates and controls the
mood of others.

The most dramatically notable report, however, occurs in the fifth act. It helps
to provide what little suspense and surprise the plot holds after Antony's death, a
main line of intrigue leading up to Cleopatra's suicide. Since it may easily be
missed in reading, let me take a moment to sketch its dramatic force. Shortly after
Caesar has left the monument, Dolabella reappears, in haste, with news of
Caesar's true intentions. His language to Cleopatra is very interesting:

---

[1]The process of transformation is further extended by the play's final procession, which represents
a transformation by Cleopatra of the triumph that her Roman conqueror has planned. Regally attired,
solemnly and respectfully attended, she is now to be carried, not to humiliation in Rome, but to a
famous Egyptian grave, and Caesar himself is glad to claim reflected glory from the spectacle. As an
Egyptian procession has brought Cleopatra on-stage at the beginning of the play, a Roman one carries
her off, but it, too, celebrates her greatness.

Madam, as thereto sworn, by your command
(Which my love makes religion to obey)
I tell you this.

(5.2.198–200)

And he tells her, concluding:

I have performed

Your pleasure, and my promise.

(203–04)

"As thereto sworn, by your command," he says, and "my promise." But what is he talking about? He has sworn to nothing; he has made no promise. No explicit order has been given. Nevertheless, something has commanded him.

On his previous appearance, Cleopatra has won Dolabella to her purposes, and the full extent of her conquest appears only here. But it is *how* she has won him that is of interest to us. She has succeeded by commanding his mood, impressing him with her greatness and the greatness of her grief. "Your loss is as yourself, great," he says. More specifically, she has won him by a report of Antony's greatness, an immense speech of praise which, even more than Enobarbus' report, has been a work of the imagination, an elaborate hyperbolic portrait, measuring Antony by the world and, finally, by the limits not only of nature but of imagination itself. It is couched in and carries to an extreme the play's language of praise for Antony:

His legs bestrid the ocean: his reared arm
Crested the world: his voice was propertied
As all the tunèd spheres, and that to friends;
But when he meant to quail and shake the orb,
He was as rattling thunder. For his bounty,
There was no winter in't: an autumn 'twas
That grew the more by reaping. His delights
Were dolphinlike, they showed his back above
The element they lived in. In his livery
Walked crowns and crownets: realms and islands were
As plates dropped from his pocket.

(5.2.82–92)

Cleopatra's praise of Antony as both equalling nature in superhuman power and going beyond associates Antony with imagination, and is in fact presented as a dream. At this point, Dolabella gently denies that there can have been such a man. But Cleopatra is ready for him. Antony is more than the stuff dreams are made on. He, too, is greater than any fancy that can outwork nature:

But if there be nor ever were one such,
It's past the size of dreaming; nature wants stuff
To vie strange forms with fancy, yet t' imagine
An Antony were nature's piece 'gainst fancy,
Condemning shadows quite.

(96–100)

It is Cleopatra's portrait of Antony that converts her audience. Again, it is no anecdote of what Antony has said or done, but simply a fantastic projection of his greatness that controls the action, transforming Dolabella from a ready tool of Caesar into Cleopatra's devoted servant, a man who imagines he has sworn an oath and made a promise.

III

The play's emphasis on greatness as imaginative command has a radical effect not only on its treatment of action but on the acting it requires of its two heroes. The actors who play Antony and Cleopatra have to convince us from the start that they are great. They have to do this not by their actions—much of the time they are allowed action that does not show greatness but at best asserts it—but by their direct command over our imagination. We must always be aware of Antony and Cleopatra's greatness as a genuine issue. Without the audience's immediate assent that this man, Antony, looks like someone we feel willing, on faith, to measure by superhuman comparisons, without this the play will be tedious, empty at the center. It will be truly actionless, for whatever unifying sense of movement we get from the play depends on our sense that from these two lovers there springs a power that can dominate memory, compel extravagant loyalty, and exact the fascinated attention of the entire world.

We might compare other tragedies in which the heroes are considered great according to one definition or another, but in which they are given early opportunities to exhibit that greatness in action. Othello illustrates his nobility, courage, composure, authority, in the first act through conflict, by challenging Brabantio and Brabantio's men, by overcoming the doubts of his fellow Senators. But Antony and Cleopatra must establish themselves in an atmosphere that comments constantly upon their greatness yet does not test it in action.[2] If anything, what they do early in the play—and indeed throughout most of it—works against their greatness, or against the ordinary measures of greatness in their world. The drama comes from their giving to all things, even the worst, a touch of majesty, making vilest things "become" their greatness.

Consider the problems of an actor who must enter on the lines:

> you shall see in him
> The triple pillar of the world transformed
> Into a strumpet's fool.
>
> (1.1.11–13)

The strumpet's fool might not be that hard to manage but the triple pillar of the world—who even as a strumpet's fool remains the triple pillar of the world! "Stand

[2]Redgrave comments, "You have to create, convincingly, the image of a man who held part of the world in thrall, and you have very little to do it with; all you have is his voluptuousness." (Margaret Lamb, *Antony and Cleopatra on the English Stage* [Associated Universities Press, 1981], p. 147.)

up, Mr. Jones, and try to look like the triple pillar of the world." It has the rawness, the unsupported nakedness of the initial awful moment in an actor's audition, which in most cases is the crucial moment—when you step out and the producer, not waiting to see you tap-dance or do your James Cagney imitation, says, "He'll do," or far more likely, "He won't do"—and doing, in fact, depends not on what you do but what you are, on something in you—that, as they say, you either have or you don't. It is raw presence that is wanted. And the play makes use of, draws its meanings out of, that raw appeal, the claim pure presence in an actor makes on an audience's minds and lives.

In the case of Antony, what the actor must have is the presence of the greatest man in the world. Caesar, by contrast, doesn't need it. If on his first entrance we discover that he looks unimposing, why that can fit into a characterization well enough. His greatness may lie in cunning, or policy, or self-discipline, or realism, or the material power behind him. But the actor of Antony must radiate a magnetism that justifies the admiration he receives.

Shakespeare has written a part that will reward and exhibit this power in the actor who possesses it. When he embraces Cleopatra on their first appearance, the convincing ease with which he requires "On pain of punishment, the world to weet/We stand up peerless" (1.1.39–40) gives an exciting resonance to their passion, which is essential to the play and which depends on our belief that this is a man who can make the world take notice by sheer charisma. When he makes his followers weep, we watch him deliberately using it. When in the third or fourth act he pulls back repeatedly from dejection, we respond to the radiance that returns.

Antony's dejection is worth further consideration here, because it helps us understand the distinctive accomplishment required of both the play's leading actors. It points not only to a side of Antony's character, but to the essential quality of his relation with Cleopatra. Antony's dejection is deep, and any production will fail that fails to stress it. It consists in his feeling that his greatness has been demolished. The land, he says, is ashamed to bear him. When he can feel a way back to asserting his imaginative command, his spirits invariably revive. Sometimes he fumbles about in his effort to reassert his greatness, as in the pathetic messages to Caesar, but he is utterly renewed even by winning a skirmish we know to be meaningless—not because he expects to win back his material power, but because his greatness is shining forth once more on all around him.

The revival of his spirits at his deepest moments of dejection depends, of course, on Cleopatra. The actor and actress who play Antony and Cleopatra not only must exercise a convincing magnetism, they must convincingly respond to its presence in each other. I know of no comparable investigation, before the nineteenth century, of the way two people in love act upon and change each other, and we must be sure to get the dynamic of their relation right. Now, some critics have taken "the expense of spirit in a waste of shame" as the emblem of Antony and Cleopatra's connection, and seen it as an example of a lust that periodically gives way to remorse.[3] This constitutes, in fact, a fair statement of the typical Roman view of sex in the play, and Antony himself seems to have it in mind early on when he says:

> The present pleasure,
> By revolution low'ring, does become
> The opposite of itself.
>
> (1.2.125–27)

But this is not what happens between Antony and Cleopatra.

Instead of attraction giving way to disgust, we find that whenever Antony reaches a peak of self-revulsion and anger at Cleopatra (never the result of sexual fulfillment, by the way), it is her sexual appeal, even, presumably, from beyond the grave, that enables him to recover. Significantly, the position he comes round to as a result is always one we recognize as more noble than the one he has taken in disgust, more appealing, more in keeping with that great property which should be Antony's. After Actium, after the whipping of Thidias, after the final defeat, Cleopatra brings Antony back from a moment in which he feels his greatness is gone to one in which we—-and his audiences on stage—feel that he is exercising it again, whether it be in revelry, battle, or suicide. After he vents his wrath on her, she wins him back to her and to himself. Their mutual attraction, their sexually charged admiration for each other, though it drives them to folly and defeat, likewise stirs them both to greatness—to renewed vitality, indifference to material fortune, and splendid self-presentation.

The sexual magnetism which Antony and Cleopatra exert on each other is very similar to the magnetism of great leaders and great actors, perhaps indistinguishable from it. What binds Cleopatra and Antony sexually is not unlike what binds the world to them and binds us to the attractive presences of the actor and actress who impersonate them. The power of presence in an actor is perilously close to glamor, but it can be taken beyond the limits of glamor by art. This is what the actors of Antony and Cleopatra are required to do, and the process works as a metaphor for the type of problematic splendor their characters manifest. For Antony and Cleopatra are most actor-like in that they exhibit a magnetism that is culturally suspect. Paramount among the vile things they make becoming to the audience are the particular vices of glamorous actors. Cheapness and self-indulgence, narcissism and whoredom, hover about all their gestures.

The challenge here is to skate as close to shoddiness, to the disreputable side of glamor, as possible, to invite demeaning comparisons, both as characters and actors. Antony strikes poses, tries to make his followers weep, takes out his frustrations on the powerless. Cleopatra bitches and camps. Yet they never entirely lose their hold on their on-stage audience, nor should they on us. Shakespeare frequently invites us to judge them harshly, but any interesting performance of the play must keep the higher valuation always before us at least as a possibility, the

---

[3]An influential and particularly explicit example is John Danby, *Poets on Fortune's Hill* (London: Faber & Faber, 1952), pp. 128–51.

sense that we are in the presence of some remarkable kind of human richness. They must be, as the text demands, showy, self-regarding, manipulative, concerned with "image"—all the familiar trappings of the glamorous "star." But while showing the seams of their talent, all the glitz of their art, they must show its irresistible power too.[4]

IV

Once we think of the action of *Antony and Cleopatra* as flowing from the glitzy/charismatic presences of the leading actors, we become aware of a larger process that is everywhere at work in the play. To describe it in the most general terms, it is the process by which things that are attractive but of questionable substance or significance exert a transforming force on the apparently more substantial and valuable world. In so doing, they transform *themselves* into valuable and enduring entities. More concretely, the process is felt in the way Antony and Cleopatra seem to make things happen by sheer magnetism, in the way Cleopatra can make defect perfection, in the way her art can transform nature and her nature outdo art, in the way imagination can alter and enhance reality.

An excellent way of appreciating the depth at which Shakespeare pursues this process is to look closely at one of the play's central terms, a word that occurs in some of its most familiar quotations:

> vilest things
> Become themselves in her.
> (2.2.240–41)

> Fie, wrangling queen!
> Whom everything becomes.
> (1.1.48–49)

"Become," in this sense of adornment or making attractive, occurs at least eleven times in the play, and is important not so much by virtue of its relative frequency as by the poetic effects to which it contributes. Shakespeare uses it to produce odd knots of meaning, where the general sense or emotion is more or less clear but an additional bend of suggestion is felt.

---

[4] In the role of Cleopatra, Shakespeare makes good use of the boy actor to reinforce this double impression. At the beginning, Cleopatra draws heavily on the boy actor's strong suits of playful bitchery, bright raillery, mockery of the "adult" Roman style, but concludes the play on a sustained level of mature emotion which severely taxes the boy's skills–even while calling attention to his limitations (including, specifically, his whory gestures). Watching the boy Cleopatra, an Elizabethan audience could feel both the theatrical shallowness of "boying" a woman's greatness and the power of *this* boy to go beyond the normal limits of his art. See my book *The Actor's Freedom: Toward a Theory of Drama* (New York: Viking Press, 1975), pp 141–45.

Let me give some examples:

> But, sir, forgive me,
> Since my becomings kill me when they do not
> Eye well to you.
>
>   (1.3.95–97)

or

>   vilest things
> Become themselves in her, that the holy priests
> Bless her when she is riggish.
>
>   (2.2.240–42)

At such moments we may be uncertain as to what is becoming to what or feel that the expected verb-object sequence has been suppressed or reversed. We would expect, for example, that attributes would become their possessors, as in *Mourning Becomes Electra*, but in some passages we feel that the relation has perhaps been altered and in others we are specifically told that the relation is reversed, that the possessors become their attributes. "Observe how Antony becomes his flaw," Caesar says (3.12.34), and Cleopatra remarks:

> Look, prithee, Charmian,
> How this Herculean Roman does become
> The carriage of his chafe.
>
>   (1.3.83–85)

This last quotation illustrates, in very few words, the complexities the use of *becoming* introduces, and, more importantly, the response to life it stands for. The general sense, I suppose, is: behold how attractively Antony carries his anger. But the words *say* the opposite. The chafe makes the carriage, and Antony adorns it. The same process is at work in Antony's exclamation, "How every passion strives, in thee, to make itself fair and admired" (1.1.51). It is not that someone's management of an unpleasant emotion is attractive. In both cases, the vile thing transforms itself into attractiveness.

Here we see a further complexity. There is, of course, another meaning to *become*—to turn or change into, to develop. The word is used several times in this second sense in *Antony and Cleopatra*, but, more importantly, whenever it is used in the first sense it also takes on suggestions of the second. A sense of transformation always flickers around its edges. *Vilest things become themselves:* the overwhelming primary meaning is that *vile things seem attractive,* but how easy it would be to say *vile things become attractive.* And the additional complication of the passage, the problem of how something can become *itself,* adds to our sense of development, of becoming as contrasted to being. More strongly still, the context of the passage firmly establishes the sense of continuing process, improvement, endless renewal:

Age cannot wither her, nor custom stale
Her infinite variety: other women cloy

The appetites they feed, but she makes hungry
Where most she satisfies; for vilest things
Become themselves in her.

(2.2.237–41)

At this point we can conveniently relate these verbal effects to the action of the play. What *becomes* of Antony and Cleopatra flows from their *becomingness*. We feel their attractiveness not only as a source of static pleasure but as a transforming force, changing lives, shaping the course of history, making things happen in the theater. It is through their charismatic appeal that Antony and Cleopatra act on each other and on their audiences. They act on and act out their becomingness, striving even in death to *become themselves*, in both senses of the phrase. Their becomings kill them, as Cleopatra says, but they eye well to us.

One of the play's great emblems of transformation, of insubstantial attractiveness making substantial change, is to be found in the speech Antony delivers in his last moment of dejection. It operates in two ways: first, by suggesting Antony's transforming power over imagination even while claiming he has lost command; second, by a description of natural objects that are at once evanescent and solid, lacking in substance yet powerfully generative of significance:

Sometime we see a cloud that's dragonish,
A vapor sometime like a bear or lion,
A towered citadel, a pendant rock,
A forkèd mountain, or blue promontory
With trees upon't that nod unto the world
And mock our eyes with air. Thou hast seen these signs:
They are black vesper's pageants.

(4.14.2–8)

On the face of it, Antony is describing the insubstantial, shifting texture of clouds. His point will be that he himself is now of no more weight or account than they. But the feeling of the passage runs quite contrary to its argument. Not weightlessness but solidity dominates our most immediate impression. The stately progress of examples suggests, not watery evanescence, but large, heavy entities, each definite and strong, and all with varying degrees of strangeness that have in common a quality of attacking and commanding power. The dragon's fire passes over into the fork of the mountain; the rock hangs pendent over us. Our sense of the clouds comes from the progression of objects. So does our sense of Antony's emotion and our emotion toward Antony. Each image is one which we can easily associate with him, with his authority, his elevation, his extraordinary capacity to fight, to rage, to brood, to inspire awe. We are not meant to feel an insubstantial Antony here, but a weighty one.

Each of us will likely differ in interpreting the individual details of this immense piece of language, and differ as well in isolating the source of its effect—but if we step back, as it were, to look at the whole passage again, we can agree that what Eros and the audience have before them at this moment is *what happens in the sky* and not its emptiness, not the insubstantiality of clouds but the sweep and scope of their transformations, a huge, strange, heavy, flowing process on the great stage of nature, nodding to the world like the trees on the blue promontory, as great as the world, for all the world to see.

Even at this low point for Antony, then, there is about him a vivid aura of imaginative command, perhaps even a shade of the old self-conscious artistry—he makes Eros weep. His imagery asserts the claims of the imagination even while reminding us of the traditional case against it. Clouds are a familiar symbol both for the imagination's vagaries and for its influence. Antony's description, while ostensibly giving a negative value to the clouds, actually awakens for us all the clouds' grand power over mood and the power of mood to spread and to infect other imaginations. Antony tells us that he is nothing, but he has not lost command over our thoughts. He rules them, like black vesper's pageants. His very loss of power is a great work of dramatic art, a pageant in which Nature and fancy outvie each other, to which we and Eros listen overwhelmed. Antony's speech is not only about his dejection but about the power of imagination to transform the world.

The passage is followed by another exercise of the imagination, a panicky lie, which has a transforming effect on the world of the play. Mardian, lying on Cleopatra's behalf, acts the part of Cleopatra dying, and this double bit of pretense finally prompts Antony to suicide. After the final defeat, then, the action is shaped by a series of deliberate manipulations of reality—deceptions (as of Antony here and Caesar later), self-dramatizations (as in the cloud speech and the conversion of Dolabella), and finally Cleopatra's carefully staged spectacle of suicide. The long concluding movement of the play, more than one-fifth its length, is dominated by this sequence of imaginative transformations, which accompany and bring about a corresponding emotional movement of enhancement—from meanness and agitation of spirit to generosity and peace, leading from Antony's rage through Cleopatra's panic, through the false report and the attempted suicide, through Antony's death in Cleopatra's arms, to Cleopatra's final sovereign moments.

V

The process I have been describing—of imaginative transformation and enhancement, of making the insubstantial substantial, the questionable valuable— is very active in those final moments, and I want to approach them by way of an important and closely related pattern of imagery. A great deal has been made, critically, of what might be called horizontal oscillation in the play, its use of a back-and-forth movement in the alternation of scenes between Egypt and Rome, in the swings of Antony's emotions, and in many images—the vagabond flag upon the stream, for instance. And this has generally been interpreted as contributing either to a sense of ambivalence or of dissolution, or both. But there is another pattern of movement in language and action which is far more vividly impressed upon us, and which both controls and gives meaning to the horizontal. It might be called vertical, for contrast. The movement is both down and up, and the effect is one not of mere oscillation or breaking apart but of enrichment, renewal, and freedom. Put simply, it is a movement sometimes of descending into, but always of rising from, the generative slime, and it makes itself felt in the stage movement, the imagery, and the psychic action of the characters. But to put it simply is to run the risk of missing the fullness of its work upon us. For it is presented with great variety and suavity.

I want to stress the larger dramatic imagery here, but I would like to begin with one of the more frequently discussed verbal images as a way of making clearer the relation I perceive between the movements I am calling vertical and horizontal. When Caesar in a famous passage refers to the movement of the tide, he is not only indulging a typical bit of Roman political analysis, he is using imagery familiar to us from *Julius Caesar*, where it also stands for those currents politicians must study and follow:

> It hath been taught us from the primal state
> That he which is was wished until he were;
> And the ebbed man, ne'er loved till ne'er worth love,
> Comes deared by being lacked. This common body,
> Like to a vagabond flag upon the stream,
> Goes to and back, lackeying the varying tide,
> To rot itself with motion.
>
> (1.4.41–47)

The tide in the affairs of men goes this way and that in both plays, and he who does not seize it at the flood is drowned in it. And when Antony sees Octavia standing, as at that moment the whole Mediterranean world stands, between the two great competitors, he calls on a similar image, though gentler and more humanely felt:

> the swan's-down feather
> That stands upon the swell at the full of tide,
> And neither way inclines.
>
> (3.2.49–51)

But like many Roman judgments in the play this version of the tide image is not final. For tides do not move horizontally but, rather, vertically upon the varying shore of the world, and it is the vertical movement of the Nile from full to ebb—not aimless but fertilizing—that dominates the play.

The process by which the rise and fall of the tides is measured and used to sow the land is described at length by Antony for Caesar's benefit during their Bacchic feast, and runs through the play's imagery. *Antony and Cleopatra* begins with an accusation that Antony o'erflows the measure, but it is suffused with the suggestion that to o'erflow the measure is to moisten the earth and renew the world. Or, put another way, the tide of the affairs of men may be an endless oscillation, but the tides of nature endlessly create.

I hope this has given a useful notion of what I am calling vertical movement. In the play's stage imagery, it is most prominent when Antony is hoisted up to Cleopatra in the monument. I doubt whether one can overemphasize the force of this daring piece of stage mechanics. First of all we must pay full attention to Antony's condition. He has bungled his suicide, and we are meant to know that it hurts. For all his fortitude, he cries out in pain at least once. As early as *Romeo and Juliet*, Shakespeare had played the neat death off against the messy one, and here the messiness of the death, in which the hero must be seen as bungling, helpless, bleeding, in cruel pain, works against and with the wit, high language, and emblematic significance of his elevation. Up comes the dying Antony from the blood and mess to a final kiss, a final drink, a final cry of pain, and a final display of nobility. At the moment he reaches the balcony, Cleopatra explicitly strikes the note of renewal:

> Welcome, welcome! Die where thou hast lived,
> Quicken with kissing.[5]
>
> (4.15.38–39)

Antony's movement here through and with what is low or messy to what is high and great is repeated more subtly but with equal theatrical force in the sequence of events leading up to and beyond Cleopatra's suicide. So much of importance is going on simultaneously in this last scene that it is difficult to talk about in any wholly perspicuous sequence. Perhaps it would be useful to begin by noting that there is more specific anticipation of the final death in this play than in any other Shakespearean tragedy. That is, there is more verbal reference to the particular circumstances in which Cleopatra will die. All the tragedies contain lines which may at least be construed as foreshadowing their end, and, not surprisingly, it is the love tragedies, *Romeo and Juliet* and *Othello*, that come closest to our play in this regard, with Romeo's dream, Othello's foreshadowing kiss, and his anticipation of chaos. But we have many more and more specific references to the nature and effect of Cleopatra's suicide—the serpent of old Nile, the breathless breathing forth of power, the am'rous pinches which are later echoed in the stroke of death like a lover's pinch, etc. I think Shakespeare may have been encouraged in this by the circumstance that this would be of all his plays the one in which the audience would be most familiar with the manner of the climactic death and most fascinated by it, and in which Cleopatra's way of dying would be one of the most famous things about this famous couple. For her death with the serpent at her breast was one way in which these lovers commanded imagination in posterity as they did in their lifetime. By anticipating it, Shakespeare is not only making capital out of his audience's state of mind, but he is using the fact of our state of mind as part of the stuff and meaning of his play. Among the other sensations of the death scene, we are aware of ourselves savoring the fame of famous events.

---

[5]Following Pope's emendation at l. 38.

In the deaths of both Antony and Cleopatra, we feel once more the force of the play's focus on greatness as imaginative command. Their deaths are insisted upon—by Shakespeare, by themselves, by the people around them—as imaginative acts that sustain and enhance their nobility, as ways of imposing their greatness permanently on the play's multiple audiences. It is not the fact that they die, or even that they die by their own hand. What matters is their style of doing it, how they conceive and describe it, how their audiences react.

Cleopatra's death is a superb piece of poetic transformation which quite insists on its poetry. Its best-known lines draw attention to their own verbal magic—their echoes, condensations, comparisons, ambiguities. The scene as a whole insists, too, on its power to change vilest things into lasting pleasures and great achievements, outreaching the Roman standard of suicide it seems based upon. Hers is no terse, stoic acceptance of a sword in the belly but a conversion of death into something gentle, regenerative, sovereign. Death is like sleep, sexual pursuit becomes a strong (and sleep-like) toil of grace; the snake is the worm that quickens Nilus' slime, a baby sleeping and feeding at the nurse's breast.

Like most of the ambiguities in the play, the treatment of the language here and the treatment of death itself works to take a relatively plain statement and promote it vertically, to invest it with greater attractiveness and value. Similarly, the events surrounding Cleopatra's suicide are arranged in a way that makes us aware of vertical promotion. Their sequence suggests a pattern of enhancement, a rising free from limit. We build up from Cleopatra as a helpless prisoner, whom we have seen struggling in the arms of her captors and kneeling to Caesar; through her scene with the Clown, with its puns and homely language, its basket and snake and talk of mud; through the play's final scene of tending and adorning, the putting on of the robe and the crown—a moment of stage spectacle that we see in the process of being created as well as in its final visual splendor. Then, of course, she dies, having become fire and air, with a great evocation of peace and gentleness.

The quality of sensation projected by the actress at the moment of Cleopatra's death is one of the play's most concentrated expressions of the entire complex of feeling we have been charting. As Lear dies in a moment of heightened perception,

> Look on her. Look, her lips,
> Look there, look there.
> (5.3.312–13)

so Cleopatra dies in a moment of heightened sensation:

> As sweet as balm, as soft as air, as gentle . . .
> (5.2.311)

Lear focusses on Cordelia's lips, as his play has repeatedly focussed on minute bodily particulars. Cleopatra dies in a large, enveloping sensual experience, which has the enriching ambiguity typical of the play. Is she describing, in these words, the gentleness of the asp like a baby at her breast, or the stroke of death like that of a lover, or is it her lover himself? For her words finally gather into that name of names, so often used simply as a superlative in the play, that infinite virtue uncaught by the snares of the world, though tangled in them, indeed adorned by them:

> As sweet as balm, as soft as air, as gentle—
> O, Antony!

VI

Like Cleopatra's death, the play as a whole can be taken as insisting on what poetry can do—and on the problematic status of that power. To make vilest things becoming, to take a gypsy's lust and, by fanning it, to convert it into a mesmerizing radiance of fire and air—well, such procedures are a kind of trick, but they also echo some of our deepest experiences outside the theater, notably the experience of sexual passion and the related phenomena of human charisma. And if it is a trick, it is not a deception; Shakespeare, like Antony and Cleopatra, hides nothing. We see the moral questionableness of the material at every step, yet the enhancement mounts. The world of the entire play is bound to weet that its heroes stand up peerless—though no one can miss the point that they are of the earth, dungy. In them, as in poetry, every passion, however mean or ugly, can be made fair and admired—and we are left astonished that this can be so.

Are we left enlightened? One way of describing the elusiveness of *Antony and Cleopatra* is to say that of all Shakespeare's plays it is perhaps the hardest to accommodate to a notion of authorial intention. As a result, it is nearly impossible to discuss the play without making some statement about how we are to receive its peculiar mixture of glamor and demystification. I would like to approach this question by way of a flight of biographical fancy, which I hope will be taken less as an assertion of possible fact than as a metaphor, a step toward describing the kind of understanding the play communicates. I find it helpful to think of *Antony and Cleopatra* as written at a moment when Shakespeare, for whatever reason, had become particularly self-conscious about his own career. At forty-three or forty-four, he would have had a reasonably clear sense of his own greatness. Even if he shared his culture's relatively low estimate of the importance of playwriting, he must have been conscious of the unusual power of his mind. The intellectual effort required to produce *Hamlet, Troilus and Cressida, Measure for Measure, Othello, King Lear,* and *Macbeth* in half-a-dozen years would have struck even the most modest of men as extraordinary. Like any great artist he might have wondered what his powers could have achieved in a more practical sphere:

> I turn away and shut the door and on the stair
> Wonder how many times I could have proved my worth
> In something that all others understand or share.

Antony, too, was admirably fitted for success in practical life—and instead both he and Cleopatra had chosen to follow an aesthetic path, the path of imagination and pleasure, had chosen to live out their mutual attraction—and attractiveness—to the full. What value, what substance, could be found in such a career?

And there was the other side of the coin to consider. What was Shakespeare's responsibility for the moral impact of his art? If, like Antony, he had followed his imagination where it might lead, placing its promptings finally before the claims of practical success, he had at the same time led a most public life. Again like Antony (and like Cleopatra too), he had continually addressed the world in the most calculated terms, attempting very deliberately to command its feelings. Like Antony, he knew how to make his followers weep. Had he done less harm than his heroes—or had he too corrupted honest men?

> Did that play of mine send out
> Certain men the English shot?

Essex's friends had of course been idiotic to arrange for a performance of *Richard II* on the eve of their rebellion, but one could see their point. Whatever Shakespeare may have intended, however orthodox the political "philosophy" of his history plays, the power of his art made the possibility of rebellion vivid, interesting, moving. In this, it loosened the fibers of authority and moral restraint. And which of the tragedies, with their immense indulgence of passion and fantasy, did not? Oh, they were perfectly correct on questions of right and wrong. *Macbeth* deprecated regicide; *Othello* made it clear one wasn't supposed to kill one's wife. But each was a risky adventure in feeling and knowledge. Certainly it could not be denied that imagination at its most importunate swept dangerously beyond moral lines. The power of language could make everything it touched precious, could, while the play lasted, make its own preciousness the center of value. In the figures of Antony and Cleopatra, Shakespeare may have recognized an appeal like that of supreme poetic fluency itself—the amoral splendor of the absolutely attractive.

In any literal sense, of course, such speculation is idle. We can never know Shakespeare's intentions, if he had any, and no intention can account for a work as great as *Antony and Cleopatra*. But the relation between poetry and the practical or moral life does give us a metaphor for our involvement with its heroes. As such it helps place the *showiness* of the play—its unparalleled emphasis on the quality of its own technique—and the similar showiness of Antony and Cleopatra. It also helps us in the difficult task of getting the play's ironies straight.

I do not think we are meant to "balance" the claims of Antony and Cleopatra with those of their critics; nor does one position dissolve or transcend the other. Rather, the main experience of the play is what I called vertical promotion. We are caught up in the process of enhancement. In the end, all the play's most questionable materials are transformed into elements of Cleopatra's final spectacle. They do not cease to be questionable, but the transformation sweeps us along. We accept it and enjoy it. At the same time, we are left with no confident way of locating or judging the process. Indeed—a further complication—we are left without a feeling of disturbance, with none of the moral vertigo, for example, that attends *Troilus and Cressida*. We are not allowed the comfort of knowing what we can "do" with the pleasure we feel; we are not even allowed the moral comfort of discomfort.

Shakespeare's position in all this may perhaps be glimpsed in the role of the messenger who brings Cleopatra the news of Antony's marriage to Octavia. What is his relation to these questionable lives he reports with such accuracy?

> O, that his fault should make a knave of thee,
> That art not what th'art sure of!
>
> (2.5.102–3)

Though the poet is not, morally, to be confused with what he describes, still the good poet must be "sure" of the news he brings—and is thus in some sense implicated in it. Neither Aristotle's nor Sidney's excuses quite get him off the hook. Poetry makes nothing happen, says Auden, but he would have been more correct had he added—except for the things that happen when we read poetry. Poetry makes life seem very interesting, and, once aroused, there is no way to confine this interest to what is healthful, prudent, or community oriented. In *Antony and Cleopatra*, Shakespeare found a subject that richly indulged the ambiguity of the poet's position, a story that both challenged the claims of raw imaginative power and seductively breathed them forth. The play mounts no case against morality and public order; for certain instants, it simply leaves them behind.

The special theatrical quality of this experience can be felt in a question: what are we to make of a tragedy that finds its climax in an *easy way to die?* Like the acting it requires from its title characters, the action of *Antony and Cleopatra* puts a premium on sensual indulgence, on the unabashed exploitation of what is immediately attractive. Not for this play the suggestion that violent delights have violent ends, the idea which makes the action of *Romeo and Juliet* feel always like fire kissing powder. Instead we are drawn into the rhythm of indulgence itself, following out its becomings, seeking its own fulfillment, the sensual moment indefinitely prolonged, remembered, desired:

> There's not a minute of our lives should stretch
> Without some pleasure now.
>
> (1.1.46–47)

> As sweet as balm, as soft as air, as gentle—
> O, Antony!
>
> (5.2.311–12)

We have seen how Cleopatra's last words focus on physical sensation. As an acting problem, that easy death must be made good by the actress' sensual conviction. Here, as throughout the play, we must be won over by the actors' ability to make the experience of sensation itself admirable and fulfilling—to demonstrate their commitment to pleasure in a way that makes an audience willing to entertain it as "the nobleness of life."

This special focus on the creation of pleasure as an end in itself—on sensuality in performance and *as* performance—places us in an unusual relation to the heroes of the play. Antony and Cleopatra are each other's best audience. They love each other, above all else, for the excellence of their performances ("Good now, play one scene/Of excellent dissembling") (1.3.78-79). If we may be said at all to identify with Antony and Cleopatra, it is their performances we identify with— with the ways in which they are most like the actors who play them, with their abnormal capacity to feel pleasure and desire and to transmit those feelings splendidly to the world. Our identification is the more breathless because we see them risking so much vulgarity and showing their bodies to be used and aging and greedy as well as attractive. We identify with their performances—rather than with the inner movement or constitution of their minds. There is nothing in Antony and Cleopatra that passes show. Indeed, the aim of their action is to find a show which passes everything—all obstacles and competitors—which shackles accidents and bolts up change.

Even more, perhaps, this is a play in which we identify with audiences, with Antony and Cleopatra as each other's audience, with ourselves as audience, and with the audience characters on stage. The play throws us into the position of Octavius in his tent, weeping at the death of a man we could not afford to tolerate among us, wondering (as we always wonder about Octavius) whether or not our tears are real. Our response to the play also resembles our response to and through Enobarbus, whose defection we regret, though in reason we cannot condemn it. As moral observers, we too would defect from Antony—yet to give up on Antony is to desert the life of the play. If we want to go on living after Enobarbus dies, we must remain loyal to this great corrupter of honest men, we must, as Cleopatra says, die where we have lived.

"Doing the Egyptian":[1]
Critical/Theatrical Performances,
Oxford and London, 1906

Barbara Hodgdon

Elizabeth and Leicester
Beating oars
The stern was formed
A gilded shell
Red and gold

> —T. S. Eliot, "The Waste Land" (1922)

And someday, when I'm old-old-old, and rich-rich-rich,
I'm going to buy me a movie projector that will run
nonstop, and I'll sit and watch Elizabeth Taylor make
her entrance into Rome until I croak.

> —Michel Tremblay, *Hosanna* (1974)

Each of these textual moments depends upon and cites a previous performance, calling attention to how "the real" is read through representation, and representation through the real.[2] This is especially obvious with Cleopatra, the figure who inhabits and joins both epigraphs, which mark the beginning and ending of a larger project that investigates the circulation of her cultural capital. Over-seen, over-represented, endlessly reinvented, Egypt's Queen is rarely "herself": instead, she is shaped and perceived in relation to different struggles over history, struggles in which producing a particular "truth" about her organizes and grounds larger cultural narratives.[3] Here, I am interested in pursuing a discrete moment in

---

This essay forms part of Barbara Hodgdon's *Restaging Shakespeare's Cultural Capital: Women, Queens, Spectatorship* (Philadelphia: University of Pennsylvania Press, forthcoming). Reprinted by permission of the University of Pennsylvania Press and the author.

[1]"Doing the Egyptian" refers to a short film (an extract from *Starlight Serenade* [1943]) featuring Wilson, Betty, and Keppel, a song-and-dance team whose specialty was a "sand dance" called "Do the Egyptian." Footage is at the National Film Archive, London.

[2]See Peggy Phelan, *Unmarked: The Politics of Performance* (London and New York: Routledge, 1993), p. 2. See also Judith Butler, "The Force of Fantasy: Feminism, Mapplethorpe, and Discursive Excess," *differences* 2.2 (Summer 1990): 105–25.

[3]For a cultural history of Cleopatra's representations, see Mary Hamer, *Signs of Cleopatra: History, Politics, Representation* (London and New York: Routledge, 1993), esp. pp. xv–xxii, 104. See also Linda Charnes, *Notorious Identity: Materializing the Subject in Shakespeare* (Cambridge, Mass.: Harvard University Press, 1993), pp. 103–47.

what might be called her citational history and in making new use of old evidence. More specifically, I want to explore two scenes of reading *Antony and Cleopatra*— A. C. Bradley's 1906 Oxford lecture on the play and Herbert Beerbohm Tree's production at London's His Majesty's Theatre in the same year—instances which map an interface between criticism, performance, and culture at a crucial historical moment. Because it is within the "discursively saturated materiality" of the historical circumstances in which a text and a performance are read that both make demands for narrative intelligibility, I am less concerned with the text itself than with what Tony Bennett calls its productive activation within intersecting reading formations.[4] My aim is to illuminate the meanings of *Antony and Cleopatra* to particular readers and spectators in a specific sociohistorical moment and so to contribute to discussions about how reading and theatrical effects shape the cultural destiny of a text as well as that of its central icon.[5] As will become apparent, certain shared contexts and constructed identities of the self in relation to historical conditions undergirding these interpretive strategies and affective responses make it possible to read these discourses as symptomatic of turn-of-the-century anxieties about the emergence of mass culture and, just as significantly, about gender, race, and nationality.

Bradley begins his lecture by ventriloquizing Coleridge's breathy assessment of *Antony and Cleopatra*—"wonderful," "astonishing"—but is quick to say it is not "as wonderful an achievement as the greatest of the plays"—that is, those considered in his *Shakespearean Tragedy: Hamlet, Othello, King Lear, and Macbeth*.[6] For when one refers to *Antony and Cleopatra* as "wonderful," one "[thinks] first of the artist and his activity, while in the case of the four famous tragedies it is the product of this activity, the thing presented, that first engrosses us" (282). Elaborating this distinction between the author's imaginative power and his own standard of textual value, Bradley notes that, although the play could be performed with "some flattening of the heroine's part," it is seldom presented. That the first signs of lack attach to an as yet unnamed Cleopatra becomes even more telling as Bradley makes her in part responsible for the play's defective construc-

[4]For the quoted phrase, see Henry Giroux, *Disturbing Pleasures: Learning Popular Culture* (London and New York: Routledge, 1994), p. 98. See Tony Bennett, "Texts, Readers, Reading Formations," *The Bulletin of the Midwest Modern Language Association* 16.1 (1983); rpt. *Modern Literary Theory*, ed. Philip Rice and Patricia Waugh (London: Edward Arnold, 1989), esp. pp. 206–7, 218–20.

[5]For historical reception studies, see Janet Staiger, *Interpreting Films: Studies in the Historical Reception of American Cinema* (Princeton: Princeton University Press, 1992), pp. 1–81. Drawing on recent theories of literary as cinematic reception, Staiger's work offers a precise materialist model. On the reception of silent films based on Shakespeare, see William Uricchio and Roberta E. Pearson, *Reframing Culture: The Case of the Vitagraph Quality Films* (Princeton: Princeton University Press, 1993), pp. 65–110. See also my "Looking for Mr. Shakespeare After 'The Revolution': Robert Lepage's Intercultural *Dream* Machine," *Theorizing Shakespeare in Performance*, ed. James C. Bulman (London and New York: Routledge, forthcoming). For an analysis of literary critics' readings, see L. T. Fitz, "Egyptian Queens and Male Reviewers: Sexist Attitudes in *Antony and Cleopatra* Criticism," *Shakespeare Quarterly* 28 (1977): 297–316.

[6]A. C. Bradley, "Shakespeare's *Antony and Cleopatra*" (1906); rpt. in *Oxford Lectures on Poetry* (London: Macmillan, 1965), pp. 279–308. To simplify citation, I use internal citations for page references to Bradley's essay. Bradley's *Shakespearean Tragedy* was published in 1904.

tion. Recalling how the scenes one remembers in the first three acts are those where she is either "coquetting, tormenting, beguiling her lover to stay," expressing her longing, or, in the messenger scenes, reacting to news of him, he writes: "we read . . . and we should witness [these moments] in delighted wonder and even with amusement," but he considers them the least indispensible to the plot, for they are not "tragic in tone" (284). This initial move pushes Cleopatra out of the (masculinist) space of tragedy and into that of spectacle, where she emerges as an exhibit or animated bauble—a performer, not a character. Yet such defects do not pertain only to her. Bradley also faults the play for not portraying Antony's "inward struggle" and for making the character of Octavius "neither attractive nor wholly clear" (285–86, 288). When measured against Aristotelian models of tragic experience, against Shakespeare's "great" tragedies, and against Bradley's own moralized characterology, the play all too obviously falls far short. Still, he readily acknowledges that the absence of decidedly tragic scenes in the first third contributes to the "peculiar effect" of its close, in which "the greatness of Antony and Cleopatra in their fall is so much heightened by contrast with the world they lose and the conqueror who wins it that the positive element in the final impression, the element of reconciliation, is strongly emphasized" (292). For Bradley, then, *Antony and Cleopatra* attains tragic value primarily, if not exclusively, at its ending, and it is from this vantage point that he can further map its sprawling terrain.

Indeed, it is precisely Shakespeare's flawed structure which permits Bradley to separate Antony *from* Cleopatra and, as though to improve upon Shakespeare, to stage his own reading of their characters. After establishing what he calls the two aspects of the tragedy—the dotage of the "strumpet's fool" and the "tragic excess" exemplified in Antony's "Let Rome in Tiber melt . . . the nobleness of life is to do thus" (1.1.33, 36–37)—he constructs Antony as a hero who, unlike Brutus, Hamlet, or Othello, is not "a man of the noblest type." Nonetheless, he writes, "we sympathise warmly with [him], are greatly drawn to him, and tend to regard him as a noble nature half spoiled by his time" (the sociologist's environmental argument); moreover, because he possesses "a large, open, generous, expansive nature, quite free from envy, capable of great magnanimity, even of entire devotion, . . . we listen to him as we do not to Richard II, partly because he is never unmanly, partly because he himself is sympathetic and longs for sympathy" (294). Securing Antony's manliness on the grounds of empathy frees Bradley to step inside Antony and inhabit his character, where he can produce the illusion of psychological interiority and the motivations he has previously found lacking. Most significantly, it is from that (relatively) safe Roman space that Bradley can not only elaborate Cleopatra's Egyptian otherness but express the desire she represents:

> When he meets Cleopatra he finds his Absolute. She satisfies, nay glorifies, his whole being. She intoxicates his senses. Her wiles, her taunts, her furies and meltings, her laughter and tears, bewitch him all alike. She loves what he loves, and she surpasses him. She can drink him to his bed, out-jest his practical jokes, out-act the best actress who ever amused him, out-dazzle his own magnificence. . . . Her spirit is made of wind and flame, and the poet in him worships her no less than the man. . . . She is his heart's desire

made perfect. To love her is what he was born for. . . . To imagine heaven is to imagine her; to die is to rejoin her. To deny that this is love is the madness of morality. He gives her every atom of his heart (296–97).

Bradley's act of envisioning Cleopatra, through Antony, bears a striking resemblance to the moment where Cleopatra herself dreams of Antony after his death, lines to which Bradley never refers but which remain crucial to his construction of her. Refusing to authorize either her voice or her highly metaphorical praise of Antony, he appropriates her discursive authority—and her hyperbole—as his own, subordinating her textual power to that of the re-textualizing critic.

But perhaps the clearest sign of Bradley's need to contain Cleopatra is that he devotes so little space to her: as he himself acknowledges, "to reserve a fragment of an hour for Cleopatra, if it were not palpably absurd, would seem an insult" (298). And then, as though aware that she might be looking over his shoulder, "If only one could hear her own remarks upon it!" (298). Indeed, Bradley mimics Antony in one of his rages, where he calls Cleopatra "a fragment of Gnaeus Pompey's," but he justifies himself by remarking, "I had to choose between this absurdity and the plan of giving her the whole hour; and to that plan there was one fatal objection. She has been described (by Ten Brink) as a courtesan of genius. So brief a description must needs be incomplete. . . . Still the phrase is excellent; only a public lecture is no occasion for the full analysis and illustration of the character it describes" (298–99). The strategy is wholly transparent. By wrapping his own opinion of Cleopatra within that of another critic, Bradley can not only bolster his own moral authority but express, without necessarily espousing it himself, the overall sense of propriety about sexual matters characteristic of a late Victorian cultural milieu, in which whores (however symbolically central) were hardly suitable topics for public discourse.[7] Yet this disclaimer also introduces Bradley's most fascinating move, through which he is able to transform Cleopatra, with Shakespeare's help, into something else. For Shakespeare, he claims, has paid Cleopatra a unique compliment by devoting the whole of the fifth act to her. Here, "she becomes unquestionably a tragic character, but, it appears to me, not until then" (299). Only when "the heroine"—a term Bradley evokes in relation to

---

[7]On the prevalent anxieties at the time, see Edward Hynes, *The Edwardian Turn of Mind* (Princeton: Princeton University Press, 1968), esp. pp. 172–211, 254–306. For the conflicts, ambivalences, and diversity of attitudes toward sexuality shaping Victorian culture, see Peter Gay, *The Bourgeois Experience: Victoria to Freud*, vol. 1, *Education of the Senses* (Oxford: Oxford University Press, 1984). Born a year after the publication of Tennyson's *In Memoriam*, Bradley died a year before the publication of T. S. Elliot's *Collected Poems*; S. L. Bethell's comment, "Shakespeare made in the image of a Victorian intellectual," illustrates the tendency of later critics, even though *Shakespearean Tragedy* was published two years after Victoria's death, to label him. See *Shakespeare and the Popular Dramatic Tradition* (London: Staples Press, 1948), p. 53. Several years later, John Dover Wilson came to his defense: "It took some pluck . . . for an elderly Victorian gentleman to echo with enthusiasm Dolabella's cry, 'Most sovereign creature!' " See the New Cambridge Edition of *Antony and Cleopatra* (Cambridge: Cambridge University Press, 1950), p. xvii. Katherine Cooke provides an account of the "Victorian" Bradley in *A. C. Bradley and His Influence in Twentieth-Century Shakespeare Criticism* (Oxford: Clarendon Press, 1972), pp. 62–89. See also Nina Auerbach, *Women and the Demon: The Life of a Victorian Myth* (Cambridge, Mass.: Harvard University Press, 1982), pp. 209–17.

Cleopatra with a difficulty that shows him wary of traditional generic categories—emerges into the recognizable space of Aristotelian tragedy already marked by Antony's (somewhat qualified) heroic masculinity does she become *decently* readable.

Even so, he approaches her cautiously, first, by praising her as an authorial creation and then by situating her with Hamlet and Falstaff as an "inexhaustible" character. "You feel," he remarks, "that, if they were alive and you spent your whole life with them, their infinite variety could never be staled with custom; they would continue every day to surprise, perplex, and delight you" (299). Appropriating Enobarbus' description of Cleopatra to characterize Hamlet and Falstaff and to frame her between them, Bradley draws her closer to the fat knight than to Denmark's prince, citing vanity as the trait joining the two.[8] And just as he marks Falstaff's character as deriving meaning from Prince Hal (who gives him "dignity" and "pathos"), what raises Cleopatra into "pure tragedy" is her love for Antony (300). That move, however, amounts to damning with faint praise, for it permits Bradley to position her in an Egyptian version of the Boar's Head tavern-brothel milieu—the space of "the popular," at least insofar as it is associated with a "low" comic Falstaff, not a tragical Hamlet. It is also, of course, the space of rejection. And that space is even more deliberately marked off when, alluding to the messenger scene in which she draws a knife, Bradley writes that "she resembles (if I dare say it) Doll Tearsheet sublimated" (301).

Unlike his interiorized map of Antony's character, Bradley's Cleopatra is constructed from externals: any "character" she possesses is written on her sexualized body. Calling her irresistible, Bradley notes that "she has developed nature into a consummate art"; her mind, he says, is saturated with desire and with her own desirability, and she glories in her sexual history even as Antony tries to shame her with it. Her "exquisitely sensitive" body is that of someone who "lives for feeling"; her egocentricity and self-presentation mark her as an eternal feminine, which is further tainted by theatricality (300). In some sense, "Shakespeare" can be held responsible for Bradley's moves. After all, once Antony dies, Cleopatra defines herself as "no more but e'en a woman." Yet what becomes increasingly obvious is that a little touch of Cleo goes a long way toward proving that she falls far short of the Victorian womanly ideal.[9] Although she is a mother, "the threat of Octavius to destroy her children if she takes her own life passes by her like the wind. She ruins

[8]In aligning Cleopatra with Hamlet and Falstaff, Bradley seems poised to anticipate present-day critical strategies figuring all three as inhabiting both masculine and feminine positionalities. On Hamlet, see, for instance, David Leverenz, "The Woman in Hamlet: An Interpersonal View," *Representing Shakespeare: New Psychoanalytic Essays*, ed. Murray M. Schwartz and Coppélia Kahn (Baltimore: Johns Hopkins University Press, 1980), pp. 110–28. On Falstaff, see Coppélia Kahn, *Man's Estate: Masculine Identity in Shakespeare* (Berkeley: University of California Press, 1981), p. 72; and Valerie Traub, "Prince Hal's Falstaff: Positioning Psychoanalysis and the Female Body," *Shakespeare Quarterly* 40 (1989): 456–74.

[9]See Auerbach, *Woman and the Demon*, p. 213. For how advertising exploited the domestic image of Victoria, see Thomas Richards, *The Commodity Culture of Victorian England: Advertising and Spectacle, 1851–1914* (Stanford: Stanford University Press, 1990), pp. 73–118.

a great man but shows no sense of the tragedy of his ruin," nor can she comprehend "the anguish of spirit that appears in his language to his servants [which] is
far beyond her" (301). Had she followed Antony directly to her own death, that
would have shown that she loved him better than her own freedom, but she is
entirely willing to survive her lover and to cheat her victor of most of her accumu-
lated wealth. Her final "fault," then, is her delay about dying, a decision made only
when she learns that she will be carried to Rome in triumph. For Bradley, to die
for love—and without material wealth—would be to die for the right reason. But
that would pull Cleopatra away from "tragedy" and into the space of domestic
melodrama, give her status as a redeemed fallen woman.

Tellingly, then, his account of Cleopatra's final moments once again improves
upon and retextualizes Shakespeare. Eliding any mention of her motherly image
or of the fantasized absent marriage so central to the close, he caps his qualified
encomium with the image of Cleopatra travelling to meet her lover "in the splendour that crowned and robed her long ago, when her barge burnt on the water
like a burnished throne, and she floated to Cydnus on the enamoured stream to
take him captive for ever" (303). Somewhat ironically, in lauding this passage
(and this essay) as Bradley's finest criticism, M. R. Ridley, the Arden editor and
the author of Bradley's biography in the *Dictionary of National Biography*,
notes what he calls a "geographical error" (presumably the reference to
Cydnus).[10] Yet that "error" tellingly conveys Bradley's desire to push Cleopatra
into the space of the captivating enchantress/prostituted other, where, safely
enclosed by a travellers' tale from "long ago," she can remain a character for the
past, not the present.

If it is as "queanly queen" that Bradley finally (if a bit grudgingly, for he never
gives her her royal title) fixes Cleopatra, he also willing admits, Enobarbus-like,
that she "laughs at definition." Citing "I am fire and air" as the moment which
comes closest to describing her, he notes this, parenthetically, as "(a passage sur-
passed in poetry, if at all, only by the final speech of Othello)." Yet her "final
ecstasy," he quickly adds, strikes readers as an effort "strained and prodigious (I
would not say factitious)": however glorious, it is not, like Othello's last speech,
"the final expression of character, of thoughts and emotions which have dominated
a whole life" (304). That it is Othello who comes to mind, drifts into view, is the
only *textual* sign that Bradley is connecting two Oriental others. Two long footnotes, however, make this move to rob her of "character" altogether by comparing
her to the masculine hero of one of the Fab Four Tragedies more explicit, for both
work to rewrite Cleopatra's sentient body into a non-Western, non-English body.
In one, he suggests that she is not beautiful but "black"—by which he means a
blackness entirely unlike that of the "*bold* black eyes" of Tennyson's Cleopatra—
and to other her as "gipsy" and "witch," thus separating her enticing difference
from an acceptable literary image of blackness (307–8). In another, he reiterates
his desire that she love Antony more, for this would gain her his admiration, turn

---

[10]M. R. Ridley, *Dictionary of National Biography* (1931–40), pp. 99–100.

her into an Imogen, Shakespeare's heroine most compounded of "fire and air," a properly British mixture which had enabled Swinburne (again, Bradley clothes himself in another critic's robes) to call her "the woman above all Shakespeare's women" (303-4; 307)

Finally, in Bradley's estimation, readers experience disenchantment, are fixed in paradox: "we are saddened by the very fact that the catastrophe saddens us so little; it pains us that we should feel so much triumph and pleasure" (304). Absent here is the "keen sorrow" produced by Romeo and Juliet, Hamlet and Othello and consonant with our judgment of their nobility and beauty, with "wish[ing] that fate had opposed them to a weaker enemy, dream[ing] possibly of the life they might then have led." Not so with Antony or Cleopatra. Writes Bradley, "It is better for the world's sake, and not less for their own, that they should fail and die" (304). Marking them as "tarnished" and "half-ruined" by their citational past, Bradley imagines a notion of "character" that writes its stable effects into, and on, the world. Although he claims to be saddened by his inability to mourn their passing, Bradley concludes by returning to the high ground of tragedy, inhabited by nobility and beauty so displayed as to elicit and command "unreserved admiration or love; or, when, in default of this, the forces which move the agents, and the conflict which results from these forces, attain a terrifying and overwhelming power" (305). Although this move offers to remove *Antony and Cleopatra* from consideration as a tragedy, Bradley quickly rectifies the dilemma he has talked himself into by saying that the play "does not attempt to satisfy these conditions, and then fails in the attempt"; rather, "it attempts something different. . . . In doing so it gives us what no other tragedy can give, and it leaves us, no less than any other, lost in astonishment at the powers that created it" (305). Given the structure of his essay, one might conclude that it is Cleopatra who has led him here, captured in "her strong toil of grace," from which he neatly steps away, circles back to Coleridge's romantic "astonishing," and defers critical activity to Shakespeare's imagination. That Bradley evokes the nexus of tragedy and authorial power to account for his last judgment strongly suggests a protectionist move associated with Matthew Arnold's cultural classicism—the need to set up boundaries around *Antony and Cleopatra* in order to recover it for high culture. But, at the last, the "something different" that *Antony and Cleopatra* represents—which he associates with flawed structure, with heroes whose lacks do not satisfy the moral prerogatives of early twentieth-century textual (and social) masculinity, and with eroticized feminine display—remains unnameable. Not, however, because it is so privately fantasized that it cannot be spoken in public. Rather, Bradley can only hint at what seems to him an improper mix of the "high" and the "low," a threateningly anarchic text in which he seems to hear a "melancholy, long, withdrawing roar" that leaves him stranded, perhaps irretrievably, alone with Cleopatra "on a darkling plain."[11]

---

[11]The phrases, of course, are from Matthew Arnold's proto-modernist lament, "Dover Beach" (1867).

What Bradley can only leave inchoate, Herbert Beerbohm Tree's *Antony and Cleopatra* at London's His Majesty's Theatre brings squarely into view.[12] For under his direction—he also played Antony to Constance Collier's Cleopatra—the play travels deep into the territory Bradley's lecture envisions but fears to name: a theatrical heart of darkness where "Shakespeare" rubs shoulders with low culture and the feminine and becomes readable along a colonial-imperial axis. If noting that the production opened on 27 December, at the height of the Christmas pantomine season, immediately situates its spectacular (and characteristic, for Tree) scenic extravagances within a mass culture context,[13] perhaps the perfect emblem for an oppositional "high-culture" spectatorship appears in the *Daily Chronicle*'s mention of two distinguished audience members, Mr. Winston Churchill and Miss Marie Corelli, facing one another in stage-side boxes: a soon-to-be representative of Empire's government and the American author of romantic sentimental novels who had invaded Stratford-upon-Avon to take up residence in Hall's Croft and later at Mason Croft, and who liked to think of herself, if not as Shakespeare's literary heiress, then certainly as a protector of his "greatness" and his name.[14] Whether or not Bradley himself may have also been a spectator,[15] it is nonetheless

[12]Prompt copies for Tree's *Antony and Cleopatra* are in the Beerbohm Tree Archive at the University of Bristol. See also *Antony and Cleopatra as Arranged for the Stage by Herbert Beerbohm Tree*, illustrated with photographs by F. W. Burford (London: Warrington & Co., 1907), a book presented on the occasion of the fiftieth performance of *Antony and Cleopatra* at His Majesty's Theatre, 8 February 1907. For a stage history of the play, see Margaret Lamb, *Antony and Cleopatra on the English Stage* (Rutherford: Farleigh Dickinson University Press, 1980).

[13]"Mr. Tree's 'Antony.' Spectacular Triumph at His Majesty's Theatre. Fine Reception," *The Daily Chronicle* 28 December 1906. The conjunction of pantomime and Victorian spectacular Shakespeare points to an intriguing syncretism of imperial (and capitalistic) values. Said the *Star*'s critic of the 1900 *The Sleeping Beauty and the Beast*, "The Drury Lane pantomime, that national institution, is a symbol of Empire. It is the biggest thing of the kind in the world, it is prodigal of money, of invention, of splendour, of men and women; but it is without the sense of beauty or the restraining influence of taste. . . . Only a great nation could have done such a thing; only an undisciplined nation would have done it" (27 December 1900). Quoted in Michael R. Booth, *Victorian Spectacular Theatre 1850–1910* (London: Routledge & Kegan Paul, 1981), p. 89. On "Egyptian" pantomimes, see David Mayer, *Harlequin in His Element: The English Pantomime, 1806–1836* (Cambridge, Mass.: Harvard University Press, 1969), pp. 147, 154–57. See also A. E. Wilson, *The Story of Pantomime* (Totowa, N. J.: Rowman and Littlefield, 1974). Egyptian tropes were also caught up by burlesque. For one that betrays British anxieties about "the East," see F. C. Burnand, *Antony and Cleopatra; or, His-Tory and Her-Story in a Modern Nilo-Metre* (1866); rpt. in *Nineteenth-Century Shakespeare Burlesques*, ed. Stanley Wells (London: Diploma Press, Ltd, 1978): 4: 141–91.

[14]Corelli had a particular connection to Tree's production. She made an excuse not to lend her rare Egyptian necklace, found during the construction of the Nile barrage and presented to her by Sir John Aird, to Constance Collier to wear on stage because she had been warned in a dream by the necklace's original owner; as the (apocryphal) story goes, the substitute Collier wore fell to the stage in pieces. See Brian Masters, *Now Barabbas Was a Rotter: The Extraordinary Life of Marie Corelli* (London: Hamish Hamilton Ltd, 1978), p. 284n. Mason Croft, located on Church Street, now houses The Shakespeare Institute. For a brief account of Marie Corelli's stormy relationship with the Stratford community, see Nicholas Fogg, *Stratford-upon-Avon: Portrait of a Town* (Chichester: Phillimore and Co., Ltd., 1986), pp. 214–18.

[15]Although Bradley is often considered an academic who knew little about the theatre, a 1909 article on *King Lear* suggests that his criticism was informed by a knowledge of Elizabethan as well as contemporary staging; the piece also suggests his dissatisfaction with Victorian spectacular theatre. See "The Locality of *King Lear* Act I Scene ii," *Modern Language Review* 4 (January 1909): 238–40. See also his 1902 lecture, "Shakespeare's Theatre and Audience," rpt. *Oxford Lectures*, pp. 361–95.

possible to imagine him present at its scene of reading, for his influence is apparent not only in Tree's view of the play as the "tragedy of a world-passion" and in his
view of Cleopatra as "the greatest courtesan that ever led man from the path of
politics—the eternal feminine that 'beggared all description' and that ruled and
undid empires and emperors"[16]—but also in the reviewers' accounts, which net in
Bradleyean interpretive strategies to frame their responses as well as to shape
their discourse.

Like Bradley, the *Times'* critic marks the first three acts as diffuse and difficult
to follow, noting constant changes of scene and variety of characters as flaws he
associates both with Cleopatra and with Clio—that is, with too much feminine display and too much history; and the *Telegraph* shares Bradley's opinon that the play
is of a wholly different design from the "major" tragedies—even a "long and sham-
bling affair," according to the *Daily Chronicle*.[17] The *Evening News* confirms that
it is only in the last acts, which become "simple, straightforward, passionate, close-
knit, [and] intense," that the representation achieves the virtues of unity accorded
to tragedy.[18] For many, it is primarily within this "masculine" space that Cleopatra
appears "right royal": mimicking Bradley's organizational strategy, reviewers
address the structural defects of the play and the production and delay considering
the more local effects of her presence until the end of their commentary. Such
pronounced evidence of traffic between literary and theatrical cultures also pervades the *Play Pictorial*, which praises Tree's ability to make "the vivid mind of the
author stand forth without burdening the poet's conception with extravagant
details" and which, by evoking Antony's "artist-nature," aligns him with
Shakespeare.[19] So, too, with the *Telegraph*'s critic, who cites "I am dying, Egypt"
(4.15.41), "Unarm Eros, the long day's task is done" (4.14.35) and "Give me my
robe, put on my crown" (5.2.279) as moments when Shakespeare's masterful
authorial voice transcended Tree's theatrical practice.

If Bradley's critical performance functions to determine and reinforce particular meanings and to mediate between text and performance, two reviewers
were willing to extrapolate his objections. Faulting Shakespeare as well as Tree,
the *Daily Chronicle* considers the "real drama" as that between "Antony's might

---

[16]Tree, "Introduction," *Antony and Cleopatra as Arranged for the Stage*, n.p. In one *Antony and Cleopatra* prompt book (Charles H. Shattuck, *The Shakespeare Promptbooks: A Descriptive Catalogue* [Urbana: University of Illinois, 1965], p. 37), Tree's marginal note reads, "Cleo the eternal new woman."

[17]"Antony and Cleopatra," *The Times* 28 December 1906; "'Antony and Cleopatra'" Magnificent Spectacle at His Majesty's Theatre," *The Telegraph* 28 December 1906. Citations are provided only for the first reference to a review. All reviews are from press books in the Beerbohm Tree Archive, The University of Bristol. My thanks to Barbara A. Kachur for providing copies. Although the review discourse configures an overall pattern of values, it is important to keep in mind that such discourse not only represents class- and gender-inflected evidence that excludes marginalized voices but works to essentialize a particular cultural positionality or identity. One way to problematize that would be to take this kind of historical reception study further by tracing the identities and penchants of the (for the most part) unnamed reviewers.

[18]"Antony and Cleopatra: Mr. Tree's Newest Production," *The Evening News* 28 December 1906.

[19]B. W. Findon, "The Production and the Players," *The Play Pictorial* 9.54 (1906), p. 226.

and Octavius' intelligence," finds it lacking, and blames Cleopatra as responsible for the result: mere "scenic display." Mirroring Bradley's discomfort with Shakespeare's mix of "high" and "low" in which public and private domestic spaces traverse one another, erasing boundaries between them, the *Saturday Review*'s critic would reconfigure the play *either* as a political affair or as a domestic romance. Citing *Julius Caesar* as the better play, to which *Antony and Cleopatra* is "merely an epilogue" able to be dismissed as "sordid and unroman-tic . . . : vulgar charm used supremely for the ends of sheerly selfish policy and vulgar lust," he would eliminate Cleopatra from history, which he views as a dis-course for men only as well as one separate from drama. Deeply sceptical of "any woman's eyes making or unmaking an empire," his fear of her gaze prompts him to argue that Cleopatra "ought to be the cause of the quarrel and should satisfy as a sufficient cause," but does not.[20] His view anticipates T. S. Eliot's objections that Gertrude's "insufficiency" makes *Hamlet* a flawed play:[21] just as Eliot's Gertrude becomes a nothing, subject to erasure, Cleopatra is "but a gorgeous prostitute, playing for her own advantage; and Antony is a poor creature who allows his politics to spoil his pleasure and his pleasure to spoil his politics." For him, the result is that all sympathy goes to Octavius—a move Bradley gestures toward but, given his distaste for the "dishonest" Caesar who would use his sister as an object of political exchange, could not bring himself to articulate. As it turns out, however, the circumstances that prompt the reviewer's comment are particular to Tree's production, where Basil Gill's Caesar presented a more attractively British exemplar of masculinity than Tree's Antony, who, according to the *Daily Chronicle*'s critic, "is for the most part an amiable, and charming, but essentially weak epicure," which made him wonder about "Cleopatra's inter-esting preferences."

If distinctions between material theatrical bodies can prompt critics to rewrite both history and play, they can also occasion a more blatant move to push Tree's production and the play's characters into a foreign space appropriate to a treatment of "sexual infatuation in the grand style." Mentioning the *chassé-croisé* of Imperial politics and situating Cleopatra as a *grande amoureuse* and Antony as the typical victim of *Venus entière à sa proie attachée*, the *Times*' critic marks the non-Englishness of the tragedy in order to establish a "healthy" Shakespeare who "knew better than to give up to a pair of *detraqués* the absolute monopoly of his stage." His string of French phrases serves to highlight a strategy of displacement that will become more apparent in critics' comments on stage spectacle and on Cleopatra—one that denies Britain's own colonial enterprise in Egypt, solidified by the terms of the 1904 Entente Cordiale, by which France gave up claims to Egypt in return for British backing for their claims in Morocco, and further confirmed by the Algeciras

[20]Harold Hodge, *The Saturday Review* 5 January 1907.
[21]T. S. Eliot, "Hamlet" (1919); rpt. *Selected Prose of T. S. Eliot*, ed. Frank Kermode (New York: Harcourt Brace Jovanovich, 1975), pp. 45–49. For a feminist critique of Eliot's position, see Jacqueline Rose, "Sexuality in the Reading of Shakespeare: *Hamlet* and *Measure for Measure*," *Alternative Shakespeares*, ed. John Drakakis (London: Methuen, 1985), pp. 95–118.

conference in January 1906.[22] Only the critic for the *Evening News*, in calling Tree's production "very timely," seemed aware that it might do more than secure a textual—or critical—real, that it might bear traces of a present-day history marked by the negotiations of contemporary imperial colonizers.[23]

Tree's own interests lay in securing a somewhat different historical real. Mapping out what at first seems a colonized reversal of empire, his programme note situates his authority in other "authentic" texts and promises to detail the political and military events that led to the "all-powerful Triumvir" becoming "Cleopatra's slave." Ultimately, however, he is less intrigued by the political than, like Enobarbus, by the lure of Oriental extravagance. Referring to Pliny's description of Cleopatra's entertainments, he positions Antony and Cleopatra at the center of an exoticized consumer society, "The Inimitable Livers," and recounts the tale of Cleopatra's banquet for Antony where she herself consumed ten million sesterces—which he estimates at £100,000—by taking a rare and unique pearl from her earring, dropping it into a vessel filled with vinegar, and swallowing the melted gem. The fellow pearl, found by Octavius Caesar among the treasures of Cleo after her death, was divided and hung on the ears of the Venus in the Pantheon at Rome—a perfect emblem of imperial control over the exotic East.[24] If, as Edward Said argues, the discourses of Egyptology, antiquarianism, and Orientalism produced Britain's *intellectual* authority over the Orient,[25] Tree's production serves as a library or archive of those discourses, their knowledges appropriated for popular pleasure. Just as Bradley had retextualized *Antony and Cleopatra*, Tree retextualizes Egypt for the material theatre. Drawing on English, German, and French texts, Tree's designer, Percy Macquoid, deliberately chose to represent Egypt as a "ruder civilization" than that of the Ptolemaic period. Although the first of the Ptolemies was a Greek by descent, Macquoid argues that "Egyptian surroundings and incidental accidents of marriage had very materially affected the personal appearance, tastes, and manners of the later branch of the family," so that Cleopatra's features are "neither Greek nor Roman, but Semitic"[26]—a racial nuance preserved in production photographs of Constance Collier in full or half-profile, demonstrating her "authentically 'Semitic'" nose (see Figs. 1 and 2). Among these material effects,

[22]See Eric Hobsbawm, *The Age of Empire 1875–1914* (New York: Pantheon Books, 1987), pp. 317–22.

[23]Work by Ralph Berry begins to explore Tree's visions of Empire, especially in relation to connections between Great Britain and Rome. See "Beerbohm Tree as Director: Three Shakespearean Productions," *Essays in Theatre* 1.2 (1983): 81–89; and "The Imperial Theme," *Shakespeare and the Victorian Stage*, ed. Richard Foulkes (Cambridge: Cambridge University Press, 1986), pp. 153–60. Barbara A. Kachur provides a fine analysis in "Tree's Scenography as Interpretation: *Richard II, The Merchant of Venice*, and *Antony and Cleopatra*," paper delivered at the 1994 Leicester conference. My thanks to Kachur for sharing her work. For a pertinent collection of essays, see *Imperialism and Popular Culture*, ed. John M. Mackenzie (Manchester: Manchester University Press, 1986).

[24]Excerpt from Tree's programme note, reprinted in *The Play Pictorial* 9.54, n.p.

[25]See Edward Said, *Orientalism* (New York: Random House, 1979), p. 19 and *passim*.

[26]Macquoid quoted in B. L., "*Antony and Cleopatra*: Mr. Tree's Production at His Majesty's Theatre," *Evening Standard* 28 December 1906.

Figures 1 and 2. Constance Collier as Cleopatra, in Beerbohm Tree's 1906 production of *Antony and Cleopatra* at His Majesty's Theatre, from *Play Pictorial* Volume 9 (#54). Courtesy of The Shakespeare Centre, The Shakespeare Birthplace Trust, Stratford-on-Avon.

Tree's programme, which describes Egyptian clothing, wigs, and birds and compares their furniture to Empire styles, notes in passing that a "favorable conceit" was figures of captive Jews and Asiatics supporting tables and chairs, and that the faces of conquered peoples were painted on the soles of Egyptian shoes. Not surprisingly, a "Nero chest" and a "Jew Table" appear in "Cleopatra's Boudoir," where an oleander bush, a "love chair," a "Hawk chair," incense burners, and animal skins fold signs of exotic passion together with those of a savage, barbaric East.[27] Like the Egyptian bazaars that had become a regular feature of world's fairs from the mid-nineteenth century forward, this particular version of the *Exposition Universelle*'s "Rue de Caire"—reproduced at the Greater Britain (1862) and Chicago Columbian (1893) expositions and in Paris in 1900[28]—was enough like these "peopled exhibits" of exotic otherness that spectators who had seen such human displays might well think they were somewhere other than His Majesty's, experiencing (like Bradley) "something else" than Shakespeare's tragedy.

Many did. Objecting that Shakespeare "has no roots in antiquarianism," the *Saturday Review* dismisses Tree's "archaeological trammels" and praises Shakespeare for "concerning himself solely with men and women"—the liberal humanist argument that betrays the critic's own preference for intimate "realist" theatre and reveals his distaste for late nineteenth- and early twentieth-century conventions of popular theatre. Circulating a familiar binary that privileges hearing over seeing, language over spectacular absorption, the *Star* opposes "History, Poetry and Dramatic Action" to "the transcendental demands of Display," and the *Pall Mall Gazette*'s critic aligns non-reading audiences satisfied by Tree's "common" spectacles and pictorial shows with Hamlet's groundlings, unable to appreciate Shakespeare's poetry but rapt by "dumb-shows and noise." Tree, he asserts, founds his production upon the assumption that Shakespeare was "an inarticulate genius, unable to explain what he imagines": "amount[ing] to an endeavour to help Shakespeare out," the whole performance is "vulgarized, modernised in the bad sense, depoeticised in every sense."[29] Clearly, such class-inflected commentary aims at guarding the Bard for a high-culture realm where poetry and artistic genius may be protected for an audience of (masculine) readers. But what also becomes clear is that the vulgar modern spectacle as well as the "noise"—the music that haunts Antony, even in Rome—are associated with Cleopatra. It is precisely through this nexus of devalued terms that reviewers push Tree's *Antony and Cleopatra* into the space of a feminized mass culture of dreams and delusions where, countering Horkheimer and Adorno, far from being

[27]See Tree, *Antony and Cleopatra* prompt copy (Shattuck's #28), ground plan for "Act II Scene 2. Cleopatra's Boudoir."

[28]See Paul Greenhalgh, *Ephemeral Vistas: The* Expositions Universelles, *Great Exhibitions, and World's Fairs 1851–1939* (Manchester: Manchester University Press, 1988), pp. 102–4.

[29]A. L. E., "His Majesty's Theatre, 'Antony and Cleopatra,' " *Star* 28 December 1906; H. Hamilton Pye, "The Worst Woman in Egypt," *Pall Mall Gazette* 2 January 1907.

the "most beautiful in the land,"[30] it can be disavowed as not English and demonized (as in the *Pall Mall Gazette*'s title) "The Worst Woman in Egypt." Moreover, it is in terms of an interface with a prefilmic and early filmic culture which threatens to absorb Shakespeare that Bradley's "something else" becomes readable in a new way.

Dissociating the play from a "well-composed" tragedy, the *Telegraph* labels it a panorama, and the *Evening News* characterizes the evening as "a trip to Egypt, personally conducted by the popular actor-manager," while the *Star* claims that Tree's arbitrary tableaux suggest nothing so much as "a course of History Made Easy: Limelight Illustrations." In particular, he faults the "magic lantern pictures of the Sphinx" which framed the opening and the close: these "remind one of nothing so much as the method they have in certain suburban theatres of wiling away the entr'actes"—a reference to the stereopticon "shows" that had become a regular feature of such venues. Objecting that the Roman scenes as well as those detailing the battles and the camp (which Tree had attempted to "weld into closer compass") become "mere kinematographs," The *Times* aligns them with the highly condensed cinematic versions of "classics"—novels as well as plays—which rendered long scenes in tableaux lasting thirty seconds to a minute.[31] This array of comments not only serves as a fascinating marker of a cultural formation at a crucial point of change but intersects with another history. The concatenation of Egypt with ancestral cinematic forms—panoramas, dioramas, and lantern shows—intensified in Britain with the opening of the overland trade route to India in the 1840s, and, although Tree's reviewers probably would not have seen the first feature-length, British-made panoramic river trip—a transparent panorama of the Nile, opening in London at the Egyptian Hall on 16 July 1849—they might well have seen Pathé's 1906 *A Policeman's Tour of the World*, which included traveling shots of the Suez Canal, or that same company's *The Life and Passion of Jesus Christ* (1902–3), where "The Flight to Egypt" was signified by the Sphinx against which Mary and the child rest.[32] Thus the *Saturday Review*'s comment—"[The Sphinx] is a bad symbol, for this is not an Egyptian but essentially a world-drama. Cleopatra herself is not an Egyptian but a Greek princess. We do not need a Sphinx to tell us that Egypt is the venue of most of the action"—can be read both as a move to distance "Shakespeare" from popular entertainments and as a

[30]See Max Horkheimer and Theodor W. Adorno, "Das Schema der Massenkultur," *Gesammelte Schriften* 3 (Frankfurt am Main: Suhrkamp, 1981), p. 305; cited in Andreas Huyssen, *After the Great Divide: Modernism, Mass Culture, Postmodernism* (Bloomington: Indiana University Press, 1986), p. 48.

[31]See Richard Abel, *The Ciné Goes to Town: French Cinema 1896–1914* (Berkeley: University of California Press, 1994), pp. 60–61, 81–86, 99, 162–67, 181–83.

[32]See Antonia Lant, "The Curse of the Pharaoh, or How Cinema Contracted Egyptomania," *October* 59 (Winter 1992): 102. In 1821, the Egyptian Hall had housed the Egyptian antiquities amassed by Giovanni Belzoni, under the auspices of Henry Salt, the British Consul-General at Alexandria from 1815–27; later added to the British Museum, they joined already substantial holdings which had come to the nation in 1801 under the terms of Napoleon's surrender and were given to the Museum by George III. See Geoffrey Grigson, *Art Treasures of the British Museum* (New York: Harry N. Abrams, Inc., 1958), pp. 22–26.

scarcely veiled attempt to deny or deflect attention from Britain's own imperial obsessions.

As Antonia Lant argues, "clearly the burgeoning of images of Egypt folds into a colonialist project that involved mapping and photographing, claiming both a territory and its subjects by reproducing them in visual form."[33] These habits are well-noted as defining characteristics of late nineteenth- and early twentieth-century politics and culture, spurred by imperialism and accompanied, as Michel Foucault notes, by the rise of the classifying disciplines of anthropology, geography, archaeology, and ethnography.[34] Just as photographic images *taken* (an operative term) outside Europe and exhibited within its boundaries functioned as symbolic markers of colonial possession, Tree's moving scenes and tableaux can be understood as another symptom of the need to conceive of and grasp the rest of the world as though it were an exhibition for Western pleasure and use. Indeed, the Roman Antony's "in the east my pleasure lies" (2.3.39) prefigures a specific traffic between the discourse of British imperial politics and the stage, for what transfers to it resembles Antony's free-floating mythology of the Orient, in which an array of figures and images—Cleopatra, the Sphinx, Isis, and Osiris—tropes its immense fecundity and mystery.[35] In making that array knowable through triumphant Western technologies—in this case, a theatrical technology of spectacular display—Tree pulled Egyptology and the stage together to meet the needs and obsessions of the early twentieth-century imagination. At its crudest, this need can be figured in terms of national identity: the Edwardian psyche aspiring to the imperial grandeur of past kingdoms while confronting again and again in this desire its recent demises and losses, its isolation from Europe, and the looming specter of a new world order.[36] Moreover, the still-dominant Victorian preoccupation with sexuality, especially female sexuality, could be thematized through an Egyptian imagery of powerful queens and bewildering Sphinxes, all made vivid through delineating the details of an everyday life that positioned the Orient as a territory watched over by a Western spectator who is the judge and jury of its behavior.

As though echoing Lord Cromer, the man who, in the words of Arthur James Balfour, had "*made* Egypt," reviewers affirm rationality as the determining trait of the British colonizer, distinguishing between the classical austerity of Tree's

---

[33]Lant, "The Curse of the Pharaoh," p. 96. See also Abel, *The Ciné Goes to Town*, pp. 256–60, 264.

[34]See, for example, Michel Foucault, *Discipline and Punish: The Birth of the Prison*, trans. Alan Sheridan (New York: Vintage Books, 1979).

[35]Said, *Orientalism*, pp. 63–65. In the late nineteenth century, Cleopatra even reached the Canadian Far West and Alaska. See Chad Evans, *Frontier Theatre: A History of Nineteenth-Century Theatrical Entertainment in the Canadian Far West and Alaska* (Victoria: Sono Nis Press, 1983), which includes a photograph (between pp. 144–45) of "Little Egypt." The last automaton, made by an American, Cecil Nixon, was called Isis and depicted "a bare-breasted, dark-skinned woman playing a zither while reclining on a couch decorated with leopard skins, hieroglyphs, and 'other Egyptian motifs.'. . . When the temperature rose above 80° F Isis moved her veil until the temperature fell." See Michael Taussig, *Mimesis and Alterity: A Particular History of the Senses* (New York and London: Routledge, 1993), pp. 219–20. My thanks to Denis Salter for calling my attention to both references.

[36]See Hynes, *Edwardian Turn of Mind*, pp. 5–53.

Roman scenes (a series of "Tadema pictures," according to the *Daily Chronicle*), which bespoke the decorum of a stately, ordered world that operates according to military precision, and the "sensuous voluptuousness" of what the *Evening Standard* described as Alexandria's "deep mysterious blues of sea and sky, frequently crowded by soldiers, slaves, singers, and dancers in dresses of dazzling colours and unaccustomed forms."[37] The *Telegraph*'s critic acknowledged a "strange pervasive influence of Oriental luxury and vice" and marvelled at how the music's "characteristic Eastern note steals into our sense as a symbol of the mingled barbarism and culture of Egypt." Overcome with the "subtle glamour of the East" fleshed out in Tree's display of what Cromer had called "subject races," he lists those aspects of spectacle "giv[ing] bodily semblance to the inner meaning of the play": "the dancing girls, with their strange emblems," the "lavish Oriental ballets," the "gaudy gold which decorates their palaces," their walls bearing "monstrous figures," and their rooms filled with "beautiful silken canopies and cushioned divans." All, he writes, was controlled by "artistic knowledge and grace" (else he could not be so thoroughly enraptured) through which "we become conscious to the full of the fatal spell which the conquest of Egypt laid upon its Western invaders." Consumed by the lure of Orientalism, he becomes a consumer of the production's excess, using it as a dreamtext upon which he can publicly write the luxuriant fantasies of his imaginative engagement as a spectator.

And he was not alone, for other reviews, notably the *Evening Standard*'s, reveal a heterodox acceptance of Tree's pictorial drama, mentioning in particular the appearance of "the barge with its scented sails and its dimpled boys" as "show[ing] us something which will linger in the memory of the eye as well as the ear." But if such phrases mark Orientalism in full flower, one tableau in particular disturbed most critics. Like Bradley, Tree was especially concerned to elucidate the sudden and unexpected transition from Antony directing Roman government to the news that he is "in the toils of the Egyptian Queen" and so took the occasion to depict Antony's triumphant return to Egypt, where Cleopatra, crowned as Isis in a gown described by the *Daily Graphic* as a sheer column of "shimmering silver embroidery, with mantle of cloth of silver, and the high mystic headdress of the goddess" and flanked by her illegitimate children, enthroned him in the marketplace (Fig. 3).[38] Although the tenor of reviewers' complaints clearly extends beyond cheapening Shakespeare with vulgar spectacle, the fully transgressive potential of Tree's tableau would not emerge until six years later, when, read through Freud's *Totem and Taboo*, it could be understood as an image of the family outside or prior to Oedipal law, ruled by a decadent *femme fatale*, and of the troubling fantasy of a polygamous patriarch who, killed outside the law, loses his legitimacy. Indeed,

[37]On Cromer as an "accomplished technician of Empire," see Said, *Orientalism*, pp. 38–44. Denis Salter calls attention to how the proscenium arch, with its origins in the Renaissance, developed in tandem with imperialism, exploration, and colonization and functioned as a brilliantly designed aesthetic and ideological instrument for the appropriation—and domestication—of exotic time and place, bringing it under the control of the symbolical domain.

[38]"*Antony and Cleopatra*: Mr. Tree's New Shakespearian Production," *Daily Graphic* 28 December 1906.

Figure 3. Beerbohm Tree's 1906 production of *Antony and Cleopatra* at His Majesty's Theatre. From *The Daily Telegraph*, Friday, December 28, 1906. Courtesy of The Shakespeare Centre, The Shakespeare Birthplace Trust, Stratford-on-Avon.

evoking Freud points to how the Orient could become a field of free play for shamelessly paranoid constructions, dreamlike elaborations of a series of Western traumas.[39] But it was also precisely through a combination of mobilizing Shakespeare's secular, licentious narrative and mining the pharaonic archive that the troubling resonances of Tree's unique blend of filmic and theatrical discourses, producing something akin to pornographic representations of the human body, could be diffused, safely channeled into a distant yet compelling culture, claimed for Britain through the imperialism of Roman Egypt and ideas about the harem, Arabian nights, and the vamp.[40]

Nowhere is that claim more obvious than in the production's discourse of costume, especially those gowns clothing the figure whose sensual body stands at the center of Egypt's "passionate" spectacle, which the *Daily Graphic* lovingly details:

> Her first costume consists of a clinging underdress of gold-spangled gauze, with jewelled girdle and breastplates, and a flowing mantle of salmon-pink silk, almost matching the blossoms of the oleander tree above her seat. The headdress has a gold disc in front, . . . red flowers at the sides, and at each ear hang jewelled medallions and chains of turquoises. [The second,] a robe of dark blue and gold shot tissue, [shows] an underdrapery suggestive of shaded green and gold feathers . . . repeated on a smaller scale in

[39]See Peter Wollen, "Out of the Past: Fashion/Orientalism/The Body," *Raiding the Icebox: Reflections on Twentieth-Century Culture* (Bloomington: Indiana University Press, 1993), p. 7.
[40]See Lant, "The Curse of the Pharaoh," p. 109.

the bird headdress, the feathers forming wings and tail to the gold neck and head of the bird. Heavy armlets and plaques are worn with this dress, also a jewelled chain around her neck, with the famous pearl as pendant. . . . In the Camp scene, [she] wears a robe like gold scale armour, with jewelled ruby velvet girdle, and a leopard skin on the shoulder. Two gold birds surmount the helmet, and she holds a ruby velvet shield, embossed with gold and green lotus flowers. After Antony's defeat [her] robe is of soft black silk, almost covered by a mantle of striped black and gold gauze. . . . Each plait of her dark hair is held by a turquoise, and a splendid emerald is set in the centre of her gold filet. The last dress is in a lovely soft shade of geranium-red silk heavily embroidered in gold round the foot, at the top of the bodice, and at the waist. The loose front piece, of purple satin, is richly worked over in gold and jewels, and matches a purple mantle, with gold border, draped on one shoulder. Rubies stud the long tresses, and in the death scene the imposing Egyptian Royal crown is set on the head, and the State mantle of gold brocade thrown round the Queen's shoulders.

Dressing Cleopatra in such authentic robes offers her body as a preeminent site where the discourse of Egyptology can be reconciled with theatrical illusion and visual pleasure. Certainly, too, the *Daily Graphic*'s review, in so far as it represents the ultimate in Orientalist consumerism, has the potential to summon up an imperialist appetite for possession, especially among woman spectators and readers. In fact, the extravagances of "The Inimitable Livers" had already been appropriated by the aristocracy and aspiring haute-bourgeoisie. When, in 1897, the Duchess of Devonshire gave a fancy dress ball in London to celebrate Queen Victoria's Diamond Jubilee, three guests came as Cleopatra: one, Lady De Grey, was even attended by a servant dressed as a Nubian slave. But, although she purportedly spent £6,000 on her costume, Minnie Stevens of Boston eclipsed her in a Worth-designed dress, described by the *New York World* as "a marvellous story in white and gold . . . simply ablaze with diamonds, rubies and emeralds": when she entered, "people accustomed to the greatest displays of jewels the world has ever known, gasped."[41] And in America, in the wake of a first generation of affluent tourists who had visited the Orient, the urban rich attended private parties dressed as harem dancers and exotic princesses—a moment celebrated in Edith Wharton's *The House of Mirth* (1905), where the adventuress Lily Bart considers posing as Tiepolo's Cleopatra, thus displaying herself "in a splendid setting" for a parlour game of *tableaux vivants*.[42]

But, although Mrs. Jameson, writing in the *Pictorial*, affirms (on the grounds that Shakespeare's Cleopatra produces the same effect as that recorded of the real Cleopatra) that she is the "real historical Cleopatra . . . a brilliant impersonation of classical elegance, Oriental voluptuousness, and gipsy sorcery,"[43] Constance Collier's Cleopatra did not attain such a perfect fusion of the historical and repre-

---

[41]Quoted by Lucy Hughes-Hallett, *Cleopatra: Histories, Dreams, and Distortions* (New York: Harper & Row, 1990), pp. 280–81.
[42]See William Leach, *Land of Desire: Merchants, Power, and the Rise of a New American Culture* (New York: Pantheon Books, 1993), pp. 104–11; and Hughes-Hallett, *Cleopatra*, p. 281.
[43]Mrs. [Anna] Jameson, *The Play Pictorial* 9.54, pp. 250–51. Jameson was the author of *Shakespeare's Heroines* (New York: A. L. Burt, 19—[n.d.]).

sentational real. Indeed, the intensified gaze generated in part by her costumes threatened a loss of meaning, a failure of identity. To appropriate Peggy Phelan's term signifying "a configuration of subjectivity which exceeds, even while informing, both the gaze and language" and points to the broken symmetries between self and other, she remained "unmarked."[44] In the case of Collier's performance, the term suggests the departure between "natural" acting—incorporating herself into the character—and standing outside of it, *looking like* Cleopatra (how could she not, in those costumes?) but marred by what reviewers perceived as a veneer of impersonation—as the *not real* of the historical (or dramatic) character. The *Star*'s reviewer expresses this perfectly: "[She] exhibited only the conventional external signs of a wayward and ardent passion. She was not regal; she was not the soul of passion made incarnate; she was one particular woman running up and down the scale of feminine vagary, quite agilely, and *that woman was an actress*" (my emphasis).

Pushing Cleopatra into the space of "faulty" impersonation is, of course, one way of displacing the effects of Collier's performance. And after all, the image a particular Cleopatra displays rarely has much to do with the subjectivity of the woman who is seen; instead, it is constituted by the desires of the spectator who sees her. If it is a timeless psychic predisposition which places a woman's body— and Cleopatra's is a special case—at the focus of the look, critics clearly wished her to remain there. The *Daily Graphic*, for instance, notes that "one or two of her gowns seemed to suffer a little from their accuracy. Gold tissue and kindred materials look exquisite while she is in repose, but in her moments of fury and agitation seem scant and unsatisfactory." Like others, he would position Cleopatra as a statuesque, static figure available for the gaze: when she acts out her own desires and passions, she becomes disturbing, "los[ing] something of dignity." Understood through Orientalism, this static/active binary represents an instance of the Western imperial spectator's forceful attempt to contain the feminized Orient by placing her in a passive, reactive position that will keep a slippery "woman on top" in her place.[45] Such comments align almost seamlessly with other attempts to draw Collier's Cleopatra into a foreign space. According to the *Telegraph*, she is a "beautiful savage thing, whose fascination is only equalled by her occasional lapses into sheer barbarism"; he calls her a "handsome, dark-skinned . . . imperial siren, . . . dominating wherever she appears," and, remarking on the famous (and much admired) messenger scene, marvels at "how close the tiger's cruelty lies under the sleek skin of the cultivated woman." It is not, of course, very far from this Caliban-ized Cleopatra to the Ten Brink–Bradley vision of Cleopatra the whore: the *Saturday Review* writes of how the "fierce unscrupulous power of the courtesan was felt; its low but lovely lure held you." To the *Pall Mall Gazette*, Collier's Cleopatra "becomes an ordinary stage adven-

---

[44]See Phelan, *Unmarked*, p. 27.
[45]See Natalie Zemon Davis, "Women on Top," *Society and Culture in Early Modern France* (Stanford: Stanford University Press, 1975), pp. 124–51.

turess. It would be no shock to see her smoke a cigarette." Drawing her into the space of popular melodrama, he remarks that "she seems all the time to be making up to Antony, much as Mr. Walter Melville's heroines exercise their venal blandishments."

It is along such lines that reviewers once again align with Bradley. Indeed, the *Times* even adopts his structure, noting first Cleopatra's "'low' feminine arts [as she] writhes, clings, caresses, then quivers and flashes with jealous rage," and saving his most fulsome praise for her final moments, where she "compose[s] herself into a set, marmorean calm" to become a "wonderful piece of work." Also like Bradley, the *Saturday Review* faults her loveless selfishness for not dying because she cannot live without Antony but because she prefers death to ignominy. Here, too, what becomes obvious is that Cleopatra's falsely sentient body is also capable of affecting those of other players. The *Saturday Review* faults the actors playing Iras and Charmian for being "just a courtesan's light though loyal companions," whereas they "should be more; they *should be men like their mistress*" (my emphasis). This, the only hint of Cleopatra's transgressive gender, expresses the fear that Antony has indeed become a woman's man—a weaker, emptier vessel who absorbs her dangerously "low" imprint. Labelling him "a wine-bibber, a libertine, a voluptuary," the *Star* then quickly pulls him away from the taint of Bradley's Falstaffian Cleopatra to name him "the finest soldier, bravest heart, and most generous mind in all Rome." Yet this attempt to shore up his imperial masculinity seems grounded more on "Shakespeare's Antony" than on Tree's performance, which he associates with "strange extravagances." "He walks to an accompaniment of music—Roman or Egyptian, according to where he happens to be at the moment. His comings and goings all are marked by imperial fanfares. Indeed, if poor Antony really lived in such a strepitous atmosphere, his flight into Egypt should evoke our sympathy. I can understand him seeking any refuge for the sake of a quiet life, away from the trumpets and the rest of the band." If the joke betrays an anxious need to recuperate the Antony described by the *Telegraph* as a "weakling weak in his virtues and his vices, irresolute and nerveless," that move becomes even more telling when the *Star*'s reviewer, calling Antony "little more than 'Master of the Show,'" positions Tree himself at the heart of, and seduced by, his own Egyptian theatre of the popular. Remarking that, at his death, "[Antony] rolls over in a last convulsion as he tries to glue his lips to Cleopatra's," the *Times* provides an image that almost seems to have been raided from an early 1906 Pathé film, *Joined Lips*, in which a bourgeois woman's maid, after offering her tongue, like a mechanical device, to wet some dozen stamps, then kisses her suitor and becomes stuck to his lips, requiring a boy to cut them apart with a pair of scissors. But, in a comic feat of reproduction, a duplicate of the man's mustache now adorns the maid's upper lip, which sends them both into gales of laughter.[46]

[46]Abel, *The Ciné Goes to Town*, p. 137. My thanks to Abel for pointing out this reference as well as for reading (and re-reading) this essay.

Figure 4. Advertisement for *Cleopatra*. *Motion Picture News*, November 10, 1917. (Courtesy of George Eastman House.)

Although it is traditionally appropriate at this point to fix on Cleopatra's final hierarchic image, I mark this particular connection between a high-culture Shakespeare and a low-culture entertainment because it intimates what is at stake in the narrative I have constructed. In that history, Tree's *Antony and Cleopatra* emerges as a special instance of Shakespeare's "fall" into the popular. Understood in terms of Raymond Williams' dominant, residual, and emergent categories,[47] his production occurs at a historical juncture where Shakespeare was being appropriated to legitimate the cinema, the century's emergent art form, and where traces of cinema were being incorporated into theatre. Indeed, as Lant argues, Egypt becomes a figure for the cinema's exotic, dark mysteries and the unsealing of the mummy's tomb a trope for its opening-out of representational economies. Shortly after Tree's production, the figure of Cleopatra becomes dispersed into mass culture, notably in one of the first fashion exhibitions featuring "The Egyptian Tendency" at John Wanamaker's department store. "Of course," read an ad in the 22 March 1907 *New York Daily Tribune*, "American women cannot be gowned in

[47]See Raymond Williams, *Marxism and Literature* (Oxford: Oxford University Press, 1977), pp. 121–27.

Figure 5. Claudette Colbert as Cleopatra in Cecil B. DeMille's 1934 film of *Cleopatra* (Paramount). Courtesy of the Wisconsin Center for Film and Theater Research, University of Wisconsin-Madison.

the flowing draperies of Cleopatra; but the graceful dress allurements of those old days that ring of Caesar, Ptolemy, and Antony, have given the *motif* for witching and daring originality."[48] And it was just a step from such *tableaux vivants* displaying "compositions" direct from Paris ateliers to putting Cleopatra "herself" on show as the cinematic subject—or object—of five silent films made between 1908 and 1918, of which William Fox's 1917 version, starring Theda Bara, is perhaps the most famous (Fig. 4).[49] By the time of Cecil B. DeMille's 1934 film, starring Claudette Colbert, Cleopatra had become aligned with the "modern woman" and firmly appropriated to mark a sensualized leisure society which would contain the emergent discourses of emancipation by turning women into consumers of "Cleopatra" negligees (Fig. 5), cosmetics, and Palmolive soap, whose ad featuring her image proclaimed, "Age cannot wither, nor custom stale, her infinite variety."[50]

[48]On Wanamaker's fashion shows, see Leach, *Land of Desire*, pp. 102–4.
[49]See Lant, "The Curse of the Pharaoh," pp. 109–10.
[50]*Cleopatra*, directed by Cecil B. DeMille, Paramount Pictures, 1934. "Cleopatra-ism" also exploded into a whole range of consumer tie-ups. Best & Co.'s Beauty Salon appropriated her bangs "for modern use, combining them with the latest in up-swept coiffures"; "authentic" costume jewelry

Figure 6. Elizabeth Taylor in the 1964 film of "Cleopatra" (20th Century Fox) as she enters Rome. Courtesy of the Wisconsin Center for Film and Theater Research, University of Wisconsin-Madison.

Those moves culminate, of course, in Elizabeth Taylor's Cleopatra (1963),[51] where the performative moment joins the real to the role to produce the image of an ultimate mass-produced Cleopatra, winking at her own excess (Figs. 6 and 7).

Given this continuing Egyptian explosion into the popular, it is particularly intriguing that R. H. Case's 1906 Arden edition of the play becomes incorporated, essentially unchanged, into M. R. Ridley's 1954 edition, last reprinted in 1977.[52] For this suggests a need to reproduce *Antony and Cleopatra* as a transhistorically fixed textual entity in the face of its reconfiguration as performance, a move that

---

appeared in department stores; A. S. Beck advertized "Egyptian sandals" in each of their fifty stores; Old Gold cigarettes, Lux soap, and Dixie Ice-Cream Cups all featured Colbert's image as Cleopatra. See Press Book for DeMille's *Cleopatra* (1934), New York: Lincoln Center for the Performing Arts Library. My thanks to Antonia Lant for sharing her research. See her "Beams from the East," *Images Across Borders*, ed. Roland Casandey, forthcoming from Editions Payot, Lausanne. See also Hamer, *Signs of Cleopatra*, pp. 120–24. For a study of consumer culture tie-ups, see Charles Eckert, "The Carole Lombard in Macy's Window" (1978); rpt. in *Fabrications: Costume and the Female Body*, ed. Jane Gaines and Charlotte Herzog (London: Routledge, 1990), pp. 100–24.

[51]*Cleopatra*, directed by Joseph L. Manckiewicz, Twentieth-Century Fox, 1964, starring Taylor and Richard Burton. A *Ladies Home Journal Special*, in an account of Taylor titled "The Burtons," includes several color photographs of Taylor relaxing on the set with a bottle of Schweppes. See *Elizabeth Taylor, Portrait of a Legend* (Meredith Publication, 1993).

[52]M. R. Ridley, *Antony and Cleopatra* (1954); rpt. (London: Methuen, 1977), p. vii.

Figure 7. Elizabeth Taylor winks in the 1964 film of "Cleopatra" (20th Century Fox). Courtesy of the Kobal Collection.

could be said to "impersonate" Bradley. Yet even at the time Bradley wrote, the text he had before him was not "the same" as that of either Tree's production or its historical reading relations; indeed, his attempt to preserve an intensely stable text that would contain Cleopatra's figure of "infinite variety" can be seen as his own ultimate protomodernist move. Some years later, Virginia Woolf, writing in "Mr. Bennett and Mrs. Brown" (1924) that "On or about December 1910, human character changed," would mark the moment Bradley's lecture gestures toward. Redeeming the myth of Victorian character she seemingly mocks, Woolf foretells the triumph of the "eternal" Mrs. Brown, a figure who (Cleopatra-like) conjoins past and future: "she is an old lady of unlimited capacity and infinite variety; capable of appearing in any place; wearing any dress; saying anything and doing heaven knows what"[53]—a regenerative capacity that would eventually produce the possibility of a woman authoring her own history. Such moves encapsulate Bradley's apprehension that Cleopatra had already escaped the sphere of high tragedy and moved elsewhere, dragging Antony with her into the realm of feminized mass culture where "the greatest hero of the world" and the feudal aristocratic military culture he stands for would become subject to intense strain.

    Indeed, one can hardly tell Cleopatra's story any more without reconfiguring it critically, as Jonathan Dollimore has done, for camp or, in the case of Michel Tremblay's 1974 *Hosanna*, for gay discourse, where, as she becomes Taylor's *Penthouse*-fantasy body rewritten on a man's body, the wheel comes full circle, returning her to the material conditions of the early modern playhouse (Figs. 8 and 9).[54] *Hosanna*'s self-fracturing dilemma, one might argue, is precisely that

    [53]Virginia Woolf, "Mr. Bennett and Mrs. Brown" (1924); rpt. (London: Hogarth Press, 1928), pp. 4, 24. See also Auerbach, *Woman and the Demon*, pp. 223–27.

    [54]See Jonathan Dollimore, "Shakespeare, Cultural Materialism, Feminism, and Marxist Humanism," *New Literary History* 21.3 (Spring 1990): 471–93; esp. 482–90. Michel Tremblay, *Hosanna*, trans. John van Burek and Bill Glassco (Vancouver: Talonbooks, 1974).

Figure 8. Geordie Johnson as Hosanna and Dennis O'Connor as Cuirette in the 1987 pro-
duction of Michel Temblay's play *Hosanna* at the Tarragon Theater, Toronto. Photo by
Michael Cooper. Courtesy of Geordie Johnson, Dennis O'Connor, Michael Cooper, the
Paramount Theater, and Canadian Actors' Equity.

faced by present-day performers, critical as well as theatrical. Thinking that he
alone "owns" Elizabeth Taylor's image, he goes to a Hallowe'en party arrayed in
her Cleopatra robes only to discover that every drag queen in Montreal is playing
Elizabeth Taylor playing Cleopatra. Given the power of such infinite replication,
can her history, like Caliban's, be reinvented? Certainly it would be difficult to
align Shakespeare's play with late twentieth-century postcolonial discourse and
decolonization imperatives; more difficult still for Hollywood to cast a white
Western star as Cleopatra. Although there are pressing reasons for such reinven-
tions and interventions, one stumbling block is that the psychic loss is greater with
Cleopatra than with Caliban, largely because celebrating her racial otherness
would cause serious interference with dominant cultural imaginaries of desire.
Perhaps, however, it is time to disown such imaginaries—a project currently
under way in critical as well as theatrical performances—and to invite their tellers
to free Cleopatra from the hieroglyphic markers that have for centuries marked
their (imperialist) fantasies of possession.

Figure 9. Richard Monette as Hosanna in the 1974 production of Michel Tremblay's play *Hosanna* at the Tarragon Theater, Toronto. Photo by Robert A. Barnett. Courtesy of Richard Monette, Robert A. Barnett, the Tarragon Theater, and Canadian Actors' Equity.

I want to conclude by briefly mapping a strand of Cleopatra-ism that travels back in time to encompass another queen, Elizabeth I. Work by Paul Yachnin and others has attempted to historicize *Antony and Cleopatra*'s Jacobean moment in terms of the nostalgia for Elizabeth during the early years of James I's Augustan reign,[55] but the chains of erotic court gossip that bind Cleopatra to Elizabeth, making them appear to be a seamless text, seem even more insistently historical when they surface within the realm of the popular. Curiously enough, given its modernist imperatives, Eliot's 1922 "The Waste Land" picks up the strand by conflating Elizabeth's barge with Cleopatra's, and Lytton Strachey's 1928 *Elizabeth and Essex: A Tragic*

[55]See Paul Yachnin, " 'Courtiers of Beauteous Freedom': *Antony and Cleopatra* in Its Time," *Renaissance and Reformation* 26.1 (1991): 1–20. Just as Octavius constructed himself as "Augustus" by naming himself after the month in which he vanquished Cleopatra, James I, setting himself in relation to Elizabeth, also constructed an Augustan image of his kingship. For Octavius, see Hamer, *Signs of Cleopatra*, p. 22. For James, see Jonathan Goldberg, *James I and the Politics of Literature: Jonson, Shakespeare, Donne, and Their Contemporaries* (Stanford: Stanford University Press, 1989).

Figure 10. Dorothy Massingham, First Act Dress, for W. Bridges Adams' production of *Antony and Cleopatra*, Stratford, 1931. Photo by Claude Harris. Courtesy of The Shakespeare Centre, The Shakespeare Birthplace Trust, Stratford-on-Avon.

History, serialized shortly before its publication in the *Ladies Home Journal*, models its structures on Shakespeare's play, while Maxwell Anderson's 1930 *Elizabeth, the Queen* appropriates *Antony and Cleopatra*'s language of hyperbole for Elizabeth's *grande affaire* with Essex.[56] Five years after the fire which destroyed the Shakespeare Memorial Theatre in 1926, W. Bridges Adams staged *Antony and Cleopatra* in Stratford's Greenhill Street cinema (now occupied by a Safeway), where Dorothy Massingham's Cleopatra appeared costumed as Queen Elizabeth; at her death, she adopted an Egyptian headdress together with her distinctly British ermine-trimmed coronation robe (Figs. 10 and 11).[57] And that curious nexus of

[56]Lytton Strachey, *Elizabeth and Essex: A Tragic History* (New York: Harcourt, Brace, 1928), serialized in the *Ladies Home Journal*, September–December 1928. Maxwell Anderson, *Elizabeth, the Queen* (1930); rpt. (New York: Harcourt, Brace and World, 1959).

[57]Reviewers not only puzzled over the anachronism but were troubled by a decision that connected Cleopatra to an *English* queen. *The Stratford-upon-Avon Herald* for 8 May 1931 noted: "In few other plays does dress take so important a place as in 'Antony and Cleopatra.' The costumes, even more than

Figure 11. Dorothy Massingham, Last Act Dress, for W. Bridges Adams' production of *Antony and Cleopatra*, Stratford, 1931. Photo by Claude Harris. Courtesy of The Shakespeare Centre, The Shakespeare Birthplace Trust, Stratford-on-Avon.

anachronisms points forward to Michael Curtiz's 1939 film, *The Private Lives of Elizabeth and Essex*, where Errol Flynn's Essex, evoking a utopian match between ideologically perfect lovers, cracks out campy one-liners mimicking Antony's "Let Rome in Tiber melt."[58] Finally, just how far *Antony and Cleopatra* travels back into popular culture can be seen in the frontispiece to the 1680 *Secret History of the Most Renowned Queen Elizabeth and the Earl of Essex*, a text belonging to a genre of pseudo-memoirs or *particular histories* (an operative term) which implicate women both as writers who focus on an interior arena of experience and as agents behind the scenes of great events.[59] There, watched by an African voyeur, a

---

the settings, symbolise the character of their wearers, and illustrate the gulf between austere Rome and burning Egypt. It was disturbing, therefore, . . . to find Cleopatra and her women in Elizabethan garb. In Shakespeare's day this may have been done, but surely on those occasions the whole company, Romans and Egyptians, would appear in the dress of the period. This is why, without wishing to condemn an experiment on sight, we cannot see the advantage of a Cleopatra weighed down with the habiliments of Good Queen Bess." Press cuttings in The Shakespeare Centre Library, Stratford-upon-Avon.

   [58]*The Private Lives of Elizabeth and Essex* (retitled *Queen Elizabeth* on video), directed by Michael Curtiz, Warner Brothers, 1939.

   [59]Anonymous, *The Secret History of the Most Renowned Queen Elizabeth and the Earl of Essex* (Cologne: Printed for Will with the Wisp and the Sign of the Moon in the Ecliptick, 1680). On the genre of particular histories, see Faith E. Beasley, *Revising Memory: Women's Fiction and Memoirs in Seventeenth-Century France* (New Brunswick and London: Rutgers University Press, 1990), esp. pp. 129–61; 190–243. See also my "Romancing the Queen," in *Restaging Shakespeare's Cultural Capital: Women, Queens, Spectatorship* (Philadelphia: University of Pennsylvania Press, forthcoming).

Figure 12. Frontispiece, *The Secret History of the Most Renowned Queen Elizabeth and the Earl of Essex* (1680). Courtesy of the University of Iowa Library, Special Collections.

Romanized Cleopatra-Elizabeth sits at the feet of an Antonian Essex, and the asp-like ribbon that floats out from her bodice, its other end across her arm, seems already to have ensnared him in "her strong toil of grace" (Fig. 12). But that, as they say, is another story.

Chronology of Important Dates

	Shakespeare's Life	Other Events
1564	Baptized April 26, at Stratford-upon-Avon (born April 23?).	Sixth year of Elizabeth's reign. She is 31 years old.
1576		James Burbage builds The Theater, first permanent playhouse in England, on the outskirts of London.
1582	Marriage to Anne Hathaway.	
1583	Daughter Susanna born.	
1585	Twins (Hamnet and Judith) born.	
1587		Death of Mary Stuart. Rose Playhouse built on the Bankside.
1588		Defeat of Spanish Armada.
1590–92	Active as actor and playwright in London. Known for success of his history plays (*Henry VI* trilogy). Early tragedy: *Titus Andronicus*. First efforts at comedy. Attacked as "upstart crow" (i.e., actor presuming to be a playwright) and defended as "upright" and "civil."	Rival playwrights Kyd (*The Spanish Tragedy,* probably an early *Hamlet)* and Marlowe (*Tamburlaine, Jew of Malta, Dr. Faustus*) active. John Lyly's plays published. Major literary works by Spenser (*The Faery Queene,* I–III) and Sidney (*Arcadia, Astrophel and Stella*) published.
1593–94	Publishes two narrative poems, *Venus and Adonis* and *The Rape of Lucrece,* dedicated to the Earl of Southampton. Becomes a principal member (shareholder, actor, playwright) of leading company of actors, the Lord Chamberlain's Men. Writes *The Taming of the Shrew, Richard III, Two Gentlemen of Verona, Love's Labour's Lost.*	Theaters flourish in London, despite periodic closings (at which time the companies tour) during outbreaks of the plague.
1595–96	*Romeo and Juliet, A Midsummer Night's Dream, Richard II, King John, Merchant of Venice.* Death of Hamnet.	Raleigh's voyages to Guiana. Spenser's *The Faery Queene,* IV–VI.

Shakespeare's Life	*Other Events*
1597–98	*Henry IV, 1* and *2.* Buys New Place, second largest house in Stratford. Mentioned as leading literary figure, for both his plays and poems. Lord Chamberlain's Men playing at The Curtain, at Holywell, Shoreditch.	Bacon's *Essays*. Chapman's *Homer.*
1599–1600	*Much Ado about Nothing, Henry V, As You Like It, Julius Caesar, Twelfth Night.* The company builds The Globe Playhouse, on the Bankside.	Essex fighting in Ireland. Death of Spenser.
1601–2	*Hamlet, Troilus and Cressida, All's Well That Ends Well.* Death of Shakespeare's father. The company very nearly gets prosecuted for play-ing *Richard II* to Essex and his friends just before the attempted coup.	Unsuccessful coup by Essex against Elizabeth. Ben Jonson emerges as playwright (*Every Man in His Humor*).
1603–4	*Measure for Measure, Othello.* The company becomes The King's Men.	Death of Elizabeth. James I succeeds her.
1605–6	*King Lear, Macbeth.*	Jonson's *Volpone.*
1607–8	*Antony and Cleopatra, Coriolanus, Timon of Athens.* Marriage of Susanna, death of Shakespeare's mother.	Midlands riots.
1609–10	*Pericles, Cymbeline.* Unauthorized publication of *Sonnets*. Company adds indoor theater at Blackfriars to its regular paying venues.	Elaborate masques become the fashion at James's court. Jonson's *The Alchemist.*
1611–12	*The Winter's Tale, The Tempest.* Retirement to Stratford.	Publication of the authorized version of the Bible.
1613	*Henry VIII.* Globe Theater burns and is promptly rebuilt.	
1616	Death of Shakespeare, April 23.	Publication of Jonson's *Works.*
1623	Shakespeare's fellow actors, Hemings and Condell, publish the First Folio edition of his plays. Death of Anne Hathaway.	

Notes on Contributors

JANET ADELMAN is Professor of English at the University of California at Berkeley. In addition to articles on Shakespeare, she is the author of *Suffocating Mothers: Fantasies of Maternal Origin in Shakespeare's Plays, "Hamlet" to "The Tempest"* (1992), in which the essay included here appears, and *The Common Liar: An Essay on "Antony and Cleopatra"* (1973).

STANLEY CAVELL is the Walter M. Cabot Professor of Aesthetics and the Theory of Value at Harvard University. His books include *Disowning Knowledge in Six Plays of Shakespeare* (1987), in which the essay included here appears, as well as *Must We Mean What We Say?* (1969), *The World Viewed* (1971), *The Senses of Walden* (1972), *The Claim of Reason* (1979), *Pursuits of Happiness* (1981), and *Themes Out of School* (1984).

SINEAD CUSACK is an actor with the Royal Shakespearean Company in England. She has played many roles, including Lady Macbeth in 1986, about which she is interviewed in the selection here, taken from the book *Clamorous Voices: Shakespeare's Women Today* (1989) by Carol Rutter et al.

JONATHAN DOLLIMORE, author of *Sexual Dissidence: Augustine to Wilde, Freud to Foucault* (1991) and *Radical Tragedy: Religion, Ideology, and Power in the Drama of Shakespeare and His Contemporaries* (1986), in which the essay included here appears, is a Reader in the School of English and American Studies, University of Sussex. He has also edited the *Selected Plays of John Webster* (1983) and co-edited *Political Shakespeare: New Essays in Cultural Materialism* (1985).

MARJORIE GARBER is Professor of English at Harvard University and Director of Harvard's Center for Literary and Cultural Studies. In addition to essays on Shakespeare, Renaissance drama, and cultural studies, she has written five books: *Vice Versa: Bisexuality and the Eroticism of Everyday Life* (1995), *Vested Interests: Cross Dressing and Cultural Anxiety* (1991), *Shakespeare's Ghost Writers: Literature as Uncanny Causality* (1987), in which the essay included here appears, *Coming of Age in Shakespeare* (1981), and *Dream in Shakespeare: From Metaphor to Metamorphosis* (1974). She was also the editor of *Cannibals, Witches, and Divorce: Estranging the Renaissance* (1987).

MICHAEL GOLDMAN is Professor of English at Princeton University, and author of *Acting and Action in Shakespearean Tragedy* (1985), in which the essay included here appears, *The Actor's Freedom: Toward a Theory of Drama* (1975), and *Shakespeare and the Energies of the Drama* (1972).

BARBARA HODGDON is the Ellis Nelle Levitt Distinguished Professor of English at Drake University. She is the author of *The End Crowns All: Closure and Contradiction in*

Shakespeare's History (1991) and has edited *Henry IV, Part II* (1993). The essay included in this volume is a part of her forthcoming book *Restaging Shakespeare's Cultural Capital: Women, Queens, and Spectatorship*.

HEATHER JAMES is Assistant Professor of English at the University of Southern California. She is the author of articles on Shakespeare and Milton, and is presently completing a manuscript entitled *The Fatal Cleopatra: Shakespeare's Translations of Empire*.

ANIA LOOMBA has taught at Delhi University and at Tulsa University. She is Associate Professor at Jawaharlal Nehru University, New Delhi, and has been a Mellon Fellow at Stanford University. She is author of *Gender, Race, Renaissance Drama* (1989), from which the essay included here was taken, as well as articles on colonial discourse, Shakespeare, and feminist theory. She is working on a book on Renaissance literature and travel to the East Indies.

MAYNARD MACK, Professor Emeritus of English at Yale University, is the author of many books, including *Everybody's Shakespeare* (1993), in which the essay reprinted here appears, *Alexander Pope: A Life* (1985), *The Garden and the City* (1969), and *King Lear in Our Time* (1965). He has served as the general editor of *The Norton Anthology of World Masterpieces*, has edited a number of Shakespeare plays, and has co-edited many books, including *Poetic Traditions of the English Renaissance* (1982).

LEAH S. MARCUS, Professor of English at the University of Texas at Austin, is the author of *Puzzling Shakespeare: Local Reading and Its Discontents* (1988), in which the essay included here appears, as well as *The Politics of Mirth: Jonson, Herrick, Milton, Marvell, and the Defense of Old Holiday Pastimes* (1986) and *Childhood and Cultural Despair: A Theme and Variations in Seventeenth-Century Literature* (1978).

STEVEN MULLANEY, Associate Professor of English at the University of Michigan, Ann Arbor, is the author of *The Place of the Stage: License, Play, and Power in Renaissance England* (1988) as well as numerous articles on English Renaissance culture and politics.

CAROL RUTTER is Lecturer in English at the University of Warwick, England. She is author of *Clamorous Voices: Shakespeare's Women Today* (1989), the book from which the interview with Sinead Cusack in this volume was taken.

MADELON GOHLKE SPRENGNETHER is Professor of English at the University of Minnesota, Twin Cities. Her publications include *The Spectral Mother: Freud, Feminism, and Psychoanalysis* (1990) and *Rivers, Stories, Houses, Dreams* (1983). She has also co-edited *The House on Via Gombito: Writing by North American Women Abroad* (1991) and *The (M)other Tongue: Essays in Feminist Psychoanalytic Interpretation* (1985).

PETER STALLYBRASS is Professor of English at the University of Pennsylvania, Philadelphia. With Allon White he is the author of *The Politics and Poetics of Transgression* (1986); he has also written numerous articles on English Renaissance culture, literature, and politics. He is co-editor of *Staging the Renaissance: Essays in Elizabethan and Jacobean Drama* (1991).

SUSANNE L. WOFFORD is Associate Professor of English at the University of Wisconsin-Madison. She is the author of *The Choice of Achilles: The Ideology of Figure in the Epic* (1992) and editor of *Hamlet: A Case Study in Contemporary Criticism* (1993). She has also written several articles on Shakespeare, Spenser, and Renaissance Culture.

Bibliography

Books and Articles on the Tragedies

Adelman, Janet. *Suffocating Mothers: Fantasies of Maternal Origin in Shakespeare's Plays, "Hamlet" to "The Tempest."* New York: Routledge, 1992.

Bamber, Linda. *Comic Women, Tragic Men: A Study of Gender and Genre in Shakespeare.* Stanford: Stanford UP, 1982.

Belsey, Catherine. *The Subject of Tragedy: Identity and Difference in Renaissance Drama.* London: Methuen, 1985.

Booth, Stephen. *"King Lear," "Macbeth," Indefinition, and Tragedy.* New Haven: Yale UP, 1983.

Bradbury, Malcolm, and David Palmer, eds. *Shakespearean Tragedy.* New York: Holmes and Meier, 1984.

Bradley, A. C. *Shakespearean Tragedy.* 1904. 3rd ed. Introd. John Russell Brown. New York: St. Martin's, 1992.

Danson, Lawrence. *Tragic Alphabet: Shakespeare's Drama of Language.* New Haven: Yale UP, 1974.

Dollimore, Jonathan. *Radical Tragedy: Religion, Ideology, and Power in the Drama of Shakespeare and His Contemporaries.* Brighton, Sussex: Harvester, 1984.

Frye, Northrop. *Fools of Time: Studies in Shakespearean Tragedy.* Toronto: U of Toronto P, 1967.

Goldberg, Jonathan. *James I and the Politics of Literature.* Stanford: Stanford UP, 1989.

Heilman, Robert, ed. *Shakespeare: The Tragedies: New Perspectives.* Englewood Cliffs, NJ: Prentice-Hall, 1984.

Holloway, John. *The Story of the Night: Studies in Shakespeare's Major Tragedies.* Lincoln: U of Nebraska P, 1961.

Moretti, Franco. "'A Huge Eclipse': Tragic Form and the Deconsecration of Sovereignty." *The Power of Forms in the English Renaissance.* Ed. S. Greenblatt. Norman, OK: Pilgrim, 1982, 7–40.

Tennenhouse, Leonard. *Power on Display: The Politics of Shakespeare's Genres.* New York: Methuen, 1986.

Young, David. *The Action to the Word: Structure and Style in Shakespearean Tragedy.* New Haven: Yale UP, 1990.

Books and Articles on Macbeth

Berger, Harry, Jr. "The Early Scenes of *Macbeth:* Preface to a New Interpretation." *English Literary History* 47 (1980): 1–31.

———. "Text Against Performance in Shakespeare: The Example of *Macbeth.*" *Genre* 15.2–3 (1982): 49–79.

Bloom, Harold, ed. *Macbeth.* New York: Chelsea House, 1991.

Brown, John Russell, ed. *Focus on Macbeth.* London: Routledge, 1982.

Calderwood, James. *If It Were Done: "Macbeth" and Tragic Action.* Amherst: U of Massachusetts P, 1986.

Cavell, Stanley. "*Macbeth* Appalled." *Raritan* 12.2 (1992): 1–15; 12.3 (1993): 1–15.

Coddon, Karin. "'Unreal Mockery': Unreason and the Problem of Spectacle in *Macbeth.*" *English Literary History* 56.3 (1989): 485–501.

Goldberg, Jonathan. "Speculations: *Macbeth* and Source." *Shakespeare Reproduced: The Text in History and Ideology.* Ed. Jean Howard and Marion O'Connor. New York: Methuen, 1987, 242–64.

Hawkes, Terence, ed. *Twentieth Century Interpretations of "Macbeth": A Collection of Critical Essays.* Englewood Cliffs, NJ: Prentice-Hall, 1977.

Kinney, Arthur. "Shakespeare's *Macbeth* and the Question of Nationalism." *Literature and Nationalism.* Ed. Vincent Newly and Ann Thompson. Liverpool: Liverpool UP, 1991, 56–75.

Norbrook, David. "*Macbeth* and the Politics of Historiography." *Politics of Discourse: The Literature and History of Seventeenth Century England.* Ed. Kevin Sharpe and Steven Zwicker. Berkeley: U of California P, 1987, 78–116.

Paul, Henry N. *The Royal Play of "Macbeth."* New York: Macmillan, 1950.

Pye, Christopher. "*Macbeth* and the Politics of Rapture." *The Regal Phantasm: Shakespeare and the Politics of Rapture.* London: Routledge, 1990, 142–72.

Schoenbaum S., ed. "*Macbeth*": *Critical Essays.* New York: Garland, 1991.

Sinfield, Alan. "*Macbeth*: History, Ideology and Intellectuals." *Critical Quarterly* 28.1–2 (1986): 63–77.

Willbern, David. "Phantasmagoric *Macbeth.*" *English Literary Renaissance* 16.3 (1986): 520–49.

Williamson, Marilyn. "Violence and Gender Ideology in *Coriolanus* and *Macbeth.*" *Shakespeare Left and Right.* Ed. Ivo Kamps. New York: Routledge, 1991, 147–66.

Willis, Deborah. "The Monarch and the Sacred: Shakespeare and the Ceremony for the Healing of the King's Evil." *True Rites and Maimed Rites: Ritual and Anti-Ritual in Shakespeare and His Age.* Ed. Linda Woodbridge and Edward Berry. Urbana: U of Illinois P, 1992, 147–68.

Books and Articles on Coriolanus

Bedford, Kristina. "*Coriolanus*" *at the National: "Th' Interpretation of the Time."* Photographs by John Haynes. Selingsgrove, PA: Susquehanna UP, 1992.

Bristol, Michael. "Lenten Butchery: Legitimation Crisis in *Coriolanus.*" *Shakespeare Reproduced: The Text in History and Ideology.* Ed. Jean Howard and Marion O'Connor. New York: Methuen, 1987, 207–24.

Burke, Kenneth. "*Coriolanus* and the Delights of Faction." *Language as Symbolic Action.* By Burke. Berkeley: U of California P, 1966, 81–97.

Daniell, David. "*Coriolanus*" *in Europe.* London: Athlone, 1980.

Dubois, Page. "A Disturbance of Syntax at the Gates of Rome." *Stanford Literary Review* 2.2 (1985): 185–208.

Holstun, James. "Tragic Superfluity in *Coriolanus.*" *English Literary History* 50.3 (1983): 485–507.

King, Bruce Alvin. *Coriolanus*. Atlantic Highlands, NJ: Humanities, 1989.

Lowe, Lisa. "'Say I Play the Man I Am': Gender and Politics in *Coriolanus.*" *The Kenyon Review* 8.4 (1986): 86–95.

Miller, Shannon. "Topicality and Subversion in William Shakespeare's *Coriolanus.*" *SEL: Studies in English Literature, 1500–1900* 32.2 (1992): 287–310.

Patterson, Annabel. "The Popular Voice and the Jacobean State." *Shakespeare and the Popular Voice*. Oxford: Basil Blackwell, 1989, 120–53.

Rackin, Phyllis. "*Coriolanus:* Shakespeare's Anatomy of Virtus." *Modern Language Studies* 13.2 (1983): 68–79.

Riss, Arthur. "The Belly Politic: *Coriolanus* and the Revolt of Language." *English Literary History* 59.1 (1992): 53–73.

Sorge, Thomas. "The Failure of Orthodoxy in *Coriolanus.*" *Shakespeare Reproduced: The Text in History and Ideology*. Ed. Jean Howard and Marion O'Connor. New York: Methuen, 1987, 225–41.

Sprengnether, Madelon. "Annihilating Intimacy in *Coriolanus.*" *Women in the Middle Ages and the Renaissance*. Ed. Mary Beth Rose. Syracuse: Syracuse UP, 1986.

Trousdale, Marion. "*Coriolanus* and the Playgoer in 1609." *The Arts and Performance in Elizabethan and Early Stuart Drama: Essays for G. K. Hunter*. Ed. Murray Biggs et al. Edinburgh: Edinburgh UP, 1991, 124–34.

Walker, Jarrett. "Voiceless Bodies and Bodiless Voices: The Drama of Human Perception in *Coriolanus.*" *Shakespeare Quarterly* 43.2 (1992): 170–85.

Books and Articles on Antony and Cleopatra

Adelman, Janet. *The Common Liar: An Essay on "Antony and Cleopatra."* New Haven: Yale UP, 1973.

Barroll, J. Leeds. *Shakespearean Tragedy: Genre, Tradition, and Change in "Antony and Cleopatra."* Washington, DC: Folger Books, 1983.

Bono, Barbara. "The Shakespearean Synthesis: *Antony and Cleopatra.*" *Literary Transvaluation: From Vergilian Epic to Shakespearean Tragicomedy*. Berkeley: U of California P, 1984.

Bushman, Mary Ann. "Representing *Cleopatra.*" *In Another Country: Feminist Perspectives on Renaissance Drama*. Ed. Dorothea Kehler and Susan Baker. Metchuen, NJ: Scarecrow, 1991, 36–49.

Charnes, Linda. "What's Love Got to Do with It? Reading the Liberal Humanist Romance in Shakespeare's *Antony and Cleopatra.*" *Textual Practice* 6.1 (1992): 1–16.

Hamer, Mary. *Signs of Cleopatra: History, Politics, Representation*. London: Routledge, 1993.

Jankowski, Theodora. "'As I am Egypt's Queen': Cleopatra, Elizabeth I, and the Female Body Politic." *Assays* 5 (1989): 91–110.

Lowen, Tirzah. *Peter Hall Directs "Antony and Cleopatra."* Photographs by John Haynes. London: Methuen Drama, 1990.

Macdonald, Ronald. "Playing Till Doomsday: Interpreting *Antony and Cleopatra.*" *English Literary Renaissance* 15.1 (1985): 78–99.

Rose, Mark, ed. *Twentieth Century Interpretations of "Antony and Cleopatra": A Collection of Critical Essays.* Englewood Cliffs, NJ: Prentice-Hall, 1977.

Singh, Jyotsna. "Renaissance Antitheatricality, Antifeminism, and Shakespeare's *Antony and Cleopatra.*" *Renaissance Drama* 20 (1989): 99–121.

Sprengnether, Madelon. "The Boy Actor and Femininity in *Antony and Cleopatra.*" *Shakespeare's Personality.* Ed. Norman Holland, Sidney Homan, and Bernard-J. Paris. Berkeley: U of California P, 1989, 191–205.

Yachnin, Paul. "Shakespeare's Politics of Loyalty: Sovereignty and Subjectivity in *Antony and Cleopatra.*" *SEL: Studies in English Literature, 1500–1900* 33.2 (1993): 343–63.